DISCARD

DARING MY PASSAGES

A Memoir

ALSO BY **GAIL SHEEHY**

WILLIAM MORROW

An Imprint of HarperCollins*Publishers*

DARING
MY PASSAGES

GAIL SHEEHY

DARING: MY PASSAGES. Copyright © 2014 by G Merritt Corp. All rights reserved. Printed in the United States of America. No part of this book may be used or reproduced in any manner whatsoever without written permission except in the case of brief quotations embodied in critical articles and reviews. For information address HarperCollins Publishers, 195 Broadway, New York, NY 10007.

HarperCollins books may be purchased for educational, business, or sales promotional use. For information please e-mail the Special Markets Department at SPsales@harpercollins.com.

FIRST EDITION

Designed by Lorie Pagnozzi

Library of Congress Cataloging-in-Publication Data has been applied for.

ISBN 978-0-06-229169-1

14 15 16 17 18   OV/RRD   10 9 8 7 6 5 4 3 2 1

To my grandchildren,
Declan, Eva, and Mairead

I THINK IT IS ALL A MATTER OF LOVE: THE MORE YOU LOVE A MEMORY, THE STRONGER AND STRANGER IT IS.

—VLADIMIR NABOKOV

CONTENTS

DARING MY PASSAGES

PART ONE

THE PYGMALION YEARS

WHATEVER YOU CAN DO,
OR DREAM YOU CAN,
BEGIN IT. BOLDNESS HAS
GENIUS, POWER AND
MAGIC IN IT.

—GOETHE

CHAPTER 1
DO I DARE?

IT FELT LIKE THE LONGEST walk of my life. Sneaking down the back stairs from the flamingo-pink precinct of the Women's Department on the fourth floor of New York's *Herald Tribune* to march across the DMZ into the all-male preserve of the city room, I was on a mission. I just had to pitch a story to the man who was remaking journalism. I could get fired for this.

My boss, Eugenia Sheppard, was fiercely competitive. She would have thrown a fit if she knew I was giving my best idea to the editor of a lowly Sunday supplement. Girls in the 1960s wrote about beauty and baking and how to be the perfect engineer of that complex machinery called family life. Men wrote about serious issues. Nobody had ever thought of turning a Sunday supplement into a classy cultural magazine. But Clay Felker did. In 1965, he was incubating the future *New York* magazine.

Just getting a job at the famous *Trib* had seemed an impossible dream. I'd read the paper religiously from my exile in Rochester, New York, where I was indentured in the early '60s as a PHT—Putting Hubby Through. My husband, Albert Sheehy, was in medical school while I worked to support us as a reporter at the *Rochester Democrat & Chronicle*. Wasn't that the way it was supposed to be? He got the degree; I was the helpmeet. That's what I thought when I married him at twenty-three, milliseconds from what was then considered a woman's sell-by date. While waiting for him to finish his fourth year, I'd studied the women's page of the *Trib*. What made it so lively? Eugenia Sheppard was the answer. She was the queen of the country's women's-page editors, the national fashion cop and keeper of the flame of a dying social register. I wrote letters asking to work for her. Nothing. Inconveniently, the great New York newspaper strike of 1962–63 began in December of that year and lasted 114 days.

The strike ended shortly before my husband and I made our getaway from Rochester to plunge into grown-up life in New York City. We were imposters, of course, still just kids. Albert would disappear into St. Vincent's Hospital for the next year. As a lowly intern, he was "on" all day and every other night, including weekends, and developed a pallor that matched his puce-green scrubs. I found a one-room garret secreted in a town house off Washington Square Park. Diane Arbus and her husband, then fashion photographers, occupied the ground floor. Never mind that we had only a pull-down Scandinavian bed, exposed toilet, and a kitchen the size of a phone booth. The garret had a big stone fireplace and lavender-and-topaz stained-glass doors that opened onto a miniature balcony. It was cheap and suited my fantasies of the artistic life.

I desperately needed a job. I paid no attention when I began up-chucking in the morning (it must be the summer heat), but when I felt a faint flutter in my belly, a tickle of life, I was ecstatic. "Guess what!" I jumped up and down on the pull-down bed when Albert came home. "We're pregnant!" He danced with me on the bed. It broke. Since he was never home long enough to repair it, I slept in a V position inches off the tile floor.

Sitting before the stained-glass-window doors in the sweltering heat of August, I bent over my Singer to sew a maternity dress. I didn't know how long I could hold out before I'd have to take a waitressing job. But I knew there was only one place I wanted to work, the *Trib*. Still no reply from Eugenia.

AN INTERVIEW WITH THE CITY EDITOR at the *World Telegram and Sun* started out poorly. He skimmed my clips. "What makes you think a little girl like you from the boonies of Rochester can write for a big city daily?"

"I didn't know geography was the measure of talent."

"I like the way you talk, sister!" He hired me on the spot.

During my first week of working on the *Telegram*'s women's page in August 1963, I kept hearing about an impending protest march on Washington. The country was on high alert. Images from the vicious response of Birmingham's police to a peaceful protest led by Dr. Martin Luther King Jr. and the Freedom Riders—seeing fire hoses and dogs turned on terrified high school students—burned in memory. Medgar Evers had been assassinated only weeks before. My reportorial juices were inflamed. The march was going to be a historic confrontation. Despite dire warnings of certain violence by the government, President Kennedy was supporting Dr. King. I knew the Washington Mall would be crammed with brave black women and men. I would persuade the editor to send me. But when I told Albert my idea, he hit the roof.

"You're pregnant, are you crazy? They're going to teargas people." I had to admit he was right.

We watched the march on TV. When I saw, I ached to be there. I was electrified by Dr. King's speech envisioning a day when children, regardless of their race, would be judged by their character. Seeing the mall dense with the humanity of many colors, I heard not a sound of violence, only silence—rapt silence. I thought about the future of the child growing within me.

It was a hundred years after Lincoln's Emancipation Proclamation, and freedom still had not been given, it had to be won. I vowed I would not spend my life watching the news on TV. I would dare to be there as history happened and write what I saw.

AT THE END OF AUGUST 1963, I was invited to interview with Eugenia Sheppard, a miniature woman perched on piano legs but a force majeure. I flattered her with my archival knowledge of her columns. She wanted me! As a feature writer! Thank God I would never again have to fake passion in print for the latest collection of Junior League tea dresses when all I wanted to do was plunge into the subcultures of New York.

I offered three weeks' notice to the editor who had hired me at the *World Telegram*. Not surprisingly, his face screwed into a bug-eyed facsimile of a jilted lover. "The *World Telegram* will not be used as a stepping-stone for *that paper.* Clear out your desk and leave."

Walking out of the paper's downtown offices into the hammering heat of late summer, I was giddy with anticipation. But what would I wear to pass muster with Eugenia when I had a telltale bulge? I had been told there were two things she found abhorrent—pregnancy and old age. I spent the next couple of days sewing an orange-and-purple-striped knockoff of a Marimekko tent dress that a pregnant Jacqueline Kennedy had worn in the 1960 U.S. presidential campaign.

In my first months at the *Trib,* I turned in the kinds of feature stories that Eugenia considered unsightly at best and radical at worst—about antiwar protesters, abortion rings, New York women doctors volunteering in Selma to sew up beaten civil rights workers, Harlem women on rent strike—while my boss was writing about Gloria Guinness and Wendy Vanderbilt and Betsy Bloomingdale and disease-of-the-month charity balls.

"Bellows wants to see you."

Jim Bellows was editor of the *Herald Tribune*. This could only mean one thing. I had violated the Chinese wall between news and fluff. He would growl something like "Whaddya think you're doing?" and tell me to stick to the soft stuff or get lost.

Bellows was a tensely coiled man with blazing dark eyes. That was the only way one knew he was passionate about what he did, since he spoke as softly as a schoolboy trying to deflect attention from his zits. "Are these yours?" he asked, holding up several clippings of my stories. I stopped breathing and nodded.

"I like this gritty stuff," Bellows mumbled, "in the middle of all the fluff. Keep it up."

Being anointed by Jim Bellows was an epiphany for me. Finding, or being found, by the right editor was as important as finding the right husband. The rare editors could be mentors, even more than mentors, coaches who dared you to surprise them, who scared you by insisting you stretch, who wanted to see you perform the equivalent of a triple Axel jump and fall on your ass on the ice until you perfected the maneuver and then went beyond.

I soon learned that Bellows was the *Trib*'s quiet radical. Named editor in chief of the poststrike paper, he saw himself as a young David with slingshot aimed at the Goliath of the *New York Times*. He was dead set on smashing the old conventional newspaper model and replacing it with bold graphics and offbeat writers. He had hired Clay Felker to tear up the old Sunday supplement and create something entirely fresh. Bellows never played it safe. He was always ready to stick his neck out to support writers or editors who challenged the status quo. I could go back to this editor and tell him the truth.

"Mr. Bellows, I'm pregnant. But don't worry! I'll work until they're ready to roll me into delivery! Meanwhile, I have an idea for using my, um, condition, for a story."

"Shoot."

I wanted to do an investigative series on the maternity clinics of

New York. The city had one of the worst records on infant mortality. By now, I was at the five-month mark in my pregnancy, exactly the point where a good prenatal exam was the best defense against complications for mother or child. If, like so many women, I could not afford to buy private insurance for obstetrical care, my chances of premature birth would be doubled. I told Bellows I would pass myself off as an uninsured waitress whose only recourse for care was public clinics. He gave his blessing.

It was a sobering experience. I sat in dingy waiting rooms and chatted with women who accepted routine abuse from the men in their lives. The bodies of most of the women were bloated with junk food, and their ankles were swollen from stand-up jobs they were sure to lose once the pregnancy showed. I could have been one of these women. We were poked and probed with indifference by trainees who didn't offer their names. No one gave us information on birth control. A day's pay was lost in the waiting. We passed the time making up nasty nicknames for the rude staff. No wonder so many uninsured women resisted this degrading and more or less medically useless experience. I swore I would reveal this disgrace.

After dragging through thirteen public clinics from East Harlem to the Lower East Side, I found it took little effort to write a series exposing unprofessional staff and dangerously careless exams. Some clinics were shut down and supervisors fired. Plans were okayed to create satellite clinics closer to poor neighborhoods. Eugenia said nothing.

ON THE EVENING OF FEBRUARY 20, 1964, I was on night duty at the *Trib* making up the women's page. That meant descending to the depths of the composing room and waddling between the rows of linotype operators to deliver last-minute copy changes. By 10:30 P.M. a proof was run off. I read backward and corrected it. Salem, the composition man, ran his razor between the leaded lines to tidy up the trays of type and off they went to be baked into the morning paper. "Looks good," Salem said. Then, noticing my ninth month of baby bulge, he sweetly suggested I take a taxi home.

"I'm fine." I had just enough energy left to take a bus to the Lower East Side where we had recently moved to dirt-cheap digs. I climbed the four flights of stairs and settled down on the sofa with the cat and a chicken pot pie. I knew I couldn't ask for time off before I had the baby; that would have classified me as a woman who was not as professional as a man. When the grinding began in my belly, I ignored it and went on watching the eleven o'clock news. The contractions began coming with some regularity every four minutes. I called my husband. He was on duty, of course, and told me to come to the hospital. I didn't ask why he couldn't get off to accompany me, but it made me sad that he didn't offer.

It was the dead of winter. February. Snow sifted under the streetlights as I took the slippery stoop step by step. One A.M. by now. It was not normal for a heavily pregnant woman to be wandering around in the wee hours without a husband, except for one reason: imminent delivery. That scares off taxi drivers. I had to ask a waiter inside Ratner's, an old-time kosher restaurant, to hide my telltale suitcase. I walked to the curb of Second Avenue and turned my back to hide my girth and hail a cab. It took some time. I heaved myself in, the waiter slid my suitcase on my lap, but the address gave it all away.

"St. Vincent's Hospital, please."

"Hold on, little lady; you'll make it or we're both in trouble."

I was set on natural childbirth, considered a way-out choice at the time. My husband had protested: "It's not evidence based." Ten hours later, after a long doze when the contractions stopped, I found the lever to release the baby's gateway to the world. Every cell in my body felt alive and in sync. A few painful thrusts and a minute later, the unmistakable cry of a healthy infant made my heart soar. Only then did my husband poke his head in. "Nice work," he said. "You did it your way." We had a daughter.

We chose the Irish name for Mary, one that meant "great" in Gaelic but was softened with vowels—Maura—it came to our lips at almost the same time.

Gail brings newborn Maura to an editorial meeting in the Herald Tribune's *"estrogen zone."*

Not long afterward, to my astonishment, I received a call from the New York Newswomen's Club informing me that I had won an award for the best feature series of the year. Unbeknownst to me, Eugenia had entered my series on maternity clinics. A formal awards dinner was to be held at the Plaza Hotel. Formal! I had a budget of $30 for a dress. I found a long flowered silk nightgown on sale at Henri Bendel. With a fake chignon from a hookers' salon, I could pass Eugenia's taste test.

NOW, A YEAR LATER, CROSSING into the clackety-clack chaos of the *Trib*'s city room plunged me into an alternate universe. Every desk was occupied by a man, and every man wore the same shirt and tie. Except two. I spotted Tom Wolfe. He looked different. His longish silky hair curled over the well-turned collar of an English-tailored tweed suit. He looked like a Tidewater Virginian gentleman, which he was. His lips were locked in a concupiscent smile. Of course, I thought, he must be flicking open his satirical switchblade to dice up the status strivings of some sacred cow who had no idea he was about to be skewered. (Tom had not yet effected the wardrobe of a contemporary Beau Brummel in white suits and spats, nor on a salary of $130 a week.)

Picking my way through the scruffy desks and crumpled copy paper scudding along the floor, I saw a cloud of smoke. A blunt head covered with black Irish curls was vaguely visible. *That must be Jimmy Breslin,* I thought. Just the way his stubby fingers stabbed at the typewriter keys let you know: back off. I knew from his writing that he was an angry man. In one of the early issues of *New York,* he wrote about posting a sign on his lawn in Queens that read WHY I HATE THESE NEIGHBORS, and he published their names. His people were hustlers, bookies, bail bondsmen, kneecappers, and his sidekick, a professional arsonist called Marvin the Torch. Breslin started every day prowling the precincts and courts to check who was getting out of prison, then returned to the city room at six to bang out his story and make the seven o'clock deadline. To loosen up afterward, he'd cross the street to hold court at the legendary Bleeck's tavern and get drunk enough to insult nearly everyone.

Wolfe's prose was the opposite. He invented unforgettable code phrases—"the right stuff," "the statusphere," and "social x-rays." He exuded excesses of hyperbole never before seen on a black-and-white page. He spotted the first "Tycoon of Teen," Phil Spector, and he was the first to explain the vision of Marshall McLuhan. The most mind-blowing of Wolfe's early articles examined the LSD life of Ken Kesey and his Merry Pranksters.

Wolfe's and Breslin's windows into New York life assaulted city dwellers with stories that rubbed their noses in the true textures of the city—from the pretentiousness of Park Avenue dinner parties to the barstool exploits of colorful hustlers. My feeling about these writers was a stew made of equal parts admiration and competition. The city room was not an alternate universe. It was *the* universe.

As often as I encountered Breslin in the elevator, he never even gave me a nod. To Breslin, women were irrelevant. Tom Wolfe did exchange a few words with me, in passing, and I hung on them. "The *Herald Tribune* is like the main Tijuana bullring for competition among feature writers," he told me. "You have to be brave."

I was little, but I liked to think I was brave. I had a taste for adventure. Why couldn't a woman write about the worlds that men wrote about? What about the world of prostitutes and pimps? The speed freaks creating a world of their own on the Lower East Side? The radical kids at Columbia beginning to make noise about Kennedy's excursions into Vietnam? But men ran the newspapers and magazines that mattered in those days. Men read the news on TV. Men wrote the editorials that told people what to think. Why should men dictate what women could and couldn't do?

Clay Felker was different. Not only was he open to women writers, he was actively recruiting and training them. Barbara Goldsmith, a socially prominent New Yorker who had a keen eye for cultural trends, was one of the first to spot Andy Warhol as the bellwether of the '60s. Her *New York Times* review of Warhol's book *From A to*

Z caught Felker's eye. He not only started her writing about the art world, he came to depend on Goldsmith and Wolfe to give him feedback on other new writers he was cultivating.

Patricia Bosworth was then a young actress playing on Broadway in *Mary, Mary*. Felker got her talking about her gabfests with other leading ingenues. He encouraged Bosworth to take notes, and he published their backstage bitching. "It made my name," Patty told me when she and I became friends. Patty dropped acting and went on to become a famous journalist and biographer.

These women were among the first female feature writers who busted into the *Trib*'s Tijuana bullring, and I wanted to be like them. But women then needed a male sponsor. The blessing by Bellows initiated a period in my life that I came to recognize, retrospectively, as the Pygmalion Years. What began with Bellows led to the feet of Clay.

MY FIRST EXPOSURE TO CLAY FELKER was his voice, a legendary voice. It roared out of his bullpen and whipsawed through the walls of the city room with the force of a busted steam pipe. None of the working reporters looked up; they had learned to ignore it. Outside his doorless lair, I had a chance to observe the man. Half-high partitions were slapped together to enclose, barely, a desk littered with newspapers and magazines, two chairs, a typewriter and a phone, which was affixed to Felker's ear while his feet rested on that desk. He was ruggedly handsome with a square John Wayne jaw and a forehead as broad as a search lamp. He further emphasized his presence by wearing an awning-striped shirt with gold cuff links. He was barking into the phone.

"What do you *mean* you don't have my reservation! *Clay Felker*, three for dinner tonight, my usual table, in the Pool Room."

The poor devil on the other end must have dissolved into broth when Felker demanded to speak to the Four Seasons maître d'hôtel. Who knew better than Felker, having invented the term "Siberia" for tables to which no-count potted plants were shown, that he and the maître d'hôtel of the state dining room for the media and entertainment elite had an *understanding*; he would be seated as prominently as a marble bust in the entrance of the Met.

"I'm taking Senator Javits and his wife out for pretheater supper— Pamela's opening tonight in *Dinner at Eight*," he told the maître d'. A long pause while the man must have been buttering him up.

"*Terrific!*" Felker's bombast of approval was as thrilling as his displeasure was terrifying.

"Pamela" could only be Pamela Tiffin, an ingenue with an angel face and cream puff of a body, who was Clay's wife. This man seemed to know everybody; he had a senator to please and a beautiful wife opening in a Broadway show. Who was I? One short-lived boyfriend had labeled me "a skinny, brainy chick," and he hadn't meant it as a compliment. Back then, few men wanted to know what a chick *thought*. But I had the one thing Clay Felker prized above all. A good story. I'd have only seconds to spit it out.

"Mr. Felker?"

He looked up. "Come in. It's Clay." He asked where I had come from.

"The estrogen zone," I said, pointing upstairs. He smiled.

"What have you got?"

The story in my mind was like Jell-O that hadn't yet set. I began clumsily explaining that it was about single guys renting co-ed beach houses on Fire Island—they were holding auditions to attract beautiful girls—they'd only have to pay for a half-share, and then—

"What the hell are you trying to say?"

I had lost his attention.

"The guys are dorks. They want gorgeous girls to act like flypaper and attract people to their parties. These auditions are funny—like specimen viewings."

"Did you go to a specimen viewing?"

"Of course."

"Then write that scene—just as you described it! We'll call it Flypaper People."

Writing scenes was something I had done since I was seven or eight years old. But writing scenes as journalism? Clay had pushed me over the edge.

I liked it there.

CHAPTER 2

CROSSROADS OF A MILLION PRIVATE LIVES

THE GUN GOING OFF AT MY BACK is what I remember best. I was five, but old enough to enter the six-and-under swimming race. Bent over in a racing dive, hanging on to the edge of a cement dock by my toes, I would look at the mean gray slap of salty waves and shiver, but my father had a gun at my back. I'm not sure now if he actually was the starter but I always imagined it was him. The shot would explode—*craaack!*—but I'd already be in the air. I was little but I was fast. I had to beat the boys. I was the only child.

Half my early childhood was spent underwater. We lived in an old Indian town called Mamaroneck. As a child I couldn't pronounce it so I'd say "mama-round-your-neck." It was one of the earliest postwar suburbs, in Westchester County, a forty-minute commute to New York City by train, but you'd never know it when you awoke to the tickle of salt in your nose and the squeal of gulls.

Our house was across the street from the fat tub of a harbor. Hurricanes could swell it up like a bath with the faucets left on until it spilled over into our street and turned into a river. Daddy let me sit in a washtub and pretend I was paddling out to sea in a beautiful pea-green boat. My father was my coach. He taught me a mean backhand and how to smack a baseball, but girls then couldn't compete against

Gail at age five.

boys in tennis or baseball so Daddy told me to stick to the water. He taught me to swim when I was three.

My father's hands were long and soft and well manicured, the hands of a salesman. My launch came from those hands. My mother was the mooring. Her hands would cup under my armpits in the split second before my head dipped below water. Times when my head did dip and my nose and mouth took in the ocean and I thrashed like a fish, my father's arms would curl me up but only for a few instants, then flip me around and set my feet to fluttering. "Kick like a frog, and you'll never go down." I would kick to my mother and her hands would reach for my stretched-out arms. Oh, Mama, yes, safe again, ready for another oceanic crossing.

Let me be clear about this. My father didn't really mind my being a girl, but I had to do double duty, as a boy-girl. He told me I could be a champion if I practiced hard enough and never gave up. The beach club he joined had a swim team. I would fly on my bike down to the end of Orienta Point to get to the club's practice lanes before anyone so I could do laps before an important meet.

Notwithstanding, the gun went off at my back summer after summer and I captured a good number of medals for my father. He built a wooden case and displayed the trophies on velvet lining and hung the case in his bedroom. But I didn't always win. "Go cut a branch off the forsythia bush," he would say in a dark monotone when we got home from a losing meet. The first time he switched my legs, they bled. I didn't cry. I tried to take it like a man. But it wasn't the switchings that hurt so much. It was the anticipation of being switched, being shamed.

No children my age lived around our house. The kids who did were mostly boys and a lot bigger than I was. Toey was the meanest one. He liked to get into fights, which is why they called him Toey, because one kid stomped on his toe and broke it. So he picked on girls.

Toey liked to push over my doll carriage. He would wait until I was distracted by pretending to buy groceries with one of my mother's pocketbooks, and then he'd rock the carriage until I screamed to see my doll falling out. Toey just laughed. One day I filled up a plastic bag with water and ice cubes and twisted the top to hold it all inside. I put the bag in the carriage. Pretending not to see him as I sauntered past, I waited for him to start rocking my carriage. Then I pulled out the water bag and twirled around with it in my hands and hit him on his backside. The bag burst open and water splattered all over. Toey didn't cry, but it looked like he wet his pants so he ran home sniveling for his mother.

"Good, you bopped him one," my father said.

It made him proud of me. So when bigger kids in nursery school tried to take away toys that I was playing with, I knew what to do.

One day I was putting together tracks for a toy train. I remember the boy with yellow hair. He wasn't bigger than me, but he kept pulling my tracks apart. I told him to stop. "My tracks!"

"No, mine."

So I picked up a piece of track and bopped him one. He cried bloody murder.

I didn't really mind being kicked out of nursery school. My mother diverted me into dancing school. I liked being a girl. I loved being able to dress up as a shrimp with two other little girls and dance in a recital at Honey Adams Dance School. My mother sewed us pink tutus and made satin headpieces with two long antennae sticking out of the tops. My father told me that shrimps have five swimming legs. After that, I tried even harder to win races for him. He loved me when I won.

GRANDMA GLADYS, MY FATHER'S MOTHER, was my polestar, a dependable navigator. She lived with us. In her room, one could dream. It smelled of lilies of the valley; a fresh bouquet was always on her dressing table. But one had to be invited into her room. She had "valuables." She didn't believe in banks. Grandma Gladys never went out of the house without lacing herself up in her corsets. She kept a suede pouch snapped on to her garter belt so she could always be sure her valuables were safe. Inside the pouch were two diamond rings. I was allowed to take them out, one at a time, but only if her door was locked. My grandmother wasn't taking any chances.

She would let me sit on her lap and punch the keys of her typewriter. I loved the *thwock* of the keys as they made the words. My fingers weren't strong enough at five to make all the letters in, say, *butterfly*. But after a couple more years of practice, I could type *prestidigitation*. Grandma Gladys said I was ready for my own typewriter, and she gave me one for my seventh birthday.

Gail's mother, Lillian Rainey Henion, modeling, circa 1932.

Grandmother Gladys Latham Ovens (center in hat) *and Gail's father, Harold Merritt Henion* (far right), *circa 1928.*

I was nine when my sister, Trish, was born. After that, things pretty much fell apart. My mother began sleeping on the couch all day. I got to be the mother. I had a real baby to walk in a carriage and feed with a bottle. My mother and father moved into separate bedrooms. I lost my own room, my own dreaming place, the writing nook that my father had outfitted for me with a desk and vanity table. Now he slept there. I was moved to the other twin bed in my mother's room. My baby sister's crib was in the corner. While my mother read paperback books with names like *Sweet Savage Love,* I would read Nancy Drew mysteries.

My father began bringing home his golf friend. Her name was Bernice and she was bigger than he was with a laugh like a man's. They liked to have wrestling contests on our living room floor. I could hear them downstairs. They didn't see me peeking between the staircase balusters. Bernice wore Bermuda shorts. Her legs stuck out, big as bolsters. She could sit on my slender father and wrap a huge leg around him and hold him down until he laughed so hard, it scared me. I remember once calling to my mother, "Mommy, Daddy's girlfriend is hurting him!"

She didn't come.

My mother would be in her bedroom with all the shades pulled down, snoring like a dog. I was scared of the smell in her room. She told me it was nail polish remover. But it came from her mouth.

I remember my mother telling me over and over about her dream to become an opera singer. Years later, I learned from my maternal grandmother how hard she had tried to make my mother's dream come true. Agnes Rooney was the only one of her seven sisters to step out of the trough of water in the Lisburn linen factory of Northern Ireland and flee to the docks, at age fifteen, where she caught a boat to America to barter herself as a mail-order bride. She was married to an engineer so miserly he bought a wife off the boat. Somehow, Agnes squirreled away the money to buy my mother opera lessons.

When the miser found out, he beat her and terminated my mother's lessons. To win her freedom from that marriage, Agnes had to barter her daughter. Forced to drop out of high school as the price to free Agnes, my mother had to work as her father's housekeeper for two years. Modeling and hairdressing on the side, she earned enough to be released at eighteen.

She must have thought marrying my father was a great step up. He was handsome and came from an affluent family. He was also a college man, with graduation from Cornell in sight until the Depression made him quit. She loved him, too; I'm certain of that now, because he was able to break her heart.

Marriage meant the end of her own aspirations. "No wife of mine needs to work" was my father's decree. It was the patriarchal edict of my mother's father all over again. Men who rode the commuter trains to New York, and competed for the prettiest split-level and the latest Chrysler model, and played golf all day Saturday had wives who did not work. They were part of the furnishings of a successful man's house. An adequate breadwinner wouldn't have a wife who worked.

My mother's attention would come and go, like clouds. She was there for me, mostly, in the daytime. But after dark my mother's bright star would float away during dinner and rotate into some realm known only to her. She would leave the table.

"Where did Mommy go?" I'd ask.

"Sinus attack," my father would say.

He didn't entirely crush my mother's dream of becoming a performer. She turned to me as the surrogate artist in the family, giving me dance and music lessons. She bought a piano at auction so she could teach me to play for her while she sang "Indian Love Call" and imagined herself as Jeanette MacDonald. My father almost killed her. She was so happy when she sang, my mother, and I loved her spirit. On Friday nights, if my father took her out to a party, she would come home singing and happy, all red and shiny. I'd play the piano for her and she would dance. Sometimes, she ~~~ boys at my birthday parties. My friends said how luck~~ such a fun mother.

ONE OF THE BEST THINGS about my earliest childhood were the blackouts. The war was far away, in Europe and Japan, but we practiced blackouts in case the enemy tried to attack our country. Around dinnertime the lights in our neighbors' windows would blink off, the few streetlights would dim, and I was allowed to strike matches to make little halos of light from candles. I couldn't wait to climb out on the roof under my bedroom window and watch the stars flung across the black sky like careless diamonds. To a child, war had a lot to offer.

When I was six, my cousin Ranny came home funny from that war. His skin was yellow from malaria, and his hands shook when he smoked cigarettes, which was all the time. He stayed with us for a while and sometimes screamed out at night. "Shell-shocked," my father told me, whatever that was. I asked my father if he would have to go to war. No, definitely not, but he wouldn't tell me why. I found out from Ranny. When they were kids playing with slingshots, Ranny had accidentally put out my father's left eye. Grandma Gladys had called upon a Christian Science practitioner to pray for the "error" to be taken away and my father's eye to be restored. It didn't work.

Nobody would answer my question: Why did my father still have two eyes? I only found out when I spied on him one night through the partly open bathroom door. He took a little box out of the medicine cabinet, opened it carefully, and took out something that glowed like a magic orb, white and shiny with a brown center—a glass eye! I formed the impression that my father had special sight. With that magic eye he could see things that nobody else could.

It wasn't war that scared me. It was Bert the Turtle. He was a toon character they showed us in sixth grade. When a firecracker went off behind his head, Bert ducked into his shell and sang, *Dum dum, deedle dum dum, Duck, and Cover, Duck, and Cover.* The singsong voice of a civil defense worker told us just what to do: *We all know the atomic bomb is very dangerous. We must get ready for it. The atomic bomb flash can burn you worse than the worst sunburn. Now, you and I don't have shells to crawl into like Bert the Turtle. So don't wait! Duck and cover.*

I don't have to tell you how reassuring this was for children. We would dive under our desks and wait for the flash. With controlled alarm, the voice of the civil defense worker would issue a final, comforting instruction: *We must be ready, all the time, for the atomic bomb.* I always wanted to ask my father if his magic eye could see an atomic flash in time to warn us.

IN THE CHAOS OF OUR FAMILY LIFE, one person's position relative to me did not change: Grandma Gladys's. On Saturday mornings she invited me into her room to listen to a radio show called *Grand Central Station.* I was enthralled by the stories, tense psychological dramas inspired by O. Henry. The sound effects pushed away the confines of our little stucco house on a tidy suburban street. Over a frenetic score, the narrator followed the rhythm of the trains as they flashed by the tenement houses south of 125th Street and dove into the long tunnel beneath the swank buildings along Park Avenue, and then . . . a screech of brakes and hiss of steam as the narrator shouted:

GRAND CENTRAL STATION! CROSSROADS OF A MILLION PRIVATE LIVES!

I began dreaming about riding into the city on one of those very trains. I just had to see those millions of private lives crashing up against one another and write about them. That was a different era: the Eisenhower 1950s. America was flush. Houses going up. Children playing hopscotch on side streets. Cars looking out for kids on bikes. Parents didn't much care where we went on Saturday as long as we were home for dinner. Bicycles made us free. My friends and I had hideouts in the woods. We roughhoused with older boys. When the ice broke up on Mamaroneck Harbor, I would go down with boots and a broomstick and pole-vault from iceberg to iceberg.

Nowadays, no doubt, someone would call Child Protective Services. My mother and father would be arraigned and sent to a parent retraining course or worse. But in that *Ed Sullivan Show* era, children were not the obsession of adults. We were there to flesh out the family album.

In seventh grade, I started to sneak into the city on Saturday mornings. My grandmother understood. She kept my secret and gave me the change to call her if anything untoward happened. The New Haven train stopped frequently at our station, a commuter hub. I bought my ticket from the old ticket master. "Tap class," I'd say, then do a little shuffle and ball-and-chain. He'd smile benevolently and punch out my ticket to the crossroads of a million private lives. My legs were too short to reach the high steps to the old washboard trains, but somebody would always give me a boost. The ride to Grand Central Station took only forty-three minutes. Then I'd run up the steps to the marble balcony that overlooked the teeming throng and become a giant telescope, sweeping around, all-seeing, able to record everyone's secrets. No one knew I was there. No one knew I was missing. Except Grandma. I was little but I was in control. I had a notebook and a pencil.

The aqua ceiling was as high as the real sky. Animals flew across it, outlined in gold stars. An invisible voice echoed off the marble walls: "Stamford, Track Fifteen!" I scribbled notes about the stick figures below. Why did the bearded man stop when he bumped into the woman with a floppy hat? She must be passing him microfilm; they were Communists, like the bad people Senator McCarthy talked about on TV. I dreamed myself into the life of the colored man who sat on the floor with one trouser leg empty from the knee down. His sign read NEED A LEG UP. Was he really a cripple? Yes, but he had a fine wooden leg at home. He would put it on and go out at night to play his trumpet and pretend to be Louis Armstrong. Who was the little lost dog who yapped and yapped and dragged his bottom across the floor? He must have dropped from the aqua ceiling. He needed somebody to put him back up among the stars.

I couldn't wait to ride back to our dozy suburb. I'd bike home to the desk my father had built beneath the window overlooking our porch and punch out little stories on my typewriter. Sometimes, I got so excited, I'd jump off the roof of the porch and roll over in the backyard. That was what they scolded me for, not for the secret rides into the city on my magical mystery train.

I ASKED MY GRANDMA GLADYS to tell me her story so I could write a "book" about her. Born Gladys Latham Ovens in 1887, she was proud to tell me that her ancestor, William Latham, came over from London on the *Mayflower* in 1620. (I had no idea then that hundreds of thousands of Americans had ancestors who somehow managed to stow away in the hold of that hundred-foot-long vessel, unbeknownst to the 102 men and women whose names were actually on the passenger list.) But Grandma had records to prove that Billy Latham really was one of the early settlers of New London. "A pretty shrewd customer," she said, making me promise not to tell that he was the town tax assessor and he cheated on his taxes! Now Cary Latham, his son, she told me, was even shrewder. He got the lease for the ferry from Groton to the other side of the Pequot River. That made him as rich as a tollbooth!

Grandma Gladys had married a man named Harold Merritt (like

the Parkway) Henion. They had one son, my father, also named Harold Merritt Henion. But until the day she died, my grandmother would call my father "Sonny Boy." Did that mean he never had to grow up? She didn't answer my question.

It wasn't until I was older that I learned about the Great Depression. Grandma's husband didn't have to jump out a window on Wall Street when he lost all his savings. He suffered a stroke at the age of fifty and died in my father's arms. Grandma Gladys had no money and no skills. She had never gone anywhere except in the backseat of a car or a horse-drawn carriage. But she remained true to the self-reliance of her forebears. She promptly learned how to drive, bought a typewriter, taught herself to type, and marched out to get herself a full-time job as a real estate agent. For the next forty years she went to work from nine to five every day. Still working, she moved in with us when I was a baby. I never heard her complain.

I would be the first of the women in my family to go to college, something I wanted desperately. My father took me out in the backyard for a serious talk. I planned to be an English major. He said he was prepared to pay my tuition to a state university, but after graduation, immediately after, I would be expected to support myself, and a B.A. in English wasn't going to earn me carfare.

"The University of Vermont has a good home economics department," he said. "Why don't you study something practical?"

"You want me to get an MRS degree?" I was crestfallen. I wanted to be a writer. Didn't he know? Hadn't he edited my copycat Nancy Drew mystery stories? He'd even read some of my stories out loud to his golf friend. "She's every bit Hal Henion's daughter, can't you tell?" But when it came to money, my father was a tightwad just like my mother's father. I could not pretend that I could make a living at writing. Who did?

Because Vermont was basically an agricultural school with a robust

government extension service, the home ec department was the closest thing they had to a business curriculum. They told me I could
take courses in economics, advertising, design, even public speaking.
I agreed to take a double major, English and—the one I never told my
friends about—home ec.

I WANTED THE FRAGMENTS OF MY YOUNG LIFE to link up and
convey the satisfying feeling one gets from piecing together a puzzle.
I was my grandmother's child: plucky and selfish, and determined to
be a writer. I was my mother's child: a cute little shrimp who liked
being onstage. I was my father's child: coached to be as competitive as
boys and sent out into the world to win, for him. But there are puzzle
pieces that I left out, jagged pieces that didn't fit into a neat coherent
picture.

It was my sister, on reading an early draft of my recollections, who
pierced my idealized rendition of our father. I'd always told people
that he encouraged my writing, how he'd get down on the floor with
me and help me concoct stories. What more could a writer want in a
father?

You forget, my sister said, you became more successful than he
was. He never read anything you published. Not one of the hundreds
of magazine articles you sent him. Not one of the books you've written. Not a word.

CHAPTER 3

FALSE STARTS

CHEERS STARTLE THE SILENT VERMONT NIGHT. A ladder slaps against the sill of my dormitory window. All along the third floor, girls in rag curlers and baby doll pajamas throw open their windows and stick their heads out, straining to witness a scene as dramatic as a high school production of *Romeo and Juliet*.

"He's here! Gail, come out!"

My roommate is calling for me, calling for the girl who was thrilled only hours ago because of a summons from her excitable boyfriend.

"I'm coming to get you," he had announced over the long-distance line in his dark and secretive voice. "After midnight. Be ready."

Tremors of dangerous delight.

"But they lock the doors after curfew."

"I don't need a door. I'll use my extension ladder. Your room's the last one on the left, third floor, right?"

"Your ladder! You're a genius."

"Wait at the window."

Ladders have always excited me. I used to climb a ladder up to the ten-foot diving board. That was a heart-in-the-mouth climb. The ladder my father put up against the little roof under my bedroom window was meant to discourage me from jumping. I used it in high school to sneak out in the middle of the night and meet my friends to drink beer and smoke cigarettes. Ladders are challenge. Ladders are adventure. Ladders allow escape.

I am in the bathroom primping, knees shaking, heart racing. How does a girl dress to elope? I'm not ready. This is only my third week at the University of Vermont. I've hardly finished unpacking. I don't have a white dress. The black-and-white polka dot I was going to wear to the first freshman dance will have to do. And white gloves, the beautiful white kid gloves my mother gave me for church. The thought of church turns me limp. I can't put my lipstick on straight. Does God know?

"C'MON, GAIL, C'MON! He's climbing up the ladder!"

I am about to be wooed away from confinement on the freshman women's campus of a remote university into the arms of a lover who will not take no for an answer. I am all of seventeen. He is a ravishing twenty-two, a real man, a brooding veteran who has seen the hell of war and has the wounds to show for it. My Romeo holds the lure of jailbreak.

I had warned him. "If the housemother sees a man on the girls' campus, my God, she'll call out the Green Mountain Boys!"

"I've got my knife, got my ladder, I'm ready for them," he said. He sounds like he's back in the swamps of Korea. He's a man on a mission. My crazy brave Romeo is going to spirit me away on his extension ladder to a life of adventure where my father can never hold a gun to my back again. All my new girlfriends are jealous.

They sing to me as I back out the window, sobbing silently. *Goodnight, sweetheart, well it's time to go, Doo doo doo de do.* One last glance at my roommate's sad face, our cozy little room, the poster of Elvis we tacked to the wall, the books on my desk that invite me into new worlds—do I really want to give all this up? *I hate to leave you, baby, and I don't mean maybe.* My foot slips, the high heel falls off—*heels, Gail, what are you thinking?* I feel his hands, big mannish hands, the hands of a tree surgeon who knows how to brace branches. His hands circle my whole waist and steady me like a falling tree. I am in his hands now.

We get no farther than the Vermont border before I ask to stop. "I need to make a phone call." I can see that McCarthy—that's his name (he likes to be called by his last name as if he's still a soldier)—is not pleased. He senses something is not right. His mission is to steal me away from college before I get any high-class ideas about another kind of life and throw him over. He drives straight through this dot of a city, past the police station, the public library, the opera house. I beg him to stop.

"I have to call my mother."

"What the hell do you want to do that for?" he demands.

"I always tell my mother what I'm doing," I fib.

"I don't like this idea, Gail."

I stare at this man's profile, his lips drawn tight as a slash, and wonder how I let him take over my life. When he turned up in town at the start of my senior year in high school, the proverbial tall dark stranger, he pursued me wherever I went, offering me rides home from school, turning up at football games, even crashing parties where he must have known I would be bored with boys my own age. He was worldly and exuded a dark and illicit energy. There were days when he would lure me to sit in the cab of his truck during my study hall break and have a cigarette with him. He brought me wildflowers and told me of the terrors of war. I thought, of course, that I could save him from his paranoid fears; I would make him believe again that people can be good.

Toward the end of the year, I would sneak out at night to meet him a few blocks from my house. He would take me to his house and make us scotch and sodas and kiss me with a violent passion. He showed me the long purplish dent in his thigh where he had been knifed by the enemy. I found it strangely erotic. When we finally coupled, the scream of pain quickly surged into a crescendo of desire that scarcely left me for the rest of the summer. I was lost to lust.

My mother tolerated him. My father wanted to kill him. *That maniac McCarthy*, he called him.

Before we cross the Vermont border, I persuade him to pull into a roadhouse. He finds the bar while I look for a pay telephone. Thank God it's in the ladies' room. I call home. I pray my mother's head won't be in the clouds. She answers.

"Hello, honey, everything all right?"

"McCarthy wants to marry me," I blurt. "We're eloping, but don't worry, we'll be fine."

A long pause, I hear her thick breathing. "Where are you right now?"

"Driving. In his truck."

"You've left school?"

"It was really exciting, Mom. He came for me with his tree ladder and all the girls—"

"Where are you headed?"

"Massachusetts. He has a nice motel picked out."

Her voice shifts suddenly into a calming neutral. "Honey, don't do anything right now. Marriage is a big step. Don't you want to have a lovely wedding? Honey?"

She must know. This isn't all the romantic getaway I'm pretending it is.

"Mom? Are you there?" She must be telling my father. I wait, trembling. When she comes back on the phone, her voice is silky as warm bathwater. She coaxes me to come home and we'll talk it all over. "You don't want to elope and miss all the fun, you know? Shopping for the dress, I can give you a new hairstyle, we can have the reception on the terrace of the new house . . ." She is making it up as she goes along, bless her heart.

"Can I speak to Daddy? It won't cost him anything, if I elope, I mean." I hear her put her hand over the receiver and my father shouting in the background.

"Your father is going to bed tonight with a gun beside him."

"A gun? Why?"

"Baby, just drive right straight home and we'll work it all out, together." I can't remember when my mother sounded so sober and sure of herself.

McCarthy has that beery look in his eyes when I find him in the bar. He interrogates me about the phone call. Foolishly, I tell him about my father and his gun. I can almost see the hairs on the back of McCarthy's neck stand up, the macho surge. Back in the truck I can't stop thinking about McCarthy's knives. He likes to show me how he can skin a rabbit with his army combat knife. His evasion knife is the most menacing, thin, black, easily hidden.

I somehow convince him that we need to see my parents together, to show them we're serious. The fight starts when we pull off the Saw Mill River Parkway. I know, he knows, once I go back home and think about sacrificing college to be Mrs. Tree Surgeon, our elopement will lose its allure. It is almost five in the morning. We are turning off the Boston Post Road onto the avenue leading to my house.

"Let me off before Claflin Avenue, okay?"

"I'm not letting you off anywhere," McCarthy says. "I love you and we're getting married, just like you said on the phone."

"But my father—"

"Forget your father. I'm going to take care of you now."

As his truck grumbles into the long climb up our hill, I am overtaken by nausea.

"Stop the car, let me out, I have to puke." He refuses. I beg. He reaches across me to try to lock my door. I grab his hand. "Don't make me bite you!"

He slows down and I bolt out. Jackknifing up from the fall, I start running, streaking across backyards, scrambling over fences; spilling out two driveways from our house, I feel my skirt catch on something, a bush? No, a hand. His big hand, he's trying to clutch at me! I feel the rush of adrenaline. I'm little but I'm fast. There's a light on in our living room. I sprint for the door.

It is my mother's arms into which I fall. I hear the swoosh of a window sash sliding up. My father's voice: "Crazy McCarthy! I'll give you a count of three to disappear—you hear—or I'll point my weapon right at your pecker!"

His truck spits gravel as he tears off. My mother nudges me to the sofa, covers me with a quilt, and brings me tea. It isn't useless to expect help from my mother, after all.

"Mom, I'm pregnant," I choke out.

"I know."

"How?"

"I'm your mother."

We sit for a long time in the dimness of a slow dawn, hands clasped. My mother begins to pray: "The Lord is my Shepherd; I shall not want. He maketh me to lie down in green pastures: He leadeth me beside the still waters."

I repeat with her: "He restoreth my soul." I start to sob. "My soul"—the shame chokes me—"my soul has no scruples."

"Let's pray to the Lord to take away your sins."

We pray. Time passes.

"Don't cry," she says. "You do not have to have this baby."

It takes time for the enormity of her gift to sink in. Gone is the cloudiness in her eyes. The whites glare like searchlights. She has stopped spinning out of the present and coalesced around the memory of a moment she lived before, the memory of a father who foreclosed her own future. Later that morning she dials doctor after doctor, then phones McCarthy and commands him to drive us in her car to New Jersey, that is, if he ever wants to see me again. She sits with me in the backseat and keeps up a pleasant pretense of conversation with him, the way people do when humoring a kidnapper.

The anesthesia of fear has robbed from my memory where exactly we went, except there was no back alley, just a normal doctor's office. Of the procedure, I remember nothing. What I will never forget is my mother's voice, singing to me in the backseat of the car as she cradled my head in her lap on the way home . . . *Hush little baby, don't you cry, Mama's going to sing you a lullaby* . . . her soft hand stroking my forehead, dabbing at my tears, mothering me. *Hush little baby . . .*

THE DEAN WAS NOT HARSH. She told me I could return to the University of Vermont but only if all of my professors agreed. I called them, one by one, and apologized for my reckless behavior. My English professor confessed that she had thought of eloping herself but was saved when her boyfriend's junk car broke down; she and I would become friends. I took a Greyhound back and walked up the long hill from the bus station and the half mile to the women's campus, longing for the very confinement that I had sought to escape. My roommate and I squealed with delight to be back in our private girl-world together.

McCarthy called my dorm night after night. My dorm mates knew to put him off. Over that Christmas vacation he drove by my house to tell me, no, threaten me, that if I didn't come back to him, he was going to marry someone else. I feigned disappointment. I never saw him again.

This is what is important: I vowed to revirginate myself. Not until I married would I ever allow myself to go "all the way" again. I kept that vow. In my junior year, however, my southern boyfriend in the Kappa Sig house next door to my sorority house made a grandstand play. We were in his car, enjoying a light makeout session, when music on the radio was interrupted for an emergency broadcast. The Soviet Union had sent something called *Sputnik* into orbit, the first artificial satellite in history. All the commentators sounded unnerved. This meant the evil rival could attack us from space. My boyfriend put his lips to my ear.

"We could be blown away tomorrow. This may be our last chance to know real love. Let's do it."

"Nice try," I said.

Countless *Sputnik* babies were conceived that night. I was proud not to be included in those statistics.

THINGS BEGAN LOOKING UP ONCE I graduated from UVM in 1958. I had interviewed for a job at the Manhattan headquarters of J. C. Penney on West Thirty-Fourth Street. My friends snickered when I came back to school from spring vacation and told them how excited I was to have a job at J. C. Penney. "What, selling long johns to old ladies?" That's what the stores in rural America were known for, of course, but I had done some research and found out that Penney's had a consumer service department, forerunner of the public relations bonanza, and it published two consumer magazines.

"No, actually," I told my friends. "I was interviewed by Mr. James Cash Penney himself."

The legendary entrepreneur from Missouri was then in his eighties and had a bushy white mustache that wagged when he smiled. He had Golden Rule written all over his face (indeed, his first stores were called Golden Rule stores). I had learned from reading about him that he always called his employees "associates." Men became manager-partners in new stores and shared in the profits. Penney's goal was not to build a chain of stores but to assemble a chain of "good men."

"What do you want to be in five years?" Mr. Penney inquired. A writer, I said, or maybe a buyer. He asked if I'd like to start in their management training program. "Do you train girls as managers, too?" I asked. He said they were just starting. "Do you pay girls the same as boys?" I dared to ask. He looked surprised. He smiled, puffed up a little, and pulled on his suspenders. "We certainly should." And so he did.

That was 1958. Unbeknownst to me, I had struck a faint blow for equal opportunity employment, which would not become a national issue for another decade. That job allowed me to travel America in a hat and gloves to put on educational fashion shows at college home economics departments, displaying Penney's fabrics. Oshkosh, Appleton, Kansas City—it was an education in small-town American values that never left me. I was also able to write for the company's magazines and work with Madison Avenue ad agencies to make informational filmstrips. This was so much more exciting than the lives of my girlfriends who had graduated with engagement rings or fraternity pins padlocked over their bras. They seemed to be time traveling straight into middle age.

I made an ironclad pact with myself: I would not marry anyone, not even Prince Charming, for at least two years after college. I wasn't going to be trapped like my mother. I just made it to age twenty-three. My suitor was a charming imposter who found me at Manhattan's White Horse Tavern on a Sunday afternoon. My roommate and I were waiting for the paint to dry in our one-room bachelorette pad a block away.

"Squadron Leader Greville Bell, R.A.F." He introduced himself in an impeccable British accent. "Fair lady, would you be so kind as to help out a stranger to your city?" I was a pushover for men in uniform, although now that I recall, this man was wearing a raincoat. But he was good-looking and so very polite and obviously helpless. He needed assistance in counting out change for a tip. "This is the pub made famous by Dylan Thomas, is it not?" he asked.

"The very one."

"'If I were tickled by the rub of love, I would not fear the apple nor the flood,'" he recited.

"'Nor the bad blood of spring,'" I chimed in. It wasn't every day that a man recited poetry to me. I could be smitten by this English-man. Squadron Leader Greville Bell was adorably sincere and worth another chance. Over the next few weeks, he called several times for dates but I was always busy. In a final attempt, he trotted out his true identity. The accent flattened suddenly to the nasality of a nice Irish Catholic boy from Connecticut.

"My real name is Albert Francis Sheehy." He confessed that he was the son of a police captain and presently living in "reduced circum-stances" while pursuing the noble aspiration of becoming a physician. I wound up laughing. Albert said if I could find it in my heart to forgive him, he would really like to take me out on a date. He courted me for a year, mostly long distance, since he was a first-year medical student at the University of Rochester.

I was happy being single and free to travel in my white-gloved job, but Albert was nothing if not persistent. He wrote to me in poetry. He could talk to me about Dostoyevsky and laugh with me over *Port-noy's Complaint*. He was five years older and horny. But even when he came to New York over vacations, I held fast to my pledge of revir-gination. I must have driven him to a frenzy of frustration. He had done four years in the air force as an officer attached to the RAF and he was impatient to get on with his life. He wanted a wife.

I loved him. And I admired his noble aspiration. He was sincerely committed to serving mankind, despite a lack of family money and loading himself with debt. My desire to be a writer paled into selfish-ness. No, worse, it smacked of ambition, and in a woman, ambition was abhorrent.

COPS NAB POET IN COFFEE HOUSE was the headline on the *Rochester Democrat & Chronicle* the day in 1960 we returned to Rochester as a married couple. We laughed. In Rochester, poets were the enemy. It was only 350 miles from Manhattan, but I could have sworn it was an iceberg broken off from somewhere in the upper Midwest that floated through the Great Lakes and grounded itself in the snowbelt of western New York State. It was always cold. The other medical school wives were even colder. Most had money somewhere in their families and were rehearsing to run Junior Leagues and silent auctions to benefit the halt and the lame. They wore cashmere sweater sets and often played bridge and drank in the afternoon. I didn't. I worked. My career aspirations were perceived as unbecoming for the wife of a future physician, even subversive.

I applied for my first newspaper job at the *Democrat & Chronicle,* a decent Gannett paper. The editor of the women's page, George Jewell, ignored the samples of my writing and went after my age and gender.

"How old are you?"

"Twenty-three."

"And married," he said suspiciously, studying my application. "How long?"

"Just a year. I want to make a career."

"Not a family?"

"Well, yes, eventually."

This was a classic example of the either-or boxes into which most females were slotted at the time: either holy mother or frigid career girl.

"So, since you've waited so long, you'll probably want to get pregnant pretty soon."

"I didn't expect this to be a maternity exam."

"I'm sorry, Mrs. Sheehy."

"Gail."

"But I don't want another girl reporter who's going to learn the ropes here and go get pregnant on me."

As I gathered up my writing samples, Mr. Jewell threw me a lifeline. "I'm going to ask our editor in chief to see you." His name was straight out of *Front Page*—Red Vag—a bantam rooster of a man with a cockscomb of red Irish hair. He liked that I was Irish, too.

"Mr. Vag, I'm married to a medical student. They make about a dollar ninety-eight an hour. I want to work. I need to work."

"What do you like to write?"

"What's going on under people's noses that they don't see—between men and women, white people and black people, stuff like that."

"I'll make you a deal," he said. "You give George three fashion stories a week to make him happy. You give me a Sunday feature on 'stuff like that.'"

"Really, Mr. Vag?"

"I can't promise they'll let me publish it, but let's you and I kick up some dust around here."

There was plenty to kick up in a town that could afford to drowse under the benevolent paternalism of Kodak. On lunch hour I would devour *The Fire Next Time,* James Baldwin's confession and sermon on racism. "You must put yourself in the skin of a black man . . ." he wrote. Try as I might, I could not begin to imagine myself into the daily blows of degradation that I had read about. My husband and I often crossed into Rochester's "colored" section to go to a jazz club, and there we felt the tremors of discontent. I wrote stories about the proud, brave, hurting people I met there. Mr. Vag didn't publish them.

My tropism had always leaned toward New York City. Now I knew why. The turbulence of those times made me feel it was my calling to be a journalist.

CHAPTER 4

DECEPTIONS

"HI, COOKIE!" His voice over the phone sounded boyish.

"Daddy?"

"How's my girl?"

First thought: I wasn't his girl anymore. I was a working news-paperwoman with two years behind me at the *Democrat & Chronicle*, thrilled to be sent to New York to write about Fashion Week. "It's been so long," I said.

"Sorry, Cookie, you've been on my mind."

"Really? Not really."

"Albert told me you're in New York. I'm coming into town to take you to lunch. How's that? The Oyster Bar. You always liked that."

It was his charming con man voice. He was an adman, after all.

"Can't, Daddy. I'm working. I'm down here for the paper with a five o' clock deadline to file my story."

"A real reporter now."

"They call me the fashion editor."

"How about that! A lunch break will do you good. Meet you at Grand Central."

"Wait! I have no time for lunch."

"Then I'll come straight to your hotel. I have something import-ant to tell you."

The way he said it made my stomach clench. When he appeared at my hotel-room door, holding a street peddler's bouquet of mums

wrapped in butcher paper, I was struck by how young and insouci-
ant he looked: like a frat boy in his camel's hair coat and casually
flipped scarf, not a fleck of gray in his thick hair, a cunning half
smile on his lips.

"I'm starting a new life."

It didn't take long for him to spill the story, as if he thought that I'd
be as excited as he was that he wouldn't have to commute anymore; he
was leaving New York, leaving my mother, marrying a young woman
he was sure I'd be crazy about—in fact, she was downstairs, just dying
to meet me.

I wished she was already dead.

In that moment, our roles flipped. My father was the adolescent,
bolting out of the family, deserting the nest, already in half flight, no
catching him now. I turned into the scolding mother.

"What are you thinking? Mom has been your handmaiden for
how long? You're going to dump her now?"

"Your mother has her own friends now. She's in A A."

His tone was cruelly condescending. This was the first I knew
that my mother had acknowledged her alcoholism. All those years
her "sinus attacks" had been the cover story for the disease of despair
she had battled alone. I felt the crush of guilt.

My father got up and went to the minibar. "Do you have any
ginger ale?"

"What about Trish?" I said. "Remember? You have another
daughter; she's only just graduated from high school." He was flipping
channels on the TV looking for business news.

"Your sister has lots of friends; she'll be fine."

My sister and I had grown up in different families. The year I
escaped to college, our parents moved to a sterile exurb in southern
Connecticut where men like my father commuted to Manhattan in
the predawn of the *Mad Men* era and competed to be top dog in their
ad agencies. Dad was a Don Draper precursor, with zipper-tight lips,

precisely barbered dark hair, square-framed aviator sunglasses, a sliver of white pocket handkerchief peeking from the breast pocket of his gray flannel suit. The mother who had been left home with my much younger sister had been a ghost mother. Trapped in her forties in the exurbs, with neither the skills nor experience to start a career, Mother had seen herself like most first wives of her era, as little more than a convenience, like a frozen dinner or a new garbage disposal. Years later, my sister told me that during her high school years, Mom had given up trying. She mostly sat around the kitchen drinking with the plumber from next door. Trish had to tell her when she needed a training bra.

My father came home in the bar car of the Metro North Railroad, flirting with secretaries who scavenged for the low-hanging fruit of frustrated marriages. A popular local politician, he had an excuse to be out almost every weeknight. His weekends were lived on the golf course. I assumed that his new girlfriend was one of those belles of the bar car and had probably taken up the role of "golf friend" when it was vacated by Bernice.

That day in the hotel room, I confronted my father: "Who's looking after Trish? Is anyone taking her around to look at colleges?"

He said he thought Mom was working on getting her into the University of Hartford. Trish was an afterthought. What my father really wanted to talk about was his own new dream, about his bride-to-be, how they had everything in common. (Really? His girlfriend was barely twenty-one.) About the branch office he was opening in San Francisco and the prize for which he had waited twenty-five years as the slavishly loyal number two—leadership of the company when the founder retired.

"Dad," I said, "you're fifty-two years old. How do you get to be the kid?"

He said he had never felt younger. "Sonny Boy" did look preternaturally coltish. I was the one who felt suddenly old. I asked my father to promise that he would fulfill his responsibility to pay for my sister's college expenses until she graduated. He gave me the doublespeak learned in the ad game. I had a sickening feeling that his allegiance had already been withdrawn from our family. He was a man caught up in a midlife fantasy of escape from a frustrating career and a dead marriage into a start-over life with a girl younger than his daughter.

I agreed to meet his new lady, but only if he would keep his promise to put Trish through college. He agreed. Before he left that day, I knew he would break his promise.

When I found Albert at the hospital that evening, his voice over the phone was soothing. "Your father's a fool. How could a man walk away from his family?" I was consoled. We were happily married. I was safe.

THE LOVE OF A HUSBAND seeps into the senses like perfume. So slowly does it diffuse, the absence of its essence can become imperceptible. I did not suspect. Two years after the encounter with my father, Albert and I were glad to be back in New York after his graduation from medical school and now living in the East Village. He was either at St. Vincent's Hospital being an intern six days a week or on call during the seventh day. I hardly saw him. But I was preoccupied taking care of our infant daughter, shopping, cooking, working, and trying to find a few consecutive hours to sleep. I began mulling over the sociological experiment we represented, a dual-career couple with a young child. We were in the professional avant-garde, and I was proud that we were doing everything right.

But were we?

In those days, I was expected to work right up until labor pains began, which I had. The two weeks I was allowed to bond with my baby were intense and joyful, but also strained by the concern that I couldn't wean Maura soon enough to keep my job. Modern breast pumps were not in existence. And I was the primary breadwinner. I stuck it out working daily from 10 A.M. until 6 or 7 P.M. at the newspaper. On the bus to the office, I would hide behind my newspapers and try to swallow the sobs in my throat. I knew that the untrained nannies I could afford were no substitute for the bonding with a blood mother. It was torture. I remember the effort it took to cauterize the emotional wound before I stepped into the elevator to the Women's Department, stung by the irony that my young colleagues and I had left our own babies at home and would be writing to other women about how to improve their lives.

I remember telling my friend Audrey about a string of sudden divorces back in my hometown. Audrey and her husband, John, were doctors in training with Albert, and we often went out for pizza as couples. "One can never tell about any marriage, anywhere," Audrey said, with a diagnostician's matter-of-factness.

One night when we had dinner at Audrey and John's, she spilled scalding demitasse over my hands. What struck me was how it wasn't our hosts, Audrey and her husband, who rushed to my aid. It was Audrey and *my* husband. They raced about together to find me some salve. Like guilty parents. After pulling off East River Drive my husband dropped his forehead onto the steering wheel and began to weep. He said he didn't know if he loved me anymore. And so it began.

Sunday night after his first blurted confession, we lay on the white bed striped black with the fingers of a fire escape lit by a streetlight and trembled. What did I do wrong?—all we've worked for—ours is one of the best marriages—isn't it?—let's go away together—who is it?—no, don't tell me—oh my God, the baby—can it be that deep?

It is not long, he tells me, but it is deep.

Cries came out of me that I had never heard before, brute sound, racking sobs. Terror overtook. We clung like children confronted with the shock of eternity. Darling, love, it will be all right, he breathed.

I'll make it all right. I did a terrible thing. Lying back, he squeezed from the last tears a promise. He could never leave me and Maura.

Don't promise me anything, I said. You must take your time. Mercifully, the sap drained from both of us. We dozed. The phone rang. When I answered, the intruder was silent. "Who is it? Who is it in my house?"

She waited, then hung up. But I felt her. This house, this marriage, this little family would never again be whole.

A YEAR PASSED AFTER THAT TORTURED NIGHT, a walking-on-eggshells year, when he repeatedly assured me that it was over between him and Audrey. I wanted to believe him. He still had three years of residency ahead of him. He had exchanged a crisp lieutenant's uniform for the pajamas of an intern. He was thirty years old and could not qualify for a credit card. We often joked with friends about our role reversal. He'd say, "My wife doesn't make bread, she earns it." Didn't we sound hip? The burn of his resentment at being dependent on me came out in ways that only I would notice. Three times a week my name was in the paper. I would leave the paper on the kitchen table open to the women's page, so when he came home late from the hospital, he would see it. He never said a word about my writing.

I CONTINUED WORKING FULL TIME at the *Trib* and hired one babysitter after another. I would come home to either a comedy or a horror show. The English nanny was a clean freak; she had probably never met a roach. She sprayed everything in the apartment with Lysol, including bedsheets, and she must have made Maura help her. I had to soak Maura in gardenia bubble bath before her father got home. The Caribbean girl who replaced the English nanny was so easygoing, I relaxed. One day I came home early and saw the white pimpmobile double-parked outside our building. I ran upstairs to find the sitter playing pinch and tickle on her boyfriend's lap while Maura played with her platform heels. Her replacement was a Cuban church lady. At least Maura was getting international exposure. But the Cuban lady liked to cook and eat nonstop, so the roaches forgot the Lysol lady and returned with a vengeance. It took me a long time to pry out of Maura why the dead roaches were all lined up along one wall when I got home. The Cuban sitter had taught her a game: give the roaches a head start up the wall and then smack 'em dead with a pancake turner. And so they went, one impossible surrogate after another. It was agonizing.

I gave up my dream job. To keep our family together, I would remake myself into a full-time mom and devoted wife, put the career on hold, and somehow find a way to make a living as a freelance writer. My refuge was St. Mark's Church in the Bowery.

A young minister was attracting an eclectic congregation of artists, writers, and theater people who were active supporters of the civil rights struggle in the South. I had written about their Easter Sunday solidarity parade and felt drawn to a new spiritual home. In college I had found fault with the religious tradition of my family, Christian Science, which denied obvious realities, like disease and accidents, and relied on prayer to heal the "error" in the world. I found in the progressive Episcopalian parish at St. Mark's an openness to people of all colors, freethinkers, and homosexuals. Once I took instruction and was baptized an Episcopalian, every Sunday I found renewed strength from the socially conscious sermons and from Jesus's words of refreshment: "Come to me, all who are weary and heavy-laden, and I will give you rest."

I begged Albert to take time off. We needed to go away, be close, disappear into the country, dance in the moonlight. He said interns couldn't take vacations. So I cooked and froze his favorite meats and filled the refrigerator with tossed salads and backups of farm-stand lettuces and veggies. Then I plundered my meager savings and swooped up my two-year-old to escape for a month to a rented sugar-house in Vermont. We lost ourselves playing in the woods and paddling in a lake and reading stories until we fell asleep under the fat tree where we were certain Pooh Bear lived. Albert came up for only one weekend. It didn't take an interrogation to know that our marriage was over.

I wanted to go back to childhood and start over. Instead, I prepared myself to take on a strange new identity for women of my generation. Single mother.

I DREADED THE HANDOVERS. The empty hours, the late Sunday afternoons waiting for the appointed return time, crouched on the top step with knees against my fluttering heart, jackknifing up from a pretense of reading the paper each time the downstairs buzzer rang or the stairs squeaked. Finally seeing Maura in her father's arms, where she belonged but could not fully belong, her head bobbing beside his chin as they rounded the banister leading to the fourth floor, singing together, *Merrily we roll along, roll along, roll along,* a song we had taught her. I chimed in from above. For instants we were a family again, *merrily we roll along,* then face-to-face, hearing the whimper start the second her father unclasped his hug. She knew this moment but she had no comprehension of its sudden cruelty, from safe and warm, brushing against the familiar scratchiness of her father's chin, to being suspended across a gulf wide as a river, an ocean, child overboard, legs helplessly dangling without support, arms clinging to her father, mother's arms outstretched—but she was never ready to surrender one for the other—and then, the innocent question, the question that had no answer: *Why can't Daddy come home?*

Her question told us that we needed to make a clear separation in order for Maura to understand how her world was altered. I had to fight against the feeling that I was at fault for the failure of my marriage. My ex-husband contributed only child support. It would have been easy to claim alimony, but I wanted no part of dependence on him. My task now was to find a way to support us and bring some delight into our new world. The greatest consolation was knowing that Albert was an attentive father.

CHAPTER 5

SEDUCTION AT THE ALGONQUIN

IT WAS A SATURDAY when Clay Felker took me out to lunch for the first time. He chose the Algonquin, I assume to give me illusions of literary grandeur. The Rose Room, scene of the famous Round Table, still held a musty glamour imparted by the savage contests of wit between Dorothy Parker, Robert Benchley, Alexander Woollcott, George S. Kaufman, Heywood Broun, et al.

I couldn't eat a thing. I watched Clay devour a mound of raw chopped beef. Actually, I didn't see him eat it. It was there on the plate, then it was gone. He was much more interested in talking than eating, and to my surprise, in talking to me. I had written several stories for him at the *Trib* but nothing so far in 1966. What was I writing these days? he wanted to know.

My pale Irish skin was aflame with sunburn and freckles. If I blushed with emotion, it wouldn't have shown. It was midsummer and I had just returned with Maura from the month's retreat in Vermont. Pouches under my eyes were filled with stale tears. He pried out of me that I was noodling in a journal to keep myself sane while my marriage was coming apart.

"Can I ask why?" he said.

"No good reason."

Clay's right eyebrow lifted, suggesting a perceptible level of interest. He wanted to hear the whole backstory. Only much later did he divulge his secret: his way of seducing writers was to get inside their heads by interviewing them, more like a shrink than an editor. He probed for your obsession, the subject you couldn't shake, the mind chatter that goes on in your head at four hundred words a minute— your holy hang-up! Then he would know how to match you with one of hundreds of ideas floating around in his brain.

The current state of marriage seemed of inordinate interest to him. I told him that I had come home from Vermont to find the note.

"What note?"

The note to my husband's girlfriend. He had left it carelessly, or conspicuously, near the phone. The year of his deceit and my denial was over. Fresh tears began filling my eyes. "I don't want to talk about this. Anymore."

Clay put his hand over mine. "I'm sorry, Gail." It was the first time he'd spoken my name tenderly, and he spoke it like a father figure. I excused myself to go to the ladies' room and finish my little cry in private. When I reemerged, the atmosphere had changed. Clay leaned in closer. He no longer seemed in such a hurry.

"Would you like something to drink, a glass of wine? Scotch?"

"Scotch," I said. "On the rocks." He ordered two Balvenie single malts, soda on the side. When our drinks came, we both sipped and sat quietly for a while. Why, he kept pondering, why is everyone's marriage breaking up?

"Everyone's?" I said.

"Mine, too."

I glimpsed in his soft brown eyes the wounded man behind his larger-than-life persona. "I'm sorry," I said.

"But why? What's going on?" he pressed. Clay was most interested in the why of things that happened.

"It's something in the air," I said. "Women getting tired of being background noise. Or betrayed."

"My wife's an actress," he said. "She's always off somewhere, like Italy, making a picture." He looked terribly sad.

"How did she hurt you?" I asked. That opened a vein. He told me he had flown to Rome to surprise her with a long weekend holiday in Venice. He found her with a married man. "A flaming Italian communist!" It wasn't clear whether the man's philandering or his politics was the more offensive. Clay had decked him. That had only made things worse.

"Sure, but didn't it feel *really good* at the time—POWWW!" I laughed.

"POWWW!" He punched the air. He laughed.

Now it was my turn to interview him. I assumed, given his nasal uptown New York honk, that he'd grown up in Manhattan. Way off, he said. "Webster Groves."

"Webster Groves! It sounds like Grover's Corners."

"It's Midwest. Missouri. A suburb of St. Louis."

"So you were baked in a solid midwestern point of view?" I ventured.

"You know the story Tom Wolfe tells about me?" Tom pretended that he went out to Webster Groves to research its imprint on Clay. Nothing, nada, no influence on Clay whatsoever. What's more, he claimed that his sister had told him that Baby Clay's first complete sentence was "What do you mean, you don't have my reservation!"

"That's Tom's gift for satire," Clay said, chuckling.

"What kind of a name is 'Felker'?" I asked.

His grandfather, Henry Clay Felker, came from a liberal German aristocratic family who fled Germany after the 1848 conservative takeover. The family changed its name from von Fredrikstein to "Volker," meaning "of the people," which was later Anglicized to Felker. His grandmother's side was Scottish, he said.

My mother's family, too, was Scottish, I said, well, Scotch-Irish, imported by the English landowners to populate the Ulster Plantation. "After the British let the Irish farmers starve in the potato famine," I added with vehemence.

"You sound very Irish," he said. "You've internalized their sense of grievance."

"My mother is a proud Irish American," I said, "but my father"—I sighed—"he wouldn't let her out of the cage to sing."

Clay was proud to say that both his mother and his grandmother had attended the University of Missouri School of Journalism, as had his father and grandfather. Journalism was a given in their family. Carl Felker, his father, worked six and a half days a week as managing editor of the weekly newspaper the *Sporting News,* and was editor of the *Sporting Good Dealer.* His mother, Cora Tyree Felker, was women's editor of the *St. Louis Post-Dispatch.* She gave it up once she had children.

"So I was acquainted early with the discontent of an ambitious, educated woman," Clay said. "Maybe like you."

This was a revelation. The fact that Clay had some concept of the discontent of women like me made him unique among the men of my acquaintance.

"Did you always want to be an editor?" I asked.

All he'd ever wanted, he said, was to have his own publication. He was around eight or nine when he printed his first broadsheet on a hexagraph in his basement, the *Greely Street News.* He hawked it up and down his neighborhood for five cents.

He told me he grew up reading the magazines to which his parents subscribed, *The New Yorker, Ladies' Home Journal,* and *Esquire,* the magazine that taught young men how to become gentlemen. He imagined the editors of *Esquire* all coming to work in black tie so they'd be ready to sail off to dinner at 21 with beautiful women on their arms. "When I actually went to work at *Esquire,*" he said, "I realized the world it created in its pages had come out of the imagination of its original editor,

Arnold Gingrich. He eventually became part of that world. I wanted to become part of that world, too."

"How long did it take you?" I asked.

His half smile had shyness in it, the perpetual awe of the outsider. "I'm still working on it."

Clay suddenly changed the subject. "I have an idea. Write that story for me."

"What story?"

"About a young marriage that breaks up for no good reason."

"It's not a story. It's life. Incomprehensible."

"That's what will make it special—being inside the writer's head while you struggle to make sense of it."

"But it's *personal*."

"Don't worry. You can change the names. I'll run it as a roman à clef. Fictionalized reality."

Clay had seduced me. I wrote the story for him. After the *Trib* folded, it appeared in the stillborn *World-Journal Tribune:* "Lovesounds of a Wife."

For the first time a man I looked up to had read my work. And published it. Was it possible that he believed in me?

CHAPTER 6

LOVE AND DEATH IN THE YEAR AMERICA CAME APART

"HE WANTS COMIN' GUP, a fancy man."

The voice belonged to the Ukrainian seamstress on the ground floor. A survivor of Stalin's genocide, she had appointed herself security guard of our rent-controlled former rooming house on the Lower East Side. Years earlier, Albert and I had moved there to accommodate the new baby in cheap digs, $139 a month.

"What's his name?" I asked over the intercom.

"He say Clay, you will know."

"Clay Felker? On the Lower East Side?"

"Look like movie star."

I burst out laughing at the absurdity of it. Out the front window I could see a sleek black town car. It must have been dropping off Clay. Tonight was the debut party of his new magazine at the Four Seasons. I wished I could have gone.

My block, East Seventh Street between Second and Third Avenues, was not accustomed to chauffeured town cars. This was a little Ukrainian village of immigrants who filled the streets with the smells of pierogi and kielbasa. These God-fearing immigrants shared the space with the new demimonde of the Lower East Side—proto-yuppies and promising artists with hair like the manes of wild animals who were happy to sacrifice safety and living space to pursue writing, acting, art, photography, or just joy, love. The most conspicuous new element in the neighborhood was the large influx of hippies, young fugitives from middle-class suburban privilege. They injected the dangerous element of speed (amphetamines). Accounts of stabbings, muggings, and robberies were becoming frequent.

I wore beatnik sandals and occasionally love beads, and I treasured the album *Rolling Stones: Now.* But with a four-year-old child, I was too responsible to spend any time being stoned.

Could it really be Clay Felker crossing the great social divide? His was the glamorous world of the Upper East Side—cocktails and canapés and charity balls for socially prominent diseases for which chic women spent the afternoon at Kenneth's getting bouffant hairdos that were perfect facsimiles of the style worn by former First Lady Jacqueline Kennedy.

"I tell him come up?"

"Give me a minute. I'm just putting Maura down."

"Okay, he's comin' gup—a fancy man!"

It was mid-April 1968. Clay had just launched *New York* as an independent weekly. The first issue wasn't off the newsstands yet and already the man was on the prowl for his next stories. I could hear him climbing the four flights of stairs, saddle-curved from a hundred years of cheap shoes, past the door of the playwright/pot dealer on two and the retired cop on three with the trigger-happy son who watched TV with the old man's service revolver on his knee. The rattle clink as I opened my three locks must have made him nervous. He burst into my apartment, pulling off his formal black tie as he peered down the long dark hall.

"Are you searching for hippies?" I teased. "There are probably some in the kitchen baking pot into brownies."

"How do you live here all alone, Gail? It's not safe."

"I bite."

He laughed.

"Can I take your coat?"

As he wriggled out of a black Chesterfield, I noticed again how unusual he was: a king-size man propped on incongruously small, princely, high-arched feet. His body seemed locked in perpetual forward motion. His hungry eyes darted about the surroundings like a house detective taking mental notes on every detail. The apartment was probably not as slummy as he had imagined: a floor-through with a real dining room, a baby's room filled with books and mobiles, and even a sitting room overlooking the street where I banged out freelance articles on my secondhand electric typewriter and often pulled all-nighters (with a little help from speed).

"Sorry to barge in—but I didn't see you at the launch party," he said as I led him into what passed for a living room and we sat down on the sofa. "I won't keep you up."

"I really wanted to go, but no babysitter," I said. "You must be so proud, Clay. To have your own magazine."

"It's all I've ever wanted."

He looked around at the homely evidence of domesticity, the scatter of toys, the odd socks, a curdle of spilled milk on the coffee table.

"You've probably never met a man like me."

"And you may not have met a girl like me."

He seemed intrigued.

"I know one thing—you can be a kick-ass writer."

"Shhhh," I said. "My little girl is sleeping."

Abruptly, he changed the subject. "Do you understand politics?"

"My father's a country club Republican, an Anglophiliac, if you know what I mean. My Irish mother is a natural-born rebel. So I guess I understand politics—it's about fighting at the dinner table."

"Then you'll understand Bobby," Clay said, moving closer. The sagging sofa threw him off-kilter; he moved back.

"Bobby who?"

"Kennedy."

"Bobby Kennedy!"

"I want you to follow his campaign."

A clutch of fear tightened inside. "Me? I'm not a political analyst."

Clay suddenly became passionate. I remember his advice as something like this: "Gail, the way to make your name as a journalist is not to do lots of little stories. No matter how good they are, they won't start a new conversation. Tackle a big story, something everybody's talking about, but they don't know the *why*."

"BOBBY," AS EVERYONE CALLED HIM, had announced his candidacy a month before, sounding very much like his idealistic older brother. He was running, he said, "to close the gaps that now exist between black and white, between rich and poor, between young and old." Much of the public was suspicious. Here was a dyed-in-the-brine Cape Cod, Massachusetts, man who dropped into New York State on a carpetbag and used his slain brother's gilded connections to help win a Senate seat.

By 1968, America was murdering its dream of itself. TV cameras were showing our dark side. We had witnessed three summers of inner-city racial convulsions; brave black students being prodded like cattle; federal troops patrolling American cities; and U.S. Marines torching thatched huts in South Vietnam with women and children inside.

In Indianapolis two weeks before, on April 4, a largely black crowd had an hour to hear Senator Kennedy speak. The city's police chief had warned him not to appear. As Kennedy's car entered a black neighborhood, his police escort veered off. Kennedy turned to his aide and asked, "Do they know about Martin Luther King?"

They didn't. On the platform, Kennedy faced the crowd and told them the horrific news: King had been shot dead that night in Memphis, Tennessee. The crowd gasped and wailed in horror. Kennedy spoke reverently of King's dedication to "love and to justice between fellow human beings" and assured the crowd that "he died in the cause of that effort." As an undercurrent of anger began to build, Kennedy reached beyond and into the hearts of the crowd to make a human connection.

"For those of you who are black and are tempted to . . . be filled with hatred and mistrust of the injustice of such an act, against all white people, I would only say that I can also feel in my own heart the same kind of feeling," he said. "I had a member of my family killed, but he was killed by a white man."

That reminder of his personal tragedy cut through the color barrier. While sixty American cities erupted in rage and grief, in the city of Indianapolis where the words of Robert Kennedy had been heard, there was no fire.

A man of enormous empathy was not what I expected from Robert Kennedy. I had read about an edge of cruelty. Even his father, Joseph P. Kennedy, an unapologetic fascist, had described his youngest son as "a hater." But during the two weeks when the world had teetered on the edge of nuclear war, back in 1962, as President Kennedy and his advisers debated what to do about photographs showing missiles on Cuban soil, it was Robert Kennedy who offered the voice of reason. In a man legendary for his aggressive behavior, it was a complete reversal of character. Here was the arch anti-Communist who represented Senator Joe McCarthy in his witch hunt now going up against the advice from almost all the members of the president's executive committee convened to respond to the Cuban missile crisis.

"I could not accept the idea that the United States would rain bombs on Cuba, killing thousands and thousands of civilians in a surprise attack," Bobby argued, as later revealed in Robert Caro's exhaustive account in *Passage to Power*. Kennedy believed the Russians had to be allowed to pull back without losing face. The rest of the advisers were surprised at the passion with which he put forward his moral argument. When Kennedy saw his brother, the president, alone, by the White House pool, he persuaded him to give Khrushchev every chance to reconsider, and above all, to avoid war by miscalculation. Bobby may have saved the world from destruction.

As a young liberal woman fiercely against America's misadventure in Vietnam from the start, I was primed to like Bobby Kennedy. I had baptized my baby in antiwar marches in Washington. And he had captured me with a speech he made at Kansas State University earlier that spring. After students at Columbia had occupied university offices and race riots had convulsed more than one hundred American cities, Kennedy's voice cracked when he praised colleges and universities that "breed men who riot, who rebel, who attack life with all their youthful vision and vigor. The more riots that come on college campuses, the better the world for tomorrow." It was a wildly incendiary thing for any politician to say, especially in conservative Kansas, but by then, even young moms like me were marching on the Pentagon while young men burned draft cards.

When Kennedy tried to depart the Kansas campus, he was overrun by adoring students who pulled at his hair and ripped his shirtsleeves. I heard my friend the photographer Stanley Tretick, of *Look* magazine, cry out, "This is *Kansas,* fucking Kansas! He's going all the fucking way!"

"CLAY, I CAN'T WRITE ABOUT Bobby fucking Kennedy!" Hanging out on the road with the big boys had already infected my language.

"Look, every good reporter has to jump in and scramble until they get it," Clay said, impatient now. "Read the clips. Read history! The same two or three political stories go on repeating themselves as if they never happened before."

"Let me think about it."

"No! The Oregon campaign starts this week. Then follow him in California, that's the make-or-break primary."

Frantically, I thought, *What about Maura?* My sister could stay with her for a few days.

Clay didn't wait for my answer. "You can do it!"

"LET'S GO!" The moment the advance man opened the door of the private air terminal at Washington Dulles, a mob of reporters rushed out like penned-up cattle, racing for the best seats on Senator Kennedy's chartered plane. All men, with a couple of exceptions. Startled, I lagged behind.

"Where are you from?" The Boston Irish accent was unmistakable. It was Robert Kennedy himself who fell into step beside me.

"Gail Sheehy, *New York* magazine."

"Happy to have you with us, Gail." He grinned, pushing the flop of wavy hair off his forehead. With his next words, he swept me off my feet. "How'm I doin' in New York?"

I couldn't wait to tell Clay: the senator from New York with the royal political family name was asking *me,* a mere pup from a month-old magazine he's hardly heard of, how he was doing with the voters of New York. Clay laughed and gave me my first lesson in political journalism: "He's trying to flatter you into feeling like you're part of his election team. Don't hold it against him, but don't buy into it."

Anyone walking down the aisle of an RFK flight would see rows and rows of seats occupied by the "Kennedy Mafia," the men and women linked to the family through friendship, marriage, work, and political alliances and ready to put their lives on hold to help any Kennedy win an election. I was so low on the pecking order behind national journalistic stars like Sam Donaldson, my chances of getting an interview with the senator were slim to none. The only other woman on that plane, a wire service reporter, tipped me off to ask for the help of Fred Dutton, Bobby's behind-the-scenes campaign manager, a rare advocate of women in politics.

Most of Kennedy's campaign flights were jolly affairs marked by singing, drinking, and practical jokes played by his resident imp, Dick Tuck. On one long night flight, Ethel Kennedy led off a songfest with "Onward Christian Soldiers." Campaign folksingers John Stewart and Buffy Ford crooned all the patriotic songs they knew while a stewardess made up the senator's bed. At 3:30 A.M., Robert Kennedy dragged down the aisle from a TV taping session, shirt unbuttoned, tie hanging. From his mouth dangled a burned-out cigar. A pretty stewardess brought him a scotch and water. He sat on the armrest in the aisle and asked for "We Shall Overcome" and then "Hymn to Young People." He kept drawing on the dead cigar, sometimes singing, sometimes leaning his head on his hand. His sad blue eyes seemed to rove planets away. Later he asked the folksinger Buffy to sit on the floor, beneath him. Now and then his hand absently picked up a strand of Buffy's long taffy-colored hair. It was a characteristic moment—the melancholy flitting through joy, the distance and the need for closeness, the complete Irishness.

On our third day in Oregon, Dutton let me know the senator was taking a very small plane to hop up and down the Cascade Mountain Range—probably twenty stops or more. "A nail-biter. You won't have any competition for a seat."

We flew over the Cascade Range of pine-studded mountains. When we landed in Roseburg, Ethel froze. Her husband had to walk through a mob of angry, rifle-toting Oregonians to debate the gun-sale issue. Rain started to fall. John Birchers were out in force, waving professionally printed signs: PROTECT YOUR RIGHT TO KEEP AND BEAR ARMS.

A woman holding a McCarthy sign stopped him; "I hear your dog bites."

"He only bites children." Kennedy's quick wit usually melted hecklers, but in this place it was not working. The woman grew surlier. "They say you're ruthless." He flashed his big, blunt, uncontainable eighty-eight-keyboard smile. "Now, can anybody with a smile like this be ruthless?"

A young man tapped him on the shoulder. "I've been waitin' two hours to tell you, I'll shoot somebody before I see a Nazi like you in the White House." Kennedy pretended not to hear. Now the senator climbed halfway up the steps of the Douglas County Courthouse. He turned, and in full unprotected view, he looked down the rifle barrels of this mostly hostile crowd and tried to engage them in a friendly debate. This was courage.

"I hear the local radio station said, 'Vote against Robert Kennedy because he's going to take your guns away,'" he said. "I'd like one of you to come here and explain that issue to me."

A young man approached him. Kennedy looped his arm over the man's shoulder. "I know some of you are volunteers with the sheriff's posse. Did you know that 90 percent of the policemen who've been shot and killed in the United States in the last two years have been shot by people who shouldn't have guns—people with criminal records or judged insane?" Murmurs of surprise. "All the law requires is that when someone purchases a gun by mail order, he must be competent to handle it." Kennedy wound up with his favorite George Bernard Shaw quote, which seemed to tame the crowd. "'Some people see things as they are and say why? I dream things that never were and ask why not?'"

Ethel Kennedy, unnerved by crowds like this, had been dropped off for the rest of the day. Only a few Oregon reporters climbed back into the little DC-3. The senator sat in front, the seat beside him empty. After takeoff, he leaned over the back of his seat. "Would you like to sit up here, New York?"

I stepped over Freckles, the beloved cocker spaniel who always dozed at Kennedy's feet. The senator was shivering from the last rain-soaked stop. He asked Dutton to hand him Jack's overcoat. For me, this was a poignant moment. Five years after his brother's assassination, Bobby was still mourning Jack's death, still wearing his brother's clothes.

The only question I remember asking Bobby is how he reconciled his attacks on Johnson's Vietnam policy with his earlier support of his brother's war. "I was involved in the decisions about Vietnam in '63 and '64 and '65," he replied bluntly. "I accept the responsibility for my part of the blame. But that's no excuse for perpetuating the error."

Wind blew a hard rain that smeared the plane's windows as we approached Seattle. The senator was in a hurry to make a national press conference. Unbeknownst to us passengers, another plane was coming straight at us. Abruptly, our aircraft plummeted a thousand feet. Men screamed. My eyes shuddered closed. While we were still dropping, I heard Bobby Kennedy quip, "I knew Gene McCarthy was desperate, I didn't think he was *this* desperate."

THAT NIGHT DICK TUCK ARRANGED for the Kennedys to be back on their big campaign plane, in the air and out of touch, when the results of the Oregon primary came in. At 10 P.M., Dutton came back to Ethel Kennedy, who was swapping jokes with newsmen over a scotch and water. Dutton moved his lips silently. "We're beat."

The senator came back from his private cabin with a smile, his hands wrapped in towels to sop up the bleeding from all the physical contact.

"Hey, how can you look so happy?" Ethel asked.

"Because I had such a good day." It was his fatalism again.

After eighty days of nonstop campaigning, Kennedy slept late on the day of the California primary and took his family to the beach. Polls closed at 8 P.M. CBS projected Bobby the winner, but other networks held back.

I had to catch the red-eye back to New York. My plane was in the air when his victory became certain. At that moment, Kennedy was hurrying through the hotel kitchen on the way to his press conference.

It was after 6 A.M. when I staggered out of the taxi from JFK and upstairs to my apartment. I had a sour premonition that something wasn't right. Maura woke when I snapped the three locks. I picked her up so she wouldn't wake my sister and carried her into the living room. The phone rang.

"Were you in the kitchen?" It was Clay, in a voice I had not heard before.

"The kitchen?"

"At the Ambassador?"

"Oh, God, no, what happened?"

"He was killed, by a Palestinian. He's not officially dead yet, but it's all over."

I went numb.

"How soon can you get me the story?"

I turned on the TV. Watching recaps: Kennedy, responding to a reporter, turned his face, looking for Ethel. I didn't see the assassin raise his arm over the senator's aides. I didn't hear the shots fired from a snub-nosed revolver inches from Kennedy's head. I didn't see Kennedy stagger and fall. I didn't hear the chaos, the yelling, "My God! He's been shot! Get a doctor! Get the gun! Kill the bastard! No, don't kill this one! Oh my God, they've shot Kennedy!"

Maura walked into the living room just as another recap showed Ethel Kennedy kneeling on the floor and grabbing her husband's hand. Blood was pooling behind his ear. Maura's voice of innocence asked the question that would cause all Americans to search our souls: "Why is the lady in white bending over the man on the floor? Did something bad happen?"

"A bad accident," I lied. "Would you like French toast this morning, sweetpea?"

I fed Maura, changed my clothes, woke my sister, and sat in front of my typewriter, lighting one cigarette after another. Clay's words played over and over in my head. "You're a journalist . . . a witness to history." I meditated for a while. A shield of detachment gradually formed around my feelings. I began typing.

It was his fatalism that carried Bobby Kennedy through, I wrote. For all his fearlessness in pleading for rational gun control, he had to know the chances were good that sooner or later, he, too, would walk into an assassin's bullets. Among his last words were "Is everybody all right?"

Even now, in the twenty-first century, America is more than ever saturated with guns and apparently guiltless about routine massacres of innocent civilians and little children.

AROUND NOON, THE INTERCOM RANG. "He's comin' gup, the fancy man."

Maura got help from my sister to open the door for Clay. I heard him enter my little study and felt his breath over my shoulder. He was reading my copy.

"Not bad," he said. I ripped the next page out of my typewriter and handed it to him over my shoulder.

"How long till you finish?"

"Two or three more cigarettes."

He massaged my shoulders. I felt the tension release. Before either one of us knew what was happening, Clay and I were awkwardly kissing. We had to have something that still mattered.

I asked him to stop. "Maura." He immediately withdrew. Nothing was said. We both retreated into our familiar safe professional roles, but a trespass of the heart and mind had been committed.

CHAPTER 7

FAILING UP

IT DIDN'T TAKE LONG for me to learn one of the most basic requirements to become a successful book writer. One has to have the stomach to take the roller-coaster lurches from failure to success and back to failure. I was fortunate. I failed early.

My roman à clef about marriage that Clay published, "Lovesounds of a Wife," created a good deal of buzz. To hear the story of an adulterous affair from inside the head of the betrayed wife was a new and unsettling experience. Wives and husbands fought about it. She loved it, he hated it. That's exactly what happened in the household of Gay and Nan Talese.

Gay Talese was already a famous *New York Times* journalist. A cocky Italian American man, he was staking claim to the sexual emancipation of the American male. In what might seem ironic, he also supported the idea that women of talent should be able to pursue independent careers, starting with his own wife. Nan Talese was beautiful, shy, and bookish. Gay encouraged her to talk to a friend of his at Random House about a job as an editor. Publishing was not a career friendly to women in those days, but Nan was hired. When I met the couple at a party in 1967, Nan and I immediately connected. Both of us looked like polite, winsome, white-gloved Anglo-Saxon young ladies who would never challenge the status quo. We were imposters. Underneath, we were both independent women-in-the-making.

I mentioned that I was writing a novel, an outgrowth of my article

"Lovesounds." Nan invited me to come to her office to discuss turning the story into a book. At the entrance to a palatial building with the nameplate ARCHDIOCESE OF NEW YORK, I stared at the marble arches in awe. This was the address Nan had given me, 457 Madison Avenue. I knew Random House was at the pinnacle of the publishing world, but I must have missed the papal encyclical that placed it under the wing of the Vatican.

Directed to the secular entrance, I climbed the broad marble stairs to the second floor. The nameplate BENNETT CERF, PUBLISHER told me I was in the rarefied executive area. I was redirected to the basement. There I found two of the only women editors in New York who edited serious fiction or nonfiction: Toni Morrison and Nan Talese.

When Nan was hired, she confided, the managing editor had dropped a careless insult. "Of course, you'll copyedit your own books and do cookbooks."

"I don't know a thing about cooking," Nan piped up in her high, airy voice. "Why don't you ask Jason?"

This was tantamount to asking Elizabeth Arden to do a client's nails. Jason Epstein was editorial director of the paperback line at Random House. His friends and colleagues knew that Jason was also a serious, even scholarly, cook. But men didn't write or edit cookbooks. That was the girls' realm. It wasn't until his eighty-first year that Jason published his version of a cookbook, a charming culinary memoir called *Eating*.

When Nan was excited, her eyebrows jumped off her forehead. "I love 'Lovesounds,'" she said. "It will be a book for the times." With conspiratorial enthusiasm, we began the editing process.

Nan had the same conflicted feelings I did about trying to balance a serious career with marriage and motherhood. The way she managed to commute between those worlds, she confided, was to live only twelve blocks from Random House, so she could walk home and give her two little daughters lunch. She and Gay rented five sepa-rate apartments on different floors in a building on East Sixty-First Street. Knowing that I needed a quiet retreat to rewrite, she kindly invited me to use a typewriter on her second floor. I could hear her prolific husband banging away on the floor below. He called his sep-arate apartment his "bunker."

Gay's incessant typing on the first floor kept me racing on the second. Nan would insist I come up to have lunch with her and the children in the zone to which they were relegated. She suggested for my book that I turn the story into a *Rashomon*, alternating chapters from the subjective point of view of both the wife and the husband. As women, I suppose, we felt we needed to represent the man's point of view. I took pains to disguise the real names and places, moving the characters up in social class to render the husband as an up-and-coming attorney who lived on the Upper East Side. That only made me an easier target.

I'LL NEVER FORGET CLAY CALLING me months later. "I just picked up the Sunday *New York Times Book Review*—you're in it!"

"What does it say?" Clay read the opening line. "'Gail Sheehy's *Lovesounds* is an angry book about a woman whose wifeliness approx-imates disease . . . She even has a child, apparently to convince her friends that she is not, to use that dreaded phrase, a 'career woman.'"

"Stop, Clay." I put down the phone and looked for a place to be sick.

When I was able to read the rest of the review, it felt like body blows directly to my gut. Only in the last paragraph did the reviewer mention the conflict at the heart of the story: the husband has been having an affair, so the wife, a successful career woman with a two-year-old child, tries for a year to be "the perfect wife." When that effort suffocates them both, the wife has to decide whether to accept the pain and humiliation of a husband who she learns is still cheating on her, or to strike a blow for self-respect and independence by getting a divorce. She chooses the latter. That, to the reviewer, is her sin.

It was a few years later, when the women's movement had surfaced and was growing strong, that I began to grasp why my book had caused such a backlash. It had been published in 1970, just as the world of unsettling change was upon us. Consciousness-raising sessions had barely begun, so those of us who were "liberating" ourselves did not have any language or emotional concepts with which to understand what we were living. The review gave me an early feel for the reactionary rage at the earthquake of gender that would shake up the 1970s. *Lovesounds* was ahead of its time. It did not sell.

Nan herself was always expecting that when she had another child, she would quit her career and stay home to be the perfect wife and mother. She never did. She outlasted most of the great male editors with whom she started at Random House and has been on the top of the heap for decades, today directing her own publishing imprint at Doubleday.

Looking back through the retrospectoscope of forty years, I appreciate how vastly social conditions have changed and improved for women. But I also see, stronger than ever, evidence of an observation I made when I wrote *Passages* in my midthirties: "Women can have it all, but not all at once." I had predicted that women who tried to wear all three hats in their twenties—marriage, motherhood, career—would likely see at least one blow off. Young women, like young men in their twenties, need time to extend their education, try out different partners and career paths, survive failure and build resilience, before they are ready to balance the competing demands and delights of marriage, family, and career.

What I didn't foresee was a truly dramatic unraveling of the American family: more and more women would rather do two things well than do all three poorly. Paycheck Mom is now the norm. In

2013, the Pew Research Center reported that in 40 percent of American households with children under age eighteen, the mother is either the sole or primary earner. That number has quadrupled since 1960. For great numbers of such women, marriage is now decoupled from motherhood. Forty percent of women with some college but no degree, and 57 percent of women with high school diplomas or less, elect to be single mothers. Why? Often, because they don't want to take the chance of having to support the baby daddy, too. It's only the elite—90 percent of women with bachelor's degrees or higher—who still believe in acquiring a mate before producing a baby. These are the enviable couples who are able to invest in their children from the resources of two successful careers, thus widening the gap between the security of the elite and the struggles of the new middle class and impoverished Americans.

MY FIRST FAILURE WAS SHORT-LIVED. Soon after the publication of *Lovesounds* in 1970, a call came from Otto Preminger himself. The world-famous Hollywood director spoke with a gurgly Viennese accent. He was interested in optioning the book for a film. How would he get in touch with my agent?

I was embarrassed to admit that I didn't have an agent. I called Clay. He said he'd get in touch with his former wife's agents, Irwin Winkler and Bob Chartoff. They invited me to lunch and offered to represent me. But weren't they Hollywood agents? I asked. Yes, but it could add luster to their résumé to have an East Coast author. I tried not to smile. Only Hollywood agents would think of a failed first-time novelist as added "luster." It's reverse snobbism; they think we're all *intellectuals*.

The next thing I knew, I was spending afternoons writing my first screenplay under the tutelage of a temperamental tyrant. Preminger was a big bearish man with a hairless ovoid head and a fleshy face. He had directed Frank Sinatra, Jimmy Stewart, and female stars such as Marilyn Monroe, whom he called "a void with nipples." His actors nicknamed him "Otto the Ogre."

He invited me to work at his classical Italian manse on East Sixty-Fourth Street, where he sat behind a massive white marble desk. Once, when I couldn't get a sitter, he invited me to bring my little daughter. Maura had inherited my Irish ginger hair and the outspokenness that comes with it. She took one look at this giant of a man and knew immediately how to tame him. She climbed into his lap. "Mr. Preminger, you're a peanut!" He roared with laughter and picked up the child in one of his basketball-size hands and lifted her over his head. She squealed with delight. From her unique point of survey, she exclaimed, "It must be so fun not having any hair to comb."

Maura at age three.

It took an Otto Preminger to option my little novel and get it green-lighted by a major studio, Paramount. Everything was on the upswing.

Three months later, on a day of drenching rain, Mr. Preminger called to cancel our afternoon meeting. "Vat gives with your agents? My studio tells me they did not get the reassignment of copyright." My work was in the public domain. The studio had found a way to keep Preminger from making a movie based on an unsuccessful book written by a nobody novelist.

It was one of those days when the roller coaster plunges down a hair-raising precipice and one's stomach surges up into one's throat. It was still pouring outside. Maura was having a meltdown. I was a divorced woman. My first movie sale was dead. My hope of making a living as a freelance writer looked dead in the water. I crawled into bed with Maura and we lost ourselves in the hilariously perverse world of Maurice Sendak, reading *Where the Wild Things Are* over and over.

"PUSSYCAT, HOW SOON CAN YOU leave for India?"

I'll never forget that rescue call. It was few months later, the end of January 1971, and I couldn't quite make the rent. The breathy voice was unmistakable. Helen Gurley Brown. She was reinventing the risqué women's magazine *Cosmopolitan,* as a guide to "mouseburgers" like Helen herself—girls with neither looks nor money who, if they learned how to be sexy and worked hard enough to afford nice clothes and plastic surgeons, could get a rich man to marry them. Helen had proved it by snagging David Brown, a movie mogul famous for producing *Jaws* and *The Sting* with Richard Zanuck.

I had only done a couple of stories for Helen's *Cosmo* while working at the *Trib,* but this was a plum assignment. She wanted me to track down the Maharishi Mahesh Yogi and his most famous new disciples, the Beatles. What could be a better rebound from failure than to strap on a backpack and plunge into the Himalayas in search of bliss consciousness and the Beatles' guru? I sensed a cultural shift in the making. Here was the first swooning embrace of Eastern mysticism by the darlings of Western pop culture. How could I pass up the chance to sneak inside the spiritual training camp of His Holiness, founder of the transcendental meditation movement? Hundreds of other journalists had staked out the compound with little chance of gaining entrance to the inner sanctum.

But what about Maura—she was only six. Albert offered to take her; he knew I needed the money.

The first and fundamental fact about gurus was revealed to me by one of the Maharishi's public relations people: The *shishya* (disciple) does not seek. When the shishya is ready, the guru appears. In point of fact, the guru himself wasn't quite ready for prime time. On the Maharishi's first visit to New York, in 1959, he had greeted reporters at the airport in Hindi-lish: "I come to spread manure on you."

I was invited to an initiation ceremony on a Saturday night at the Barclay Hotel on East Forty-Eighth Street. The man behind the peephole of the Maharishi's suite was not the ascetic Indian mystic. He was a Norwegian opera singer, Richard Fleur, a big strapping Siegfried who instructed a gathering of decorative young New York neurotics to remove our shoes and kneel to offer thanks and gifts to our teacher, Guru Dev. (Who he?) No answer.

We were coached on how to meditate. Most of the shishyas drifted off to sleep. Then came the big moment. Each of us would receive our "customized mantra." The mantra, Fleur said, is a sound, a vehicle; we travel with it to the innermost core of our being. "To receive the mantra possessed of the right vibration and mystical power for the individual," he emphasized, "one needs a guide." Then the fast finish: "Anything good costs a lot of money." The price he quoted was roughly equal to an average week's salary.

"You understand this sound must never be told to anyone or written or even spoken aloud to yourself," Fleur said solemnly. "It must be kept as part of your pure being. Do you agree?" I agreed. However, the picture of a robust Siegfried tossing water over the shoulder of his business suit and moving grains of rice between brass bowls while chanting Sanskrit in a Norwegian accent put a certain strain on reverence. Each of us was asked five questions, presumably to allow Fleur to penetrate our pure being and divine our unique sound.

Forty-five years later, I think I am reasonably safe in revealing my personalized mantra, since it is merely a hitching of half my last name to the oldest of sacred sounds, OM. It is—forgive me, Guru Dev—Shee-Om. That's it.

"Now I will have to ask for the contribution," Fleur said. "It is for the Guru Dev, not for me."

Fumbling with pen and checkbook in the darkened and densely incensed hotel room, I felt like we were kids playing dressup.

"Where *is* the Guru Dev?" asked one intrepid shishya.

"He is everywhere."

So I bought my mantra and headed off to India with more than a dollop of skepticism.

I CHOSE TO MAKE THE JOURNEY from Delhi to Rishikesh by bus. Three dollars. Racing around the bus yard looking for the No. 1871 bus among forty skeletal conveyances, all piled high with bedrolls and numbered in Hindi, was the first test of the staying power of bliss consciousness. I failed. It was miserable.

The road through 140 miles of flat Gangetic plain was a river of bullock carts, rickshaws, and columns of men who looked headless under bundles of wash, wood, or sugar cane. At the foothills of the Himalayas, the driver motioned for me to get off. "You wait. You sit. It coming." In a while a horse-drawn tonga appeared and carted me to a notch in the hills at the headwaters of the Ganges. I scrambled down to the clear green water. Stranded on the wrong side of Mother Ganga, I didn't have to fret for long about how to cross to Rishikesh.

"Hey, American girl, over here!" A power boat was swerving in my direction. What a welcome sight, a bunch of tangle-haired American hippies! They welcomed me to spend the night in their Hash Ashram. That was a trip in itself. A traditional *ashram* is a spiritual hermitage hidden in a forest or mountains where Hindus seek tranquillity and perform some sacrifice. The Hash Ashram was a joyful happening where the only sacrifice was privacy. A motley collection of young men and women—stoned-out visa violators and guitar-toting trust-fund babies—crowded around an open fire in their stone abode. Joints were shared. We sang folk songs and Beatles favorites, *I get by with a little help from my friends, I get high with a little help from my friends,* until near dawn when everyone spilled out onto the bamboo deck, as if on cue. We slept until the sun rose too high to ignore.

Walking up the burning sand in the noonday sun, with two heavy bags and no idea where to find the pathway to bliss consciousness, I practiced meditating. Amazingly, it sort of worked. My walking meditation was indeed quite pleasant. As if by divine mercy, a boy appeared and piled my bags on his head. He led the way to the side of an unmarked cliff and pointed up. I climbed about a mile up a trail from the beach. WELCOME! Pastel flags flew from the outpost of the Maharishi's sixteen-acre compound, which was encircled by barbed wire.

I was detained at the guesthouse outside the compound. Dutifully, I submitted a copy of my written request to interview the Maharishi. Five o'clock. A light Himalayan wind sprang up. Monkeys descended to snatch the banana I foolishly peeled. The Beatles were not yet in residence, I learned. Mia Farrow was en route. Where would I sleep?

"You wait. You sit. It coming. Just now."

Then I heard it. The unmistakable California sound of a high-pitched male voice mingled with guitar. Emerging from the trail was

Mike Love, blessed Beach Boy, draped in a purple satin hooded rajah coat and singing "Good Vibrations."

Mike was full of smiles. He had renounced drugs. But even he had to sit and wait. He asked for tea and we were served. He talked excitedly about how meditation had changed his life. I told him I had been practicing. Don't worry, he said, he would make sure the Maharishi gave me a proper initiation. Did he always find the time and quiet to practice meditation in the hectic show-business life?

"Oh, well, you blow a meditation now and then."

We were joined by an English journalist. Like most Brits, Peter Drake avoided sincerity at all costs. "I don't buy the Maharishi's Kool-Aid," he said, "but I can offer you other forms of libation." He revealed a fifth of Gilbey's gin and several bottles of tonic in his backpack. We asked our minder if we could have some ice—for our tea. After an hour of happily drinking and chatting, Peter and I were admitted to adjoining rooms in the guesthouse. We smoked some hash I had brought along from the night before. I relaxed into the delicious abandonment of responsibility with this handsome fellow vagabond. Before I knew it, Peter and I were in the same bed. The night turned into a rediscovery of the joys of eros. What had I been missing! Peter was a sexual athlete. Tussling for what seemed an eternity ended with us asleep on the floor when our minder knocked. Morning already?

"You come. You hurry. Maharishi ready. Just now."

THE MAHARISHI MADE AN APPEARANCE in a pastel two-hundred-seat hall. He took the lotus position on a goatskin. Sprigs of jasmine nestled in his flowing white hair and long beard. And what he did was—nothing. For ten minutes. He said not a word. He smiled beatifically. He looked upon each face, row by row. Soon everyone was smiling. Laughing. Bringing him flowers and fruit. Spontaneously, a dialogue began. For two hours it never palled.

Then we adjourned to a porch to practice with our guides. Signs were hung from the backs of bamboo chairs overlooking the Ganga.

DO NOT DISTURB—MEDITATING.

Teenagers with blankets over their heads sat beside middle-aged English ladies with cashmere sweaters under their saris. It looked like an old people's home with young people. I was summoned to sit on the roof with a German-speaking guide. By evening, it was hot as hell. Peter and I blew a meditation and enjoyed another night of gin and sin.

Finally, the Maharishi summoned me to a private lunch in his "bungalow," a marble-terraced, five-room villa. Skittering old women in stockinged feet brought trays of vegetables and chapatis hot off a handheld charcoal stove.

"I am chief guru of the Western world," the Maharishi said with a beguiling blend of boyishness and barking mad messianic zeal. "I need one meditation center per every one hundred thousand population. Yes, so. To bring bliss consciousness to the whole world." This was the message he wished me to take back to America.

I had to acknowledge that the Maharishi was the only thing about India that did not say, "You sit. You wait. It coming." The Maharishi said *now!*

IN A SOFT SPIRAL NOTEBOOK I had recorded my wanderings in the foothills of the Himalayas and my audiences with the Maharishi. That precious notebook was wedged next to my rump in the back of my jeans all the way from India to JFK and on a subway into the city and on a final sprint up Lexington Avenue to meet my ex-husband and reclaim my daughter.

I swooped Maura into my arms and we twirled round and round and then skipped across Central Park. Somewhere in that dizzy re-union, the notebook left my person. It was never to be found.

While I played with Maura and made her favorite meals, in the back of my mind was the panic about returning from a hugely expensive trip with nothing to show for it. Once Maura went to sleep, I skipped dinner and lay on my "bed of nails," playing Beatles and Beach Boys records. Gradually, I was able to return to the languid tempo of Rishikesh, recall the most vivid conversations, and finally feel the warmth of bliss consciousness again. This was one meditation I was not going to blow. Then I wrote the story.

"I'M JUST CRAZY ABOUT YOUR WRITING and I just *have* to have you in my magazine." It was Helen Gurley Brown, gushing, which was how she won people over. "Pussycat," she purred, "I can pay you fifteen hundred dollars a story if you'll give me one story a month for the next year."

I didn't have to meditate on it. If it would pay the rent, I'd play pussycat.

CHAPTER 8

THE *NEW YORK* FAMILY

"LOOK WHO'S HERE!"

That was the sonic boom of recognition we all longed to hear from Clay, the welcome that made it worth it to climb the four flights of gravity-defying stairs to the top of the old Tammany Hall clubhouse at 207 East Thirty-Second Street to the garret occupied by the brand-new *New York* magazine. It launched in April 1968.

"What do you have for me?" he would demand, like a little boy expecting a chocolate bar. Everybody would look up from their desks: Who was the star of the day? Clay would be all ears. The poor wretch, marshaling every bit of bravado, knew he or she had just thirty seconds to make the pitch. If it wasn't interesting, the next time that person appeared, Clay would have forgotten his name. I knew he wouldn't forget my name, because I was one of only a handful of women at the beginning.

Milton Glaser, Clay's partner in the start-up, owned the historic four-story building where his Pushpin Studio offices were located. He rented the top floor to *New York*. Messengers would appear breathless and ashen faced at the top landing, looking minutes from needing CPR. The historic patina came with a leaky roof, wavy floors, and a single closet of a bathroom. More than forty family members were squeezed cheek by jowl into a railroad-car-skinny space only twenty feet wide and a hundred feet long. This meant that a hive of staffers had to find perches wherever they could, but it worked.

An office without walls was Clay's idea. Everybody heard every-thing. He believed it reflected the egalitarian spirit that animated Americans to do their best work. There were no secrets, no favor-ites, no blood-on-the-walls rivalries like the contests he remem-bered from his days at the old *Esquire*. What there was in abundance was noise.

Clay's enthusiasm for a sound piece of work—whether it was a photo, a drawing, or a piece of writing—was broadcast widely. He would roar "Fabulous!" or "Knockout!" or "Never read anything like this before!" He also roared when a writer refused to answer the phone as the deadline ticked away. He roared when the truck carry-ing storyboards to Buffalo bogged down in snow. He roared when the kid messenger showed up at the last moment with the printed dummy in hand. "Goddamn hero!" He roared for the helluvit. Clay was so su-perhumanly animated, some staffers wore earplugs or even earmuffs, which came in handy during winter days when the heat went off. I always layered up with sweaters and boots, but my skirts were short enough to reveal my blued knees.

FROM THE START, the new independent *New York* was a family. This family was unusual in that it had two fathers, Milton and Clay. Milton was the perfect grounding for Clay, whose personality acted as the lightning rod of creativity and animosity. The son of a tailor marinated in the knish culture of the Bronx, Milton would grow to become both a fine-arts painter and one of the most influential graphic designers in the world. Perhaps his best-known achievement was designing the ubiquitous logo I ♥ NEW YORK.

At first glance, he and Clay appeared to be opposites. Milton always wore jeans and big ties printed with fruit or vegetables, his black hair hooked over his big ears and what looked like foot-long sideburns to make up for the hairless highway running from front to back of his head. Clay bought his Turnbull & Asser striped shirts on London's Jermyn Street with cuffs that required cuff links.

Milton's eyes had become somewhat jaded by growing up street-smart in New York. Clay brought to the magazine the curiosity of a perpetual outsider. "Clay was obsessed with the city's power establishments, the lives of the rich, the talented, and the perverse," Milton said. "He never developed the thick skin of cynicism, as so many editors do."

Milton, too, had other interests: the Lower East Side, left-wing politics, and cheap food. Milton and his writing partner, Jerome Snyder, founded a column, named by Clay "Underground Gourmet." It continues to run in *New York* magazine to this day, fifty years later.

Clay and Milton argued often and loudly. Their shouting matches were usually about the same thing.

"Make it bigger!" No matter what it was, a photograph, the headline, the pull quotes, the text type, this was Clay's recurring demand.

"It's already big," Milton would protest.

"Make it BIGGER!"

Before he lapsed into profanity, Milton would insist, "When everything is big, nothing is big."

Commonly, the relationship between editor and art director resembles that of Cain and Abel. But the tight daily working relationship between Clay and Milton evolved into one of those mysteries of human affection that endure not despite but *because* of the obstacles. Both needed an opposing force with equal talent, and they came to understand they were better together than separate.

"Milton and I feel committed to one another in a personal way, beyond the professional," Clay said one evening when the three of us had dinner together. Milton agreed: "It's as mysterious as why people fall in love."

Nonetheless, everyone was relieved when Walter Bernard was lured away from *Esquire* to join Milton, his teacher and mentor, to become the full-time, hands-on art director. Walter's emollient personality was the salve that healed rifts between Clay and Milton. With his infectious smile and blue aviator glasses and unflappable ability to solve design problems, Walter looked the part of the magic genie who pulled the magazine together. I remember leaning over the art table to look at any one of the covers to illustrate my stories and yelping with delight.

GLORIA STEINEM WAS THE SISTER everyone would have loved to have. She had started out as a receptionist at *Esquire* in 1960. Every man who entered that magazine office gaped at the long-stemmed beauty.

It was Gloria who was first to answer Clay's plea for help in raising money to start *New York*. At an endless series of lunches, she "tap-danced for rich people," as she called it, which meant being witty and charming. Clay wanted Gloria to write a story for the maiden issue. She came up with the idea of writing about Ho Chi Minh's travels in New York and other parts of the United States as a young man. Oddly enough, she said, the Vietnamese leader had been an ally of Roosevelt's and helped to rescue downed American fliers in the jungles of Vietnam during World War II. Clay liked the offbeat idea. Gloria tried desperately to contact the president of Vietnam, but Western Union operators couldn't grasp the spelling of a name with all those consonants. When Gloria showed up late clutching her story, she found Clay flailing to pull together the issue.

"What have you got for me?" he moaned.

"Ho Chi Minh in New York."

He grabbed the manuscript and without a glance handed it off to a messenger to take to the printer.

"But, Clay, you haven't read a word. You might hate it," Gloria protested.

"How could I hate it?" he said. "It's here."

WORKING ON THE FOURTH ISSUE, a worried Clay shoved a manuscript and a few photographs into Tom Wolfe's hand. "Take a look at these, Tom, and tell me if you think we should run them." The magazine was a newborn, only two weeks old. "The advertising department tells me if we run these photos, we'll lose every high-end retail account we've got."

Barbara Goldsmith's article entitled "La Dolce Viva" was an inside look at the sadomasochistic world of Andy Warhol's Factory. It featured Viva, one among the posse of models who appeared in his home movies, which the art world was now taking seriously. These movies were endless-loop bacchanals with no director, like *The Lonesome Cowboy,* where Viva was the focus of heterosexual seduction, homosexual sex, masturbation, talk, lots of stoned talk, and the target of a faux rape. Barbara was one of Clay's star writers and an original investor, and here she was telling the world what it was really like in the roachy inner belly of Warhol's infamous Factory with its indiscriminate couplings and wasted "superstar" models who enslaved themselves to the high priest of pop culture.

Barbara had become friendly with the ascending artist when she reviewed Warhol's ghosted book for the *New York Times, The Philosophy of Andy Warhol: From A to B and Back Again.* The last sentence of her review read: "Some people say that California is the bellwether of the nation, but I say it's Andy Warhol." A surprisingly insecure Warhol called her up and said, "You really think I'm a bellwether?" The New York School of Art was a fertile breeding ground for new talent—

with Jasper Johns, Roy Lichtenstein, Larry Rivers, Jim Dine, and others—but Andy's genius for marketing himself and the circus of his life would have the most lasting impact on the culture.

Clay had okayed the story on Warhol's Factory and told Barbara, "Don't be so careful." He had assigned Diane Arbus as the photographer, whose eyes inevitably found a pocket of Marquis de Sade perversions beneath the most plain-brown-wrapper of a person. Goldsmith recalled for me, "Once, when we worked together on a story, she said, 'I have a very loving eye; I don't know why people say that I'm perverse.' She was painfully shy. It was her own vulnerability that allowed her to penetrate to the dark side of another's soul."

Viva had greeted the writer and the photographer in her apartment in red slacks and a half-buttoned blouse with her delicately featured face unmade-up and a huge tangle of dark hair pulled back. After a long loopy monologue about the vicissitudes of her life, Viva casually stripped and lay back on a ratty Victorian couch with no part of her anatomy concealed. Barbara wrote down her desperate self-description: "I'm nude because Andy says seeing me nude sells tickets . . . I think I look like a parody, a satire on a nude, a plucked chicken."

The article was dynamite. But the full-page photograph of Viva with her shrunken breasts and eyes rolled up under her skull like a stoned-out zombie was apocalyptic. It may have been the first photograph to tear down the wall between public and private identity. Both Clay and Tom sensed that Arbus would change the way we looked at photographs and cast them as art, and they were right.

Tom looked up from the photo at Clay and said, "I don't see how you can*not* run it."

"That's the way I feel," Clay said. And he did run it. The full story and several photographs appeared in the third issue of *New York*.

The morning after the Viva issue appeared, Jane Maxwell, Clay's executive assistant, was bombarded by furious phone calls. That was the morning that Jane, a zaftig redhead, became the mother of our fledgling family, protecting Clay from the raw rage of the advertisers, knowing full well he was not going to apologize to a single one of them. The advertising department reported that every high-end retailer on Fifth Avenue had canceled its ad buy for the full year.

The board called Clay, on the carpet of Armand Erpf's Park Avenue apartment, fuming that their investments were certain to be wiped out. They were ready to fire him. Erpf elevated the discussion to a moral plain and praised Clay for his vision and balls. This was his boy, his wunderkind, and he was putting more money into the magazine; he wanted Edgar Bronfman and the others to follow suit. "This magazine is going to be a big success, so don't thank me," he said. "You're going to love this investment."

Over the summer of '68 hung the fear that cash-flow problems would hold up people's paychecks. Fashion writer Priscilla Tucker was hired to lure back the retail advertisers. Still, chatter on the street persisted: Would the magazine fail? It was a scary time. Yet no one quit. Clay's writers and photographers were moved by the evidence of this editor's loyalty to them. Clay was rare among his ilk, willing to brush off the business side if he believed in a great story and startling photographs. We all began to breathe the elixir of Clay's own ambition. It was our own dolce vita.

I WAS LUCKY TO HAVE STARTED PREVIOUSLY with Clay at the scrappy Sunday supplement in the *Trib*. Now, at the independent *New York* magazine, there was a new manifesto: No more limits to nonfiction . . . if you have the stamina and the courage to do the reporting and the talent to tell a story as compelling as a literary short story, do it!

Inspired by Gay Talese and Tom Wolfe, some of my colleagues and I began borrowing the dramatic techniques used by novelists—scene-by-scene construction, dialogue, and use of status details to denote social class. We treated the protagonists of nonfiction stories like characters in a novel. What was their motivation? What were they thinking? What was it like living inside their reality?

The New Journalism would grow into a movement. But the form wasn't really all that new. Clay had stumbled upon it back in the Duke library when he came upon bound volumes of the Civil War–era *Tribune*, Horace Greeley's famous nineteenth-century newspaper. He began to read gripping accounts from the Virginia battlefield, not from a disinterested correspondent, but vivid stories with narrative structure written by soldiers in the trenches.

Most of us were on the cusp of a new generation, precursors of the counterculture. We began setting the agenda for the jumbo-size baby-boom generation that came on our heels. Mostly fugitives from the suburbs or small-town Midwest, we wanted to escape the conformity and cookie-cutter marriages and the materialist fixations of our parents and explore the new urban lifestyles. Each of us brought with us a fantasy of New York. We projected those fantasies through our writing and the art direction of the magazine. Clay sought writers and artists who reflected the many different New Yorks.

My New York was the Lower East Side. I saw myself as half hippie/half striver. I did have a very clear dream. I wanted to be a journalist because that would give me license to ask questions of anyone about anything I wanted to know. One of my first attempts at literary journalism I wrote while I was in graduate school at Columbia University in 1969. Clay asked me what I thought about the student "revolutionaries" uptown at Columbia. "What are these privileged kids revolting about?" he wanted to know. "Why are they playing with violence?"

After weeks of hanging out in meetings of affinity groups, I gave Clay my perspective. Young white liberal males, handsomely supported by the very suburban elite parents they were expected to repudiate, were desperate to be taken seriously as revolutionaries. They felt themselves shamed by the Black Panthers, men with warrior Afros and Cuban shades who were actually prepared to die to expose racial oppression.

Clay gave me an idea for how to tell the story: "Seek out a young bomber struggling with this challenge and follow him, try to get inside his head." I found Marc, a mild-mannered graduate student from St. Louis whose wife was on the radical feminist fringe and goading him into violent activism. Recently, Ted Gold and his companions had played with dynamite while planning a violent action and were entombed in a town house on West Eleventh Street. Poor Marc was losing weight and preparing himself to die.

For some young white radicals it was enough to participate in the chic of rage and the ecstasy of despair. Not long after the excitement of trashing Columbia, some of the participants called another tactics meeting. I sat next to one of those despairing radicals. He dropped his head into his hands: "We'll never have a revolution in this country. Too many people are happy."

Clay loved that line. He never believed for a moment that the United States would allow another revolution, but he had a natural nose for spotting new trends at least ten minutes before history. And the '60s and '70s spawned more new lifestyles than could be contained in any magazine. Only in retrospect did we appreciate our good fortune in being part of a utopian experiment in American journalism. At the time, we were too busy having fun.

THE MOST CONTROVERSIAL of Tom Wolfe's many indelible pieces for *New York* was the cover story "Radical Chic," which took up twenty-six pages in the issue of June 8, 1970. This was a chronicle of the infamous party at Lenny and Felicia Bernstein's thirteen-room penthouse duplex on Park Avenue, where the Black Panthers were celebrated and fawned over and bathed in humbly mumbled liberal white guilt while munching on little Roquefort cheese morsels rolled in crushed nuts, offered to them on silver platters by maids in black uniforms with hand-ironed white aprons. (It was okay, they were white maids.) We had all seen the bloody pictures in *Life* magazine of police shootouts in Chicago where Black Panthers were treated like the Viet Cong. So what were they doing being pampered in a Park Avenue salon? Tom would tell us as only Tom Wolfe could.

"When you walk into this house," the host, and maestro of *West Side Story,* apologized to Don Cox, the Panther's field marshal from Oakland, "you must feel infuriated!"

The man with a giant Afro and black turtleneck looked embarrassed, wrote Tom. "No, man . . . I manage to overcome that . . ."

"Don't you get bitter? Doesn't that make you mad?"

"Noooo, man . . . I'm over that."

"Well," said Lenny, "it makes me mad!"

Lenny's wife, Felicia, was "smiling her tango smile at Robert Bay, who just 41 hours ago was arrested in an altercation with the police, supposedly over a .38-caliber revolver that someone had in a parked car in Queens . . ." The revolutionaries were surrounded by stars: Jason Robards, Steven Sondheim, Lillian Hellman, Mike Nichols, Otto Preminger, Larry Rivers, Aaron Copeland, Barbara Walters, Jerome Robbins, and countless others. Tom, who had RSVPed on an invitation borrowed from David Halberstam, politely introduced himself to the host and hostess with his pen and reporter's pad in plain sight. Tom thought he'd fallen into a scene that Hollywood couldn't have cast any better to reflect the comedy of manners that masqueraded in the 1960s as a revolution. Years later, he described his delight in a *New York* magazine tribute to Clay: "The sight of the rich, the famous, and the brainy kowtowing to a band of black radicals from Oakland, California, in Leonard Bernstein's living room, baring their soft white backs the more poignantly to feel the Panthers' vengeful lash, then imploring them not to kill their children—no writer would have ever dreamed of a bonanza quite this rich."

"Radical Chic" stood the test of time as the earliest social commentary on political correctness. The title also was only one of many popular phrases that Tom introduced to written and spoken language, along with "the Me Decade" (sometimes altered to "the Me Generation"). He also liked to use *nostalgie de la boue,* which is literally translated as "nostalgia for the mud," but which Wolfe used ironically to skewer the newly rich for romanticizing the trappings, fashion, style, and even radical philosophies of the underclass in pursuit of social aplomb and prestige.

CLAY TOOK ANOTHER CHANCE when he allowed himself to be one of the first male chauvinists enlisted in the movement for women's equality. Gloria and I both believed that he could be educated. Simultaneously, he and Gloria picked up on a brilliant idea floating in the atmosphere of free radicalism.

"Let's test the idea of a magazine reflecting the philosophy of women's liberation," he suggested to Milton. They discussed testing it in the year-end double issue. With so many women working for *New York,* the two men thought they had a ready-made staff of writers.

"And you are the perfect editor," Clay told Gloria.

Gloria retaliated. "How can you publish a credible voice for women's liberation in a magazine owned by men!" It took Clay a few days, but he told me when he had the epiphany: "It doesn't make sense for a company run by men to be the publisher of such a magazine. But I could let Gloria use the pages of *New York* to launch a sample issue."

Separately, Gloria and her sisters at Women's Action Alliance had produced a dummy issue of *Ms.* magazine. They'd had no luck in raising money for it. Clay went back to Gloria with a generous proposal.

"I can add one hundred pages to our double issue for January," he said, "so we could print thirty pages of your *Ms.* and fold it inside *New York.* Like a sample issue. We could test it for you as a one-shot."

Gloria was impressed. Clay paid her writers' fees and all the expenses of production. Eager to repay Gloria for helping him to launch his publication, he gave Gloria full ownership of the new magazine.

The cover of the preview issue of Ms., added as an insert in the January 1972 *New York* issue, featured Kali, the multiarmed Hindu deity, pregnant, and attempting the impossible balancing act performed by women who tried to be perfect in all their roles. Gloria went on a publicity tour and ran into male TV commentators who ridiculed Ms.: What could women possibly have to say after the first issue? More troubling were the call-ins from viewers who complained they couldn't find Ms. on their newsstand.

Gloria called Clay in a panic. He laughed. "Our year-end issue usually sells forty thousand copies. All one hundred thousand copies of the Ms. issue have sold out. Congratulations!"

Four decades later, Ms. still had plenty to say in its fortieth anniversary issue, and by 2012, it had gone global.

CHAPTER 9

"I'LL MAKE YOU A STAR"

THIS WAS CLAY'S SIGNATURE PROMISE. He delivered on that promise many times over. As Richard Reeves said, "He was a Godfather, but actually, he didn't *make* his star writers. It was much better than that. He gave us the freedom to make ourselves."

At a party barely weeks after *New York* launched, Clay walked up to Reeves, a *New York Times* political reporter, and said, "How come you never write for me?" Reeves quipped, "You never ask me to write for you." Clay said, "Well, I'm asking you now." The handsome single young stud with a sterling silver byline on the Old Gray Lady looked at this rude interloper whose tiny rag wasn't yet out of infancy and said, "Trade the *New York Times* for a dream? No thanks."

If Clay read the work of a writer and wanted him or her to join the family, he never gave up. It was a year or so later that Reeves happened to walk out his door on West Eleventh Street and was startled to see a line around the corner to get into a hole-in-the-wall soup and sandwich joint. What the hell was going on? He found out that Milton Glaser had touted the place in his "Underground Gourmet" column. There went the neighborhood. The next time Reeves saw Clay, he told him the story.

"Write for me," Clay repeated. Reeves did join the *New York* family and became a major political star who went on to write an acclaimed trilogy on the presidencies of John F. Kennedy, Richard Nixon, and Ronald Reagan. He was never sorry he made the move: "Being part of *New York* was so much more fun." Whenever he wrote pieces for the *New York Times Magazine,* people would come up to him, obviously impressed, and say, "I saw your piece in the *Times* on Sunday." From the first time he wrote for *New York,* people would stop him on the street wanting to argue: "Listen, when you say Rockefeller and Nixon . . . blah blah blah . . . you don't know what you're talking about!"

Reeves introduced Clay to his best friend, Ken Auletta. Nobody thought that a former political campaign manager could write. But Auletta had great sources at city hall. "The city is lying about this fiscal crisis," Auletta told Clay in 1975. Using all kinds of fiscal chicanery, the city was hiding the truth of how deeply it had gone into debt. Auletta had a fresh point of view: "Ford is doing New York a favor, pushing the city to the wall to save itself." Going against conventional wisdom tickled Clay. He hired the feisty young man to write a series on the fiscal mess.

Auletta's most memorable piece brought out the best of the collaborative process that was encouraged by Clay and Milton. When Franklin National Bank collapsed, it was the biggest bank failure in the country up until then. Auletta fingered the city's top bankers along with its top politicians. Clay called Milton and Walter Bernard and his top editors—Byron Dobell, Jack Nessel, and Sheldon Zalaznick—around the art table, along with Auletta, to brainstorm about how to give this shocking story maximum impact.

Milton pulled out a big sheet of paper and started to draw thumbnail sketches of a lineup including banker David Rockefeller, Vice President Nelson Rockefeller, Mayor Abe Beame, and a dozen other big shots. Then he drew a box around them and prison bars to which they were clinging.

"Should These People Go to Jail?" Clay called out the headline. It all happened in a matter of minutes. The artwork was assigned to a brilliant British artist, Julian Allen. That story, like many others, proved that the editorial team was not tied to either political party but on the side of the citizens of New York. That was a good part of the magazine's success. (Auletta is renowned today as *The New Yorker*'s window into our media democracy, in his influential column, "Annals of Communications," and his many books, including *Googled* and *Greed and Glory on Wall Street*.)

Clay's approach also worked because he hired several brilliant editors to provide adult supervision of the wild-eyed wunderkinder he was hiring fresh out of college and graduate schools. Sheldon Zalaznick was his senior managing editor, an intellectual's intellectual with a dry sense of humor. He was a teacher to his perfectionist core. Shelley knew how to spot a story and help an untrained writer to weave it into a solid magazine piece. It was he who found Andrew Tobias.

In 1970, Tobias was a brainiac Harvard graduate who had already become vice president of a conglomerate, the National Student Marketing Corporation. The company used its inflated stock to buy up all kinds of unrelated businesses, and the scheme was wildly successful until its fraudulent accounting was exposed. Six months before Tobias could cash in stock options worth a small fortune, he watched the company's stock plunge. Quick to try to turn lemons into lemonade, Tobias wrote an amusing piece, on speculation, about his exploits. It was rejected by so many magazines, he forgot about it. He was a graduate student at Harvard Business School when the phone rang in his dorm room and a cultivated voice said, "Mr. Tobias, please."

"I'm twenty-three, unshaven, sitting on my bed in shorts in Cambridge," Tobias remembers.

"This is Sheldon Zalaznick at *New York* magazine. I am terribly sorry that it has taken us so long to see your piece. By any chance, is it still available?"

"Confessions of a Youth Marketeer" featured Tobias on the cover of *New York* teetering inside a bubble. Ten pages were devoted to the first magazine piece he'd ever written. It was a huge success. But there was a subject closer to his heart, the new gay culture. "I was going to Harvard Business School for something respectable to do while I went to gay bars every night," he told me. Tobias planned on becoming a little tycoon.

"No, no, you should be a writer" was the advice he heard from Clay and Shelley. Tobias worried that his straight bosses would be put off by his admission of being gay; his parents didn't even know. "But Clay and Shelley took it in stride," he recalls. They published an excerpt from his autobiography, *The Best Little Boy in the World*. Tobias did indeed become celebrated for writing amusing articles and books about investing and later as a powerhouse fund-raiser for the Democratic Party.

Clay had to lure Nick Pileggi away from the bosom of a flush wire service to take the leap into New Journalism. Pileggi's New York was the criminal underworld. He was a nimble AP reporter who often slept in precinct houses, waiting for one of the detectives to show up too drunk to go out on a call so he could take his place. Clay liked Pileggi's colorful stories. In his piece about Joe Colombo, a top Mafia boss, he described the "lump job" administered to his head by a couple of FBI agents in a street brawl. Pileggi was the first to suggest that Colombo might soon be taken out in a mob power struggle. Two weeks later, at the Italian Unity Day rally, Colombo was shot in the head; he ended up paralyzed and lived for the next seven years as a vegetable. Pileggi produced a dozen stories in the first year. Right behind Mario Puzo, he became a Boswell to the Mafia and later wrote the hit film *Goodfellas*.

One morning Clay was supposed to be interviewed about the competition between *New York* and *The New Yorker*. When the doorbell rang early, he went to the door of his apartment in his boxer shorts. A tall, lanky Texan appeared in the doorway and pretended not to be startled. Aaron Latham, an Amherst man and an editor at *Esquire,* was known for his often lethal interview style. Deadpan, he would ask a question and then shut up. He had no trouble with awkward silences, patiently waiting for the hang-yourself quote.

Clay sat opposite him with a breakfast tray on his lap, a poached egg propped on an English muffin. During one long silence, Clay lifted the whole egg on a fork and bit off half. The egg exploded like a yellow grenade all over his face, all over his white shirt. Clay wiped off his face with a cloth napkin, ignored his shirt, did not laugh, did not speak. Aaron hid his own embarrassment. He proceeded to his next question as if nothing had happened. Clay admired his sangfroid. A few hours later, Clay called Aaron and offered him a job.

The Texan turned out to be a natural stylist for *New York*. His vivid depiction of displaced frontiersmen driven to displaying their manhood by riding a mechanical bull in a downbeat dive was the basis for his screenplay of *Urban Cowboy,* a hit movie. He would become Clay's adored surrogate son.

NEW YORK WAS A WEEKLY with the ambition of interpreting the news like a monthly. No independent weekly had attempted that before, except for *Time, Life,* and *Newsweek,* all with their massive corporate resources. Clay's operating theory was disequilibrium, guaranteed by the frenetic weekly tempo. You might be working on a piece for a month, and when you thought it was done, Clay would change the lead, cut it in half, or demand, "What the hell are you trying to say?," and you would crawl back to your keyboard and force yourself to find out.

Clay did more reporting than all of us put together. He had very little time for a romantic life in those days. He was out every night cruising the latest openings, screenings, book parties, art galleries; then on to dinner parties with power brokers who dropped tantalizing hints about political scandals or Wall Street shenanigans; followed by drop-ins to East Village joints to hear Jefferson Airplane or the next-next hot music group.

He demanded that his writers and artists have a point of view. "Clay knew just enough about almost everything that he could give the writer some context," noted Amanda (Binky) Urban, who started out as Clay's executive assistant and was promoted many times over until she launched her career as a high-powered literary agent at International Creative Management (ICM). Clay would send a writer off with several key questions: Why are things the way they are? (Sniff out the latest trend); What led up to this? (Give us the historical background); How do things work? (Who is pulling the strings or making the magic or making fools of us?); How is the power game played in your corner of New York, or in the White House with a new president?

What he never wanted was what journalism schools often teach—a "nut graf"—meaning a lead paragraph that sums up what the story is about. Clay's style was the opposite: tantalize the reader with a compelling opening scene but don't give the story away. He told writers, "Take me inside the world you know, where readers don't have any access, and tell me a great story."

I came to understand that for Clay, for any influential editor, the instinct for spotting a story is inborn. It cannot be taught. His hunch was often more prescient, more edgy, more easily supported by anecdotes than hard reporting, and that could lead to arguments with his most independent reporters. This was particularly true with women journalists. Taking direction from a male editor, especially if the subject was the emergence of feminism, ran up against a built-in resistance. Julie Baumgold, a self-described Upper East Side Jewish princess, specialized in mocking feminism and arguing with Clay about it. Jane O'Reilly was a wild spirit who also resisted direction. She wrote a famous story about the click!—the moment of truth—that turned housewives into rabble-rousers for women's lib.

Along about this time, *Esquire* editor Harold Hayes grew jealous of Clay's success. "Felker's got a group of terrific women writers over there," he told Lee Eisenberg, his assistant editor. "Why don't you take them out to dinner and try to steal them for us." Eisenberg did indeed invite Julie, Jane, and me, separately, on consecutive nights, to "seduction" dinners. We might have felt free to fight with Felker, but when it came down to loyalty, he had us.

TALENT ATTRACTS TALENT: that was another of Clay's secrets. It was how he persuaded Stephen Sondheim, already a matchless composer and lyricist who in the 1970s turned out ten hits with Hal Prince, to create puzzles for the magazine. The irrepressible Woody Allen wrote several stories for early issues. Clay even drafted the nearly eternal *Village Voice* cartoonist Jules Feiffer, who went on to write many plays and over three dozen books.

Michael Kramer was fresh out of Amherst and Columbia Law School when Clay asked him to come to talk. Kramer's book *The Ethnic Factor* had been well reviewed by the *New York Times*. When he came into the office, some of us chuckled: his suit and tie were incongruous with his cascade of unkempt hair. Kramer spoke in staccato bursts, but he had a lot to say about Clay's favorite subject: politics. Gloria was giving up the "City Politic" column to work full time on developing her own magazine, *Ms.* "I'd like you to take over the column," Clay told Kramer.

"I've never been a journalist before," the young man confessed.

"Don't worry about *that*. Here's my advice. Just write like you talk." It was the energy and rawness that Clay wanted in political columns. Kramer's first was due in ten days. Terrified, he called his father: "What can I write about?" His father, who'd worked for two New York governors, suggested he interview his old friend former mayor Bob Wagner. Kramer groaned. "But he's never given a single quote worth printing." His father tipped him off that Governor Nelson Rockefeller had just appointed Jerry Finkelstein, a fat-cat business-man, to the board of the New York Port Authority. This was a pow-erful fiefdom that controlled every form of transportation on land, water, and underground in both New York and New Jersey. Kramer went into his interview with Wagner not knowing that beneath the mayor's hypnotic monotone there blazed a vicious hatred of Finkel-stein. Innocently, Kramer lobbed a last question. "What do you think of Rockefeller's appointment of Finkelstein to the Port Authority?"

Wagner sucked in a breath and let go. "All I know is, if I were Nelson, every morning when I woke up I would count the bridges and tunnels to see if they were all still there."

"What have you got for me?" Clay demanded when Kramer strode into the office. The greenhorn delivered the ex-mayor's punch line with the same cold scorn used by Wagner. Mouth agape, Clay mar-veled: "You're the greatest reporter of all time!"

BYRON DOBELL WAS THE EDITOR Clay hired away from *Esquire* with the promise that he could come up with one fresh cover story idea every month. Byron had an antic mind, attuned to art, history, love styles of the rich and famous, you name it. I recall laughing until my sides hurt when Byron and I got up a wicked fantasy piece for the Valentine's Day issue of *New York,* about a radical woman holding up a sperm bank, titled "The Great Valentine's Day Uprising."

Jack Nessel was the quirkiest of the three line editors. A rumpled Berkeley graduate with a California sensibility, he was first to em-brace the edgy humor of Lenny Bruce. I loved working with Jack. His DNA tended toward the sarcastic, but if you could make him laugh, you had him. He never gave up on me when we suffered hours of prose scrubbing and line cutting on pieces that then ran as long as eight thousand to ten thousand words.

Clay spotted Steven Brill while he was still on scholarship at Yale Law School. Brill was a poor kid from Queens, but when Clay took him to lunch at the Four Seasons, the kid puffed up and talked with jaw-jutting bluster about the business of law. Clay hired him on the spot. Why? Because, as Clay told me, he wanted to find out more about Manhattan's powerful law firms. Brill's most memorable story for *New York* dug into the anti-Semitism that prevailed within white-shoe WASPy firms. Brill predicted that with the advent of hostile takeovers in the 1970s, it would be two Jewish lawyers—one a fat, habitually farting proxy fighter named Joe Flom, the other the son of a Jewish immigrant factory worker named Martin Lipton—who would elevate their respective firms to the pinnacles of success within ten years. Indeed, as corporate raiding become the rage on Wall Street, Skadden, Arps, Slate, Meagher & Flom, and Wachtell, Lipton, Rosen & Katz would become the go-to firms. And Clay would later turn to both Flom and Lipton to save himself.

Brill asked Clay to help him launch his own magazine, *American Lawyer,* and one of the first reality shows, *Court TV.* All Clay had to do was call the moneymen who would later back his purchase of *Esquire* and tell them he was sending over one of his writers with a terrific idea for a new magazine. It took Brill all of thirty minutes to persuade the British press lord, Vere Harmsworth, to invest in the young man's winning idea.

THE FAMILY HAD TWO MOTHERS. Jane Maxwell knew the boss, literally, inside and out. He told her to go into his pockets after lunch and pull out his Hermès diary to note his guest in his expense record. "His entire life was the magazine then."

The other mother figure was Dorothy Seiberling, a senior editor at *Life* when Clay started out as a young reporter. Dottie had taken Clay under her wing and together they had made a romantic grand tour of Europe where she tutored him in the masterpieces of art and architecture. She was able to soothe the ruffled feelings of staffers on whom Clay unloaded one of his cloudbursts of pique. "Don't take it personally," Dottie would say, "he's already forgotten about it. Clay is just so passionate about what he's doing, he expects everybody else to be the same way."

"Clay created an atmosphere that encouraged maximum quirkiness," remembers Debbie Harkins, the demon fact-checker who saved us all. "He let us be who we all were, and we loved him for it."

Ruth Gilbert was the Mother Goose of the place. She always looked as if she was about to hatch a bunch of chicks, but instead, she hatched her own eccentric page to write about whatever she felt was stylish in the city at the moment. Furtive in her mischief, she might insert a ribald verse at the top of a page just before the issue closed, for example,

> hoorary, hooray,
> the first of may
> outdoor fucking
> begins today.

The deluxe litter box for Randolf the cat sat under Ruth's desk. He was a congenital plagiarist, always getting into Clay's open briefcase and eating up other people's stories. "Randolf, get out of there!" Clay would scold. Randolf would wait until evening to retaliate, then climb up the cork walls to claw the pushpins out, sending the artwork to the floor. Clay never did fire Randolf.

TWO OF THE SUPREME CARICATURISTS of the last forty years brought their own visual storytelling to enhance the articles. Edward Sorel's covers skewered our political and artistic pretensions with hilarious visual irony. David Levine's pen-and-ink drawings got under the skin of the people being profiled and rendered them vulnerably human. Some issues featured serious oil paintings of major national events by Julian Allen, Jim McMullan, Burt Silverman, and others. Even establishment newsmagazines such as *Time,* and elegant monthlies such as the *Atlantic Monthly* and *Fortune,* sought face-lifts by *New York*'s design duo, Glaser and Bernard.

At that time it was possible to run a magazine from the point of view of its editor and art director without the chill hand of a corporate owner weighing on their shoulders and carrying an implicit threat. The heyday of magazines spanned the mid-1950s to the late 1970s, before a general decline of editorial voice began as a handful of large media companies came to control all print media.

"Every week, you couldn't wait to see the cover of *New York,* couldn't wait to read it; everywhere you went it was the conversation at lunch or dinner," a latter-day editor of the magazine told me over lunch at Michael's. Joe Armstrong, an amiable Texan, recounted with vivid nostalgia the galvanizing effect it had on so many lives. "It made New York the most exciting city in the world. Clay's *New York* had the greatest impact of any magazine."

It was the Golden Moment.

CHAPTER 10

HIDING OUT AT WOODSTOCK

WHILE THINGS WERE RAMPING UP in my career, a slow-motion train wreck began accelerating in my family. The origin lay in the year our father abandoned the family. My sister's life had come apart. Tuition payments stopped, promises forgotten. Trish had dropped out of college in the winter of 1967 and ski-bummed until spring when she came to live with me in the East Village. It was a sweet interlude. She took care of Maura during the day while I was writing *Lovesounds,* and she got a waitressing gig at night. Glad to be freed from preppydom, she shopped for the most ethnic sandals and began wearing the earrings she strung and sold and a leather jacket with long floaty skirts. She still failed to pass for a hippie—too adorable and clean.

Her down-to-earth sense of humor kept me laughing. We could even chuckle about "Pretty Boy," her nickname for our narcissistic father. We had a plan. I would take her to Paris in the summer, certain I could get an assignment from *Cosmopolitan* with her as my assistant. The next fall she hoped to start at the School of Visual Arts. I would find a way to help her with the fees.

All bets were off when I came home one day to find a note she had left under my door. She had moved in with a "friend" in the East Village. No forwarding address. Maura was downstairs with my

Ukrainian neighbor. Beneath my sister's bold declaration of independence, I sensed a cry for help. When I returned from another presidential campaign trip in June, I tried desperately to reach her again. People at the restaurant where she worked said they hadn't seen her in two months.

Trish lived in my blood as thickly as if she were made there. I had to find her. My neighborhood being a haven for wigged-out runaways, word on the street finally tipped me that she "belonged" to a well-known druggie who lived near a Hell's Angels clubhouse.

The Angels' fortress dominated a block in the East Village not far from my apartment. Outside Dr. Cornblaster's drugstore on the corner I found an old man pulling open the grate across his shop. I asked if he had seen a girl who looked like me. "But much younger."

"The shiksa goddess?"

"Maybe so."

"She's with the doctor, so-he-says doctor. Blue door, upstairs."

A doctor? She hadn't mentioned any friend who was a doctor. Then I remembered with a shudder of guilt. I'll call him Nate. The previous winter when Trish was living with me, new and lonely in the city, I had invited Nate to come for dinner. That's when Trish met a man I should never have introduced to her. He was just back from Ibiza, Spain, looking drop-dead handsome, shirtless to show off a deep tan from hanging out in the yard. "The yard?" we'd asked. "The prison yard," he said casually. "Trumped-up charge, a girl overdosed." I couldn't get much more out of Nate, except that he was acquitted.

Of what? I persisted.

"Oh, just murder."

Nate could make a joke out of anything, and we thought this story must be a joke. This man had been one of Albert's best friends in medical school, after all. Nate Unterberg was a diabolically charming personality, a heartbreaker from the Bronx with riveting blue eyes and music in his fingers who could make all the girls cry, whether he played Chopin on his harpsichord or laid a guitar across his groin and belted out "The Ballad of John Henry." In medical school he had had the brilliant idea of becoming the junkie's doctor. He would have to experience every kind of drug, study its pharmacology, physiological effects, and so on, and then, of course, beat it. His experimentation was so "absorbing," he told Albert, he had to drop out of med school. He was going to save his generation.

I found the blue door on East Third Street and walked through the unlocked entrance and upstairs past walls bubbling like fish roe in the humidity. Steel bars padlocked the doors. It looked like a slaughterhouse. I knocked on the first door.

Nate's blue eye was unmistakable in the peephole. "Yes?"

"Nate? Do you have my sister in there?"

"Gail? Let me get some pants on."

Through the dimness lit by a ten-watt hung over a mattress on the floor, I glimpsed Trish, stumbling off the mattress in a black baby-doll.

"We, uh, were just sleeping, for like, ten hours."

"That's a funny time to sleep, honey, through the whole day."

"I'll wash my face." She reached for the Noxzema over the tub-in-kitchen and buckled in the knees. Her questions dribbled out. What time is it? What day is it? Do you want coffee? Where's the cup? Nate will go next door for a cup. I stared at her eyes. Transparent. Nate came back with a cup. I asked why Trish was shaking. Nate said it was the middle of the night for Trish. How could anyone tell what time it was, in here?

"There's nothing to you, honey." I was staring at her legs. The calves were as bony as chicken wings.

"People tell me I look great! It's nice to be on the thin side for once."

"Your legs look like Mom's when she was drinking."

"Trish hasn't had a drink since Christmas," Nate announced with righteous indignation. Trish nodded. She nodded at everything that Nate said.

"Know what we had New Year's Eve?" she said. "Chocolate mallows and milk."

I noticed an empty jar of chocolate syrup and a box of sugar doughnuts on the counter. The apartment was furnished like a dollhouse, little boxes with tiny pillows for seats, a doll-size trunk from the street. I knelt next to my sister. "I'm really worried about you and I want to help."

"I don't need help," she said, belying the plea in her note. "I'm happy and I'm doing what I want to do."

"But we had a plan, remember, honey? You were going to stay with me and save money to go to school."

"Mmm-hmmm."

Looking up at Nate with her moon-blank eyes, she murmured that he had given her a wonderful gift on the first day of spring. The magic vitamin. Speed.

"Amphetamine?" I shuddered. Yes. It made her feel beautiful and confident and as if she belonged, she said. He could slip the needle in for her so it didn't even hurt. The rush from vein to brain took seconds. The old Trish she hated had died. She was reborn. Nate had renamed her Joy.

I wanted to kill Nate. How could I have allowed this sociopath anywhere near my sister? She was just twenty-one. I had already crossed over into the enemy camp, having turned thirty. I took my sister's hand and tried to talk her back to herself. "What does 'Joy' want from life?"

"Actually, I just want to think about the big things. So many things going through my mind . . ."

"What things?"

"Why time doesn't really exist."

Nate smiled, obviously proud of a fragile new mind under his control. Albert had told me that Nate claimed to have made it through hashish, barbiturates, and mescaline, relying on cocaine to keep him awake all night so he could study pharmacological texts. Nate boasted that he had even pulled people off heroin and shaken it himself.

"What about speed?" I asked Nate now.

"Acid is over. Speed is the real magic. It makes everyone feel like they're eighteen again," he exulted.

"But, Nate, you're older than I am."

He ignored my interruption. "Imagine what it can do for the revolution—young speeders, running on moon-shot time!" He was proud to say that he had enlisted Trish in his Grand Magic Vitamin Experiment.

"Which is?"

"I have so many subjects lined up for my study, I can't take care of them all."

"So you're a dealer."

"No. I'm the Pied Piper."

"You're going to lead the children to Nirvana on speed, is that it?"

"Believe me, they go willingly."

I moved closer to my sister, putting my lips to her ear. "Come home with me, sweetie." She looked at me blankly. "This is what you need to know. The Pied Piper led children to their deaths."

FOR THE FIRST SIX MONTHS of 1969 I followed Nate's Grand Magic Vitamin Experiment, now wearing my journalist's hat. I won Nate's cooperation by offering him the most potent drug of all for sociopaths—notoriety—saying I might write about him for *New York*. It kept me in touch with my sister. She and his other "study participants" assured me their efforts would be a roaring success by summer.

Slowly they grew thinner. Their faces hardened with cunning. Help from city institutions was virtually nonexistent. My apartment became a pathetic substitute for a mental health clinic.

Mother drove down from Connecticut and as backup brought along her new boyfriend from AA. Big Al came from the tough-love school. He wanted me to call the police to arrest Nate. "Then put the girl in a state hospital and let them pull her off dope, and a psychiatrist can straighten out her thinking."

I told Big Al that I couldn't get Nate arrested; amphetamines weren't illegal. The problem in Trish's thinking was mind control. When I took Mom and Big Al to see Trish, they tried to use their own recovery from alcoholism as an argument. Mother's boyfriend tried a Bill W. intervention.

"I'm a grateful recovering alcoholic," Big Al said. "My life is already happy, joyous, and free, and I have another life ahead of me. But you people want to retire at twenty-one!'

Laughter broke through the generation gap.

Nate said he was gathering followers. It was easy work, and the future would be lucrative.

"But to retire *before* you've lived, why?"

No reply.

"Why can't you answer these questions?" our mother wanted to know.

"They asked Einstein the same thing," Nate said.

"Einstein had direction," Big Al said.

"We're finding beauty in Florida," our mother said.

"The day we found beauty with speed, we made a sign," Nate said. "It's illegal not to be free."

"That and thirty cents will get you a beer," Big Al said.

"We don't drink."

"I NEVER KNEW ANYONE who stopped shooting by themselves," Marge told me. She was a smart twenty-four-year-old veteran of speed who was a counselor at Encounter, the first drug treatment program to accept amphetamine addicts.

"Then how do people stop?" I asked.

"Three ways. Number one, death. Two, move on to heroin. Three, somebody pries them away from the provider." She added as I was leaving, "I hope you're aware, your daughter could kill herself any day."

"My sister, you mean."

"You called her your 'daughter.'"

IT WAS SUMMER WHEN MY FATHER made an unannounced visit to my apartment on East Seventh Street. He was not as carefully dressed as the last time I'd seen him, two years before. His gray-striped seersucker business suit was rumpled. Beads of sweat ran from his forehead—maybe it was just from climbing my four flights. But new folds of flesh draped the corners of his eyes.

"Very California," I said, trying to start things off on a light note. It didn't help.

"That SOB," he swore. "Marr promised me that job."

I knew right away where this story was going. His San Francisco dream had collapsed. The company he was meant to inherit from the founder had gone bankrupt. He was back east and his new wife had to take a job at a local bank back in Wilton, Connecticut. Everybody he knew would see her there. The story got worse.

"I commute in from Connecticut every day," my father said. "Well, not the same commuter train my old bridge buddies ride. I go later. Answer ads. Sit in waiting rooms. Nothing pans out."

"Daddy, I need you to help me, with Trish—"

He continued his monologue without hesitation. "You know, I should have had that job, goddamnit; Marr had promised me that job."

"Daddy, we have to do something drastic."

He could not hear me. He went on to describe in detail what it was like to stand on the subway platform in midafternoon, pretending to read the *Post*'s afternoon edition. Not wanting to go home to his wife with nothing to show for it.

"I can't help wanting to look down at the tracks," he said. Alarm bells went off, of course. The air grew unbearably thick with the unsaid. I knew what was coming, but I didn't have the heart to hold him off. All at once he brightened. The old spit-and-polish salesman began laying out a new pipe dream. He was about to start his own advertising agency. He could run it out of his home. He just needed a little start-up loan.

I told him I would mail a check when I sold my next story.

"Thanks, Cookie."

I was not just a single mother anymore. I had a sister and a father both on the verge of suicide.

ON THE MORNING OF JULY 21, 1969, my cover story in *New York* hit the newsstands with a shocking image by Milton Glaser. A Day-Glo snake coiled out of a drug capsule under the headline: "SPEED CITY. The Amphetamine Explosion by Gail Sheehy: An Intimate Story of the 'Magic Vitamin' and Its Consequences."

At that exact moment, Trish and Nate were leaving their room at the Plaza Hotel. They picked up a copy of the magazine at the hotel newsstand. "We're famous!" Nate chuckled. "The new Bonnie and Clyde!" Moments later, Trish and Nate were arrested for using stolen credit cards.

"That was the beginning of the end," said my sister when she later filled in her side of the story. I saw a girl brought into the courtroom who appeared remarkably clean for having spent two nights in the infamous Women's House of Detention. Her scowl softened when she saw me sitting in the second row. She looked scared. I petitioned to have her released into my custody. The judge agreed, provided that I and her parole officer would see to it that she entered a drug treatment program.

I found a hospital in Connecticut that would accept her for observation, but she fled within days. The next stop was a locked ward at Bellevue, a prison ward, because she had attempted suicide. I had to demand that she again be released into my custody, arguing that she wasn't a criminal, only a drug user, and amphetamines were not illegal. The warden was only too eager to have an excuse for disposal. Her discharge card read: Bellevue Reject.

Later that month, I took my sister home with me, fed her, brushed her hair, bought her a new dress. Things went reasonably well for a few days until Nate called, homicidal over the "suspension" by law enforcement of his Grand Magic Vitamin Experiment. It wasn't safe to have Trish living with me where Nate could find her. And I had a five-year-old to protect. Maura was going to a church day camp. I could not bear for her to see her aunt having withdrawal agonies or a panic attack.

I called Clay. He offered to arrange for me to take my sister up to Armand Erpf's estate in a remote upstate county. Isolation was the last thing she needed. I sat my sister down and told her, gently but firmly, there was only one choice left: Encounter, the first drug treatment program designed for speed addicts. Encounter was run by counselors who were ex–speed users, a new concept at the time. From the first day Trish spent with the Encounter people, she felt safe and even happy. She attended every day, and within the first few weeks, she was on her way to being clean. Meanwhile, Nate was arrested for car theft and I had to go to court to testify against him. Damned if his mother didn't get him out on bail. I worried that he could come to my apartment looking for Trish.

Serendipitously, my wonderful editor, Nan Talese, told me she and Gay were decamping for the summer to their Jersey Shore home. Would I like to babysit their apartment? I asked if I could put up my sister there. Bless her heart, Nan agreed.

On Saturday, August 14—only in retrospect does the notoriety of that date matter—I took Maura to her father's for the weekend. It was early that evening when a pounding at my door made me jump. Why hadn't my Ukrainian lookout announced the caller? Wary, I slid open the peephole. A man with a red bandanna around his forehead looked back. The eyes, glassy blue and big as saucers, belonged unmistakably to one person.

"What do you want?"

"I have some things to give you," Nate said.

"What things?"

"Joy's things."

"I'm not dressed," I lied.

"I can wait. All night if I have to."

"You're barking up the wrong tree. Trish isn't here."

"That figures. I'm not surprised. It's you I want to see, the good girl Gail. Can you spare a Coke?"

"Only the kind that comes in a can."

"That's cool."

It was the first time I'd heard that expression. I had to see this creep and warn him to stay away from Trish. I let Nate in. I brought him a Coke and we sat on the sofa.

He told me he knew where Trish was, in an apartment uptown, and he wanted the address. She needed him, bad, he said.

"She has other friends now; her sanity is returning."

He insisted I tell him where to find her. As if playfully, he pulled off his red bandanna and tried to tie it around my forehead. "You'd look good as a hippie, just relax." He was high, alternately laughing and threatening and flirting. I lied, "Albert will be here any minute, bringing Maura home." Suddenly he shoved me down and threw himself on top of me.

"Just tell me the address," he demanded. "It's no fun to hurt someone I like."

"You don't like me."

He was stuffing the bandanna in my mouth. I reached for the Coke on the coffee table and threw it in his eyes. With a rush of adrenaline strength, I managed to wrestle myself free and bolt for the door, run down a flight, and bang on the door of the cop below. His fat teenage son was sitting in front of the TV with his father's service revolver in his lap, as usual. "Intruder in my apartment!" I said to excite him.

The boy took a long time working his half-bushel haunches out of the depths of the sofa, too long to catch an intruder. I heard Nate's big feet clambering down the stairs. He would still be on the loose. By this time, I had little faith that law enforcement would get this menace off the streets. My strongest instinct was to collect my sister and get as far away from Nate as possible.

I'd read in the paper about a music festival upstate. A huge crowd was expected. Call it crazy, but there was great appeal in getting lost in a crowd. I called Trish at the Talese apartment. "I'm coming to get you. Pack your medicine and your sleeping bag, we're driving to Woodstock."

"What's in Woodstock?"

"A whole lotta people—Nate will never find us there."

ONCE I HAD TRISH in my little green Beetle, I stopped to pick up my Indian friend Chota Chudasama, a travel executive, to ride shotgun. Trish hid in the backseat as we lost ourselves in the tide of humanity headed for the rock festival. The more impenetrable the traffic jam, the happier I was; we were less detectable than amoebae. Darkness fell, rains came, we arrived at a mudfest. Walking around was surreal. We were the only people there who were not high, dead sober, without even a reefer among us, feeling really square, but glad of it. There was more marijuana than music, billowing clouds of it; you didn't even have to smoke to get high.

Trish began to break out in hives.

"Don't worry," she said, "it's just my body reacting to the weed." I'd heard the Hog Farm commune was there to help with drug problems. We found their Tripper's Tent. Trish lay down on a cot and felt better right away. Then she took on the role of counselor and helped stoners come down.

When Joe Cocker took stage to scream "Let's Get Stoned," Trish looked longingly at people lighting up. Chota and I took her off to the Food for Love tent. In the background, we heard Jimi Hendrix's whining guitar playing his own version of "The Star-Spangled Banner." As word passed in the wee hours of Saturday morning that Joplin was finally about to appear, the three of us nudged our way close. A blue angel under the lights in her Indian jacket and bell bottoms, she was obviously feeling no pain, leaping up and down with a river of hair spilling over her face, singing in a hoarse voice "Ball & Chain" in ecstasy and agony—*Nevuh nevuh nevuh.* She spoke to the crowd. Did we have everything we needed? Were we staying stoned?

The beauty of it was, at that moment, my sister didn't need to be stoned to be happy. Amid half a million people, my sister and I felt connected by music and youth. We were closer than ever before. For years afterward, we relived our hilarious escape from drugs at the biggest drugfest in the history of the world.

———————————

WHEN SHE FINISHED HER YEAR with Encounter, I finally did take Trish to Paris. She was my "researcher" for a *Cosmo* story on why Frenchmen make great dates. We woke up in a funky hotel room and threw open the heavy wooden shutters to see the painters setting up their easels along the Seine, and we welcomed a new stage of life. We could now be pals, not big and little sister, but soul sisters. Our relationship would probably outlast all others.

Trish never went back to drugs. She did eventually go back to college, with my help. With her third marriage, to Larry Fantl, a charming, laid-back psychologist, she got it right. I could not have been prouder when my sister, Patricia Klein, stepped up to collect her Ph.D. diploma from Fordham University and became a professor of creative writing.

CHAPTER 11

PLAYING HOUSE

CLAY TOOK ME TO HIS HOME for the first time on a wintry Sunday afternoon. We had met in Central Park to discuss a story. Ostensibly. The cold was shattering. It was well after his separation from Pamela and my divorce. We had been seeing each other, sub rosa, since the Kennedy piece. This was the first time he suggested we go to his apartment.

The building, not far from Sutton Place, looked like an embassy. The sleepy doorman tipped his hat. My Ukrainian seamstress was a far more formidable lookout. When the elevator opened on the seventh floor, there was only one door, his. It led into a red-carpeted foyer that floated like a parapet over a vast salon. I had never seen anything like it. We stood there, awkward, wary, two wounded soldiers of the '60s divorce wars, suspended like a dash in the middle of an unfinished sentence.

"Would you like some hot tea?" he said.

"Can I make it?"

He told me the kitchen was downstairs, then disappeared down the long hall of his duplex to change his clothes. Left in the foyer, I leaned over the wrought-iron railing to look down on the living room and felt dizzy. The windows were two stories high, ornately draped in gold silk. A lake of buff-colored carpet lapped up to a brass fender wrapped around a baronial fireplace. Lions everywhere; they must be his avatar, I gathered. A giant oil portrait of George Washington was guarded by two white terra-cotta lions. All the tabletops were bare. Gilt sconces on the walls and museum art books stacked on the bookshelves and an oversize pinch-pleated leather sofa all suggested a fine English men's club. Totally inanimate. Not a plant or flower or any evidence of human inhabitation. The dying light of a winter afternoon muted the room still further. It was a stage set.

I was overwhelmed by the absence of smell, sound, light, movement—the absence of life. I could not imagine how such a thunderous man who supplied the energy for so many talents survived in such a place. It was meant to be filled with people and laughter. Or late at night with two bodies, dancing in their private ballroom with all the abandon afforded by that grand space.

I ran out to the corner deli and bought two bunches of giant yellow mums and a dozen blueberry muffins. The flowers lit the room. The muffins emitted a sweet smell from the idle oven. Only then did I feel able to call to him. He asked me to come up and bring the tea.

He was a ghostly presence, sitting on the white spread of his king-size bed. A pale giant in a white shirt surrounded by a mass of white newspapers. White shades were half drawn under sheer white curtains. In one corner a white hospital scale, in the other a gumball machine. If it hadn't been for the gumballs, I would have thought I was in the Plaza Hotel.

"Let's go downstairs to have tea," I said.

We sat on the leather sofa. We spoke briefly about what was most important to us. I said honesty. Learning to be honest with myself. He said it was the same for him. All at once we were enveloped in each other's arms. It was an erotic eruption. He seemed as startled as I. His next words were prophetic:

"Who seduced whom? I don't know if it was you or me."

Neither did I.

———————————

WHAT FOLLOWED WAS A YEAR of furtive sleepovers. Every other weekend, when Maura was with her father, I often spent with Clay. This was not the "honeymoon phase" that women's magazines promise. This was heaven and hell, the push-pull of attraction and withdrawal between two high-strung people scared of committing again. I remember thrilling highs, when we would dance together at a party in the Rainbow Room, and tender moments, lulls when he would dare to confide a past hurt or yearning of the heart, but these were often followed by flashes of temper. He did not like to feel vulnerable. Not infrequently, I was the one to lurch out of his bed in a primal fury over a remark, some nonchalant reference to how beautiful or smart he found another woman. I did not like to feel less than number one. I would crawl out in a drizzly dawn and walk the empty corridor of Second Avenue, feeling like a lost puppy.

One night about a year later, Clay appeared at my apartment house in the wee hours, a little tipsy, judging by the gruff dismissal he received from the Ukrainian seamstress. She didn't want to let him up. Her frantic ringing of the intercom failed to arouse me. Suddenly, I was awakened by a loud banging on my door. I grabbed a robe and opened the peephole. There was the hulk of Clay, chesterfield blown open, black tie hanging askew, looking like big Lab who had lost his way home. I could barely get the locks undone before he uttered a loud lament:

"Come home with me!"

"What? It's the middle of the night."

"I can't stand it anymore."

"Can't stand what?"

"Going home without you."

"Are you crazy? I have a child."

"I want to see more of Maura, too."

"And the dog?"

"You don't have a dog."

"I know, but we were thinking—"

"Gail, I want you with me at dinner parties." He was dead serious now. "I want your softness beside me when I go to sleep. I want to show you my favorite jazz clubs. I want to go through the papers with you over breakfast—you have so many ideas—I can't stand this anymore—you have to move in with me!"

Of course it was absurd. I laughed, but even now, writing this, I feel a faint surge of the magnetic pull that defied all reason. The romantic obsession that had been building between Clay and me for the previous two years had elements of the Pygmalion myth. The original narrative from Ovid's *Metamorphisis* depicts a sculptor who created an ivory statue of a woman so pure and realistic, he fell in love with it. Venus granted his wish to turn her into a real woman. With a kiss, the sculptor found her lips warm, and touching her breasts, he found the ivory had turned soft. They fell in love.

I liked the erotic imagery. But I wasn't an inert piece of marble that required a man to bring me to life. I was an ambitious woman who needed to write. I think I gave Clay a brownie and milk and sent him home like a truant schoolchild. The next day I climbed his stairs, all four flights to the funky *New York* office. It was crammed with freelancers waiting to pitch Clay stories.

"Look who's here!" he shouted from one end of the long hall to his office. I didn't deserve his enthusiasm; my story wasn't finished. I was writing a piece about the suburban dads, like my father, who commuted to New York and the "Belles of the Bar Car" who waited for them to fall out of their marriages. Clay escorted me down one flight to a boardroom used only occasionally by Milton's Pushpin staff. He made sure I had a working typewriter, copy paper, carbons.

"You'll have it finished to give to fact-checking by five?"

"I'll do my best."

It was all very businesslike.

Sometime around four, Clay slipped into the boardroom. Not a word from him. Nor from me. As if in a stupor, we stepped through the world into another, smaller room and I was on my back on an Oriental carpet and I saw him far above me. My nipples hardened. I ached with desire. He was touching my breasts. My hands clutched at his shoulders. The innocence was gone. It was on every count utterly, shockingly, rapturously wrong.

I DIDN'T THINK ANYONE at the magazine knew that we were involved personally. And I knew for sure that he did not favor me over other writers. Whenever there was an assignment that I really wanted, he would say astringently, "Gail, when the assignment's right for you, I'll give it to you." But so-and-so is better for this one, he would say. Nonetheless, moving in with him would at least keep our uncontrollable attraction aboveboard, and out of the boardroom. But here was the problem: I couldn't picture myself living on the Upper East Side. Foreign country. I didn't even own a proper suitcase.

The next day, a Friday, I dropped Maura off to spend the weekend with her dad. I stuffed a tote bag with a few things and shopped for a weekend's worth of groceries. (Tom Wolfe later told me about the day he stopped by to see Clay at his Xanadu on Fifty-Seventh Street and found him putting together some income-tax data. "Look at this," Clay exclaimed with pride as he riffled through his date book, "I only ate dinner at home eight times last year!")

Sitting on an uptown subway with the three flimsy bags under my feet, I felt like a runaway. *I must be totally mad.* And I was—I was mad about this man. The uniformed elevator man looked at me dubiously but silently rode me up to the seventh floor. Clay's door was wide open. Right away, entering the ruby-carpeted balcony, I looked over the wrought-iron railing into the sunken living room, and again, my knees went weak. Clay sat filling a big club chair by the fireplace. Buttons on the phones were blinking. The intercom was buzzing. He was talking to a guest perched on the fireplace fender while a big white phone receiver was tucked under his ear. There was no seam between the fabric of this man's life and his work. He announced me like a headline.

"Gail is here! C'mon down!" His voice filled the vast room. "Where's Maura?"

"With her father for the weekend."

"I'll be up shortly. We've been invited to a cocktail party for Pamela Harriman."

The situation was ludicrous. Here I was, hot off the subway in my jeans and boots with two bags full of groceries, imagining I'd cook us a cozy little supper. Instead, I was expected to be suited up in a chic little cocktail number for a party to celebrate the marriage of one of the most famous courtesans of the twentieth century. Pamela Digby Churchill Hayward Harriman, once described as "a world expert on rich men's bedroom ceilings," was the daughter-in-law of Sir Winston Churchill. The very day after her second husband died, she had gone back to her old lover, Averell Harriman. A month later, she had walked the venerated seventy-nine-year-old ambassador down the aisle.

"Tonight?" I gasped.

"Friends are giving them a little party," Clay said casually. "Drinks at six."

I set my humble bags down in the bedroom. The room smelled of roses; he had put a vase of yellow ones on the night table. A nice touch. But I couldn't help feeling like a letter slipped under the door marked Addressee Unknown.

NOT A MOMENT TO CATCH my breath from the day we moved in. Mornings were a rush to get Maura off to school. During the day, I was always on deadline for Clay's magazine. He'd dash past the desk while I was desperately trying to close a story by six o'clock—

"Why aren't you home? Dinner's at eight."

He just assumed I'd also be home and dressed in time for a command performance as his companion at a plated dinner party where most of the other women would have had their nails lacquered like Chinese empresses, their pores glazed like English porcelain, and their lashes thickened like privet hedges, the better to make eyes at the richest men. I would usually be the youngest female at the party, but an ink-stained working waif by comparison, with waves of unmanageable red hair and wearing a then-twenty-nine-dollar Diane von Furstenberg wraparound dress.

WITH ALL THE FRENETIC ACTIVITY of sharing life with Clay, I was worried about the impact on Maura. She had started kindergarten at Grace Church School, a wonderfully nurturing primary school where the children began the day with organ music and the Lord's Prayer in the chapel of the imposing Gothic-style Episcopal church. But for Maura, then five, Clay's apartment was a castle beyond imagining. She slept like a princess in the four-poster. Carved on the headboard were fantastical wooden animals. Her tiny school uniforms hung in a closet that she could reach only by standing on a footstool. Her own recollections, which she gave me permission to include, are more vivid than any I can render, since she knew Clay's world from the point of view of a young child:

> I was five or six when I began to form the impression that Clay was magic. Whenever he thrust out a hand for a taxi, a checker cab appeared, even though there were hardly any left in New York at the time. I'd look up Second Avenue, or wherever we were, at the tide of charging yellow and there wouldn't be one in sight. I'd think, "It's not gonna happen this time," and the next thing I knew I was climbing into a checker and opening up the jump seat, trying to remember when I looked away.

The door to Clay's apartment on 57th Street was always wide open, propped by a solid brass lion. Clay didn't need a door, he just needed a portal, a threshold. The world wasn't supposed to stay out; it was supposed to come in. The buttons on the phone were always alight, people always calling, always coming over, always talking, meeting, asking, answering, eating, reading, listening, arguing, pitching, laughing. There was magic throughout the place.

Clay wasn't like anyone else. He didn't laugh like anyone else. Just a single, HA! And maybe a second, ha!, if he was really amused. He spoke in headlines and exclamation points; "The kid's home from school!" From Clay's life, I learned about passion for one's work. Not driven duty but the deepest possible creative fulfilled engagement. I saw him inspire legions, especially my mother. If he thought you could do it—and he always seemed to—you could.

In the city when we went somewhere with him, he'd often just start off walking, impossibly fast, as if pushing against the atmosphere. Down some dark street the wrong way from home, I'd yank my mother to keep up, which couldn't be done in her heels. If I asked how much longer, he'd just stab a pointed finger into the air and grunt "just . . . just . . . just . . ." and suddenly he'd stop and there would be a door where it never seemed there would be one and we would go in and there would be some great music, a splendid room, some unbelievable delight. People, sounds, something happening. It was magic.

As I grew up, most of my childish impressions were corrected by the world. But not this one about Clay being magic. Instead I realized that everyone else thought so too.

It was going to take a long time to get to know this man in all his contradictory guises. He wanted me in his life yet he warned me more than once not to become emotionally dependent on him. "My emotions move with glacial slowness." On the other side of our most tender moments, I felt those icy crevices open and swallow him. I brought the adulation of a young disciple, the sutured heart of a betrayed wife, and the insecurities of a child-woman who didn't know how to play the part of hostess to the great man. But when it was good, it was very, very good.

CHAPTER 12

FEAR OF FEMINISM

CLAY STAGED AN EARLY FIRST SKIRMISH between the sexes at an unforgettable dinner party in February 1969. The setting was the Park Avenue apartment of Armand Erpf, Clay's most faithful benefactor. His living room was a billion-dollar art gallery with Impressionist paintings casually interspersed with priceless Renaissance art. An elfin man over seventy, Armand's most recent acquisition was a bewitching wife. Almost twice his girth and roughly forty years younger, Sue Erpf sat opposite him at the end of a stately dining table, black eyes blazing, black hair curling over her shoulders, breasts proudly displayed in an empire gown. Armand had found the perfect complement to his aging Giacometti ascetic, a flesh-and-blood incarnation of a nineteenth-century Courbet nude.

To provide the evening's entertainment for Armand's rich donor friends, Clay had invited two of his most formidable women writers, Gloria Steinem and Barbara Goldsmith, along with me. We were meant to be bait for the star guest, a biological anthropologist named Lionel Tiger. He had written his first book, *Men in Groups,* expounding a deterministic thesis meant to prove men's biological superiority as hunters and women's subservient purpose as breeders. His own biological superiority was not immediately obvious, although his unusually short stature and chimp-shaped ears did clearly link him to a primate past. Mr. Tiger's book had not been published yet; Clay was eager to hear our reactions. And we wanted to perform for Clay.

"We are entering a period of intense personal acrimony between the sexes," Tiger began pontificating. Stony silence. "The seriously competing woman between the ages of thirty and forty must forget about having children."

Goldsmith and I squirmed. We both had children already, and we certainly had not dropped out of the competition. But we said nothing.

"The prerequisite is to forgo offspring," Tiger repeated. "Or drop out and lose her place in the pecking order."

Gloria was single and childless, by choice. I waited for her to pin his ears back, expecting her to say something like, *To "forgo offspring" is a choice women can now make. The Pill gives us control over reproduction. You must know, Mr. Tiger, this is the bedrock of the feminist revolution.* But Gloria, too, said nothing. She remembered later that Armand and his wife both sounded off when I spoke approvingly about seeing male graduate students with baby carriers strapped to their chests. "How pathetic," Sue Erpf said. "So unmasculine."

I had just published a cover story in *New York* titled "The Men of Women's Liberation Have Learned Not to Laugh." I was still a graduate student at Columbia University and in a prime position to observe a fierce and often funny lashing out at men by the brightest of young, outspoken women. I had written about Polly, who went nowhere without her latest copy of *Aphra,* the first feminist literary pamphlet. Her boyfriend, Jerry, was used to treading on eggshells for fear of unconsciously dropping a male chauvinist remark just as they were cuddling into precoital mode on some sunken couch in the common area of his dorm.

"The way I look at it," Jerry told Polly, "about the worst goddamn thing to be these days is a white, middle-class, Anglo-Saxon American male." Polly gave him her byzantine stare. "What I mean is," he tried to explain, "you haven't got a damn thing to be oppressed about so everyone treats you like a crumb." Polly fixed him with her blinkless stare.

"You just try being a woman in this society. It's like being a cripple. For nineteen years I thought it was just me, but now we're getting a sisterhood together. I'm sorry, Jerry"—she slipped off her engagement ring—"we've come to the period of separatism."

Jerry was left speechless.

"I suggest," Polly said, as she rolled his pants and shorts into a neat bundle and lobbed it into his arms, "you form a men's consciousness-raising group as fast as you can."

This may sound like dialogue you just heard in the next seats at the movies. One might have hoped that fifty years after the arc of male privilege began to end, only the angriest white men would still feel a sense of aggrieved entitlement. But there you are.

AS COFFEE WAS SERVED in the Erpfs' living room, Clay raised the subject of women in politics. Gloria had begun raising money for women as political candidates.

Tiger ridiculed the idea that women could be effective in politics. "The problem women have is they can't bond with one another." That touched a raw nerve. Of course we didn't know yet how to bond; we had been competing for crumbs from the table. Gloria made a provocative suggestion. A woman might run for president in the next election. (No one had yet dreamed that an African American woman, Shirley Chisholm, would do just that a year later.) Tiger's face gave a shrug of disbelief. Gloria looked to me to back her up. Here, I must confess that my memory may have rearranged the climax of that evening. I would like to think that I came up with some smart riposte to Tiger's hyperchauvinism. I must have voiced at least some lame defense of the right to self-determination that was surging in women like Gloria and Barbara and myself. When I later asked Gloria for her recollection of the evening, she gently administered the shock of counterfeit memory.

"It was at that dinner that you said women had 'labial personalities,'" she wrote to me. "It came across to me that you were taking sides with the biological determinism of Lionel Tiger, who was a clear adversary. To be truthful, I had hoped you would be an ally."

Did I really say "labial personalities"? What on earth did that mean? That women's heads were dominated by their carnal desires? I don't think I was aware yet of the manifold delights of the female erotic response system, much less their anatomical names. I'd certainly never uttered the "v" word; it would take thirty more years for Eve Ensler to make *vagina* a household word. I might have said women had "labile" personalities, which wasn't much better. That would just have reinforced the stereotype that women's emotions were in constant flux. What was I afraid of? Clay thinking that I was one of those ball-busting barracudas who seemed to be taking over the fledgling women's movement at that time?

Whatever words I used, I am ashamed to admit that I let Gloria down.

Rather than allow Tiger the triumph of goading two women into disagreeing with each other, Gloria remained silent as we finished coffee. The dinner party was becoming unbearably uncomfortable. Clay tried to lighten things up. "When I was at *Esquire,* I gave Gloria the assignment to write the first article on the Pill. She came back with an exegesis on the science behind birth control."

Gloria laughed. "Clay told me, 'You have performed the incredible feat of making sex dull.'" Tiger wouldn't let it go. "The Pill is the biggest put-on of the century," he declared. From notes, I recall him stating that the Pill maintains women in a constant state of counterfeit pregnancy, thereby rendering men highly dispensable and no threat.

That was a clue to men's fear that drugs and technology could make them irrelevant (not an unfounded fear, as it turned out). Armand Erpf weighed in. "Men have the power. We will always be dominant." His wife, happy chatelaine of his vast apartment and his thirty-two-room country estate, nodded and raised her crystal goblet in a toast to the status quo.

The dinner party didn't so much end as dissolve, with each of us fumbling among the hanging coats for something safe and familiar. Gloria and Barbara rode down in the elevator together. Standing on the street to hail a cab, Barbara looked at Gloria and vowed, "I will never, ever, ever again in my life keep my mouth shut." Gloria looked at Barbara and repeated the same vow. I heard later that Gloria let loose with one of her zingers: "Tiger wouldn't be so addicted to his idea of 'masculinity' if he were three inches taller."

Clay hailed a taxi and opened the door for me. I glared at him. "I can take care of myself, thank you." Inside, I couldn't wait to light up. Fumbling for the box of Newports in my bag, I remembered that Clay disapproved of smoking, especially in women. I took my sweet time opening the new box, tapping to tease out one long tube of pleasure with its fine white filter, probably replaying in my mind the commercial of a young couple playing tag in the waves and then flopping down on the beach so he could light up a Newport for each of them. This was my pathetic little passive-aggressive retaliation for the evening's scenario. All the way back to his apartment, we snapped in personal acrimony. Clay never lit my cigarette. This was the paradox of our early radicalization. I still wanted to be the girl.

"YOU'RE NOT GIVING YOURSELF the huge credit you deserve for changing, as most of us were doing profoundly, in different ways," Gloria wrote to me after reading the first draft of this chapter. Gloria's recollection of that early period in the movement was that "Women began to actually tell the truth and not to 'Uncle Tom' and be 'feminine.' We were less likely to seek a derived identity through men—and thus manipulate them or expect the impossible."

What made me fear changing was the prospect of choosing between an either-or. I was not then, not ever, willing to give up being feminine. And neither, by all evidence, was Gloria, which is what made her so effective. With her low, creamy voice and natural beauty, Ms. Steinem as she came to be called, having invented that simple honorific, rarely if ever antagonized men. On the contrary, she charmed them, played games of wit with them, politely listened to them, and never argued without insulating her words with a warm laugh. Men often found themselves nodding to curry her favor, until they got home and analyzed her actual words and had a virulent attack of indigestion.

Here was the dilemma for me in those early times: how to preserve the best of our inborn feminine nature—our nurturing, compassionate, and ferociously protective instincts, our insights, our powers of love and, yes, female attraction, which are vital in ameliorating the more aggressive nature of men—while we discovered our power to say No! to inequality.

Up to that moment in 1969, I didn't consider myself a feminist; I thought of myself as a humanist. Gloria was a few years older and far more sophisticated politically, but she wasn't a card-carrying feminist yet, either. Yet she was breaking new ground. Clay had given her "The City Politic" to write. She was one of the first women to pen provocative essays on politics. Gloria had no interest in marriage or children. In her spare time she raised money for female political candidates and flew to California to organize protests for migrant workers. I wondered when she had time for men. In fact, she was one of the more sexually prolific women of our generation.

When my early dream of working to put hubby through graduate school was smashed, I'd had to start all over again. Who was I if not my father's little winner? Who was I if not my husband's helpmate? I didn't even have a name to call my own. "Sheehy" belonged to Albert. Who would I be when I didn't belong to anyone? These were the kinds of shattering questions that millions of women were being forced to confront. Gloria had been invited to join Betty Friedan's new organization for women, NOW. She had politely refused. When asked by NOW to join a sit-in at the Plaza Oak Room in February of 1969, she begged off. You will find this hard to believe: for women to be served lunch there, we had to be accompanied by a man. Nine years earlier, in 1960, four brave black American male college students had seated themselves at a lunch counter at Woolworth's and remained seated when they were refused service. Their passive resistance helped to ignite a sit-in movement all over the South to challenge racial inequality. Yet here we were, fortunate northern white women in one of the most liberal cities in America, becoming aware that we were being discriminated against in the same way.

Friedan had picked the Plaza to attract mainstream publicity. She urged her group of demonstrators to wear fur coats, intending to differentiate the proper upper-middle-class membership of NOW from the radical feminists who had recently been ridiculed for burning their bras at the 1968 Miss America Pageant.

Arriving at the Plaza in black mink and dark sunglasses, Friedan hardly looked like a revolutionary leader. Her group brushed past the maître d' to seat themselves at a round table in the center of the room. They were ignored. Finally, waiters hoisted the table over their heads and left the women sitting in a circle like kindergartners waiting for the teacher. Friedan turned to reporters and announced triumphantly that they were being refused service. That simple action thrust NOW to the forefront of leadership of the nascent women's movement.

Back in 1969, Gloria believed that Clay would like the idea of opposing us. News is conflict, after all. But Clay saw the larger shift that needed to take place in the culture: women would have to set aside our conditioning to compete with one another; we had to bond if we were ever going to coalesce around common goals for the women's movement.

"I want you to sit down with Gloria and compose your differences," Clay told me one night in his paternal voice. He wanted us to be allies. "You're not that far apart, and you need each other." He invited Gloria and me to have lunch with him at the Oak Room, no less. I squealed in protest. He looked smug. Whether or not the threat of a cover story in *New York* was responsible, the hotel had agreed to lift the ban on unaccompanied ladies having lunch. Clay had set the stage for a propitious conversation between two women he respected.

WITH AN ELABORATE FLOURISH the maître d' beckoned Gloria and me through the French doors into an expanse of Old World luxury beneath an arched Gothic ceiling: the Oak Room. A men's drinking room, a favorite haunt of Fitzgerald's character Gatsby, was now open to women who were writing a new narrative for the New World. It felt good to be seated prominently at an oak table. Impishly, Clay pointed up to the chandelier. On it figures of lusty barmaids hoisted beer steins. While munching on bread sticks, Gloria and I began a friendly discussion only to discover that we had many points of agreement.

"I'm afraid the ball-busting faction seems to be getting all the attention," I said, "after the bra-burning in Atlantic City. And I'm not anti-men. I don't think you are either."

"Some of my best friends are men!" Gloria gave one of her disarming chuckles. We both smiled at Clay. "But we were raised in a culture that taught us to expect the normal male-female relationship was 70-30. That has to change."

"What makes you think I'm against that?" I asked.

"You wrote about a woman left by a man, in your book, *Lovesounds*. I gathered you see women as victims."

"I wrote that novel to understand what I was living. Thank God, because it turned my head around."

"Great! That's why we have to keep writing."

"And speaking out," I added.

Gloria confessed that speaking in public terrified her. She had no stomach for confrontation. We agreed this was something we had to learn, like a new sport.

We agreed that we had Kate Millett to thank for defining Friedan's "problem without a name." Millett's solution to women's helplessness was to "demolish the patriarchal system."

That would take something like the Peloponnesian Wars, I was thinking. Patriarchy was as old as civilization, older; Cro-Magnon man was not into power sharing. No dominant group shares power unless it is persuaded that being blindly autocratic could undermine its status. What weapons did we have?

Numbers, for starters, Gloria said. At the time, women were moving toward becoming a majority of the American population. As we talked, and traded experiences, we began to grasp the concept that writer Robin Morgan was popularizing: the personal is political. As women dared to tell our real-life stories in public, it would expose gender inequality in every aspect of daily life. We could change the culture without going to war against men. That was a breakthrough for me.

The lunch that Clay had arranged for us turned into a consciousness-raising occasion that was being duplicated all over the country as women came together in living rooms and basements and on picket lines and antiwar marches and began to share our common experiences and join forces.

IN AUGUST 1970 OUR WORLD began to change. Betty Friedan's culture-busting book, *The Feminine Mystique,* had been passed around among millions of tranquilized suburban housewives over the seven years since it had been published. I had found a paperback copy of it hidden under my mother's bed in 1964. It was the blueprint of my mother's life, but when I tried to talk to her about it, she clammed up. She had to keep up the illusion that she was totally fulfilled by the wife and mother role, when we both knew she had the DNA of a businesswoman and desperately wanted to use her mind. She dulled that lively mind with alcohol. I was hell-bent on escaping her fate. But I was also afraid of being linked with the extremist feminists like Redstockings, Radical Mothers, BITCH, WITCH—no joke—these were angry women whose resentment was turning the sterling silver concept of equal rights into corrosive man-hating sexual warfare.

It was comical to read deadly humorless treatises elevating the clitoral orgasm to a sacrament that would free women from dependence on the male penis. The media loved sensationalizing the man-haters as the face of the movement. Friedan, too, was worried about this radical offshoot scaring off not only men, but the mainstream working-class and middle-class women who were needed for a broad grassroots movement. Women were already a majority—51 percent—of the population, yet we were still stuck in second-class status. Slow, incremental changes were not going to get us anywhere. But how could we show the world we were mounting nothing less than a revolution?

The brilliant stroke came in August 1970. Friedan called for a Women's Strike for Equality to celebrate the fiftieth anniversary of the women's suffrage amendment giving women the right to vote. Not just one march up Fifth Avenue, but marches all across the country.

Walking toward Fifth Avenue, I felt my heart palpitating for fear a feeble turnout would bring ridicule by the media. Male TV commentators would laugh us off as a bunch of hotheads. But as I turned the corner and was stopped by a police barricade, my heart swelled to see legions of women converging from all directions. Our good liberal mayor, John Lindsay, had denied Friedan a permit to close Fifth. But looking down the avenue, all one could see were hordes of female heads bobbing and signs waving.

"Stay on the sidewalks!" police shouted. The sidewalks could not hold us. Mounted police tried to corral us into a single-file line. One line could not contain us.

"Lock arms, sidewalk to sidewalk!" Betty shouted.

The police gave up. The women did not.

Like the full expanse of Fifth Avenue, the world began that day opening up for us, for women and for men. Sons could be raised as feminists, too. We were leading the second great social revolution of twentieth-century America—what a thrilling time to be a woman!

CHAPTER 13

WOMEN HELPING WOMEN

WHEN I BECAME SINGLE AGAIN, I felt free to enjoy over a decade as a gay bachelorette, assuming the same prerogatives that single men had always enjoyed. But I was clear about adopting only selected aspects of the way Helen Gurley Brown and Gloria Steinem made their way in the world. In one core area, I was not at all like them.

Helen chose never to have children. Her *Cosmopolitan* magazine rarely mentioned children. Gloria chose never to have children. Her *Ms.* magazine rarely mentioned children. I loved having a child. And I longed to have another, but only if and when I was in love with a man worthy of being a husband and father. It might take years until all the pieces fell into place. I was prepared to wait. I was still a young woman. I wanted to walk up and down and around the world, free to invite adventures and write about them. Singlehood offered me a second chance.

But I had a child. Readers young enough to be part of the third wave of feminism may be shocked to learn how far the pendulum swung in the '60s and '70s. Married women with children sometimes bailed. Just like that. Up and left their husbands and children to seek the self-fulfillment they now saw as their political right. Some left to join communes. Lesbians came out for the first time, writing poetry and plays, proud of their new political identity. But none of those options was right for my daughter and me.

It was Margaret Mead who pulled me across the passage that I would come to call Catch-30. When I was awarded a Rockefeller Foundation fellowship to graduate school at Columbia University, it allowed me to study for the year 1969–70 under the professor of my choice. I was thrilled to become a protégée of the renowned anthropologist Margaret Mead. She was already an iconic figure in academia, but with the expansion of television, she was becoming a Socratic gadfly, popping up on talk shows and being invited to speak all over the country. She was the new American cultural prophet. It was when I came under her tutelage that my intellectual life began to take shape.

Short and solid as an oak stump, Mead planted her forked walking stick with an authoritative thump at each step and moved through time and place like a tribal elder who transcended cultural boundaries. I was in awe of her in our first classes. I soon learned that Margaret Mead was another model of hard work and self-discipline.

The new living space I'd found to be nearer to Columbia was a sunny sublet on the Upper West Side; serendipitously, it was only blocks from the Beresford where Dr. Mead lived. Just to know she was there inspired me to work twice as hard. On those mornings when I wanted to crawl away from a deadline or a decision and burrow under the pillow of self-doubt, sucking on some primal injustice of gender, I could almost hear the predawn engines of the Indomitable One. Curly head bobbing, she would already be pounding the portable electric on her dining room table. Getting the job done.

When she discovered that I lived near her, she offered to let me ride with her to and from school. It was the chance of a lifetime to be exposed to a great mind. She found our friendship useful as well. Mead was a general among the foot soldiers of feminism. She enlisted me as one of her grunts. As a journalist, I could investigate cultural trends that interested or troubled her. In a series on "The Fractured Family," I wrote about women who were choosing to be "Childless by Choice" and about "Bachelor Mothers," the earliest experimenters with a lifestyle that would grow to represent more than 40 percent of all births. The idea made Mead furious. "I am continually frustrated by the refusal of Americans to learn from the mistakes of their history!" she fumed when I showed her the issue of *New York*. She insisted that children would develop well only if they were nurtured by both a male and a female parent.

She was chillingly clear in her views: "One child does not necessarily interfere with a woman producing important work. One child can always be put to bed in a bureau drawer. It's having two children that really changes a woman's life."

Our rides together led to a more personal conversation. Mead was then almost seventy and the consequences of her lifestyle choices were established. She admitted that her efforts to be a collaborating wife, trying to combine intensive research and an intimate private life, did not work. She and Gregory Bateson, a fellow anthropologist, divorced. Mead stayed on in a joint household where another man's wife looked after her daughter until Catherine turned fifteen. Mead and her daughter, who became an esteemed published writer, subsequently became estranged.

This was definitely not a model I wanted to emulate. But while I rejected the pattern that Mead had worked out for her personal life, she gave me brilliant instructions for how to become a cultural interpreter.

"Whenever you hear about a great cultural phenomenon—a revolution, an assassination, a notorious trial, an attack on the country—drop everything and get on a bus or train or plane and go there, stand at the edge of the abyss, and look down. You will see a culture turned inside out and revealed in a raw state."

I took her manifesto and ran with it.

CHAPTER 14

REDPANTS AND REGRETS

"YOU'RE GOING OUT IN THAT?!"

It was 10 P.M. Clay looked up from his reading chair and eyed my costume: blue suede hot pants that left a lot of leg showing before reaching the white vinyl go-go boots that sheathed my calves.

"I'm going out to follow the working girls."

"They'll think you're a streetwalker."

"That's the point—I want them to talk to me."

In the summer of 1971, a prostitution crisis was gripping New York and driving tourists away. I couldn't wait to immerse myself in the subject. Saturation reporting is fun. It often requires taking on a false identity, like an actress playing a role, and there was a secret thrill in seeing what it was like to walk on the wild side.

"I knew you wanted to do a story about hookers, but this is a new breed," Clay protested. "You told me yourself, they're violent."

I assured him that an off-duty cop had agreed to stroll with me, playing the part of my pimp. And I had found the perfect source: Bobby, the night guard on the Lexington Avenue door of the Waldorf Astoria. He was a natural-born sociologist who knew all the girls: the old ones, the new ones, the pecking order. Bobby would help me to understand the life cycle of a streetwalker.

"Don't wait up, I won't be back until four."

"Four in the morning—that's *crazy!*"

"Working girls' hours."

Considering the sudden proliferation of singles bars and coed dorms and all the willing divorcées with water beds, one might have thought that prostitution would become a dying art. On the contrary, prostitution was booming *because* of our so-called sexual liberation. Men were retreating from the free giveaway. Most of them didn't know what to do with it.

"Mature" men in particular had learned the erotic gospel according to *Playboy*. To be good guilty fun, the bedmate must be a plaything, a depersonalized no-no. All these young girls who said yes-yes, but on their own terms, were, well, scary. A paid girl relinquishes all rights to make emotional or sexual demands. She would never call his office the next morning and leave an embarrassing message. It is her stock in trade to *encourage* men's sexual fantasies and exploit them.

No surprise, then, that New York in the early '70s was fairly swarming with prostitutes. The youngest and prettiest streetwalkers were migrating from the seamy doorways of porn parlors in Times Square to work more prosperous precincts on the Upper East Side. Every weeknight, at any one time, thirty or forty girls would be strutting their competitive stuff up and down Lexington Avenue between Forty-Fourth and Fiftieth Streets. The Waldorf Astoria was home plate.

They stood framed in the stone shallows of darkened office buildings like . . . cave art . . . fanning their quick, toxic eyes with double tiers of Black Spider lashes; teasing, taunting, flouting the public's most tender mores by turning men on. They walked or ran some five miles a night on white gladiator boots with an apricot of flesh oozing through every peephole. Salesmen in town for a convention would dally with them for one mad capricious moment before their suburban wives draped in faux diamonds yanked them onward to their promised night in the Big Apple.

What intrigued me was that these working girls belonged to a violent new breed. They worked on their backs as little as possible. More often they worked in cars, with partners, sashaying through the theater district and parading around the grand hotels. The goal of their night's work was not the dispensation of pleasure for simple cash payment. It was to maximize their profit by swindling, mugging, robbing, knifing, and occasionally even murdering their patrons.

I had become fascinated by the subculture of deviance among women while I was studying under Dr. Mead at Columbia. She told me that she'd learned from her anthropological research that when women disengage completely from their traditional role, they can be more ruthless and savage than men. Men and male animals fight for many reasons. They fight as a game. They fight to show off, to test their prowess, and to impress females. They have built-in rules that often inhibit their willingness to kill. Women and female animals, when they do fight, are fiercely defensive. There is no game about it. They kill for survival.

Statistics backed up the phenomenon of increased violence by women, who were then becoming major criminals at a much faster rate than men. (The steady rise in female criminality would continue into the next century.) As America was beginning to take notice of female discontent, the awakening assertiveness of women could be seen most starkly at the farthest distance from the conventional center—in the netherworld.

The old journalism with its who-what-when-where-why rigidity was inadequate to convey the wild gyrations of gender and politics, music and mind-blowing drugs in that era. It would be like filming Woodstock in black and white.

For six weeks I followed and taped and sometimes befriended the streetwalkers, capturing their dialogue on my cassette recorder. I'd hired a bearded Christian brother to be my research assistant. An odd choice? Christian brothers belong to a scholastic order of the Roman Catholic Church and are trained as teachers. Brother Bernie was a redheaded Irishman who'd had enough of the ivory tower and was eager to see something of raw unsheltered life. Was he game to pose variously as a "john" or a peep-show operator or a pimp? Yes, he promised. We got pimps to brag about their exploitation of the girls and followed johns into hotels; we ran from police prostitution vans, developed blisters, and soon felt as degraded and defensive as the hustlers whose lives I wanted to chronicle.

We also had a lot of laughs. One evening, a prostitution hotel operator who called himself Jimmy Della Bella wanted to show off. He suggested I slip my tape recorder under the bed in room 3. He introduced us to his most prized girl, Suede, who was taking a new trick upstairs. She was tall and rawboned, recognizable on the street by her pink suede boots. She signed the register. A card at the desk stated that the management was not responsible for valuables. The preliminaries were always the same, as dull as preparing for the dentist's chair.

> SHE: You have to pay me first, okay? Twenty dollars.
> HE: I have to pay you now? Got any change?
> SHE: No change.
> HE: This okay?
> *He peeled a fifty out of his money clip.*
> SHE: You get change, after, we see.

Through the open window the frantic loneliness of Times Square played back . . . gears stripping, kids yelling, the long hot scream of a police siren.

Up the stairs they climbed, a fumbling, frightened, pathetic man and a cold, contemptuous, violated woman—prepared to exchange for twenty dollars no more than ten minutes of animal sex, untouched by a stroke of their common humanity. It was not the habit of these girls to undress. Listening to the tape later with Brother Bernie, all we heard was *Zip!*

HE: You sure I get my change back?

SHE: Relax. If you're so worried about your money, honey, lay your head on your pants. What'll it be? Half and half?

HE: Yeah. (he moans)

SHE: No kissy kiss . . . When you have sex, you have to use this.

HE: No!

SHE: Take your hand away now.

HE: Why?

SHE: Honey, I cannot have sex with you unless you use this.

HE: I want my money back.

SHE: You wanna catch a disease?

HE: I don't want it. I want **you.**

SHE: Nooo, no, no, no. Not for no twenty dollars.

HE: I just want to—

SHE: *We don't do all that!*

These were the most awkward, unromantic, nickel-and-dime conversations I'd ever heard. Listening, Brother Bernie blushed.

I also interviewed police commanders and assistant district attorneys and followed the fraternity of prostitution lawyers from criminal court to their favorite hangouts. But the best sources were the eyes on the street: all-night countermen, news hawks, and hotel staffers.

The main contribution of the New Journalism was conveying factual information in vivid scenes. Here is one scene from my story "Redpants and Sugarman."

"This is a rough street now," Bobbie tells me. He is the night guard on the Lexington Avenue door of the Waldorf-Astoria. "These new girls comin' from outta town are pullin' knives and drivin' around in rented cars, bustin' heads. Say around four o'clock in the morning, if a guy comes up the street, five or six of them together will tear his clothes off and rob him blind."

He points up Lex to a tacky white Chevrolet illegally parked just outside the Waldorf garage. The horn is blaring. "Two girls got a retired Florida detective pinned inside," Bobbie grouses. "One's probably gettin' him hot while the other's pickin' his pocket. I tell these dumb johns but they won't listen." He is sure the detective is leaning on the horn for all he is worth.

"Here come the poh-leece," Bobbie says. A sense signal passes from corner to corner. Well before an actual siren answers the car horn, the foot girls start sprinting from all corners to their hideaway in the Waldorf garage. One of the car girls darts through the back lobby of the Waldorf. Without missing a beat, poised to whirl through the brass-trimmed door onto Lexington, she kicks off her Gucci shoes at Bobbie the guard's feet.

"Redpants, that you?" His voice leaps.

"Hold my shoes!"

A younger girl flees past Bobbie and drops something black. Traveler's checks. As he bends to retrieve them, a man's arm sheathed in chocolate net scoops under his nose and grabs the checkbook. It's Sugarman, Redpants's pimp. Then the pimp is gone too.

By now police are swarming through the garage. They smoke out all the wrong girls, any streetwalker they see. A prostitution van is filling up on Lexington. One face turns and through the rear window she catches the guard's worried eye. Redpants blows a kiss.

Bobbie the guard stoops for the shoes she kicked off. He runs his hands over the pitted soles, shakes his head. "She was the prettiest brown-skinned girl I ever seen on the street . . . She used to be tall as a tree and she had a shape and she was beautiful. Bought everybody presents too. I mean Redpants, she was makin' so much money she didn't know what to do with it."

A relief man arriving for the night shift says she didn't look so good tonight.

"You wouldn't either!" Bobbie snaps. "After two years on the street, runnin' from the cops, climbin' these stairs, livin' on hot dogs, they decline. Pimp took alla Redpants's money. Now she's thirty. She ain't got no money, she ain't got no looks, she ain't got no shape, so she's just out there a scavenger. She's done."

Bobbie rolls up Redpants's shoes in the *Daily News* and tucks them under his arm. "What're you bothering with her shoes for?" the relief man asks. "They locked her up."

"She'll be back," Bobbie says. "They always come back."

The real reason Bobbie the Guard served as my best resource was because he cared; in particular, he cared about Redpants. He knew her whole story. I observed Redpants until finally, through Bobbie's efforts, she agreed to see me. Before our appointment, word passed like brushfire on the street: the other girls would cut her up if she talked. Then she disappeared. Word came to Bobbie that she had been banished to the Holland Tunnel for holding out on her pimp. Bobbie the Guard knew how most of these stories ended, and he found two other streetwalkers who knew Redpants and were willing to talk to me.

Saturation reporting requires re-creating the characters' pasts: Where did these girls come from and why? What had happened to generate this violent new breed? Did they ever fulfill the fantasy, make it off the street with enough money to buy their own swanky house and start a legitimate business with their pimp? I had prefaced the Redpants narrative with a long reportorial article: "The New Breed," published in July 1971.

But for the story of "Redpants and Sugarman"—which took up nine thousand words in the same issue—I wanted to convey in a dramatic narrative the whole arc of a streetwalker's life. In order to pull together my weeks of reporting into a unified narrative, I used the literary device of a composite character. Drawing on transcripts of exact quotes from other streetwalkers and a "retired" pimp, as well as other eyes on the street that had watched the short, brutal life cycle of prostitutes from their teenage heyday to their accelerated middle age at thirty, I fleshed out the Redpants story to the bitter end.

The cover art—a pair of women's red shorts held up by a bullet belt and, opposite, the rakish brim of a pimp's hat—created a sensation. Tom Wolfe sent me a handwritten fan note. "You made us see and care and run with these girls—remarkable enough! But your piece wasn't only an eyewitness account of the trade; you always gave us an analysis of prostitutes as a status group with six distinct social gradations. Thank you for being the hooker's Boswell!"

We were riding high on the great buzz created by the piece. Much later—and I don't remember the source—the *New York Post*'s Page Six? or the *Washington Post*—the backlash began. I was ripped for making up the character of Redpants. I was shocked. At some point I called the *Washington Post*'s executive editor, Benjamin Bradlee. I told him that Redpants was a real person. She had been a notorious streetwalker, known by many in her world whom I interviewed. After she was banished to the tunnels, I couldn't get her to agree to more interviews for an obvious reason: her pimp would have killed her. So I filled in the latter part of the life cycle of a streetwalker from accounts of Redpants's cohorts. I had explained my technique in the third paragraph. Every description and quote came from a real person. Bradlee was sympathetic. He asked me how I had phrased the paragraph.

I looked again at the magazine as published. My God! Where was that paragraph of explanation? Missing! In a panic, I called my *New York* magazine editor on the piece, Jack Nessel. How could the explanation have been left out? He didn't know either. I went to the office and asked everyone what had happened. No one would admit to removing it. I was sick. The controversy would give ammunition to the increasingly vocal critics of the New Journalism.

Using the literary devices of scene setting, dialogue, and the expression of a person's inner thoughts was new and startling at that time. Today, it is expected. It's in the leads of the *New York Times,* for heaven's sake, and liberally used by such respected practitioners of biography as David Maraniss in his book about Barack Obama. It all started with Gay Talese's famous profile for *Esquire,* "Sinatra Has a Cold." Unable to talk to Sinatra, Talese spent weeks doing saturation reporting—he called it a "writearound"—with people who knew and often saw Sinatra. Then the journalist used literary techniques to create scenes showing Sinatra in action. The resulting story is the holy grail of journalism, taught in colleges and universities to this day.

Under attack for months, I was tormented by my conflicted feelings. I was proud of my work, I felt it was one of the best pieces I'd ever written, and I knew that I had provided an explanation that had mysteriously landed on the cutting-room floor. But I was ashamed that my work was being used to cast doubt on the veracity of New Journalism. One night, months later, Clay found me sobbing over my typewriter.

"What on earth is wrong?" It took me a long time to give him the answer.

"I can't write anymore."

"Don't be ridiculous. You're the most prolific journalist I know."

"Anything I write is going to be picked apart. Clay, I can't write if I have to take the life out of the story!"

"That's why I took out your explanation of technique—it would have slowed down the story."

"You! You took out the paragraph?" I wanted to slug him. He muttered excuses, looking guilty, reaching back into the history of journalism for a rationale. "Hell, *The New Yorker* is famous for stories by writers who used composite characters. Joseph Mitchell's character sketches."

I was struck dumb. How could he have done this without asking me? It felt like the most intimate betrayal. He was contrite. He promised to call the *Columbia Journalism Review* and other editors to take the blame. It was too late to undo the damage to my reputation and left a blot on the magazine. In Clay's defense, newspapers and magazines at that time did not offer explanations of a journalist's methods or disclose much about sources. The use of anonymous sources peaked in the 1970s during the "golden age" of journalism. In more recent decades, journalists almost always explain why they grant anonymity and give their reason for protecting a source.

What defused the chill in our personal relationship was our redoubled commitment to continue the exposé of prostitution's impact on the city. I went on to write five vividly detailed articles for *New York* about the spread of a violent sexual subculture. The crime wave to which pimps and prostitutes contributed was killing business around luxury hotels and in the theater district. A blue-ribbon commission had been named to find out the cause. I pored over city real estate records to uncover the real identities of the prostitution hotel and massage parlor owners. Late one night, under poor light, I began finding the names of so-called respectable real estate moguls who sat on the cleanup commission. The final cover story, "The Landlords of Hell's Bedroom," exposed the men who were profiting handsomely from the very blight they appeared to condemn. That article set Fun City on a serious cleanup operation.

Mayor John Lindsay lambasted his watchdogs, telling them to "get off your tails and get to work." Investigations and prosecutions were pursued and within a few years, Eighth and Ninth Avenues were virtually free of prostitution hotels. Inspector Charles Peterson, the police commander of the bedroom district with whom I had worked closely, gave me a patronizing compliment in *Newsweek:*

"She showed what a little girl with a lot of drive can do."

I was thirty-five but still seen as "a little girl." It felt much better to read in a print interview that Mayor Lindsay called me "a natural resource." The series won me another New York Newswomen's Front Page award.

The best defense was to write another book—this was becoming a habit! *Hustling* was my fourth book. A contract from Delacorte gave me six months to follow the subculture of prostitution from the street up through the status ladder to call girl and ultimately courtesan. ABC Entertainment was then pioneering "long-form" TV movies. President Brandon Stoddard bought the Redpants and Sugarman story and a hunt began for who could play the charismatic hooker.

When Lee Remick accepted the role of the journalist (me), she used up most of the budget. Jill Clayburgh was an eager pup of an actress in 1972 when she snagged the part of Redpants. She woke me at 7 A.M. in the Beverly Hills Hotel to insist we have breakfast so I could teach her all about the world of streetwalkers on Manhattan's Upper East Side.

Jill was a dog with a bone. She walked Forty-Second Street day after day, practicing her skills at catching tricks. She couldn't wait to show off her Oscar-worthy performance. I watched her stop a tall black dude with a brimmed hat and chains. When their dialogue stalled, I strolled over to catch the drift. The dude was smiling.

"Wassa matter with you, sugah? Ah'm a pimp!"

Jill came back to me. "Well, sugah, guess you better teach me saturation reporting." Ultimately, her performance as a spent streetwalker was raw and heartbreaking.

CHAPTER 15

SECRET OF GREY GARDENS

THE REST OF THAT SUMMER of '71 was a schizoid mix of slogging my way through the gritty subculture of prostitutes and pimps and repairing to the Hamptons for weekends of bodysurfing and tending tomato plants. Clay and I had rented a tumbledown house on West End Avenue in East Hampton. It overlooked the gentle swells of Georgica Pond and, beyond, a bucolic farm dimpled with orange-and-white cows. We loved sitting at the window at sunset and watching the pond, landing pad for hundreds of Canada geese that practiced their graceful migratory maneuvers. All was well until another story—this one truly loony—found me. Somebody should have stopped me before I started writing again.

This time what made me take notes was a gothic tale of greed and lunacy within an exclusive precinct of East Hampton. "The Secret of Grey Gardens" was the first story to reveal the bizarre lives of Big and Little Edie Beale, the reclusive relatives of Jacqueline Bouvier Kennedy and her sister, Lee Radziwill. I stumbled upon the mystery quite innocently.

Maura had found a box of abandoned kittens in our driveway and had come running to me to say, "Can't we take them home?" I told her they would never survive the train ride back to New York. She suggested we take them across the street to what she called the

"Witch House." With all their cats, she said, the owners must like animals. We ducked under ropes of bittersweet hanging from a pair of twisted catalpa trees and tiptoed between the humps of cats, too many cats to count, crouched in the tangled grasses, rattling in their throats, mean and wild. Suddenly, we found ourselves at the tippy porch steps of an Arts and Crafts house. Refuse littered the porch. A hand-lettered sign hung from the door: DO NOT TRESPASS, POLICE ON THE PLACE.

There was no turning back.

"Mother?"

We whirled at the sound of the tremulous voice. A middle-aged woman was coming through the catalpa trees, dressed for church but most oddly: a sweater wrapped around her head, and her skirt—believe it or not—on upside down. Her face was oddly young, as if suspended in time, faintly freckled and innocent, but painted with thick dark lipstick and heavy eyeliner. It struck me that she looked strangely familiar . . . like . . . like who?

"Are you looking for Mother, too?" she asked, even more unnerved than we.

My little girl held out the box of kittens.

"Did you think we care for animals here?"

My daughter nodded solemnly.

"You see! Children sense it." The woman clapped her hands in delight. "The old people don't like us. They think I'm crazy. The Bouviers don't like me at all, Mother says. But the children understand . . ."

My little girl said it must be fun to live in a house where you never have to clean up.

"Oh, Mother thinks it's artistic this way, like a Frank Lloyd Wright house. Don't you love the overgrown Louisiana Bayou look?"

Maura asked if there really were police on the place.

"Not really, but there are boys who come over at night sometimes and try to club the cats to death."

I suggested the boys might just be prankish.

"Oh no, they're dangerous. I can tell what's inside a person right away. Mother and I can see behind the masks; we're artists, it's the artist's eye. Jackie has it, too."

"Jackie?"

"I'm Jacqueline Bouvier's first cousin. Mother is her aunt. Did you know that?"

"No, we didn't."

"Oh yes, we're all descended from fourteenth-century French kings. Did you like the Kennedys?"

Now it clicked. The woman before me was a version of Jackie Kennedy coming back from church on a Greek island, but this was Little Edie in the summer of her fifty-fourth year.

"You . . . resemble your cousin," I stammered.

My daughter wanted to know if she knew President Kennedy well. Maura remembered having been introduced to the Kennedy clan when she was four years old, watching the TV image of a fallen Robert Kennedy and asking me, "Why is the lady in white bending over the man on the floor? Did something bad happen?"

"Jack never liked society girls," Edie offered, "he only dated show-girls. I tried to show him I'd broken with society. I was a dancer. But Jack never gave me a tumble. Then I met Joe Jr. at a Princeton dance, and, oh my!" She swooned. "Joe was the most wonderful person in the world. There will never be another man like him . . ."

From then on, I was invited into the private world of the Beale ladies, two outcasts of a wealthy and famously dysfunctional branch of the Kennedy dynasty—the Bouvier-Beales—who were being hounded by county health officials threatening to evict them. Lee Radziwill, Jacqueline Kennedy's sister and a fashionable princess reputed to be worth more than five hundred million, wanted her relatives out and the house sold. When Little Edie led me through the decaying house that summer, it was a chilling version of Jackie's famous White House tour. The wood floors of this once-proud mansion were lumped and crusty with old cat feces; the roof was punctured with raccoon holes. Mother remained upstairs, summoning the services of her daughter by banging her cane on the floor and calling out in full operatic tremolo: "EeeDIE! Where is my champagne cocktail?"

Little Edie would then perform her secret act of subversion, spooning out cat food and shaping it into a proper mound, garnished with a twist of lemon. She winked at me. "Mother's pâté."

ALMOST EVERY WEEKEND for the rest of that summer, I went to the beach with Little Edie to hear more about her family and her own story. She would pick up exactly where we had left off in the last conversation, heartbreaking evidence of her isolation. Sometimes, I would see her come flying off the dunes with her long scarves waving.

Little Edie told me how attached she and her mother were all through her growing years. "I was my mother's crown jewel," she said in a whisper of awe. "She even kept me out of school for a year, two years, and took me to the theater or movies every day." Mother, having been a frustrated actress herself, assured that her daughter would be just as stagestruck.

As Little Edie grew into a voluptuous young woman, she told me with devilish delight, she had dived into the pool at the prudish old WASP Maidstone Club in a flimsy tank suit. When it slipped off, she brazenly paraded the full length of the pool, in the buff, hoping to be famous for something other than being Jackie's cousin. Desperate for attention, she ran away to New York and modeled for Bachrach. "I was just waiting to audition for Max Gordon [a famous Broadway producer]"—she was breathless with the memory—"and he told me I was a natural musical comedienne! But someone squealed to my father."

Her father, Phelan Beale, had reputedly marched up Madison

Avenue and put his fist through Bachrach's window. Scandalized by the theatrical behavior of both his wife and daughter, he divorced Big Edie—by telegram—and ran off with a young thing, leaving the ladies in the twenty-eight-room house a block from the sea.

"Did you ever go for the audition?" I asked, eager for the end of the story.

"Oh, no. Mother fell into depression, and she got the cats. That's when she brought me down from New York to take care of them."

Over the rest of that summer, Edie Beale would invite me to meet her at the beach (away from Mother) to hear about her many aborted attempts to escape. She talked about dating Howard Hughes and marriage proposals from Joe Kennedy Jr. and J. Paul Getty. But always, Mother drove her suitors away, she said. In a final act of negation, she tore out the faces of her boyfriends from the photographs she saved, so only her image remained, solitary and sad.

A fit of rebellion may have occurred shortly after Little Edie moved back to Grey Gardens. Her cousin John Davis told me about a summer afternoon when he watched her climb a catalpa tree outside Grey Gardens. She took out a lighter. He begged her not to do it. She set her hair ablaze. And in that act of self-immolation she sealed her fate as a prisoner of the love of her mother.

The resolution of the two discards was to become defiant iconoclasts. If they couldn't have a public audience, they would live out the musical in their heads and use each other as their audience. Until, sweet revenge! In the 1960s, they were suddenly being indulged by a nervous White House. Secret Service cars were posted outside. The private family party after Jack Kennedy's inauguration gave Little Edie a chance for her own theatrics. She reminded Joe Kennedy Sr. that she was once almost engaged to his firstborn son. And if Joe's plane hadn't gone down while he was bombing Nazis, "I probably would have married him," she told her fantasy father-in-law, "and he would have become president instead of Jack and I would have become First Lady instead of Jackie!"

Guests told me that Joe Kennedy Sr. drank heavily at that party.

AFTER MY STORY WAS PUBLISHED in *New York*, it was Jacqueline Kennedy Onassis who came to the rescue of the ladies of Grey Gardens with a $25,000 check for a cleanup, on the condition the town would allow them to remain in the house. In 1975, the Maysles brothers persuaded the Beales to vamp for a documentary they were filming. Little Edie told me she loved doing her Isadora Duncan dance and flirting with the two men. She and her mother also hoped to get money from the deal, she told me, but they never saw a penny. It did, however, make them famous.

When Big Edie died two years later after a fall, no one believed that Little Edie could survive their folie à deux by herself. But her optimism was only part delusional. It helped her to live another quarter century on her own. She held out against selling Grey Gardens as a teardown, until, in 1979, the *Washington Post* power couple, Sally Quinn and Ben Bradlee, bought it for $220,000 with a promise to restore it.

Something in the wild nature and tragic vulnerability of these two creatures, who resisted capture at all costs, made them appealing to broader audiences in multiple mediums long after my article appeared. The Maysles brothers' documentary *Grey Gardens* became a cult classic. In 2006, a mainstream Broadway audience made a roaring hit out of Doug Wright's musical, starring Christine Ebersole and Mary Louise Wilson, which won three Tonys and played to enthusiastic audiences in London. The musical was a re-creation of *Grey Gardens* in all its glory, with Mother singing racist show tunes and the butler twirling a silver tray while Little Edie is breathlessly preparing for her fictional engagement party to Joe Kennedy Jr. HBO recast Drew Barrymore and Jessica Lange as the pre-Camelot stars of the Kennedy clan.

To this day, when autumn riptides slash the shoreline and divots in the sand swallow the late-day sun in purple pools, I sometimes walk the beaches of the Hamptons and recall one of my last conversations with Little Edie. I imagine seeing her again, the prisoner of Grey Gardens, freed by the empty postseason beach to appear in her black net bathing suit, streaking down from the dunes trailing a long silk scarf and plunging into the embrace of waves. In our final conversations, she had moved back to New York City, at last. She was making a splash by singing in Manhattan cabarets. They paid her well enough to keep her in a hotel. I read critics mocking her, but Edie seemed to be oblivious of her detractors. Her exhilaration made her sound nineteen again. I loved her spirit.

CHAPTER 16

FIGHTING IRISH WOMEN

IN JANUARY OF 1972 I BEGGED Clay to send me to Northern Ireland to write about the fighting Irish women involved in the Irish civil rights movement. After the wholesale roundup of their Catholic husbands to be imprisoned without charge or trial, as suspected terrorists, women and children became the warriors, vowing to defend their civil rights to the death. My muted Irish ancestry was inflamed.

Margaret Thatcher had sworn to crush the movement. She had decreed the Special Powers Act that allowed British soldiers to launch the roundup of Catholic men. "It would be a perfect story for your St. Patrick's Day issue," I said.

"Why would that interest readers of *New York?*" he wanted to know.

"You're kidding," I argued. "New York City has the largest number of Irish Americans of any city in the country. And I have to believe a lot of them are fighting mad about the British stomping on the Irish Catholics—*again!* I am too!"

"You'd be crazy to get mixed up with the IRA."

"I can get a great story from the women," I said to placate him. They were out in the streets every night banging garbage-bin lids to warn their men before the British soldiers made a raid. And these were among the fiercest women on the planet—some of them fighting with guns. The women's angle sold him.

IT HAPPENED SO FAST, I couldn't believe it. Weren't we just standing in the sun, relaxed and triumphant, after a peaceful civil rights march in Derry? Hadn't we done all the script called for in these deadly games? Met the British soldiers at the barricade. Vomited tear gas. Dragged those dented by rubber bullets back to safety. Then a young boy and I climbed up on a communal balcony along a block of flats to survey the crowd.

Only seconds before the massacre started, I was asking the boy, "How do the paratroopers fire those gas canisters so far?"

"See them jammin' their rifle butts against the ground?" the boy was saying when the slug tore into his face. I tried to think how to put his face back together again. Up to that moment in my life I thought everything could be mended.

This is a scene from 1972 that I have relived hundreds, maybe thousands of times. I wrote about it in the opening of *Passages;* I have described it in lectures and interviews. I have struggled to write it afresh here—and failed. It is engraved on my brain as if on a gravestone.

There was no time to think. British armored cars were plowing into the crowd. Paratroopers jackknifed out with black gorilla faces behind gas masks. High-velocity rifle fire sang into the unarmed crowd. More fire coming from the roof—IRA sharpshooters? This was making no sense. Prime Minister Margaret Thatcher had sworn to crush the Irish Republican Army for good, but the IRA had not provoked anything today.

"Get down; cross fire!" A man grabbed my legs and pulled me down. I lifted my head to see the boy's face. A bloody socket where one eye should be. What monsters shoot children? I crawled toward the boy, reached for him. The man shouted, "MOVE!" Dazed bodies pressed in on us. Entwined like a human caterpillar, we inched on our bellies up the steps of the exposed outdoor staircase.

"Can't we get into somebody's house?" I shouted. No response. Someone would have to crawl out in the cross fire and bang on the nearest door. I heard a man wail, "My son! It's my son!" His voice propelled me across the balcony. A bullet whizzed past my head—time floated—and stupefied, I watched it penetrate the brick wall and throw out spalls of plaster. I hurled myself against the nearest door. We were taken in.

After the massacre, all exits from the city were sealed. Anyone inside the Catholic ghetto was officially under the authority of the IRA. An IRA commander politely explained he would have to confiscate my film. "Otherwise, the Brits'll strip you and throw you in the lockup for forty-eight hours."

I told him my tape recorder was running the whole time. I had a story to write. "Good lass!" He put an arm around my shoulders. "I'll have one of the boys escort you uphill to a safe house."

Climbing the hills from the Bogside, we were pressed into a huddle of thousands of protesters scrambling to hide within the bungalows of the Catholic ghetto. One man carried his son, his still limbs dangling. Could it be the boy who was shot beside me? I tried to ask, but the father was too distraught. Armored cars rumbled past us through the narrow streets. The warning *pffftt* of rubber bullets punctuated the air. My escort dropped me off at the house of an older couple proud to say that their son, a priest, had fled over the border with a carful of his Provo pals—IRA volunteers. Mothers shooed their young ones into the bathtub to stay out of trouble. The wee voice of a child came from somewhere: "What were they marchin' for today, Mum?"

The old woman offered me tea. I could hear soldiers kicking open the door of a nearby house; their shouts did not ruffle her. She turned up the volume on a recording of men singing Long Kesh Prison songs. Some safe house.

"What will you do if the soldiers come in here firing?" I asked her.

"Lie on me stomach!"

I started to shake. What happened to the boy with the bloody face? Surely, he died. What will happen to us? Fears gurgled up past the taut chest where I trapped my feelings. My throat burned. I was not a reporter now; I was a frightened child. *Please, God, throw me a lifeline.* I asked the old woman if I could use the phone. Yes, one call. I called Clay. My love would say the magic words to make the horror go away.

"Hi! How are you?" His voice was breezy; he was in bed in New York.

"I'm alive."

"Good, how's the story coming?"

"Fourteen people were slaughtered here—"

"Hold on. CBS News is talking about Londonderry right now—"

"They're calling it Bloody Sunday."

"Now look, you don't have to get in the front lines. You're doing a story on Irish women, remember that. Just stick with the women and stay out of trouble. Okay, honey?"

I was dumbstruck. For the first time, Clay didn't get it. My last wish for deliverance was squandered. As I joined the others lying on their stomachs, a powerful idea took hold: *No one is with me. No one can keep me safe. There is no one who won't ever leave me alone.*

BEFORE BLOODY SUNDAY, I had driven out of Belfast to look up my great-aunt Sarah. Actually, I was driven by an IRA commander who worked under Martin McGuinness, second in command of the Derry IRA. Once my guide realized we were going to Lisburn, he yelped, "That's the bloody headquarters of the British army!" Slamming on the brakes, this hard-bitten car bomber dove to the floor of the car. I couldn't help laughing. Taking over the wheel, I eventually found the ancestral home on Waterloo Road, a seventeenth-century stone farmhouse with a parlor draped in company slipcovers. At the kitchen door, the very fantasy of my great-aunt Sarah emerged from the scent of baking biscuits: a raspberry-cheeked, blue-eyed woman of considerable stature. Long widowed, she managed the modestly successful farm with paid farmers of her own.

"Och, it's Lillian's daughter, aren't you now?"

We were immediately family. As we sipped strong tea and nibbled her sweet biscuits, I was shocked to see a photograph of her deceased husband dressed as the leader of the local Orange Lodge. This is the Protestant-loyalist organization that perpetuated British rule and kept a boot at the throats of native Irish workers, treating them as the equivalent of blacks in the American South. With great trepidation, I asked my great-aunt if she was a supporter of the Orange Lodge.

"Och, no, it's a wicked way to run down your own kind," she said. Aunt Sarah abhorred the long civil war in the North. She employed both Catholics and Protestants on her farm and fervently wished to live to see the Republic united, North with South. I was relieved that at least one of my forebears had rejected the path of violent repression. A woman, of course. But back then, in 1972, at the height of confrontation between Derry's Irish revolutionaries and Prime Minister Thatcher's militaristic response, I couldn't imagine that peace would ever end this centuries-old religious war. Martin McGuinness was twenty-one years old at the time of Bloody Sunday. Who would have thought that forty years later he would be deputy first minister of the parliament of Northern Ireland? The fearless women of Northern Ireland, like Aunt Sarah, would be the peacemakers. They would shame the men into giving up their guns and sitting at the table until they reached the Easter accord. But who could have foreseen that one day, in 2012, Queen Elizabeth herself would visit Northern Ireland and Martin McGuinness would take her white-gloved hand in his and bless her in Gaelic, "*Slan agus beannacht*: Good-bye and Godspeed."

AFTER BLOODY SUNDAY, I escaped Derry in a bumpy getaway car over pastureland and was more than grateful to see signs to Dublin. So was my photographer, Rima Shore, a Zionist at heart, who kept saying, "How the hell did I get mixed up in *your* war!" We checked into the Shelbourne Hotel and Rima disappeared into the bathtub. I met with our IRA contact in the lounge. Heavyset as a bar bouncer, he was all business. Given that I had a tape recording of Bloody Sunday, I was a valuable asset. In the seven-hundred-year war between the British and the Irish, there was no possible way of talking to both sides. Once under the protection of the IRA, one had to stick with the IRA. And after Bloody Sunday, the Republic was roiling with revolutionary fever.

The contact whispered in my ear. "Yer're not wantin' to stay here." It was an English-owned hotel. "We might be doin' the Shelbourne tonight."

"Doin'" meant bombing. I raced to the room and called to Rima in the tub. "I don't mean to torture you, but it's not over. We're on the run again." While she scrambled to dress, I ran out to buy a bottle of strong Irish whisky and a chocolate cake. One always needs articles of appeasement. The next days and nights were a blur of mounting paranoia. We were led far out of town to another "safe house," a deserted school with drawn shades. This was the hideout of Rita O'Hare, a young Belfast mom who shot a British soldier in her backyard.

"Rita Wild." She introduced herself with her code name. Short with swirls of ginger hair and a rosebud smile, she looked harmless. She was a great interview. I heard the story of how she'd been protecting her husband while he made a getaway. She was shot in the hip, stomach, and head. As she lay in her backyard, she heard a British soldier shout, "Here's one of the bastards here, dead!" Another soldier cocked a rifle at her skull. All she could think to do was pull back her hood and say, "I'm a girl." The soldiers kicked her in the head and dragged her into their vehicle and took her to Armagh prison. Awaiting a show trial certain to end in a severe sentence, she escaped and fled into the Republic.

Her nuclear family now consisted of her five-year-old son, Rory, and two IRA goons for protection. For our evening's entertainment, mother, child, and goons sang their favorite rebel songs:

> *The night was icy cold I stood alone*
> *I was waiting for an army foot patrol*
> *And when at last they came within my sight*
> *I squeezed the trigger of my armalite*
> *Oh Mama, oh Mama, comfort me*
> *I know these awful things have got to be*
> *But when the war for freedom has been won*
> *I promise you I'll put away my gun.*

It was Rory's birthday. I brought out the cake. Rita Wild told her little son to fetch a big knife. Moments later, I saw the boy sneaking up on Rima's back with a carving knife held like a dagger.

> *Oh Mama, oh Mama, comfort me*
> *I know these awful things have got to be . . .*

"Rory!" His mama stopped the boy but did not scold him. She was homeschooling him as a child soldier. When the goons showed us the room where we would all sleep together on the floor, I asked if they worried that Rory might get hold of their guns. Oh, no, they said, they slept on their guns.

"But the boy's always getting into the gelly," one says.

Gelly?

Gelignite, the explosive commonly used by the IRA.

The appeal of a "safe house" was lost on me. I tried to sound polite in suggesting that we find a nearby inn to stay the night. Checking in did not go well. When I produced the license-plate number of the rented wreck, I was told I must see the manager. A dour man, he noted that the car had been rented from outside of the Republic. "You'll have to take it back to Belfast."

On the run, again. We sprinted through a downpour to the rented wreck and screeched into the airport, left the car hot at the curb, and caught the next thing smoking out of Dublin for the United States. The plane pitched and tossed. Fingers kneaded rosaries. Crucifixes bobbed on trembling chests. The fear did not leave me for another year.

AFTER FLYING HOME FROM IRELAND, I couldn't write the story. Every time I tried to listen to the carnage captured by my tape recorder, I felt the panic rise again. After a week of my evasions, Clay erupted in frustration: "If your story isn't in by noon, the ship is sailing without you." He still didn't get it. I managed to drag out a routine story. My quick Irish temper served to overpower the panic attacks, but at a great price. Outbursts at those closest to me lengthened into diatribes, driving away the very people who could have helped me confront my fears.

As spring came, I hardly knew myself. The rootlessness that had been such joy in my early thirties, allowing me to burst the bonds of old roles, to be reckless and selfish and focused on roaming the world on assignments and then to stay up all night typing on caffeine and nicotine—all at once that didn't work anymore. Some intruder shook me by the psyche and shouted: *Take stock! Half your life has been spent. What about the part of you that wants a home and talks about a second child?* Before I could answer, the intruder pointed to something else I had postponed: *What about the side of you that wants to contribute to the world? Words, books, demonstrations, donations—is this enough? You have been a performer, not a full participant. And now you are thirty-four.*

To be confronted for the first time with the arithmetic of life was, quite simply, terrifying.

SIX MONTHS LATER, I had to travel to Miami Beach for the Democratic National Convention, July 1972. Maura was safely installed with her father for the week. Clay had persuaded me to stay with him at the Jockey Club (a friend described it as a high-class brothel, where they rang a bell at 5 A.M. and everyone changed beds). I should have been filled with excitement at the chance to see and write about my first national political convention. Instead, when I found my lovebird dead, I burst into uncontrollable tears. I barely made the plane.

Flying had always been a joy to me. It was different now. Every time I went near a plane I saw a balcony in Northern Ireland and the boy I couldn't save. The fear of airplanes had blossomed into a phobia. I'd heard a weather report for Miami that contained the word *soupy.* From the safety of the entrance canopy, I called in to the pilot, "Have you had experience with instrument landings?" By now I had no shame. I asked for the aisle seat in the tail of the plane so that when we crashed, I would be the last one to see the ground.

I began to suspect that I was cracking up. I was overwhelmed with a sense of uprootedness. Well, yes, all the ins and outs and ups and downs with Clay; I'd had four different addresses in the previous two years. I couldn't even keep a lovebird alive. No sooner had I single-mindedly willed the 727 to clear Flushing Bay than the intruder was back: *You've done some good work, but what does it really add up to?*

Too nervous to eat, what I didn't know is that a combat between two opposing medications, prescribed by different doctors, had begun in my gut. One was for a lingering intestinal flu, the other for the panic attacks after the Ireland trauma. Onto the angrily separating oils and waters of that digestive system, I threw champagne and cognac.

Clay was already at the convention commandeering his reporters. I let myself into our hotel room and decided to be mindlessly mechanical. Open the suitcase. But right there, a pair of red leather heels had bled onto a white skirt. Like the bloody socket of the boy's eye. I slammed the case shut. Listened to the radio. "Temperature eighty degrees in beautiful Boca Raton. Don't miss the eclipse tonight—but experts warn not to view the eclipse directly, to avoid permanent eye damage."

That night, I was drawn to the balcony. With morbid fascination, I monitored the eclipse. Even the planet was suspended in an unstable condition between intervening forces of the universe. Heat lightning sparked off the towers of Miami Beach. The impulse was to let go and float with it. Parts of myself buried alive with an unreconciled father, severed husband, misplaced friends and loves heaped on me in a mass of fractured visions, all mixed up with the bloody head of the boy in Ireland.

Clay came back. I couldn't talk. I sat through the night on that balcony in Miami, trying to get a fix on the moon.

The next morning I called both doctors who had given me pills. I wanted a nice, neat medical explanation for the debilitating fears and mental confusion that had stricken me for the last half year, beginning with the Redpants blowback. The concept of posttraumatic stress syndrome was not yet recognized. Doctors confirmed that the two drugs (one a barbiturate, the other a mood elevator) were colliding in a violent chemical reaction. All I had to do was stay in bed for a day and wait for it to go away. But "it" was much bigger than that.

Around 8 P.M. I snapped off the idiot box. It didn't go off. I passed in front of the TV set and bent over to pick up a chain-link belt. A hissing sound escaped from the set. I felt current sizzling through me. The shock knocked me over. I looked back. A jellyfish of fiendish hues was spreading across the screen. Was this a drug trip or was I coming undone?

The phone was in the other bedroom. It was beyond the window wall with its balcony hung over the water. Black water sliced by silver knives. The sliding doors were open. Wind sucked at the curtains. Suddenly, I was afraid to walk past that window wall. If I so much as went near that balcony, I would lose my balance and go over the edge. I crouched down. Crablike, I inched across the gaping room. I tried to tell myself this was ridiculous. But when I stood, my limbs went wobbly. The thought persisted, *If only I can reach the right person, this nightmare will go away.*

Ireland could be explained. Real bullets had threatened my life from the outside. My fears were appropriate. Now the destructive force seemed to be inside me. I was my own event. I could not escape it. Something alien, unspeakable but undeniable, had begun to inhabit me.

My own mortality.

CHAPTER 17

KISSINGER AND THE KITCHEN WARS

"KISSINGER IS COMING TO DINNER on Saturday," Clay announced casually. "We'll have to expand the table to seat ten."

I choked on my breakfast muffin. Henry *Kissinger,* President Nixon's henchman? How could Clay play host to such a person? He might personally find Kissinger's politics abhorrent, but he was an editor, and editors have one criterion: Will it make a good story? Clay was also fascinated by power—who had it, how they used it, and how high-octane power brokers used one another. He knew the best way to see this dance play out was to give a great dinner party.

This was the same interminable summer of 1972 and I would have less than a week to pull the party together. Clay told me not to worry about the dinner, his housekeeper would handle it. But I had to design the menu and choreograph the evening, and, up to then, I'd barely been able to cross the threshold of his kitchen without feeling like a trespasser. The kitchen was the domain of Angeles, Clay's formidable Filipina housekeeper. She'd presided over Clay's domicile before and after Pamela. Even though Clay and I had been living together for almost three years, I kept a separate office on East Forty-Ninth Street. My daughter and I made a point of avoiding Angeles at all costs. She was not about to relinquish her prime ministerial role to some young "heepie" who had turned up from the Lower East Side.

On weeknights when I tried to make dinner for Clay and me, she'd shoo me out. She now stood before me in the dining room, muttering in her high-pitched voice inscrutable phrases in Tagalog.

"Dis is a ting from hell!"

She was wearing rubber gloves and holding her nose as she extended a baggie full of food.

"Oh, dear. It must be the salmon from Sunday night. Let's find the deodorizer," I suggested with studied containment.

"I do my way. Don't bodder me in kitchen."

"Angeles, please, let's don't fight. This is a very important dinner party, and I need your help. You know where everything is in this kitchen—and I don't." Gently, I introduced an idea suggested to me by a friend. "We can order tenderloins from the Perini Ranch in Texas. You don't even need a steak knife, I'm told. You just breathe on them and they'll slice themselves."

Angeles was not into power sharing. She wanted to do all the cooking. "Cooking and serving for ten is too much for one person, Angeles. I'll order the tenderloins. You won't forget to take them out of the freezer . . ."

"You forget. I not forget."

". . . five hours before the guests come," I continued, "because they're supposed to be served at room temperature."

"What you tink? I'm neen-com-poop?"

"Of course not, but now that I'm living here, I need you to tell me how Clay likes things—like which silver and china to use."

"I know. I know ebrey-ting." She turned toward her realm. "You go play with your typewriter—I work."

CLAY WANTED TO BUY ME A DRESS for the party. It was one of the more benign customs of male chauvinism, but I could see that he wanted to costume me as his hostess for a formal social-political dinner party. I agreed only on the condition that I pay for the dress with my own money. He made an appointment with a personal shopper at Worldly Things on Madison Avenue. Like a proud Pygmalion, he sat in an armchair while the shopper selected several long dinner dresses. I swirled out of the dressing room to show them to Clay, feeling pretty. Clay chose red, the power color. A red silk crepe with shoulder pads and a peekaboo slit at the bustline, cinched over a long wraparound skirt slit up to the knee—a costume unlike anything I had ever worn. Very Kate Hepburn. Clay's favorite movie was *Woman of the Year* with Tracy and Hepburn playing journalists from different worlds who wind up marrying only when he persuades her that he doesn't want her in the kitchen.

As we walked down Madison, eyeing one window after another displaying women's fashions, Clay blurted a rare admission. "Now I can't look at any mannequin without seeing you in the clothes. You've besotted me!"

I laughed at the accusation. Clay had difficulty saying "I love you." I would settle for besotted.

CLAY BRIEFED ME on the secret agenda of our party. He had invited Katharine Graham, owner and publisher of the *Washington Post*. They were close friends. Clay knew it would be valuable to his good friend Kay to feel out Kissinger on just how furious Nixon was over her 1971 publication of the Pentagon Papers and what he might try to do about it.

At that time, Kay Graham did not have a great deal of confidence in herself as a publisher, and even less confidence in herself as a woman. Little wonder. Her once larger-than-life husband, Phil Graham, had cruelly belittled her, been shamelessly unfaithful, and ultimately taken his own life in the most violently angry way, shooting himself with a .28-gauge shotgun at their Virginia country estate.

I had never questioned Clay about the nature of his relationship with Kay. I understood that he had to court the royalty of journalism, and Mrs. Graham was becoming the queen of social Washington, entertaining presidents and prime ministers in her elegant Georgetown mansion. She obviously adored this fair-haired prince of New York publishing and often invited Clay to join her weekend house guests at the manse. She held seventeeth-century-style levees. On rising in the morning, she would have her guests shown into her boudoir where they would discuss the papers with her from a settee at the foot of her bed while servants delivered breakfast.

I wondered, Did people sleep together at levees?

One night, a year before, Kay had turned to Clay in a moment of crucial decision. On June 13, 1971, the *New York Times* had published the Pentagon Papers, the Defense Department's secret history of the Vietnam War. No sooner had the *Times* published the first installment than Nixon's attorney general ordered the paper to halt further publication under threat of criminal prosecution. This was the first attempt in American history by the federal government to restrain the publication of a newspaper.

Kay had telephoned Clay from her home in Washington. I answered. She told me that she needed to speak to Clay urgently. When I passed the phone to Clay, he shooed me out of the room. I felt like a child being sent away because the grown-ups needed to have a serious conversation. In fairness, this was a top secret matter. Earlier, Clay had gotten wind from journalists in Washington that the *Post* also had the documents. He left a message for Kay: *Can I help?* At that moment her editors and lawyers were all frantically reading through a box full of more than four thousand pages of disorganized photocopied sheets. Her corporate attorney had warned her that the paper was vulnerable under the Espionage Act. If found guilty of a felony, the *Washington Post* company could be stripped of its license to operate TV stations.

Kay was distraught. She confided to Clay that her company was about to go public and if threatened with criminal action, the underwriters could withdraw without penalty. Clay's instincts were strongly in favor of publishing. If she held back because of government pressure, the *New York Times* would beat her, and the paper's reputation could be destroyed. He told Kay he felt the soul of her newspaper was at stake. His views were echoed by her editors. She understood that if she didn't publish, she would lose respect and loyalty on the editorial floor. Courageously, she gave the go-ahead.

A pinch of jealousy had begun to muddy the reservoir of respect I had for this gutsy woman who was preserving her paper's journalistic integrity against intimidation by the president and his gang. She was at the center of a national crucible. Clay was in awe of her. The Pentagon Papers showed a deep cynicism on the part of the military, and bald-faced lying by the previous president, Lyndon Johnson. Nixon knew the whole sordid history but was perpetuating the big lie as the centerpiece of his reelection campaign.

Clay also knew that Kissinger avidly courted Graham. Her newspaper was the Rosetta stone in Washington. It was written in two languages: one for recording policy documents and boilerplate statements from politicians, and another for leaks, where the real news was couched in unsourced quotes. Kissinger took every opportunity to soften up the liberal media with such leaks. His aim was to elevate himself to the status of America's Bismarck, the German statesman who created "balance of power" diplomacy that preserved the peace in Europe from the 1870s until World War I.

Kay and Henry were surprisingly cozy. They sneaked off to the movies together. She gave small, off-the-record parties for him at her home. This baffled me. Kissinger had done his best to squash publication of the Pentagon Papers; Nixon despised the *Post*. So how could these two, on opposing sides of the Vietnam War, and pulling with all their powers in opposite directions in the political war for the hearts and minds of the American people, be such close friends?

Power loves power.

Clay had also invited Joseph Kraft, a high-profile *Post* columnist. Clay had tapped Joe to write stories for *New York* because he was not as easily manipulated by Kissinger as other political writers. Even when Joe outed Kissinger for his double-dealings in helping to elect Nixon in 1968, the journalist didn't lose access. On the contrary, Kissinger was even more willing to take his calls. Joe and Clay had become great friends. On summer weekends, he and Clay and I would ride bikes to Georgica Beach and go bodysurfing. Then the two men would sit on blankets and talk Washington politics, in a shorthand I could barely decipher. This dinner party would offer Joe a golden opportunity to needle Kissinger about Nixon's bizarre turnaround, from hiding his secret bombing of Cambodia to ballyhooing his expansion of the Vietnam War in that sovereign country as a brave new policy.

Finally, learning that David Frost was in town, Clay asked him to join the table. Frostie had sought out Clay in the mid-1960s to help him with ideas for his first American TV show, *That Was the Week That Was.* The two men had a ball creating sly, British-style political satire and the kind of zany skits that live on today on *Saturday Night Live.* Frost had an agenda of his own; he wanted to seduce Henry Kissinger, the president's closest confidant, into appearing on his syndicated talk show.

I understood that Clay needed to stay close to the biggest ears in Washington, D.C. Nothing tickled him more than a dinner party that brought together masters of manipulation from the political and media worlds, hip to hip, around his table. He would start off spinning the top by tossing out a provocative question. He counted on the writers he'd invited to ask the follow-ups. Guests would grow dizzy with the velocity of views and quips and counterarguments until, in the competition to sound like the smartest one in the room, they would forget what they shouldn't say. Clay would slip out of his breast pocket a small Hermès notepad and a gold pen and jot ideas. This is how he made certain that his magazine always stayed ten minutes ahead of history.

DURING COCKTAIL HOUR before the dinner party, tall candles on the fireplace flickered in the convex mirror overhead. The flames reflected outward, shooting like golden stars around the room. The whole space glowed. Peonies on tall stalks spread their pink petals and added a seductive scent to the room. Clay smiled approvingly. I had set the stage well.

One by one, guests entered from the foyer above, looked over the balcony at the elegant scene below, and made their entrance down a spiral staircase. Cheek-to-cheek kisses. Flutes of champagne. Angeles passed a platter of pâté and cheese puffs, displaying a deference that I had never seen before. I tried to follow her into the kitchen to check on the Texas tenderloins, but she stopped me at the door to her realm. "Ebrey-ting under my control."

I yanked up my sliding shoulder pads, feeling like a little girl playing dressup. Kissinger, in his sauerkraut mumble, introduced the subject of his recent world-shaking trip to China with Nixon. He let others fawn over his stunning feat of diplomacy. Nixon may have shaken the world by making the first presidential visit to Communist China, but who opened that door? Kissinger, of course, whose instinctive feel for power and conspiracy allowed him to play Beijing against Moscow and win the trust of another subtle statesman, Chinese Premier Zhou Enlai, who issued the invitation to Nixon.

Yet Kissinger had his own dark anxieties, tinged with paranoia and insecurity. I picked up the signal when his hand reached into the bowl of potato chips. Clay had turned up his nose when I'd set out this pedestrian dish, but I'd read that Kissinger fancied such comfort food when he was tense. He asked Kay, "What's the matter, don't you think we're going to be reelected?"

Kay assured him that she was reading the same polls that he was reading. "I haven't the slightest doubt that Nixon will be reelected," she said without inflection.

It was Kay's turn to pry information out of her dear Henry. "We all know Nixon loathes the press. If he is elected . . ."

"*When,*" Kissinger interjected.

". . . will he try to get even with the *Post* for running the Pentagon Papers?"

"Wouldn't you?" Kissinger exclaimed, followed by a gravelly chuckle to indicate he was only needling her. He wanted to make it clear that he was never part of any actual discussions with the president that related to threats (this statement by Kissinger was later revealed as false), but that he knew Nixon wanted to get even with a lot of people following the election.

Clay asked the direct question that Kay could not. "The president already threatened the *Times* with criminal prosecution. How far would he be willing to go to muzzle the *Post?*"

That gave Kissinger an opening to warn his friend Kay. "As you might imagine, he is most antagonistic toward the *Post*. Whether true or not, he believes the paper has it in for him."

It wasn't hard to read the tension in Kay Graham's face. She smiled to cover it and lightly put a lid on the topic with a quip. "I know I can count on you, Henry, to appease his paranoia."

This was when I first began to understand that power brokers like these are symbiotic. They cling to each other like lichen to a rock. They feed off each other. They cannot do without each other. For Kay and Henry to meet and talk over a small private dinner party in Manhattan, beyond the eavesdroppers lurking behind every column in the Capitol, was an opportunity not to be missed. That night I saw how Clay set the stage to gain context for a story that he suspected would eventually shake the country.

Joe Kraft bounded down the stairs and immediately began tracking Kissinger like a bloodhound. He brought up a little-noticed story that had appeared in the *Post* about a month before. "Tell us, Henry, why would a gang of Cubans wear surgical gloves to visit the Democratic National Committee Headquarters?" With a sly smile, Joe asked, "Were they planning to perform an operation?"

He was referring to the first Watergate story, given a giant eighty-three inches of copy in the *Post* on June 18, 1972. Readers scarcely paid attention. But it had awakened suspicions in Joe and Clay.

Kissinger froze on hearing Joe's question and muzzled himself with another fistful of chips. "Bungled burglars," he mumbled finally. "Cuban exiles, you know, crazies."

I thought I caught Kay's eyes shoot Joe a warning look. Joe backed off. Unbeknownst to me, but not to Clay and Joe, two "kids" on the *Post,* as Bob Woodward and Carl Bernstein were called around the newsroom, had begun digging up evidence against the president. They were just beginning to burrow into the cracks behind the bizarre account of a break-in at the Watergate by a motley crew carrying a stack of sequential one-hundred-dollar bills, forty rolls of unexposed film, and bugging devices that they were attempting to plant behind ceiling panels in the office of the head of the Democratic Party election campaign. Cops had interrupted them at gunpoint. The revered *Times* had been out in front on the Pentagon Papers story. On the Watergate story, the scrappy *Post* was way ahead, but dangerously alone.

Kissinger, who looked like a scared rabbit, suddenly underwent a change of political coloration worthy of a prize chameleon. The superhawk began to drop clues about Nixon's obsession with enemies, which Nixon suspected surrounded him on all sides. Even he, Kissinger said, was kept at arm's length because of his liberal leanings.

"Liberal leanings!" It escaped my mouth before I could call the words back. Kissinger gave a forgiving chuckle. He reminded us that he had been an adviser to "Nelson" (Rockefeller, the liberal Republican former governor of New York), as if that was where his heart of hearts resided. But things being the way they were now, his best efforts went toward restraining Richard Nixon's more exaggerated personal—well, he didn't say *neuroses* but managed to imply it by emphasizing the word *personal*—suspicions of hostility.

(Sweet irony: In June 1973 we would learn that Kissinger himself masterminded the bugging of many of the hundreds of reporters and others on the president's enemies lists, which included none other than Joseph Kraft.)

David Frost was late. Oozing charm and apologies, he soon had us roaring with laughter at his subtle British parodies of guests on his show who were full of themselves while quite unaware of how foolish they appeared. His date was Diahann Carroll. She was ravishingly beautiful, the first African American female star of a popular TV series, *Julia*.

Kissinger couldn't take his eyes off Diahann. He fancied himself a "secret swinger" who famously boasted, "Power is the ultimate aphrodisiac." Diahann disported herself on the fender in front of the fireplace, confident of her allure. She had left a marriage and cast off an affair with Sidney Poitier, leaving a vacancy that was about to be filled by Frost.

Clay gave me the nod; time to sit down to dinner. I headed for the kitchen. The swinging door was blocked. "Angeles?" Again, she protested that all was under control. "I'm coming in—to help." I leaned on the door and stumbled in, immediately chagrined to see that she had the twenty precious Texas tenderloins all spread out on baking dishes and ready for heating up. I took a fork to test their fabled tenderness. The tines trembled but did not penetrate. I tried puncturing another chop from the top. No give. I picked up a serving fork and stabbed the damn thing. It flipped off the table onto the floor where it landed like a brick.

Ohmygod, these babies are still frozen! "Angeles, didn't you take them out five hours ago?"

"You tell me five minutes."

"Five *hours*."

"Minutes."

The absence of remorse in her face gave it away. Angeles was a kitchen saboteur. She would now have the pleasure of gloating while I seated ten hungry people around the table and tried to make small talk as we snacked on leftover pâté. I would have to tell Clay. Fight-or-flee reactions collided in my stomach. I felt overcome by the fever of failure. It was as bad as when a cover story comes in a holy mess at the last moment before deadline. "Get me rewrite!" is the classic panic call. I beckoned for Clay to come into the kitchen.

"There's been a communications problem . . . we need a total redo on dinner." Huddling in the kitchen, we ran through one miserable alternative after another. Then I hit on a solution.

"Peking duck!"

"Peking duck?" Clay repeated dumbly.

"I can call Mr. Chow's downstairs. They'll deliver chop chop."

"Perfect!"

Clay was already working out the new scenario. It would be a tribute to Henry, as if we'd planned it all along. "He can replay his trip to China—he'll love it."

As it turned out, the duck was a great hit. Kissinger was euphoric as he traced his triumph in China straight through to dessert. Kay Graham appeared charmed. But before she left, she confided to Clay that from the subtext of Kissinger's remarks, she had the feeling that a *High Noon* situation was developing. Could the White House be planting false leads intending to draw her reporters down a road to discredit the paper? Clay promised her he would keep his eyes and ears open.

David Frost was elated by the evening. He had ingratiated himself with Kissinger by hanging on his every word, angling for a future interview with the president. He and Diahann let me know they were about to be engaged. Gushing on, they said they couldn't think of a more perfect place to have an engagement dinner party than in our apartment. If only they had known about the beef on the floor and the emergency duck.

Upstairs, alone together at last, I moaned, "Oh, God, Clay, can you forgive me?"

"Forgive you?" He threw his arms around me and lifted me off my feet. "You pulled a rabbit out of the hat!"

"You mean, a duck."

"You made the evening look as easy as duck soup. I'm crazy for you!" He led me to our bed and moved a hand up the slit of the Hepburn dress. I'll never forget how quickly he changed from the big game hunter into a most tender lover.

THE REVERBERATIONS FROM THAT DINNER PARTY continued for years. Clay suspected all along that Kissinger had been behind the campaign to smear the *Post.* The ultimate personalized threat was voiced by Attorney General John Mitchell to a *Post* reporter: "Katie Graham is going to get her tit caught in a big fat wringer." Clay assigned Aaron Latham to write the cover piece for *New York.* Latham followed Woodward and Bernstein as they tracked down the story of their generation: "How 'The Washington Post' Gave Nixon Hell."

On the morning of October 10, 1972, the lead story in the *Post* established that the Watergate bugging incident was part of a massive campaign of political spying and sabotage directed by top officials of the Nixon government and, by implication, the president himself. It took two more years for the American public to catch up and for Nixon to be impeached.

Frost finally got his audience with Nixon five years later, in 1977. Twelve sessions over four weeks. He asked Clay to be one of his advisers. After the session on the Vietnam War, Frost was downcast. Nixon's early paranoia and mistakes had not been revealed. Approaching the final interview, Frost was desperate to get "the confession." He asked Clay to fly out to give him some insights for the follow-up interview. Late into the night at the Beverly Hilton, Clay and I sat with David and his vivacious new girlfriend, Caroline Cushing Graham, my colleague from the *Trib*, until finally Clay urged David to be "less British, less polite."

"Ask him straight out if he's ready to admit he made a mistake."

Frost asked Nixon if he believed the president could decide to do something illegal if he thought it was in the best interests of the nation.

"Well, when the president does it, that means it is not illegal" was Nixon's stunning reply. Having struck gold at last, Frost was keen to extend the conversation. He sat forward: "You mean as a matter of course?"

Nixon nailed it: "Exactly."

Later in the interview, Nixon confessed that he regretted that he had resigned. By doing so, said the man who could not admit a mistake, "I impeached myself."

Frost had scored one of the "Greatest Interviews of the 20th Century," according to the *Guardian* newspaper. I came to realize that Clay was a master catalyst, able to influence culture in ways that were not obvious.

David would die prematurely in 2013. Two thousand people were invited to his memorial service, held with full pageantry in Westminster Abbey as the bells pealed out across London. The royals came to pay their respects to a working-class man who was honored like a king. David would have loved (and laughed) to see that the man who elevated television to a respected repository for history had his flagstone set in the abbey's Poets' Corner, close to Shakespeare's.

Clay and Gail toasting David Frost's triumphant Nixon interviews, 1977.

CHAPTER 18

STEPPING OFF THE PEDESTAL

WITH THE COMING OF SUMMER in my thirty-sixth year, I felt a surge of impetuous energy to contend with the battering of time. If even earth and sea are subject to death, as Shakespeare tells us, then bring on the waves! I had always envied how effortlessly Clay bodysurfed. As the sweet honeyed days of summer came, I felt able to dive into the sprawling explosive surf on the day after a storm and let my body be tossed about like a toothpick.

My turbulent love affair with Clay had begun five years before. Five years since the silent kiss as he pulled pages of my Bobby Kennedy story out of the typewriter. Three years of living together. And where were we? Can love hold back "the swift foot of time"? That summer of 1973, Clay rented a larger summer cottage for us in East Hampton. It was a gift to me. I could stay out there with my daughter and write. Maura was now nine. Clay would join us for weekends. I will never forget the splash of earliest morning sun on the tile floor of the large funky living room. It lit the inside windows in both Maura's and my bedrooms at either end of the big room. Together, we would emerge and throw open the glass doors and run barefoot over the dewy grass to stick our toes in a warm inlet of Georgica Pond.

After breakfast we would walk down to the ocean beach early enough to pick out some flounder and maybe even blowfish from the squirming, honking, battling catch in the huge nets dragged ashore by the last of the seine haulers. We might go to one of the local farms reddening with strawberries—pick all you can eat—then go home to make shortcake. I would write while Maura read books until it was Friday and time to drive to the airport and wait for "Big Daddy," as we jokingly called Clay, to emerge from an improbably small commuter plane. On Saturday mornings Clay always drove with Maura to pick up the papers. He took the *New York Times*. She appreciated that he showed equal respect for her choice of reading material, that is, comic books.

She and I planted a vegetable garden and raced the rabbits to the lettuce every day. Joe Kraft might drop by in late morning to kibitz about politics. Clay would drive over to Truman Capote's house, dreading to find the once-beautiful boy genius, now paunchy and bald, in a boozy haze and mumbling excuses for why he couldn't finish a cover story. Shana Alexander, one of the first female journalists to become a big name on television, would often invite us for lunch with an eclectic cast of writers, musicians, and politicians. We would all laugh over the running sketch on *Saturday Night Live* where Jane Curtin and Dan Aykroyd would parody Shana, as the feisty liberal on CBS's *60 Minutes,* going head-to-head with James J. Kilpatrick, as the sexist conservative. Aykroyd, in the Kilpatrick role, would begin his crude rebuttal with "Jane, you ignorant slut."

Given these manifold delights, why did my feelings of unease persist?

We were a "let's pretend" family. The '60s had spawned so many options, marriage was seen as unnecessary and definitely unhip. A lot of people we knew were experimenting with "open marriage." I saw that as a dispensation for adultery, and those couples usually erupted in savage jealousies. Divorce was as popular as a new sitcom; it seemed everyone was trying it. Having been through the hell of divorce, Clay and I were both wary about being burned again. We were deeply attached emotionally and professionally and drawn to each other sexually as if by magnetic force. Yet marriage was too big a leap. So we just made it up as we went along.

Not by coincidence, the piece I was working on for New York's Valentine issue was called "Can Couples Survive?" For the story I interviewed Dr. Ray L. Birdwhistell, a communications professor at the University of Pennsylvania's famous Annenberg School. Birdwhistell was aptly named for a happily divorced pioneer in the study of nonverbal communication between men and women. He had left the nest of his conventional wife, he told me, when women's liberation made him a "free bird." His theory was that "the closed dyad"—couples who expected all their emotional needs to be met through the spouse contract—was lethal to prolonged love and good sex. Both partners should accept the need to make valid social contracts with other people.

It made me look at Clay dispassionately. Here was a handsome, magnetic, heterosexual bachelor-about-town in his midforties. At the office he was surrounded by comely young staffers. After dark he was in demand to fill the single-man quota at uptown dinner parties given by "social x-rays," as Tom Wolfe memorably labeled the spareribbed ladies of a certain age who hungered for the attentiveness no longer paid them by their bored philandering husbands.

For my part, I had three lives, which only occasionally overlapped: Maura's mother; Clay's partner and hostess; and Gail the writer and breadwinner. Every day I felt as if I were running a minimarathon, dashing past Clay's office with my story unfinished in time to pick up my daughter from school or have dinner-bath-and-books with her before I had to be dressed to the nines as Clay's partner for the evening's events. Clay often said, "I can't get enough of you." There wasn't enough of me to go around.

And I wasn't crazy about the prospect of a closed dyad either. I felt eager to stretch. As a single woman who attracted flirtations from other smart and sexy men, what was I missing?

Maura's father and I had worked out a civilized, even cordial, relationship as coparents. We agreed not to argue about possessions or custody or holiday calendars. We realized that we had a responsibility that superseded all those issues and it would last for our lifetimes. I assumed full custody but shared our daughter with Albert every other weekend and alternate holidays and for two weeks in the summer. It didn't occur to me to ask for compensation for working as his PHT (Putting Hubby Through) partner. Only fifteen years later did courts consider restitution for PHT services through expanded alimony or a division of property rights in the wife's favor.

Pride kept me from asking for alimony, and Albert contributed only child support. I made a conscious effort to sideline the hurt and anger and to put on a happy face whenever our paths crossed. Those repressed feelings would later erupt during Maura's adolescence. But for now, we concentrated on smoothing the jolt of transitions and sharing the daily decisions that would nurture a child we both cherished.

Had Clay and I married then—and I knew it even at the time—we would most likely have turned into a variation on the marriage in Noël Coward's *Private Lives,* living on snappy dialogue with every other sentence a dagger between the ribs. When I raised the subject of children, Clay would get fidgety, like someone stuck between floors in an elevator. He knew that I was keen to have another child. He might have been persuaded to accept the idea, but he told me he couldn't see himself dragging strollers through airports or sitting up with a colicky baby when he had a cover story to close. The message was clear: I could have a baby, all right, as long as I was prepared to be alone with it in the kitten box for the first five years. But I did not want to be a single mother, again.

"Can Couples Survive?," an excerpt from my book in progress on couples, stirred a lot of talk when it appeared in a special issue of *New York* in February 1973. Aspirational women were just beginning to recognize that early marriage usually foreclosed the possibility of a career dream. Feminists started the trend toward postponement of marriage, much to the dismay of many men who expected a wife to carry the husband's dream.

Honesty prompts me to admit a larger obstacle to marriage for both Clay and me. Neither of us had yet met the criteria of the psychoanalyst Erik Erikson, who had given a pretty good definition of intimacy as the capacity to live with another person in an emotionally attached, interdependent, and committed relationship. That task was supposed to be mastered in one's twenties! But I had already advanced to my midthirties, and Clay was twelve years older—what was wrong with us? As George Vaillant learned by following the men in the Harvard Grant study from college into their nineties, the mastery of intimacy depends on first mastering identity. In Vaillant's 2012 book, *Triumphs of Experience,* he reported that some of the study's men didn't become capable of true intimacy until after age seventy!

Clay was utterly confident about his ideas. But despite his larger-than-life persona, he did not feel confident, in private, that his identity as an editor and publisher was secure. Publishers from rich and powerful families could, at whim, buy or sell or shut down small successful publications such as his. He did not have a father's missionary zeal behind him, like Henry Luce, or a titled family like Lord Beaverbrook, or a family castle like William Randolph Hearst. As a self-made man, Clay was always dependent on the kindness of wealthy strangers.

My identity was even shakier. It was time for me to loosen the coils that kept me still dependent on my Pygmalion. I was ready to become my own woman. Time was pressing. Intimations of mortality continued to invade my thoughts after the confrontation with death in Ireland. I believed I had to prove to myself, and to the world, that I could write a book on my own terms, live on my own income, and combine raising my child with fulfilling my own dream.

———————————

SERENDIPITOUSLY, I WAS INVITED in midsummer of 1973 to take a trip to the Soviet Union. This was the most frigid era of the Cold War, but somehow, Columbia University had arranged for a small cultural group, Citizens Exchange Corps, to take a handful of American students who wanted to meet their Russian counterparts. It was an extraordinary opportunity. Clay encouraged me to go. Maura was already scheduled to spend those same two weeks with her father.

At the end of our trip, I was detained at Moscow Airport. "Icon!" snapped the emigration officer. "*Nyet, abstrakni,*" I said. The officer had torn off the paper from a tourist-only berioska shop with which I had attempted to camouflage an abstract oil painting I had bought from an underground artist. It was a collage of a church with every window and door barricaded. But it wasn't the religious theme that upset the officer; it was his total unfamiliarity with abstract art. He was pulling off all the collage pieces in a manic attempt to find the precious gold icon he was certain lay beneath. My arguments were futile. Even after he had destroyed the painting, our whole group was detained for hours.

I had to let Clay know I would miss my plane and be delayed getting home. An offer of dollars to "compensate" the officer for having to stay so late on my account was remarkably effective in disarming him. He granted me one long-distance call. It was 8:30 P.M. in Moscow, 4:30 A.M. for Clay. He was in East Hampton. An odd uncertainty in his voice surprised me; I sensed someone else was there. Before I could pursue my suspicion, the line went dead.

When I returned a day late from the Soviet Union, something was different in the atmosphere of our weekend cottage. Clay wasn't there, but something feminine, a scent not my own, lingered in the bathroom. Had another woman left a cloud of dusting powder, bubble bath, a hint of roses? Then I remembered. He had asked if a new staffer he had hired could stay in Maura's vacated room for the weekends when I was away. Nancy was freshly divorced from one of

Clay's oldest friends, dumped in New York from her previous life in Paris, and feeling like "a wet cat looking for a home," she had told me. Clay had promised her a job at the magazine. Remembering the terror of dislocation after divorce, I had sympathized with her.

I said nothing when he arrived, nor did he. But the morning after my suspicions had been aroused, I awoke in our cottage bursting with righteous indignation.

"Did Nancy take my place while I was away?" Clay stammered until he gave up trying to craft an alibi. I packed up my belongings and called a taxi to go to the train station. Clay kept protesting, even begging, until my Irish temper broke. "I hope you and Nancy will be very happy together. I have a book to write. AND I DON'T NEED YOU!"

He ran outside in his boxer shorts to stop me from getting into the cab but I had the last word, a slammed door.

He returned to the apartment on Sunday night, but that night and the entire following week, I slept in Maura's room and refused to speak to him. I began making inquiries to find my own apartment. He moped around and had breakfast solo. The next weekend, facing the prospect of a long Labor Day holiday alone while Maura went to her father's, the armor of righteous indignation began to wear off. The magnetism resurfaced. Clay pleaded with me to go with him to the country. Of course I declined. He left for the four o'clock train, alone.

The therapist I had been seeing to sort out my conflicted feelings about Clay had warned me: "You go from one extreme to the other. You tell yourself to give him up altogether, but you seem incapable of cutting the cord. So you throw yourself into a full commitment to him, again, and then are disappointed when he doesn't reciprocate."

I couldn't resist. On Saturday morning, after a sleepless night, I picked up the phone at seven and called him. His voice was stiff. "It's too early to call."

"I miss you."

"This is not an appropriate time to talk."

"Why? Is Nancy there?"

"And you're not."

"Is this an ultimatum?"

"Take it as you wish." He hung up.

Yes, of course, his fling with Nancy was his ultimatum: live with me or I'll find other women to play with.

Consumed with the jealousy he had intended to sow, I had to find some way to distract myself. I tried to write. My fingers soon tired of hitting the stuck keys on my aging typewriter. As the day lengthened and loneliness swelled to fill the hours, I remembered a party invitation. It was a PR event for politicians and media types, and it was that night, but in Washington, D.C. An attractive senator I met on an interview had tried to persuade me to come down. I'd sent my regrets but now, defiant, I slipped into a clingy summer dress and high strappy heels and hailed a yellow cab for LaGuardia, intending to catch a shuttle.

The cabdriver warned me the Bos-Wash corridor was drenched with rain. At the airport they said freakish lightning was on its way. Nothing was going to fly. I walked back to the same yellow cab, grounded, glum.

"Tough luck," the cabbie said.

"Yup." Now what—home to eat sprouts and start packing?

As the cab crowned the Triborough and cut over toward the Manhattan exit, I said, "What would it cost to drive to D.C.?"

"Two hundred and dinner."

"Really?"

It was an excuse to visit his "little lady on the side" who lived in D.C. "Let's go."

The drive was surreal. The sky thickened to the consistency of cooking fat. We were looking for a popular hangout on the edge of Georgetown but not much of anything was visible, not even the Naval Observatory Tower. Ridiculously late, we found the right street but we couldn't read the number or even the names of the restaurants through the curtains of rain. Zeroing in on my best guess, I urged the driver to pull up onto the curb: "Yes, point the lights at the sign over that window."

A crowd of laughing faces suddenly filled the window. A New York City yellow cab was crashing their party! A man rushed out with an umbrella. It was he, the very senator who had flirted with me when I interviewed him.

"Hey, New York!" he shouted. "Don't drive in—I'll carry you in!"

He scooped me up and carried me to a barstool amid cheers. The cabbie was carried in, too, on a brace of two pairs of shoulders, and plied with drink. Guests raised a toast and began singing as the band broke into the Rolling Stones end-of-the-world rocker, "Gimme Shelter" . . . *I tell you love, sister, it's just a kiss away.*

We all drank beer and sang our favorite Stones and Beatles songs, and the band did riffs on Eric Clapton and Cream. The senator couldn't stop laughing about my zany escapade. He got cozy and asked if he could take me to my hotel. "I don't have a hotel," I said. "I have a milk train to catch."

"The Capitol's so gorgeous by night, why don't we walk through and look at the art?" he proposed. "It's the best gallery in town."

"Won't someone be waiting up for you?"

He assured me he had no time for marriage; he was a freshman senator. By 1 A.M. the air was drying and sweet as he swept me off in his convertible. His offer, of course, was a high-powered variation on "Come up and see my etchings." But it was magical to stroll the portrait gallery with an amorous guide. He took pains to point out the painting of an attractive woman in a blue suit sitting at a desk: "Eva McCall Hamilton, the prettiest suffragist," he said. "She was fearless, like you. She drove a horse-drawn float through Grand Rapids with a huge banner proclaiming 'Vote for Women,' and that was in 1910."

He kissed me under Ms. Hamilton and said he would like to continue seeing me. I was not naive enough to think this was his first time moonlighting as a docent to a single woman. After more kisses in the car, I began feeling like Birdwhistell's "free bird." There was magic in this night. The senator pressed me to stay over. I had to get home before Maura returned the next morning, and it would have spoiled things.

On the dreary milk train ride back to New York, my thoughts returned to Clay and I was caught in a whipsaw: *You have to leave him, Gail. Yes, but I don't want to lose him.* How perverse we women are! Another scene from *Woman of the Year* flickered through my mind. After Hepburn pushes Tracy too far by adopting a child and expecting him to take care of the boy, he leaves her. She lures him back by letting herself into his apartment and making breakfast for him. She wakes him up. He says he doesn't want her in the kitchen, but he falls for her all over again.

If it worked for Hepburn . . .

CLAY RETURNED FROM THE COUNTRY at about seven on Monday night. The flicker of candlelight in the living room must have caught his eye. He leaned over the balcony railing. "Who's there?"

He must have seen the placemats set out on our favorite oval cherry table, a bottle of wine chilling in a Georgian silver bucket; he must have smelled the rosemary-stuffed lamb chops and potatoes baking.

"Gail! Thank God. I thought you'd left, I mean, for good, you didn't answer, last night, I kept calling . . ."

"I'm here. Are you alone?"

"Of course!"

I wasn't sure that Nancy was totally out of the picture. But this was not the time to fuss over our recent dalliances.

"Look at the lovely supper you've fixed for me," he said, diving down the stairs. He wanted to give me a big hug, and I let him, but I didn't dare allow a kiss.

"Let's talk," I said. He opened the wine and brushed a kiss on my neck as he poured me a glass, then began trying awkwardly to apologize. "It was a dumb fling. I was feeling like you forgot about me."

"It's more than that."

Over salad, I told Clay I needed solitude to get serious about writing the book that occupied my mind. "I can't do it with all these distractions."

"Like what?"

"Our on-again, off-again romance," I said. "I've become too dependent on you. I don't want to stop seeing you, but—"

"You can't leave," he protested. "You belong here."

"There comes a time when the apprentice has to leave the mentor."

"But Pygmalion got the girl—she literally melted into his arms."

It took all the gumption I had to resist falling into his arms. "You need freedom, too, Clay. You're still a wild bird. You're not ready to nest."

He didn't argue. I remembered being unhappy about the way he had treated me when we'd spent a weekend at the Virginia retreat of the *Washington Post* publisher.

"Where do things stand with you and Kay Graham?"

"I don't know what you mean." He had a goofy grin.

I was tired of his evasions. "Are you pursuing her, I mean, personally?"

"Would I have insisted you live with me if I were trying to capture Kay?"

"Maybe I'm your cover. You wouldn't dare let her courtiers see you as a rival. But I could tell at our Kissinger dinner. She's in love with you."

He brushed it off by saying something about how much older she was, and besides, he would never be a kept man by a rich woman. I let it go. I realized it would be foolish, and probably futile, for me to insist that he break off his relationships with some of the most powerful women of the day. They had together what Birdwhistell called "a valid social contract."

Why did I have to leave him to grow? he demanded. Didn't I understand what he had told me after the dinner party from hell? He didn't want me in the kitchen. He wanted my ideas. He wanted me at his side, at the table with his circle of writers, he wanted my insights about New York's movers and fakers. He wanted me in his bed. Suddenly, he was desperate to claim me.

"Why now, why couldn't you make a commitment before now?" I asked.

"You never gave me an ultimatum!"

I couldn't help laughing. Clay being a man who could not abide being told what to do would have dug in his heels and said, "No woman dictates to me."

He tried another approach. "With all our fights, we've taken a lot out of each other this past year. When I first knew you, and your life was coming apart, you were only, what?—twenty-eight or something? I thought you looked worn out. But you know what? Today you look more beautiful than ever."

"Then I hope you can wait until I'm ready." I stood up, an announcement that I was ready to leave. "Clay, I adore you. But it's time for me to break away. Can you understand?"

His face reddened. In a burst of frustration he said, "I love you so much, I could KILL you!"

Whatever the outcome, I knew I had made the most daring decision of my life.

PART TWO

THE PASSAGES YEARS

PROBABLY A CRAB WOULD BE
FILLED WITH A SENSE
OF PERSONAL OUTRAGE IF
IT COULD HEAR US CLASS IT
WITHOUT ADO OR APOLOGY AS
A CRUSTACEAN, AND THUS
DISPOSE OF IT. "I AM NO SUCH
THING," IT WOULD SAY; "I AM
MYSELF, MYSELF ALONE."

—WILLIAM JAMES

CHAPTER 19

LOVEBIRDS

THE DAY IS WHITE AS A BLANK SHEET. The windows are open and naked. A breeze caresses my face with the scent of fall. I can hear trees out there rustling. The bed is vast, unfamiliar, suitable for two, three, children and dogs. Where am I? Oh, yes. Not in Clay's world.

This is one of the first mornings in a place of my own. A friend steered me to this furnished sublet on the Upper West Side. A sprawl of a place, but sunny with polished oak floors and a full dining room, a lazy living room with deep armchairs, a marble bar in the mirrored closet, and a bedroom for Maura the size of a small kindergarten. All this for the sacrifice price of $700 a month.

Here, I feel free of the usual to-do list. I can stretch and let my mind play in the swinging door between imagination and consciousness. I am beginning to intuit the idea that will underlie my next book. When we come to a dead end, if we dare to make a major life change, we will grow from it. When one door closes, that makes room for another to open.

The doorbell rings, an unfamiliar ring. It takes a long time to roll out of this bed. Feeling like Goldilocks, I stumble to the windows and find myself looking down at the tops of trees in Central Park. I take a deep breath and count my blessings. It's autumn 1973 and I'm in a new world. Gail's world.

I PULLED ON A COTTON CHEMISE and padded barefoot down the long hall and peeked out the peephole. It was filled with a big handsome face, lots of brown curls, a much younger man than Clay. He was holding some kind of a cage.

"Who is it?" I called.

"Robin. I come bearing a bird."

"Robin? Oh my God. Robin Costelloe, how did you remember about the lovebird?"

Robin was a dreamy Irish sculptor I had met in Dublin while escaping from Bloody Sunday. I had told him how shaken up I was after coming home from Ireland to find my lovebird dead—what kind of loser couldn't even keep a bird alive? "Robin, I don't know how you found me, but you caught me sleeping later than I ever have in my life. Can you give me a few minutes to get decent?"

In that charming Irish accent that runs sentences up a hill ending in a question mark, he said, "I'll pop 'round to Chock Full o' Nuts? What kind of coffee would you be liking?"

What crossed through my mind was: *Do I really want to open this door? I've just closed the door on one life in order to find the solitude that a writer needs to do an important piece of work. Maura has more of her mother here and we have a whole park across the street as our front yard.* All I wanted to do was take my daughter to the park and teach her how to ride a bike. And while she was having a playdate, I'd sit down at my brand-new board-over-fileboxes desk in the bedroom and start writing.

I went into Maura's room to wake her. "Quick, get dressed, honey! I want you to see the surprise on our new doorstep!" I pulled on jeans and a shirt. Maura squealed over the bird.

"How did it get here?"

"It's from Robin, my Irish sculptor friend. He remembered about our lovebird."

Robin returned with jelly doughnuts and coffee and a bunch of jolly yellow mums. Maura fixed the flowers while I made us eggs.

Robin was in the United States as a visiting writer at a North Carolina university. He wanted to invite me to come down for a weekend book festival that fall.

Maura asked if the bird would sit on her finger. "Oh, yes, they're very tame," Robin said. "Try it."

The baby parrot was peach faced with a green body and looked like he was blushing. We were all captivated. Who knows what false move spooked him? Suddenly he was flapping around the dining room and then disappeared. We found him in my bedroom where the windows were wide open. Maura shrieked, "He's going to fly into the park and get eaten by crows!"

"No he's not!" I said. I slammed down the windows, one after the other.

Robin, the only one with the composure to find towels, led us in the chase. It turned into a great scramble with the poor bird squawking and flapping. Each of us failed by inches until Maura delicately dropped a blanket over the bird. The noise stopped. I lifted him back into his cage and covered it to calm him down. Up until this point, I had sworn to be guided by the Chinese proverb about cultivating creativity, "Before spontaneity comes discipline." I was pretty good at discipline. Robin was all spontaneity. His presence reminded me that we need a healthy dose of both.

OVER THE NEXT YEARS, I enjoyed an emancipated bachelor woman's life.

Traveling for research and speaking engagements brought me in contact with intriguing new men. Like most women in their mid- to late thirties, I was probably at the peak of my physical attractiveness. And being single, I was shamelessly flirtatious. The senator often came up to New York, and our romance blossomed, but like a day lily, not a perennial. I enjoyed dates with a dashing foreign correspondent, and dinners prepared by a documentary TV producer, curly headed and concupiscent, who once danced me through a rainstorm on the beach. My friend Chota at Air India introduced me to his eclectic clan of diplomats, filmmakers, and foodie friends. And how could I forget the painter with the body of a ballet dancer?

As I sit here collecting these memories into a list, I realize that it may sound as though they were superficial flings. On the contrary. They all evolved from infatuations into relationships and grew into lifelong friendships that I cherish. And then there was Jack and the spell of Sligo in the Celtic twilight.

Jack Deacy, a red-bearded Irishman with a perpetual laugh, was a writer I met while we were both contributing to the Irish issue of *New York*. When I was offered the loan of a house in Dublin by an Irish government official, it seemed curative to go back to Ireland under more promising circumstances. Once ensconced in an elegant Georgian town house with a lovely garden and mild weather, I yearned to throw a party. I discovered that Deacy was in Dublin and invited him. He brought along the actors and playwrights and newspaper people he knew. It turned into a long, lugubrious night at the end of which Clay called from London to ask me to join him for the weekend at David Frost's. Deacy answered the phone. Clay was not pleased. Assuming that I was having a flaming affair—and worse, with another Irishman—he accused me of betrayal.

"But I can't have an affair—we're not married!"

As the English say, I might as well be hung for a sheep as a lamb. Deacy wanted to show me the west of Ireland. We drove up to Yeats country, reading to each other from *The Collected Poems of W. B. Yeats*. After driving around the shivering deep blue of Lough Gill, we found a beautiful old hotel, the Abbey Inn, in Dromahair. We had just finished reading a Yeats poem about Dromahair, "The Man Who Dreamed of Faeryland." Deacy had an uncle, a musician-farmer, who lived nearby. He brought his traditional Celtic band to the hotel to play for us. The frenetic tin whistling and reel after reel of furious thumping on goatskin drums got us up and dancing until we ran out of breath. When we walked outside for air, astonished at the green of the fields lit by the full moon of a late Celtic twilight, we noticed a two-story stucco house next door. A For Rent sign hung on it.

I dreamed that night of living in this magical land.

The next day we met the genial owner of the hotel, Jack McGoldrick. He showed us the house with its six bedrooms and kitchen and commodious common room. If we knew any Americans who wanted an inexpensive getaway, with a bar and restaurant right next door . . . the owner had read my mind. When something sounds too good to be true, it probably is. But by then, I was hopelessly beguiled by the poetic Irish soul and the mellow beauty of Yeats country.

"What if we got some of our Irish writer friends to go in together and rent the place?" I said to Deacy over our picnic lunch. "We all need an inspiring oasis to write our books—each of us could maybe take it for part of the year."

"A writers' collective; I like it," Deacy enthused.

And then we read another Yeats poem. I can't resist reprinting the final stanza of "The Song of Wandering Aengus":

> Though I am old with
> wandering
> Through hollow lands and
> hilly lands,
> I will find out where she has gone,
> And kiss her lips and take her
> hands;
> And walk among long dappled
> grass,
> And pluck till time and times are
> done,

> The silver apples of the moon,
> The golden apples of the sun.

Why wait until we were "old with wandering" to make this little dream come true? The poem had given us a title for the writers' house. Mr. McGoldrick, an uncommonly enterprising man, showed up the next morning with our title freshly painted on a sign.

GOLDEN APPLES OF THE SUN

SILVER APPLES OF THE MOON

A WRITERS' COLLECTIVE

Then he quoted an unbelievably reasonable tariff. That clinched it. I telephoned Pete Hamill—he loved the idea—and Dennis Duggan, the bureau chief of *New York Newsday*—he couldn't wait. It was agreed we would each take four months of the year. Before Deacy and I left, Mr. McGoldrick brought around his finest horse. "Would your daughter fancy him?" he asked. As I looked on the noble black stallion, haughty but friendly, all rationality deserted me. Maura loved horses and had been riding since she was a young child. A penny was pressed into my hand and I pressed it back into the owner's hand, sealing the deal, Irish style. I went back to New York with a house and a horse. Of course, when it came time to collect for the shares in the house, everybody backed out.

I was able to negotiate my way out of the rental, but I was responsible for the animal's keep, and he ate like a horse! Keeping him in hay was costing more than I paid for the meatless spaghetti that kept my child and me fed while I wrote the book. Fortunately, my good friend Tom Baer, a top-tier corporate lawyer, offered to take on, pro bono, what he called "the Dobbin case." He saved me from a lifetime of supporting Dobbin.

MAURA WAS AT THE AGE to leave the relaxed, nurturing environment of Grace Church elementary school and move up to middle school. To my delight, she was accepted at the Brearley School, an all-girls enclave with a sterling reputation. This was one of my most cherished dreams: to provide my daughter with a first-class education. I used the full palette of the con artist in every good reporter to persuade my bank officer to give me a loan: "If you help me to pay for my daughter's private schooling, I'll give you my first mortgage." He laughed, he sympathized, he signed. If I could give my child a better start in life than I had, I would work my heart out for the rest of my life to pay for it.

"Mommy, you gotta believe me, it's like a game with too many rules," Maura whimpered after the first few days at Brearley. The school had exceptionally high expectations for each student to shine. Maura was bothered by a not-so-subtle class bias against anyone who didn't belong to the privileged East Side establishment. Some of the mothers wouldn't let their girls cross town to play with her, as if the West Side was some depraved lower depths populated by theater people, artists, writers, musicians, and flaming former Trotskyites (which it was).

Even though I was there every day when she came home, Maura did not have my full attention. When her eager face tipped up and the flood of words burst forth describing her day, my mind might still be tangled up in the knot of a chapter that I couldn't unravel. Or fretting about how to pay the bills that week. When my bank balance was precarious, I would have to scare up a magazine assignment and rush off to profile a newsmaker. The life of a freelance writer is a roller coaster, but the ride shifts from full speed to sudden jolting stops. I was exhilarated by the scope of the book I had undertaken. But most of the time during Maura's childhood, while I was struggling to find my way as a single mother, I looked only for external validation. I desperately needed to be successful as a writer. That was the ticket to self-esteem, since I had failed at marriage and was only half a parent.

I relied on Maura during those dutiful ages of nine to twelve to Xerox and file and assuage the volatile moods of an isolated freelance writer. My flashes of temper were sudden and sometimes extreme, like an Irish cloudburst. For me, moments later I could feel the shaft of sunlight, a calming. Yet anyone who had experienced that storm would feel drenched in apprehension and anger, and not fully safe around me again. I never blamed Maura, but being a child, she naturally felt somehow responsible for my distress. She was my comforter. When I slammed the closet door, she would write me a note saying she was sorry to have upset me, when she hadn't. She took care of me as much as I took care of her. It wasn't a fair swap.

What stays most vividly in my memory about those next three years is how attached Maura and I became once Clay's demands no longer came between us. Her personality began to bloom. She had always made friends easily. Maura had a double set of intuitive antennae, reading people better than I could, inhaling everything deeply: adult conversations, dramatic plays, books. When we went skiing with a controversial author (who wrote for Clay), Jerzy Kosinski, and his girlfriend, Maura became engrossed in Kosinski's most phantasmagorical novel, *The Painted Bird*. She couldn't be pried off her air mattress until she'd finished all 234 pages. "That's the best novel I ever read," she told the author over dinner. It was the first adult novel she had ever read. She was only ten, but she got it.

Maura had a droll sense of humor. I loved seeing through her eyes the comical side of what was going on around us. And she certainly saw the comedy of me. She kept after me to give up cigarettes. "I'll stop as soon as I finish this story," I must have said countless times. One day she crossed her arms and stared at me: "Mom, writers are never finished." That stopped me.

We got our first dog, a Lhasa apso, and named her Ms. in recognition of the new feminist appellation. Ms. went sledding with us on snow days and snuggled with us while Maura and I read together. I often fell asleep beside her. Then, around nine or so, a second wind would send me back to my bedroom and my brand-new IBM Selectric typewriter. Chewing on celery sticks and carrots, I would write until past midnight.

In the fall of '73 I had to go on a tour for *Hustling,* my book on the world of prostitution. It started with my first national TV appearance, on the late-night Jack Paar show. It was a disaster. The aging comedian had planted a prostitute in the studio who shouted insults at me for exposing a "noble profession." I called my mother right after the show to ask how badly I'd handled it.

Her answer spoke volumes. "I'm flying up to New York, honey. I'll go with you on your tour." How wonderful to have a mother who was now well and was able to be there for me.

But I had developed a fear of flying. Not the kind Erica Jong made famous with her startling book of that name. It wasn't the "zipless fuck" that I was afraid of; it was death. Immediately following the traumas in Ireland, I had fled home on a turbulent flight and my anxieties became attached to flying. "Conversion reaction," they call it. After appearing on *The Phil Donahue Show,* the flight between Dayton and Cincinnati through an electrical storm was a nine on the terror scale. My mother and I bailed on the connecting flight to New York and took a sleeper train. It was so bumpy, my mother fell out of her berth. The next morning I developed a new appreciation for a smooth jet plane ride to New York. And a surge of appreciation for my sweet sober mother. I took her to lunch at the Four Seasons and put her on a plane back to Florida.

I needed a wife.

God answered my prayers. She came in a guise that I didn't recognize, as so often happens with God doings. When I opened the door for Ella Council, a dark-skinned African American woman sent by a household employee agency, my first thought was, *This won't work*. We sat together on the sofa and had coffee and the interview was more than satisfactory. But I couldn't ignore the elephant in the room.

"Ms. Council, let me be frank. Do you think, at this time of racial tensions, that a black woman can work for a white woman and not burn with resentment?"

Ella Council tilted her head and surveyed my face, then tilted her head the other way and stared me straight in the eye, and said, "Ms. Sheehy, I like your smile."

Gail's support system: Ella Council and Gail's sister, Pat (Trish) Klein.

That was it. Almost. Ella and I had to test each other. Two weeks after she started, her Harlem apartment was robbed. Shaken, she asked to borrow the money to buy a decent security alarm; she would pay it back from her next paycheck. When she did, our bond of trust was sealed. Ella Council turned herself inside out to be my household manager, and when I traveled, she slept in to be Maura's surrogate mother. She would stick by me, and I by her, for the next thirty-six years.

CLAY HAD HIS OWN FLINGS, with Barbra Streisand (I think) when she was flogging the dubious talents of her hairstylist boyfriend, Jon Peters, and wanted Clay to publish an article he had written about producing her remake of the film *A Star Is Born*. Clay played with the fire of mother-daughter rivalry by dating Kay Graham's daughter, Lally Weymouth. As an Anglophile, he was easily captivated by the talented English novelist Sally Beauman, until she tried to browbeat him into espousing her Eaton Square Marxist views. Years later, I was touched to read a letter that his ex-wife, Pamela Tiffin, had written to him during that period of our estrangement. "I hear that you have stopped seeing Gail Sheehy. Don't be foolish. She is a woman of fine character and great talent. Be good to her."

The magnetism between Clay and me never did subside. Although we gave ourselves to others, we never gave up on each other. Once I buckled down to doing the research for the book on couples, I made a point of staying away from him, even from the editorial lunches he held at the Palm restaurant. I missed seeing the "family." I missed giggling when Clay's attention would be occupied by the slow transit of a slab of steak while he tried to listen to the drone of a boring mayoral candidate, his chin bobbing up and down to his chest, until he dozed off. I missed *him*.

Rumors swirled that Clay had bought the *Village Voice*. All the *New York* magazine contributors were summoned to the office for an important editorial meeting. I wrestled with myself but finally went. I said little at the meeting and avoided his glance. Stepping out of the closet-size toilet room, I was surprised to see him waiting for me. Would I ride uptown with him? I was speechless. My stomach wrenched like an old-fashioned washing machine, go, don't go, yes, go, no no. He picked up my work bag and slid an arm around my back, his hand warm and possessive against a place that had not felt a man's hand in a while.

As he got into the taxi behind me, he blurted, "It was so painful and exquisite to have you in my office again today. I was overwhelmed by longing. Gail, we're part of each other. We're each other's history."

I must have given him a cool and guarded look, so defended was I against falling into another loop of passion followed by his retreat from commitment. Outside of his building, he stood on the curb with the cab door open. "I just have to run in and pick up my bags. I'm going to Europe for a week's vacation."

"How nice, with whom?"

"With myself."

"What a waste."

The mask of command slid off to reveal a boy's eyes pleading for affection. "You wouldn't ride out to the airport with me, would you?"

I hesitated. The churning. The door stood open.

"Hey, mistuh, you goin' or comin', I gotta start the meter again."

"Run the meter and keep the lady happy," he told the cabbie and, smiling, disappeared into his building.

Once inside the taxi, he resumed his role as my mentor. Had Dutton agreed to let me change the focus of the book from couples to the stages of adulthood? Yes. How was the writing going? It felt like swimming the English Channel. Would I still write for him? Of course. Suddenly, his head was nudging into my shoulder, his mouth nibbling my lips. He was hungering for the very certainty from which he would surely later back away. He said he was hoping his vacation in Europe would give him time to decide.

"But I've already decided," I said.

He didn't give me time to talk. He pulled me into his arms. "I don't want to lose you." He pulled his raincoat over us. We fondled and stroked each other. The world dissolved. I felt my power, the power women have to make men fall in love with us.

"Oh, Gail, you are the center of my life."

"You want the center of my life to be your world. I can't give you that now. I've been giving myself to the book and it's working."

"Can I still see you?"

"From time to time."

At the airport, he opened his wallet and showed me my picture. "I always carry it with me." A quick peck on the cheek. I watched from the cab as he disappeared through the glass doors of the BOAC terminal.

CHAPTER 20

BIRTHING *PASSAGES*

CLAY AND I WERE SEPARATED, but not really; still crazy in love, but reluctant to make a commitment—oh, so very avant-garde. Much wilder experimentation was going on among women and men in the 1970s—casual sex, communes, open marriages, living together, bachelor mothers, gay and lesbian liaisons, and even some church weddings—leaving the very idea of what constitutes a couple open to question.

My *New York* magazine article "Can Couples Survive?" had attracted book offers. Sam Cohn, my fabled ICM literary agent, was not your ordinary cigar-chomping salesman. During tense book auctions he chewed paper. He didn't have to chew very long to win a contract for me with E. P. Dutton for an "untitled work about couples." My advance was a modest $9,375. When and if the manuscript was accepted, I would get a second payment in the same amount, and a final payment on publication. This would not be an easy birth. Labor pains would probably last for three years. My advance would put me below poverty level. But I was thrilled.

Once I had the advance I went on a spending binge, but not for designer shoes and showy jewelry. I blew a wad on tomes I ordered from Foyle's, the famed British bookstore, and then slogged through all of Freud, and the antidote, the works of Carl Jung. This launched my lifelong habit of catch-up self-education. Freud, of course, had handed down the assumption that our personality is pretty much determined by the time we reach the age of five. I enjoyed a little shrug of insubordination by dismissing this canon of the twentieth century. Longitudinal studies that I consulted showed that most people did change from one period of adult life to another. Sometimes radically. Historical biographies revealed even more dramatic evidence of people who made a leap of growth from one stage of life to another, or, by contrast, suffered through periods of stagnation or regression.

With the advance, I was able to cast my net more widely for men and women of all ages to interview. My subjects were recommended by friends. I usually met them for our two-hour sessions in cheap, brightly lit Chinese restaurants. Once the first forty interviews were transcribed, I began to see a larger theme emerging. In similar comments made by both women and men in their late thirties and early forties, I heard evidence of a period of disequilibrium:

"I have a hurry-up feeling."

"Time is running out."

"Is that all there is?"

Suddenly I had an insight. None of my subjects had actually experienced a life-threatening event or been exposed to an external trauma like Bloody Sunday in Northern Ireland. Yet I found evidence in every one of them of discontent, ranging all the way from mild to a full-blown crisis. I came across a paper by Elliott Jaques, a Canadian psychoanalyst, which introduced me to a new concept. Dr. Jaques had studied the careers of many artists and composers and found leaps of creativity or declines in productivity between the ages of thirty-five and forty. He coined the term "midlife crisis."

At the deepest level, a midlife crisis was triggered by the first awareness of mortality. For some among my subjects, it was when they went home after a long absence and were shocked to see that Mom or Dad had crossed over from high speed to low velocity. *Oh my God, if it could happen to them, it could happen to me. I'm not going to live forever!* Most of the people I interviewed in their forties had to give up some illusions around the dream of their twenties. Some realized they really hated what they were doing or had outgrown their marriage. To give up after all that investment felt a little like a rehearsal of dying. I wrote that it was normal to feel a "little death" at some point in midlife or, for some people, in later middle age. But that was the precursor to growing a new life on the other side, what I would later name our "Second Adulthood."

The great hope I found in this work was to see that *change,* which most of us fear, was *good.* How could I present change in a more positive light? One night in a seafood shack on the Sag Harbor dockside, I found myself staring at a tank full of lobsters of all sizes. One little critter had wriggled out of his shell and was suddenly a pale, translucent, trembly blob. I looked up the evolution of crustaceans. This is how lobsters grow, I learned, by developing and shedding a series of hard, protective shells. Each time it expanded from within, the confining shell was sloughed off. The lobster was left exposed and embryonic again, until it grew stronger and developed a new shell to replace the old.

In that tank was a perfect analogy! We, too, shed an old self as we grow and expand our personalities. For us, a transition may take several years or more. Coming to the end of a transition, we enter a longer and more stable period in which we can expect a sense of equilibrium regained.

It was tempting to tie our transitions to *marker events.* Graduations, getting or losing a job, marriage, children's births, divorce, parents' deaths, and retirement are the concrete happenings of our lives. But a developmental stage was not defined in terms of marker events—it was defined by a change that began from *within,* whether or not it was accentuated by a marker event.

As I gathered more life histories, I found myself drawn to a subject infinitely more complicated than couples. Not only were there other critical turning points than at midlife, but they came up with some

Gail pitching Clay, ca. 1986. ©2014 *The Estate of Cosmos Andrew Sarchiapone*

Clay at *New York,* ca. 1970:
"I'll make you a star."
©Burton Berinsky/Landov Media

Gail at *New York,* 1969.
Author shot for "The
Amphetamine Explosion."
*Photograph by Dan Wynn/Courtesy
Demont Photo Management*

The *New York* magazine "family" in their 100-foot-long garret.
(*Left to right:*) Dottie Seiberling, Walter Bernard, Milton Glaser,
Aaron Latham, unknown (*partially hidden*), Clay Felker.

©2014 *The Estate of Cosmos Andrew Sarchiapone*

Tom Wolfe in full regalia,
ca. 1970. ©2014 *The Estate of Cosmos
Andrew Sarchiapone*

The Pursuit of Social Realis...

Horse race of the New Journalists. This illustration by Arnold Roth, titled "The Pursuit of Social Realism on the Field of Fame, 1972," appeared in Esquire magazine and depicts the leading practitioners of what was known as "the New Journalism," including *(left to right:)* Jack Newfield, John Sack, Michael Herr, Pete Hamill, Jimmy Breslin, Hunter Thompson, Norman Mailer, Terry Southern, Gay Talese, Tom Wolfe, and Gail Sheehy (the sole female representative, leading the pack).

The hound being trampled by the New Journalists' horses is labeled "The Underground Press"; the leading hounds are labeled *(top to bottom:)*

Esquire, The New Yorker, Harper's, The Atlantic, and *New York.* Their quarry, the fox: "Social Realism." Note the abandoned hound to the rear of John Sack: *Life* magazine, which ceased weekly publication in 1972.

In the back, to the left, is a group leaving the hunt, labeled "American Novelists." Breaking off from them and trying to catch up with the New Journalists are Gore Vidal, William Styron, Truman Capote, George Plimpton, and James Agee. Above Agee, on a cliff, are "The Critics." © *2014 Arnold Roth*

"Redpants and Sugarman" cover story by Gail, 1971. ©*New York Media LLC*

"The Midlife Crisis" cover story by Gail, 1974. ©*New York Media LLC*

Tom Wolfe's iconic *New York* cover, "Radical Chic," 1970.
©*New York Media LLC*

Debut of *Ms.* magazine inside *New York*, 1972.
©*New York Media LLC*

Gail writing *Passages,* 1975. *Courtesy of the author*

regularity at around the same ages. People would describe feeling unfamiliar stirrings, sometimes surprising changes of perspective, often mysterious dissatisfactions with the course they had been following with enthusiasm only a few years before. Those times were often followed by surges of creativity or accelerated personality growth.

It was an *aHa!* moment. We didn't just move from the whirl of adolescence into one long boring plateau until we hit senescence. We continued to grow through stages of development. I began to see turning points, or crises, in adult life that were *predictable.*

ERIK ERIKSON HAD LAID OUT the original concept that adulthood continues to proceed by stages of development throughout the life cycle. Each stage, he proposed, was associated with a specific psychological struggle. For example, the struggle of the twenties is between intimacy and isolation. Erikson had laid out eight stages across the life span. He ascribed only three stages to adulthood, sketching them out very loosely, inviting others to fill out the picture.

The budding social scientist in me was thrilled to hear a graying professor of social psychology from Yale, Daniel Levinson, give a symposium on "Normal Crises of the Middle Years." Dr. Levinson and his team had been studying forty men in different occupations between the ages of eighteen and forty-seven. He proposed that adults, like children and adolescents, continue to develop by periods. Each period engages them in specific tasks. His study found that men only moved on to the next period of development when they began working at a new task and built a new structure for their lives.

I approached Dr. Levinson for guidance on how to work with the biographical method. He generously offered to read some of the biographies I had been collecting. We met several times. "They're excellent interviews with lots of good quotes," he told me. "Which means you're getting the person in his fullness or emptiness." That gave me confidence. "But when they want to talk about something important, let them go on." That made me wonder whether I would be a geriatric case before I could transcribe all the tapes.

The rigidity of Dr. Levinson's thesis bothered me. He proposed that each stage of development had to follow as A to B. One could not jump from A to C, or postpone the tasks of B while dealing with the challenges of C. I argued that most women had to dodge and weave around their husbands' career paths. And when women had children, they usually put their own development on hold and only later tried to catch up.

"If women are expected to pursue the same linear track that you are laying out for men, wouldn't that drive both of them crazy?"

Levinson laughed. "That's nice—that fits." He concluded that it probably was not possible for a woman to work out a combination of two careers—domestic and professional—until she was thirty or thirty-five. "The chances are that by the time she has begun to arrive at the integration necessary to do it all, so many other things have gone haywire that she has probably divorced or the family has been impaired in ways that can't be fully remedied."

"Thanks a lot!" I exclaimed. "But we can't just write off the struggle of women to combine roles as leading to divorce or family impairment. Who is studying the developmental patterns of women's lives?" I asked.

Dr. Levinson shook his head. "Nobody." He encouraged me to take on that inquiry. His groundbreaking book, *Seasons of a Man's Life,* would be published in 1978.

The subject of adult development was only beginning to germinate. When I sought out researchers at Harvard, Berkeley, and UCLA, I was startled to find that almost no cross-pollination had taken place. What little research I found was being done by men who were studying other men.

How could we possibly expect to understand the development of men until we also learned about the women who raised them? The women they love and hate, and depend on, and who are dependent upon them.

The old, closed family structure showed signs of cracking. With the publication in 1971 by the Boston Women's Collective of the breakthrough book *Our Bodies, Ourselves,* women were beginning to take control of their anatomy, open their minds, and strike out into unfamiliar territory to pioneer new ways of living in the world.

That led me to wonder: Did men and women go through similar stages at the same time? Obviously not. They were often out of sync. What would that mean for couples? These ideas became a lens through which I saw my friends, my parents, and myself and Clay.

I asked Clay if he hadn't noticed that men often hit a crisis point in their midforties when they might have to give up the illusion of a grand, youthful dream. He realized that he was seeing it all the time in younger men who worked for him; when their lofty expectations were not met, they hardened into resentment. This predictable period of de-illusioning for men, I proposed, might well coincide with a predictable phase of re-imagining for their wives. With their children semi-independent, women often returned to school in their mid- to late forties to complete their own education and give birth to new dreams. A man's lapse into stagnation might hit the couple just as his wife is feeling a sense of exhilaration, having finally completed her business degree, and is raring to open a boutique.

This suggested a natural dyssynchrony between men's and women's development. If I could make clear that this was normal, it might lead couples out of conflict and toward cooperation. He supports her new dream—she will, in turn, support his. That struck Clay as a premise worth serious investigation. He asked me to write about midlife as a crisis time for couples. I had to smile. He and I were prime suspects.

There was another challenge: how to describe the times of turmoil in between the more stable periods of adult life. They are not always crises. It is in these bumpy transitions that we have the opportunity to make a leap of growth. But what to call them? I tried all kinds of names. It would take another two years before I found the right word.

IN THE MIDST OF ALL THIS YEASTY INTELLECTUAL FERMENT, my wonderful editor, Hal Scharlatt, dropped dead on the tennis court. "He was only forty-three!" bemoaned the shaken publisher of Dutton, Jack Macrae, who called me the same day. Since Macrae was of similar age, this tragedy took on an exaggerated value in his mind. Weeks later, he invited me to lunch and offered to take over as my editor. By now, the book was exploding in my mind and had taken on a theme much larger than the relationship between couples.

"How large?" he asked with a worried frown.

"As large as adulthood itself," I said, smiling as if I were joking. Before I explained, I had to get him into the tent. So I interviewed him about his life. That intrigued him. Then I spelled out three objectives for the book. The first was to locate the individual's *inner* changes in a world in which most of us are preoccupied with externals. The second aim was to compare the developmental patterns of women with those of men. It was a natural progression to the third objective: What, then, were the predictable crises for couples? He was hooked.

As I began turning in chapters, Macrae handed them off to someone I had never met. He said she was an offsite copy editor who would ultimately save us time while I continued to write. But customarily, a copy editor is not involved until the editor has finished working over the manuscript with the writer—for structure, tone, voice, and where to cut—all the elements that make the real difference in quality of the work. Copy editing is about grammar and continuity. My early chapters were coming back badly bruised with the copy editor's blue pencil marks; I called her the Blue Meanie.

The very first section, which described my brush with mortality in Northern Ireland and my breakdown of nerve, was crossed out completely. "They'll think you're crazy" was the Blue Meanie's comment. I asked Macrae if I could at least talk to this copy editor. He declined, advising that it was better to keep the relationship strictly professional. I held my ground on the first chapter, pointing out that my personal experience with a traumatic passage was the foundation of my credibility. After I rewrote that chapter at least twenty times and showed it to Macrae himself, he accepted my argument.

I began to suspect that the Blue Meanie was not an offsite copy editor but an in-house editor, smart and prickly with her own point of view. Over my chapter about women's life patterns she had scrawled, "All your women are wimps! You need some hotshot younger women."

With a slightly devious plan in mind, I waited one day until the occupants of Dutton's editorial offices spilled out for what was the leisurely two-martini lunch, typical of those times. Cruising in and out of offices, I scanned for handwriting that matched the Blue Meanie's. There it was—at the desk of a junior editor. After lunch, playing dumb, I told Macrae that I needed to find a trailblazing young woman to flesh out my interviews. Would he have anybody like that on his staff?

That is how I met Laurie Colwin. I asked to interview her for the book. Peppery with a sharply angled face softened by a corona of dark curls, this was a woman in her early thirties who had many passions—for writing the great American novel, for cooking, for love. At nineteen she had made a jailbreak from her possessive family, dropped out of college, left the older man with whom she had been living, and found a job as an editorial assistant.

Where did this confidence come from? I asked.

It wasn't confidence, Colwin said. It was determining clearly what she *didn't* want to be. "I wasn't going to end up like the kids I knew in the suburbs."

She sold her first short story to *The New Yorker* at twenty-five and ran off with another man, believing it was a blazing love, and hit the ground rather hard when it fell apart—a typical Catch-30 passage. Now thirty-two, she had fallen in love again. Her first novel was receiving good reviews. But for all her boldness and persistence in pursuing a singular career path, Colwin wrestled with the same conflict that bedeviled me and legions of other women who wanted to make something of ourselves. All along she wondered, "Why couldn't I have been the sort of person who just settles down and doesn't give anyone a moment's trouble, meaning, have a baby and the whole thing." She kicked off a shoe as if in exasperation with herself. "I didn't want it! But I felt I *should* have."

At her happiest, she disregarded "the shoulds" that I had written come from the imprint of one's peers. She had pursued her own dream. "In my most unhappy moments, I would say, 'Well, it's clear you're just nuts and no one will ever have you.' But I was always very smart, cold, clear and uncomplicated about my own work. I love to write. I want to have everything. And I don't see why I can't."

I saw in Laurie Colwin a harbinger of the New Woman. She built a devoted audience through her five novels, married an editor at thirty-eight, and found the courage to open her heart to the risk of intimacy. She had a baby after forty, which in the days before the reproductive revolution was considered just short of magic. Entering midlife, she found a way to balance mature love with creative success and family.

TOWARD THE END OF MY RESEARCH in the second year, I flew to Los Angeles to interview a psychiatrist, Roger Gould, who had done a preliminary study of white, middle-class people, including women from ages sixteen to sixty. He invited me to talk at his home in Beverly Hills. Once I described my thesis to him and the broad research I was doing, he became keenly interested. He proposed that we collaborate on the book. I was startled. For more than ten years I had been an independent writer.

The psychiatrist was relentless. He insisted that I needed him because no one would take me seriously. "You're just a journalist," he said with undisguised scorn. Those words were lifted right out of the mind chatter in my brain. The psychiatrist had no trouble locating my weak spot; he struck at the vulnerability all writers feel. But a voice inside me shouted, *No!*

I politely dismissed the idea of collaborating. To soften this rejection, I foolishly agreed to allow Dr. Gould to read some of the case histories I was collecting. He sent me some of his interpretations.

In my third year of work, I ran out of money. The Alicia Patterson Foundation came to my rescue with a $10,000 fellowship to enable me to write the book. My obligation for the fellowship was to write for its free newsletter, the *APF Reporter.* In an article about several academic researchers, I quoted Dr. Gould. *New York* magazine reprinted my pro bono article. The psychiatrist then resumed his campaign to convince me to take him on as a collaborator. His threat rang in my ears: *No one will take you seriously—you're just a journalist.*

I sensed what Erikson meant when he described each stage of adult development as marked by a crisis. "Crisis" connoted not a catastrophe, but rather, *an inner impulse toward change,* a crucial period of increased vulnerability and heightened potential. Something important has changed in the way we think about the meaning of our participation in the external world. At such points either achievements are won or failures occur. It signals that we know ourselves better.

This was just what I was writing about: questions of how our values, goals, and aspirations are circumstances invigorated—or violated—by the present being of our lives. How do we balance family and social roles with our work, our purpose? Is there a rising fire of individual expression that we can no longer deny?

Yes! It was rising within me. If I had been ready to break free of Clay as my mentor, I should be ready to take the leap of faith and be my own author. My final conversation with Dr. Gould was a textbook example of a concept that we had discussed. As adults, we often re-place the "inner dictator"—our leftover parents' voices—with a mate or boss or mentor we cast as "the strong one."

"I believe I have outgrown the need for a strong one," I heard myself calmly telling the psychiatrist. "You don't need me, either. We both have a clear point of view. We can both write our own books." It was my personal declaration of independence. And it felt good.

Imagine the shock, then, when the psychiatrist sued me. His in-tention was to enjoin publication of my book—before I had even finished writing it! The claim was that I had plagiarized him in the newsletter article. The charge was patently absurd. I had quoted him in a pro bono newsletter with full attribution. Everyone at *New York* magazine, including the attorney, was appalled.

But I was dead broke. I couldn't afford an attorney to defend myself. A family market around the corner gave me an account to charge food and was lenient on being paid. Ella found an apartment across the street so she could sleep in when needed. She stretched my budget by making veggie burgers with salad for suppers for Maura and me. Mornings I powered up by holding my nose to drink a god-awful health potion with yeast, called Adele Davis's Milk Pep-Up. Evenings I was often cheered by my warmhearted neighbor, Muriel Bedrick. She would bring over a casserole or leftover cake from one of her three daughters' birthdays. A poet herself, Muriel read drafts of my book and found the perfect verse to illuminate each of the seven stages.

My accountant strongly advised that I offer the psychiatrist some-thing to make his suit go away. Certain that my book would never make any money, I offered Dr. Gould 10 percent of my royalties. Dumb mistake? Yes, but what was the alternative? To be stopped two-thirds of the way through gestating a book was unthinkable. I had to deliver.

IT HAD BEEN A BRUTAL YEAR. When summer 1975 came around, I needed solace. Clay appealed to me to share weekends with him again. Being together in the sweet rented house in Wainscott contented Maura and me, all three of us.

By August, Jack Macrae was coming out to work with me in all-day editing sessions. After five o'clock, Macrae and I would be fainting from the heat. Biking to the beach, we would climb up to the lifeguard's chair to find a breeze, survey the ocean, and talk of anything but the book.

When I finished the first full draft in mid-December of '75, I was shocked by its heft. Almost one thousand double-spaced pages. Macrae told me it needed to be cut by at least one-quarter. And this massive editing job had to be accomplished in three weeks to meet the production deadline. I had to hire a freelance editor, Carol Rinzler, to help me slash without burning. We worked every night from 8 P.M. to 1 A.M. Then I had to hire two typists to perform the equivalent of a twin-piano act as they banged out fifty pages of notes and sources for an on-time delivery.

Macrae invited me to the Four Seasons for a celebratory lunch. Over flutes of champagne, my publisher raised a burning question, one I had been evading for months.

"Well, what's the title?"

I had played with every variation on changes, transitions, stages, you name it. Sitting there, eyes closed, mind relaxed, a name for my baby leaped to mind at the last moment.

"Passages."

Macrae looked puzzled. It was such an unfamiliar use of the word. "They'll think it means 'excerpts.'"

With a confidence that surprised me, I said, "Until they read the book."

CHAPTER 21

FEAR OF FAILURE OR FEAR OF SUCCESS?

MARCH 1976. THE COUNTDOWN WAS ON. Three months before *Passages* was to be published, *Time* magazine was sending its back-of-the-book editor to my apartment with a photographer. It would be my very first interview in a national publication. I suited up in my best jeans, boots, and a fitted shirt, had my hair styled as if it weren't, and set out coffee and cookies, naively imagining this would be a friendly conversation. When I opened my door, it was to a scornful man.

"I should have written this book," he growled. I had struck a fatal blow to the ego of a high-status editor of what was then the most powerful newsmagazine in the country. *Passages* had taken three years to write and thirty-seven years to live; it was not, as his article would dismiss it, a "pop phenomenon."

Clay called and with sweet conviction said, "I bleed for you, honey. I've never seen such a blatant example of male jealousy."

One Sunday I got a call about a review appearing that day in the *Chicago Tribune Book World*. It slammed the book for "a shocking lack of research." My head dropped to the kitchen counter. Fifty pages of footnotes laboriously dredged up from many hundreds of sources, typed and retyped countless times on copy paper with multiple carbons—all were ignored. Why? When publishers send out early review copies, they are labeled "uncorrected proofs" and do not include footnotes, bibliography, or index. Strict warnings are given that the reviewer must wait to get the final hardcover before writing an assessment. This critic had broken the embargo on publication date and ignored the accepted rules. What to do? Again, nothing. One can never argue with newspapers; they come out too often.

My first invitation to appear at a bookstore was in early May at a small Brentano's in Greenwich Village. I wore heels and stockings and a hot-pink cotton suit for the appearance. The sales manager gave me a chair by the window to sit in and sign books. I sat alone. I looked out the window. Nobody came. I felt like Rapunzel.

"Could I use your phone?" I asked the sales manager. I called my freelance editor, Carol Rinzler.

"I'm coming right down," she said.

She showed up within twenty minutes, stepping into the store impeccably turned out in hat and gloves. "We have reservations at the Waverly Inn," she announced, and swept me off so I could hold my head up high.

These early insults were discouraging, but friends kept surrounding me with cheerful messages and book parties. The party I remember best took Clay and me out to Sag Harbor. Our hosts were Robert Emmett Ginna and his wife, Margaret. They were both editors of taste and originality who found their way to this historic whaling town in Eastern Long Island along with a batch of *Life* magazine people. Sag Harbor and its environs were becoming a refuge for authors of the post–World War II generation such as Edgar Doctorow, Peter Matthiessen, and James Salter. I was thrilled to be in their company. Everyone asked what my next book would be. I hadn't the foggiest.

"So what *is* next?" Ginna pressed me.

"Now is what's next. I'm going to go out there and talk to everybody I can—on the street, in coffee shops, on the bus—and get them reading this book so I find out whether it speaks to them."

WORD OF MOUTH WAS ELECTRIC. For several weeks ahead of the official publication date, I spoke anywhere I was invited. I still had no experience with public speaking, but audiences grew. Dropping into the largest independent bookstore in Los Angeles, I was surprised to learn that a dozen customers had the book on order. I felt a tingle of excitement when I overheard two women at a bus stop talking about "Catch-30"; when I heard a hairstylist comparing notes with a manicurist about their "jailbreak marriages"; when I followed a political story to a plant opening and found two lunch-pail guys discussing "man-o-pause."

The only thing these folks had in common was belonging to the boomer generation. The common denominator seemed to be their excitement about the possibilities of change. Instead of being confined by old roles and rules, they found validation for busting out and trying to be something more. The book was also being introduced in a period when our culture was already fiery with protest movements by women and minorities. *Passages* was not an angry book. It encouraged revolution, but revolution from within.

The book was often labeled "pop psychology," which I took to mean it wasn't academic, it was accessible. Jack Macrae, my publisher, told me, "Great word of mouth is often touched off by books that have no precedent, like *Passages*. People like discovering a book on their own, better than having it shoved down their throats by promotion."

A great part of the book's appeal was Milton Glaser's cover design. A staircase of assorted colors had brightly colored block letters marching diagonally up the steps to spell PASSAGES. Delicious as a pack of Lifesavers, it also conveyed the promise of adult life as a progressive ascent, rather than a decline.

Most authors I asked about book tours told me they were hell. Nobody has time to read your book. You're always worried that your hair won't dry so you can look good on TV at 7 A.M. God forbid the makeup lady doesn't show up. I learned fast how to "make the eyes pop" and warm up my oatmeal-fair skin with bronzer. But once the makeup lady takes over, your eyes and lips no longer belong to you. They are her creation. When you catch a glimpse on the monitor of hooker-heavy eyelids or chimp lips, it's too late to cry, "That's not me!"

You move across country on an invisible conveyor belt, appearing every morning on a facsimile of the *Today* show. A pair of hosts who look identical to yesterday's hosts apparently move along the time zones just ahead of you. They always seem to be called Sandy and Dave. After engaging in essentially the same patter from Philadelphia to Dallas, I once dozed off during a commercial break.

I decided that the best way to approach this new role was like an actress opening out of town. Two great costume changes and a spiral notebook full of my best anecdotes would make me feel like a pro. Oh, yes, and I would remember to lie to the makeup lady that I had a cold sore on my lips, don't touch. When my tour hit Los Angeles, Clay happened to be there on business. He took me to a boutique on Rodeo Drive. I picked out two fitted silk shirts, one pale pink, one baby blue, with matching scarves, and an orange wraparound skirt to wake up the interviewers. My "show wardrobe" cost $500, the most I'd ever spent on anything that I couldn't live in.

My first lecture about *Passages* was in a prime venue: Marin County. This was the City Arts and Lectures crowd, superhip culture vultures raised on Allen Ginsberg and Joan Didion. Roughly three hundred people were stacked in bleachers to hear me enlighten them about the "Predictable Crises of Adult Life." I was scared to death. My voice faltered. When I couldn't be heard, people started climbing down from the top rows of the bleachers and walking out. I dropped my note cards.

Finally, I noticed in the front row the wife of a man I'd written about in the book, in a chapter called "Living Out the Fantasy." Her husband had left her to live high on a commune in Mexico with a Latin dancer. Notwithstanding, she looked strong and radiant. I took strength from her and belted out the remainder of my speech. The half of the audience too polite to walk out did applaud.

I called my friend Lesley Stahl to tell her how poorly I performed. She urged me to see her speech coach. Dorothy Sarnoff was a former singer and Broadway star who had incorporated the positive rein-forcement strategies of the human potential movement. "I don't criticize," Miss Sarnoff told me off the bat. "I'll give you loving sug-gestions." She had me stand behind a lectern. "Stay on both feet, no shifting weight. Lock on my eyes; ninety percent is eye contact. Nice smile, but don't overuse it. Animate. That's it. You LOVE being here. Now give me the vibe of authority."

Then she turned on the TV camera and recorded me. Just clean-ing up the "ums" and "uhs" and "you knows" was like learning English all over again. But after three sessions, I began enjoying the experi-ence of talking through the camera to an imagined audience of one person in her living room, engaging her, persuading her, making her laugh and think. The secret was all in one's imagination.

Once the official book tour launched, I began enjoying it. Media heroines of mine, such as Susan Stamberg on National Public Radio and Nancy Dickerson at the Washington, D.C., public TV station, were such smart interviewers, they made me sound good. Milt Rosen-berg was a fixture on WGN in Chicago, where I was paired with the *Washington Post*'s gossip columnist, Sally Quinn, for two hours of small talk masquerading as social psychology.

However, some interviews were endurance contests. Newspaper-men in their twenties wanted to play Woodward and Bernstein and find the smoking gun. Men as smart as Ken Emerson interviewing me for the *Boston Phoenix* just couldn't imagine that any passages described by men over thirty would be relevant to them. They had life all figured out. I decided this is the way the young male psyche is built, which is why so many can be sent off to war without considering the possible side effects. My debates with these younger men could stretch up to two hours. The only argument I could not use was to state the obvious: That's all right . . . it's just the stage you're in.

BY JULY, THE BOOK HAD RECEIVED a very good notice in the *New York Times Sunday Book Review* and a rave in the *Washington Post*. Interview requests from notable journalists were piling up. I was sure the bubble was about to burst. This could not really be happening.

Was it fear of failure? Every writer has it. What we write is so much of who we are. To be rejected for who you are is about the worst fate one can imagine.

Fear of success? Foolish as it may sound, I suffered from it. Success is much more devious than failure. Success is the whole object of the American dream. But do people love you for it? I was fortunate in that the man in my life was totally behind my aspirations and benefited from my success as a writer. But the prospect of achieving what I most wanted—that is, to be taken seriously—could also open me to unexpected consequences.

What if, based on the observations I made in my book, people risked dramatic changes in their lives? Like divorce. What if women struck out to finish their college degrees in their forties, overshadowing their husbands, and their marriages fell apart? What if some guy quit a safe job to try a bold new career path and wiped out? Or the opposite: one man told me when he read about the Catch-30 transition, he gave up the illusion of rock stardom and was much happier as a record producer. So change could go either way. Nonetheless, I had periodic attacks of the what-ifs. What if a few years down the road, the doorbell rang and there was a line around the block of people shaking my book at me, saying: "I want my old life back! My new life stinks!"

It was time to get out of Dodge.

I COULDN'T BELIEVE MY GOOD FORTUNE when *Paris Match* offered me an expense-paid trip to France to write a comic story about how the French behave on the northern beaches of Brittany. It was a wonderful chance to take a break with Maura and have fun. We stayed in a small auberge and followed the parade of vacationers as they trudged to the beach, rain or shine, outfitted with umbrellas, short pants, striped socks, pipes, and maybe a homburg. Like Jacques Tati playing Monsieur Hulot, they moved as if in a migratory pattern essential to long life.

Back in Paris, we had a short stay at the Hotel L'Abbaye while I worked with an editor on my story. I took Maura to the Piscine Deligny. She loved doing cartwheels off the diving board as the pool rocked on its barge at the side of the Seine. I remember feeling that this was like rocking on a cloud over the peak of life.

Then it was time to drop out entirely. We pushed on to Italy to connect with my best childhood friend and her children for a holiday weekend in Venice, planning to wind up in Florence to meet Clay and steep ourselves in Renaissance art. I swore not to give *Passages* another thought.

Susan Schmedes Dando picked us up at the Venice Marco Polo Airport in her little red Fiat. Crammed in with her nearly six-foot-tall daughter, Holly, Maura's age, and her towheaded son, Evan, we had a hilarious drive to Venice. We sang along with Evan who was already writing music at age nine, songs destined to make him a rock star with his band, the Lemonheads. We caught a vaporetto across the Venetian lagoon to the island of Lido and planted ourselves by the pool of the fabulous Excelsior Hotel. For two days we alternated between watching the children swim in the pool and in the sea while Susie and I talked ourselves back to our reckless childhood selves. The burden of the book and fears of success were dissolved.

Then came a late-night call from Clay. Would I accept? Dreading the worst news, I closed my eyes as he began to speak: "You better be ready to pick up the *International Herald Tribune* tomorrow."

I knew it, another nasty review.

"You're numero uno in the *New York Times Book Review!*" he said.

I was dumbstruck. Number one? This was beyond my wildest dreams. I had expected *Passages* to sink with little trace. It wasn't written by an academic with an alphabet of letters after his name. I had thought the pleasure of research and completion of writing would be my reward.

That night Susie, the kids, and I put on fancy dress and Venetian masks and found a friendly trattoria where we could celebrate. Italian patrons were curious when they heard these boisterous Americans singing "Lucy in the Sky with Diamonds." They chimed in on *tangerine trees and marmalade skies*. What was the occasion? In my best Berlitz Italian I explained that I was a *scrivere* whose book was number one in the United States. I bought Prosecco for the house. The title was passed around. A chorus of *"Passagi!"* rang out and was incorporated into a chorus from Verdi's *Rigoletto*. This is what I most love about Italians. Any excuse to turn life into opera.

THE EXCITEMENT OF PUBLIC SUCCESS was accompanied by a disequilibrium in the privacy of my soul. The more I looked into the blind eye of a TV camera, the more I began to understand why Native Americans distrusted photographers, believing them to be voyeurs who robbed them of their spiritual identity. Although I was thrilled that the book was received as breaking new and positive ground, I hadn't figured on losing my privacy. That is to say, my normalcy. Most authors, even household names, couldn't be picked out of a lineup. The more I looked into the face of TV cameras, the more I was complicit in my transmogrification into a different life-form—a quasi celebrity.

Every one of my relationships was distorted by my new status as a bestselling author. Writer friends now saw me as competition; if I was on the bestseller list, I had stolen their rightful slot. My father now turned to me as an ATM machine. He wanted me to take out a second mortgage on his house. It would be for only a few years, he promised, until he built his own advertising business. I wanted so badly to believe him, to help him believe in himself. I could not say no. What's more, to have money for the first time in my life made me nervous. Knowing nothing about how to manage money, I was sure I would let it slip through my fingers.

These were luxury problems, of course. But I prayed for help in getting my feet back on the ground. I did not feel my uncertainties to be unique. I was a woman, like any other woman of my time, who had to discover how to make her way in a world constructed by and for men. My lot was not much different from all women and men. We have the same longings, the same fears and frustrations, the same fleeting successes and inconsolable losses, the same secret shame and muted self-doubts. I believe that if and when we face our flawed likeness, and find the courage to change what we can, we may be able to accept being merely human.

The softcover edition of *Passages* was published in 1977 by Bantam Books, the king of quality paperbacks, when that house was run by the triumvirate of Mark Jaffe, editor in chief, Oscar Dystel, president, and Esther Margolis, a publicist so clever I believe she could have outsold the Bible with *Lady Chatterley's Lover.* She booked me for feature interviews in every major and minor newspaper. Word of mouth kept spreading like wildfire. People couldn't wait to read about what stage or passage they were facing. Curiously, they rarely read *ahead* of their age; they didn't want to know. TV interviewers almost inevitably began asking about their own stage. Except for Johnny Carson. I was warned, "Don't get personal with Johnny. He'll cut you dead."

Esther suggested we go with the fun of a guessing game with Carson. "Give him a few characteristics of three major passages and let him guess which one he's in," she advised. We knew he'd want to be as young as they come, so we front-loaded the choices with the Trying Twenties. He went for it and made jokes about trying out a new identity every night, on air. I was amazed at being able to forget myself and enjoy playing the game with a genius of comedy.

"I'VE FOUND YOUR HOUSE!" It was my friend Margaret Ginna.

"My house? I'm not looking for a house."

"Yes you are." Her confidence resided in a Zen sensibility. "You hate leaving the Hamptons every fall. And now you don't have to. You've worked hard for this."

It was Labor Day weekend. I was bemoaning summer's end as I packed up the linens and pots to vacate our rented cottage. *Passages* had only been out in softcover for three months.

Clay took a look at the hundred-year-old farmhouse with Margaret and urged me to take her advice. Within a matter of minutes of seeing the secluded house and grounds, I fell in love. It was a ramble of cozy bedrooms with fireplaces, a study, and a big barn of a living room with two window walls that looked out on a rolling lawn and lots of places to plant a garden.

It was a relief to dig a hole in the sand and imagine stuffing the *Passages* money beneath a house and forgetting about it before I blew it. Who knew how long the book sales would remain strong? Besides, how could I qualify for a mortgage? I had no credit history. My friend Ted Kheel, the renowned labor lawyer, offered to vouchsafe to Chase Bank that I was not a deadbeat. The owner of the house, a Broadway producer, Fred Coe, agreed to sell me seven beds and a starter set of early-American antiques. The closing was accelerated in hopes that I could take occupancy before Thanksgiving.

NOVEMBER 27, 1977. IT'S MINE! I had waited so long for a family life, I just had to turn the house into a home—in a day. My birthday.

Up before dawn in New York, Maura and I finished packing dozens of boxes and hurled them into a rented station wagon. We took back roads, bleary with fog. "Mom! A deer! Watch out!" We barely missed brushing the white of his tail. Inside the chilly house, we emptied the boxes and flapped out seven sets of sheets to make up the beds. I lingered in each room, acquainting myself with its individual charm.

My mother and I were both embarking on new and exhilarating passages. She and her new husband, Al, were driving up the coast from their home in Florida and out to near the end of Long Island to celebrate my taking possession of my very first house on the occasion of my fortieth birthday. I wanted to celebrate my mother's emancipation into the woman she was always meant to be: a businesswoman. She now bought and redesigned houses for resale. Once released from incarceration in a cold, conformist suburb and a faithless marriage, she had recovered her self-respect in AA and become a sober woman and a contented wife. The divorced engineer she had met in the program adored her and brought his building skills to their collaboration in buying, renovating, and selling houses in Florida. All this as my mother approached sixty. She was a poster woman for a passage into the Age of Mastery.

Clay was expected on the four o'clock commuter plane at East Hampton airport. Sister Trish and her husband were coming later by train, and stepsister Susie from a different direction.

Maura had already made her signature lemon bundt cake and put it in the oven. I dashed outside to clip holly bushes bursting with red berries and found a huge copper container to display them and brighten the living room. Wood had to be chopped, the table had to be set. Oh wait! Farmer Ludlow was killing a twenty-pound fresh turkey for pickup at two. We drove to his farm. Maura helped me lug the bird in through the kitchen door, watch out! Ms., our emotionally needy Lhasa apso, got tangled up in our feet. A resident raccoon was flushed from the laundry room. Just then tires could be heard chewing the gravel as my mother and Big Al approached.

I greeted them with hot cider and cinnamon sticks and shortbread cookies. My mother surveyed the living room and sweetly dissembled: "I can't believe you have everything in place." I took her by the hand to the piano. Clay arrived in time to set the fire as Mother was warbling her third chorus of "Indian Love Call." *I am calling you-who-who-who-ooh-ooh-ooh . . .* I was seven again, accompanying her on the piano my father almost killed her for buying at auction so we could make music together. *That means I offer my love to you-who-who-who-ooh-ooh-ooh . . .* We took a simple supper by the fire. After tucking everyone in, I snuck outside to circle my new home and murmur prayers of thanksgiving. Looking back from the fringe of woods under a clouded moon, the hulk of white became the silhouette of a cruise ship. The ocean was close, licking and gnawing at the shore. We were safe. How long I had waited to reconstruct the lovely chaos of family life.

Inside, in the dark of a hall, Maura surprised me. She hugged me tightly, her cheeks hot and damp; this would not be another solitary Thanksgiving. "Oh, Mommy, I love it! This house makes up for all the moving around—and it's going to work!"

PASSAGES REMAINED ON THE BESTSELLER LIST of the *New York Times* for three years straight. It was published in twenty-eight languages and went through countless reprintings. A survey by the Library of Congress named it "one of the ten most influential books of our time."

CHAPTER 22

FATAL ATTRACTION

THE VISITOR HURTLED DOWN the spiral staircase in Clay's apartment and assumed a gladiatorial crouch.

"Dolly signed!" he bellowed triumphantly.

It was the evening of November 20, 1976, and Rupert Murdoch had planted his flag on a new continent. It was Clay who had introduced him to the famously tough proprietor of the ultraliberal *New York Post,* Dorothy Schiff. The Australian newspaper magnate had been cultivating his relationship with Clay for a couple of years by then, to ease his entry into the clubby world of New York journalism. He had been in a pugnacious mood ever since we'd met him, waiting for the right moment to pounce on the only surviving afternoon newspaper in the Big Apple.

"How did you close the deal?" Clay asked.

Murdoch boasted about spotting her weakness: "We had lunch. She was tired, older all of a sudden, the *Post* was losing money." With lightning speed he struck a deal for $32.5 million. "I may have paid too much for it, but it was the chance of my lifetime." He had bought a powerful mouthpiece in the media capital of America.

Clay was impressed. The connection between the two men resembled a friendship, but I was wary from the start. Editorial integrity was irrelevant to Murdoch. I had no doubt that he would renege on his promise to Schiff to maintain the *Post*'s liberal outlook, and, of course, he did. He had already built a newspaper empire of some ninety publications in Australia and England before the age of forty-five. Clay wanted to know how he did it.

"The way to operate is with OPM," Murdoch would tell Clay. "Other people's money."

That touched a sensitive chord in Clay. "Since I had no track record and nothing in the bank when I launched *New York*," he confided to Murdoch, "I had to take money where I could get it. You can pay too much for money by giving up too much control."

I brought out a tray of hors d'oeuvres and Clay broke open a bottle of champagne to celebrate Murdoch's triumph. The combatant was still too full of fight talk to sit down. "If the *Daily News* tries putting out an afternoon edition, I'll put out a morning paper and we'll have a good old-fashioned newspaper war," he barked. "Nobody will win, but they'll know they've been in a hell of a fight!"

Back then, I have to admit, I thought Murdoch looked like Humphrey Bogart: the dark eyes crouched under a thick shrubbery of black brows, the dissolute dents in his cheeks, the pouting lower lip. For all his legendary ruthlessness, Murdoch also had a sly charm. He turned it on full force around Clay, just as he had with Dolly Schiff, just as he would later do to woo Clay's enemies and countless government officials all the way up to presidents and prime ministers—whomever he needed to build his media empire.

What attracted Felker and Murdoch to each other puzzled me for a while. They couldn't have been more different in temperament. Clay was an impresario. He had the volatile personality of a creative editor: he was fanatically loyal to his tribe, the writers and editors, artists and photographers, and they returned his loyalty. Murdoch was a juggernaut. He had to overpower. When he and Clay and I first met over a social weekend at *Washington Post* publisher Kay Graham's Virginia farm, Murdoch played tennis not well but savagely, noticeably ignoring the proper nuance at a polite country weekend. Forget friendship, Rupert Murdoch played to win.

I remember telling Clay at some point that Murdoch was not his friend. "He will court you, promise you, pick your brain pan clean, but he is a cannibal—the kind of guest you invite to dinner and he eats the host."

But Clay was seduced by being close to powerful men and women; he wanted to learn their secrets. He offered Murdoch a respectable entrée into the stratosphere of New York. He mistook Murdoch's interest in him for friendship. It would prove to be a fatal naïveté. Clay's other fatal flaw was his inability to fake friendship with his moneymen. As fascinated as he was by power, he did not know how to be manipulative. He didn't know how to play people off against one another and he didn't know how to protect himself. Worse, he didn't think he had to; after all, his board of directors saw Clay as the golden goose of editors. But they also shared the assumption that he, like all artistic people, was clueless when it came to business.

Business mesmerized Clay. He even took classes in corporate accounting, determined to teach himself to be a good businessman. He was convinced this was the only way he would be able to maintain control of the media empire he intended to build. But it was the moneymen who held the strings to his corporate purse. And some of them, jealous of Clay's entrée, wanted to be wooed and introduced around town to elevate their social standing. Clay couldn't bring himself to chum around with them.

We often went to dinner with the Murdochs. I liked his then wife, Anna, a softly contoured blonde with a subversive agenda. She had been a reporter on Murdoch's *Sydney Daily Mirror* when they married, and Murdoch commanded her to resign. Anna obeyed, but she never forgave. Whenever she raised the subject around the four of us, goading me to make some feminist comment, Rupert would laugh and move his chair away from the women.

"I've made the breakthrough," she proudly confided one evening. "I'm starting at Fordham to finish my undergrad degree and then I'm going on to grad school in psychology. I'm going to be my own woman!" To my ears, that statement of liberation was the death knell of the Murdoch marriage.

TO FURTHER CELEBRATE MURDOCH'S COUP with the *Post,* we repaired to Elaine's, the legendary uptown bistro that attracted Manhattan avatars like Woody Allen and Mayor Ed Koch. The proprietor, Elaine Kaufman, indulged her pet writers. Wriggling between tables with her half-bushel hips, she doled out witty vulgarities and a free drink here and there to the likes of George Plimpton, Kurt Vonnegut, Mario Puzo, even Pavarotti. The food was overpriced and just palatable, but Elaine's regulars accommodated with an excess of drink. Elaine always welcomed Clay; he brought to her establishment the faces that would be all over the news in the future. Everyone enjoyed Clay's access to the newest media curiosity in the Big Apple.

The biggest contrast between Clay and Murdoch was the scale on which they did business. Murdoch's empire was then worth hundreds of millions and was controlled by a family holding company. Clay's company had a market value somewhere between $10 million and $20 million and was controlled by investors. Nonetheless, that evening at Elaine's, they talked like publishing peers, offering each other advice: "The one you should hire to find gossip for the *Post* . . ." and "What you should do with the *Voice* . . ." When Clay mentioned the *Village Voice,* there was no mistaking the delight in his purchase of the premier alternative weekly with its Peck's bad-boy irreverence. But Clay spoke like a proud father of his firstborn, *New York.*

Murdoch was envious. All was not galloping down the glory road for him. Over the exultation of his first major conquest in the New World there hung a cloud of probable rejection in the Old World. As contemptuous as he pretended to be of the "establishment," Murdoch's strategy was to court the very aristocrats and prime ministers he was presumed to hate, then invade their hierarchies and usurp their power. Without question, the route to respectability for Murdoch was to buy a prestige publication in Britain. He had begun expanding from his native Australia into the United Kingdom in 1968 when he took over the populist *News of the World* and immediately established his reputation as a purveyor of tits-and-ass photos and lurid crime and scandal tales. A year later he bought the *Sun* and turned it into a tabloid with the same hugely successful down-market format.

In 1973, he made one fatal turn. His Sunday *News of the World* caught the conservative Lord Lambton with a prostitute and exposed him in photographs as a symbol of decadent British aristocracy. The establishment ostracized Murdoch. That had driven him to sell his home in England and move lock, stock, and silver chests to America. Just that winter another chance had arisen in England. A venerable British institution, the *Observer,* was for sale. Murdoch was so certain about buying his first establishment newspaper that he and his wife had taken a new flat in Mayfair.

"Anna and I went over there earlier last week to put finishing touches on the flat," he told Clay at Elaine's. "When I found out all of a sudden that Dolly was willing to sell the *Post,* I flew back."

"Did you sew up the *Observer* deal?" Clay wanted to know.

A great shrug lifted Murdoch's cheeks and then dropped them even lower. "Crybaby liberals are throwing fits." His fighting words masked the nasty reality. Murdoch leaned over and confided to Clay that in the past forty-eight hours he'd had word that the board was blocking his bid. Journalists at the *Observer* refused to work if Murdoch took over. As we left Elaine's in Murdoch's limo, it was Clay's turn to confide that he was having problems with his board.

"You've had a lot of experience with these things, Rupert. Maybe you can give me some advice."

"Let's get together and talk about it."

Six weeks later Rupert Murdoch would smell the weakness in Clay's hold on the board of his publishing company. Gladiators have to win; they can't afford friends.

CHAPTER 23

POWER FEVER

WATCHING CLAY DRESS FASCINATED ME. He had gained in girth. He puffed out proudly in his custom-made Turnbull & Asser shirts, his chest an awning of bold stripes in tangerine silk or cornflower blue. His suits had the unmistakable high-cut sleeves and narrow cuffs of custom tailoring from London's Savile Row. If his shoulders weren't already broad enough, piling on a Huntsman camel's hair overcoat gave him a positively equine silhouette. Okay, I'm exaggerating, but it was the contrast of the top heft to his feet that made it almost seem so.

Clay's feet were positively balletic, I mean tiny, with the high arch of a Baryshnikov. I would watch him shoehorn those delicately articulated tootsies into the polished oxfords bench-made for him at John Lobb. Could he really support himself on them? Yes! He'd leap up and I'd almost expect him to pirouette out the door and prance off across East Fifty-Seventh Street like a Lipizzaner stallion.

But a very human appetite often slowed him down. He was a collector. I sometimes wondered if that instinct was encoded in his DNA. Too many mornings, on his way to work, he would shout to our taxi driver "Hold the cab!" and dive into James Robinson's shop to indulge his taste for antique silver. Of course, the last thing he needed was another silver biscuit basket, or another English porcelain dinner platter, but he couldn't help himself. His assistant, Jane Maxwell, later told me how she used to come over on Saturday mornings and shuffle his bills—which ones to pay this month?—while Clay would be out perusing the lots up for auction at Sotheby's, hoping for a bargain on a Della Robbia terra-cotta sculpture or a Majolica painted lion to add to his collection. He once told Maxwell that he believed a man should always live beyond his means.

I was worried about the feet of Clay.

CLAY WAS HUNGRY BY 1976. Why not? *New York* magazine was fat and happy by its eighth year in business. The family of writers, editors, and contributing artists and photographers had grown to include more of the most noted journalistic talents to come out of the late 1960s and 1970s: Kurt Andersen, Pete Hamill, Anna Wintour (who would become the queen-mother editor of *Vogue*). John Simon became a fearsome theater critic.

"If you wanted to learn about magazine writing, editing, or design, all you had to do was keep your eyes peeled and your ears perked—it was all being done out loud, with great sweeping gestures and the unforgettable sight of Clay's fist crashing down on the art counter, making all the X-Acto knives and glue pots jump into the air," said Elizabeth Crow, who went on to become editor of several magazines. "You'd pick up enough information to run a magazine of your own."

Clay backed Judith Daniels to start her own magazine for women, called *Savvy*. Michael Kramer, the political writer, was encouraged by Clay to start his own magazine, *More*. Joan Kron, the home decorating editor, gave birth to the high-tech movement, using industrial objects for interior furnishing, such as operating tables for bar carts or police barricades under a tabletop. It only became a movement because Clay later published an excerpt from the book Kron wrote with Suzanne Slesin, another visionary of interior design who wrote for *New York* and authored twenty books of her own. Clarkson and Potter, their publisher, hated the title, demanding: "What does it mean?" Kron refused to give in on her title. Once Clay owned *Esquire,* he ran it bigger than a title, as a banner across the August 29, 1978, cover: "HIGH TECH: The Industrial Style and Source Book for the Home." The idea swept the country in the '70s and spawned office furnishing and big-box stores decades later.

AN INSTINCT FOR THEATRICS also came naturally to Clay. I'll never forget the celebrity-studded party he took me to at Lally Weymouth's East Side apartment in 1977. To begin, I was suspicious of Clay's friendship with Lally, a social colossus with a smoldering ambition to become the greatest journalist of her day. Lally was the daughter of Kay Graham, whom she openly accused of following the archaic practice of primogeniture by grooming her firstborn son, Donald, to take over the helm of the family business, rather than Lally. Clay tried to play the peacemaker between mother and daughter, which only exaggerated their rivalry and focused it on a competition for Clay's ardor.

At the party, I was left in the hallway as Clay plunged into the gilded crowd. Right behind me, Jacqueline Kennedy swept in on the arm of the handsome Harvard economist John Kenneth Galbraith. She was immediately enveloped in a bear hug by the guest of honor, Lord George Weidenfeld, a Holocaust survivor who had elevated himself to a British lord and powerhouse publisher.

I followed Jackie into the main salon and watched with my reporter's eyes as she sat at a cocktail table and was immediately surrounded by men. They virtually bowed their heads like vassals. She selected them, one by one, her enormous eyes fixed on the elderly filmmaker Sam Spiegel, then the CBS chairman Bill Paley; these and other tycoons melted in the resplendence of her full attention. She listened. That was her secret. When finally her breathy childlike voice spoke, it touched them like an anointing. I had watched it happen with Clay.

He had described for me a telling vignette from the time he

went to the Kennedy compound on Hyannis Port in the summer of
1953, a new reporter for *Life,* to interview the attractive new senator from Massachusetts. John Kennedy, then only thirty-five, scion
of the state's most prominent Irish Catholic family, had displaced
the WASP dynasty of the Lodge family in a stunning upset. Clay, as
usual, had spotted a comer. Only a few months before, Kennedy had
proposed to Jacqueline Bouvier. The twenty-four-year-old daughter of a prominent New York family, Jackie was working as a street
photographer for a Washington newspaper. Clay was invited into the
family's screened-in porch for the interview.

Jackie, wearing shorts, literally knelt at the feet of Jack. Her 2.88-
carat diamond and emerald ring blazed in the sun as she rested her
hand on her bare knee. Jack sat forward in his chair, relaxed in an
open shirt and shorts, facing the green reporter and waving his sunglasses to emphasize his points. Later, while the Kennedy boys were
playing touch football, Jackie invited Clay to sit beside her and watch.
The embrace of her full attention made him feel cocky enough to ask
a flirtatious question.

"What do you see in this guy? Why do you want to marry him?"

Her answer gave Clay a clue to the future Camelot. "I like the life,"
she said.

At Lally's party, Clay came up from behind me and slipped his
arm around my waist. "Where have you been? I want you to watch
something. Mailer's already drunk. He's stalking Gore. There's going
to be a fight."

Sure enough, the bullheaded Norman Mailer was circling his
nemesis, Gore Vidal. Too short to take on tall men, Mailer preferred
butting heads so he could force his opponents to bend down. He
edged into the circle around the nearly six-foot Vidal, who was fully
engaged, as usual, in talking about himself. Mailer threw his drink in
the elegant author's face. Gasps, shrieks, laughter, an electric charge
ricocheted through the crowd. Mailer, shoulders hunched, charged

forward like a minotaur. Gore bent to meet him but Mailer pushed back hard. I think it was here that Gore got off his famous line: "Once again, Norman, words fail you." This was not just another highfalutin verbal brawl; this was the literary version of the Liston-Ali fight!

Lally looked around frantically. "God, this is terrible, please, somebody, do something!"

Clay leaned close to Lally. "Shut up, this is making your party!"

How right he was. That party has lived on from Liz Smith's column to Murdoch's *Sun,* to newspapers in every corner of the world and multiple memoirs and, recently, in a review by Graydon Carter of the biography by J. Michael Lennon, *Norman Mailer: A Double Life.*

RESTAURANTS WERE ANOTHER of Clay's myriad fascinations. Back at the *Trib,* he had sent Gael Greene to write about the reopening of La Côte Basque. She had talked her way into the confidence of Henri Soulé, the snobby king of haute cuisine, and penetrated his inner sanctum to write a dishy piece about how the place worked. When Clay called in 1968 to spring on her the offer to be his restaurant critic, she was stunned, thinking how reckless to tap an unknown to compete with the Great God of Gourmands Craig Claiborne. But Clay's eye for casting had spotted her unique approach.

"You make food sensual," Felker told Greene. "You'll be great!"

Mimi Sheraton's food criticism was an enticing addition to Gael Greene's restaurant reviews. Sheraton won Clay over with her first big story for *New York* in the early 1970s when she discovered the hottest gourmet food shop in town and ate her way through more than a thousand products. The headline was "I Tasted Everything in Bloomingdale's Food Department." She went on to write for just about every print publication in existence as well as to produce sixteen books.

Nora Ephron wrote some funny pieces for Clay, but she didn't like competing with the other women writers at *New York.* She wrote occasional essays for *The New Yorker* and directed some of the era's most popular romantic comedy films and mined the self-hating feminine eye in her books.

Mary Ann Madden delighted readers with her topical crossword puzzles and literary competitions, calling for readers to submit humorous poetry or other clever wordplay on a theme she changed each week. Her contest hooked even star writers like David Halberstam, David Mamet, and Woody Allen.

EVEN WITH AN UNRULY FAMILY that extended from L.A. to London, Clay was not satisfied.

When Clay hired his own chief financial officer, Kenneth Fadner, his board saw the move as a slap. Clay sent Fadner out to meet with Carter Burden, the young prince of the city who owned the *Voice*. Born to wealth and with the delicate blond beauty of a fawn, Burden straddled the worlds of party-giving dilettante and progressive city councilman representing the Upper East Side. His exquisite Lalique figure of a wife, Amanda Burden, had killed his fantasy of becoming president someday when she was rumored to have had an affair with Teddy Kennedy. During the year of his divorce, 1974, he went virtually missing in action from the city council.

Clay's hunch was that Burden preferred an all-cash deal because he didn't want it known that he owned a media property that covered politics, and especially not a pinko tabloid in Greenwich Village. Fadner was able to borrow $1.5 million from Chemical Bank and, with the excess cash the magazine had, meet the $5 million asking price.

But when Clay and Fadner went to the board with their proposal to buy the *Village Voice* for cash, they were treated like crazy dreamers. "No, no, no, it's not good for the company to borrow money," argued Alan Patricof. He was a forty-year-old venture capitalist brought onto the board by Armand Erpf. Patricof represented "other people's money," but for him personally, the magazine held a certain je ne sais quoi that doesn't spring to mind when one thinks about the meat distributing business or the animal feed supplement business, two of the major clients Patricof attracted to his private investment company. Raised in Manhattan, this natural-born dealmaker had always been close enough to the parade of the talented and glamorous. The primary reward he looked for in his association with *New York* magazine was social cachet. "I wanted to be Clay's friend," he often told me, meaning he expected to be introduced to the governor and the mayor and other big shots naturally attracted to the parties of a big-city editor.

But long before 1974, any trust between Felker and Patricof had been fatally shaken. Clay's benefactor, Armand Erpf, liked the idea of maintaining a "creative tension" between the artistic wildmen—Clay and Milton—and the staid moneymen. Clay was wary; he had almost lost the magazine in the late '60s. Back then, George Hirsch, the self-congratulatory publisher, had enlisted writer Jimmy Breslin in an attempted heist. When Erpf found out, he fired Hirsch. Patricof appealed, saying, "Hirsch is just like me," but Erpf prevailed. Breslin resigned. And Patricof became chairman of the board. Clay won that first power struggle, but he never trusted Patricof again.

The bitterness over that attempted betrayal set the stage for a "Spaghetti Eastern," a shootout waiting to happen.

Clay's and Patricof's philosophies on how to run a publishing business were in constant opposition. Clay wanted to plow profits back into operations in order to expand the business and, in the long run, the profits. Patricof, having come of age during the go-go years on Wall Street, was fixated on maximizing short-term profits to raise the price of the stock.

Patricof's insistence that Burden take stock in *New York* magazine rather than cash had the effect of dangerously diluting Clay's small equity in the company he had started. Clay had given a generous spread of stock ownership to key editorial people, including Wolfe, Breslin, Steinem, Peter Maas, and Jerry Goodman (none of whom would later go along with the patricide plot). Burden and his business partner Bartle Bull got a total of 34 percent of the merged company's stock. That gave Burden and Bull the largest block of votes. And they were no friends of Clay Felker.

As early as '73, Clay's board had begun getting nervous about his spending habits. By '76, despite the fact that he had built a company that was a model in the publishing world, Clay's equity was now confined to only 10 percent of the value he had created. He decided to live with that situation if the board would compensate him with an increase in salary or a share of the profits. Patricof was fit to be tied. Jealousy flared so brightly, it could almost be seen like lightning.

"I was not going to stand by and be the quiet, nice guy anymore," Patricof told me in an interview after the crisis was over. "I was only getting $12,000 a year for being chairman. I gave the editors lots of tips on merchandise that would be perfect for 'Best Bets'—do you think anyone ever paid attention?"

Several times during our interview I asked Patricof, "If being on the board brought you so much grief, rancor, and humiliation, why didn't you resign?"

"That's a good question, Gail, a good question," he said with a shrug. At the end of our two-hour interview, I suggested an answer: "Prestige?"

"Yes, I enjoyed the prestige. People think being chairman of the board is an important role. But I'm not known in every restaurant. I don't get invited to special screenings. I don't have a press card to use…"

IN 1976, MEASURED BY PUBLIC ACCEPTANCE, Clay Felker had achieved his dream. Measured by the balance sheets that year, when the city's economy was still in free fall, the company had overall revenues of $26 million. *New York* magazine itself earned $1.2 million. The *Village Voice* earned $649,000. Clay began to believe in himself as a businessman. This was his Achilles' heel.

He set his sights on California for the next expansion. He first looked at *Los Angeles* magazine, which at the time was a glossy version of a Chamber of Commerce magazine, beautiful but boring. He offered $500,000 for it. His board of directors went berserk, arguing that the company didn't have enough money. "Clay, being so instinctive, knew it was worth much more than half a million, and it later sold for something like twenty million," Ken Fadner once told me. Clay's hands were tied. He backed off. But the rancor with his board developed into a bitter estrangement.

Then Clay decided to make a drastic move—to launch another start-up. He was completely comfortable with chaos, which as an artistic spirit he believed was necessary to create something new. His idea was to reproduce the excitement of an urban magazine in Los Angeles. He would call it *New West*. Nothing pleased him more than brokering movie sales for his writers from articles they developed for *New York*. California became a great romance for him, with its raw-boned politics, its history and cultural heroes, its energy, its cults, and its crazy variations on the American dream.

The announcement of *New West* kicked up great excitement in L.A., where magazine journalism was a low-end product. Clay plucked one of the top business journalists in the country, Frank Lalli, from *Forbes* and made him the founding executive editor. Lalli's talented wife, Carole, lost her reluctance to leave New York when Clay hired her as the magazine's food writer.

Costs began to break the budget early on. Soon, Clay began calling to ask me to come out and write a cover story for his new magazine. I was still caught up in promoting *Passages,* but I welcomed the distraction. My Columbia mentor, Margaret Mead, was delighted to hear I had another news outlet. I must do an exposé on the dangers of nuclear power, she commanded. A little research uncovered a popular protest in the San Diego area against the Diablo Canyon Power Plant. It was discovered in 1973 that it sat on a seismic fault, a fault that had already generated a 7.1 magnitude earthquake. On the California ballot that year was a referendum on the safety of nuclear power plants. It was a made-to-order investigatory story. And it allowed me to take Maura to L.A. for spring vacation.

Maura sat at the pool of the Beverly Hills Hotel all day spying on stars, while I inhaled nuclear power publications, then swam with her and wrote half the night nourished by room-service salad. We met the designer Diane von Furstenberg in the coffee shop over perfectly made omelets; Diane was funny and real and we became good friends. Once Clay joined us in the bungalow, the magic really began. His friend the moviemaker Peter Bogdanovich invited us to visit the Twentieth Century Fox lot to watch him direct Ryan O'Neal in *Nickelodeon*. Lunch at the Fox commissary was a further occasion for star spotting. And that night, we were invited to watch the Academy Awards at the home of Irwin Winkler, producer of the Rocky films, who was making *They Shoot Horses, Don't They?* with Jane Fonda.

Why not move here? Winkler coaxed us. The next day a gaggle of New Yorkers gathered for lunch by the Beverly Hills Hotel pool, all of us splotched with two-day tans and red half-moons where our bathing suits had ridden up. Lunch over, we went back to our lounge chairs. "Time for turning!" chirped the cabana boy, pointing to a sun now at two o'clock. We all ran guiltily to our rooms, fearing that if we adopted the laid-back L.A. lifestyle, we might melt down to a dribble of Hawaiian Tropic tanning lotion.

BY AUGUST, PATRICOF WAS READY to move on a campaign to oust Clay. He arranged separate meetings with each board member and pushed the story that the company was in trouble because it had run out of cash.

"The idea that we were in financial trouble was totally preposterous," insists Ken Fadner. "The board had voted unanimously to wipe out earnings to start *New West,* in order to allow the government to finance half of the costs." Nonetheless, the board denied Clay a new contract. A brawl broke out at the September 1976 board meeting.

"If I've told you once, I've told you fifteen times, Clay, you don't have to be a superstar all over town for paying writers well," Patricof scolded.

"*New West* has exceeded all our expectations in terms of circulation growth, advertising, popular acceptance," Clay countered. "It's making us temporarily victims of our own success—but just temporarily. It's grown so rapidly that the costs have outrun the original budget."

Glaser looked at the men around the room. "This has been a launch of unprecedented success," he intoned, "and you guys are crying because there's little money in the bank. The fact is, we are at the healthiest point in the company's whole existence."

But egos had been too bruised for healing. Glaser later lamented to me, "Clay and I weren't wise enough to make that board of directors feel part of our community. They always felt on the outside. That guaranteed that they would act only in their own financial interests; they would have no family ties."

WHO WOULD HAVE GUESSED what unpredictable forces would come together in the same week of November 1976? Murdoch, recoiling from his humiliation at the hands of the British upper class in refusing his bid for the *Observer,* collided with Felker, wrestling with hostile directors over control of his three periodicals.

But Murdoch was first to seize his moment.

Clay had been trying since the start of summer to coax Burden into naming a price for his shares so Clay could make an offer. Burden's mode for dealing with stress was avoidance. At the first hint of the necessity to make a tough decision, he would start rolling up into a ball and the ball would wedge itself into a corner until there was no way at all of getting at it. "I couldn't fish or cut bait," Burden himself told me later.

But Patricof knew he had a live buyer. He gave Murdoch's investment banker, Stanley Shuman, the names of all the major stockholders and told him who was particularly unfriendly to Clay. The backroom deals between raider and insiders had begun.

Sensing connivance in the making, Clay grew rigid with paranoia. At this very same moment, Clay's father was slipping away in a blanket of minor strokes. After flying home weekends to Webster Groves, Clay would return on Sunday nights, sad and shaken. I would coax him to go to a movie and we'd come home to warm milk and brownies. Chocolate always worked on him.

But one Sunday evening, Felix Rohatyn, Clay's financial guru, came over. Clay loved learning about finance from the senior partner of Lazard Frères's investment bank, who was successfully maneuvering to save New York City from bankruptcy. Rohatyn enjoyed being exposed to the world of ideas from the man whom many were now calling "Mr. New York." We sat in the living room while Clay told Rohatyn he was worried about the sudden increase in trading of *New York* Magazine Company stock and the rise in the price. He was worried that one of his unfriendly directors might be making a market on insider information. And he was uneasy about Murdoch.

"Uneasy?" Rohatyn said. "Have no illusions. Murdoch is a ruthless man."

"Who can we find to buy out Burden?" Clay asked.

"Kay Graham." Rohatyn knew how close Clay was to the publisher of the *Washington Post*.

"I can't ask Kay," Clay said.

"She would be hurt if nobody did," Rohatyn said. "I'll call her."

CHAPTER 24

MURDOCH MAKES HIS MOVE

ABOVE THE JOLLITY OF FRIDAY NIGHT at P. J. Clarke's tavern on Third Avenue was a no-nonsense law firm where the lights burned all night. Skadden, Arps specialized in the traumatic law of tender offers. It was the home of Joe Flom, the groundbreaking attorney who made Skadden, Arps the go-to firm for clients enmeshed in hostile takeovers. Steven Brill, the lawyer who had written the prophetic piece about Flom for *New York,* walked Clay into the Skadden, Arps office late one night. Lawyers there quickly developed a cynical view of human nature. People came at their worst. Either they wanted to learn the art and artifice of being a raider, or, in a panic, how to save their hides as victims.

This is where I found Clay in the dying hours of that fateful year of 1976. To me, the inside of the building felt like a hospital. Meals were served on trays from a twenty-four-hour kitchen. A limousine waited perpetually just outside, ready to rush clients to court or pick them up from a bloody board meeting. The attorneys slept on couches, the floor, or not at all. They sent out for cigarettes, aftershave, clean shirts from Brooks Brothers.

Clay smiled as I slipped a cup of strong coffee and a crème-filled pastry lobster tail in front of him. He was on the phone with his friend and advocate, Rohatyn. "Burden has been screwing around with my offer for a month," Clay muttered. "Of course he can make up his mind. I told him we were prepared to raise our offer above Murdoch's and give him $7.50 a share." Rohatyn himself was ready to kill. Once again, he dialed Carter Burden's lawyer:

"Get that yo-yo off the slopes!"

All day the lawyer for Burden, Peter Tufo, had been telling Rohatyn that his client couldn't be reached—he was in Sun Valley, skiing.

"Peter," said Rohatyn, "there is no snow on the slopes out there. Stop bullshitting me."

"You're just going to have to give me more time," the lawyer said.

"We'll give you till four," Rohatyn said darkly.

He was sitting in *Newsweek*'s Manhattan offices with Katharine Graham and her attorneys. Over the next two hours, the humiliation level in the room rose considerably. As queen mother of one of the most highly respected publishing organizations in the world, the *Washington Post* Company, Graham had been trying for two days with increasing desperation to buy *New York* Magazine Company. Clay and Rohatyn had been trying with mounting frustration to sell it to her. Burden was treating them all like pathetic passengers on the wait list for a flight that was never going to take off.

At 4:45 Tufo called back to tell Rohatyn, "Look, I've talked to Carter, and it cannot go your way."

"You mean it can't go our way at any price?" Rohatyn asked in astonishment.

"I can't tell you more than that," Tufo said.

The people in the room could not believe what they were hearing. They had been working around the clock to prevent the great magazine raid. If it went through, it would be the first hostile takeover of a publication since the 1920s.

What none of us knew was that between Christmas and New Year's, Murdoch had obtained oral "understandings" from enough board members to sell to him if the price was right. Graham took the phone with its last feeble connection to Tufo. On a conference call connection we heard her implore: "What is it you really want? Should I fly out to see Carter, is there anything humanly possible?"

When no answer came back, she whispered, "What can I do for my darling Clay?"

"Kay, don't," we heard Rohatyn say. "It's demeaning to you, the whole thing is obscene; at least keep your dignity."

In the virgin hours of 1977, Murdoch and his forces sped by private jet to Sun Valley to start the New Year by sewing up Carter Burden.

IN THE MIDST OF ALL THE CHAOS, I decided to move back in with Clay. He was always there for me when I was being attacked, well, almost always. He needed me now. We needed each other. I knew Clay was still under the illusion that there were people who would commit to him and save the company out of loyalty. I was doubtful.

We spent the rest of New Year's Eve cuddling up with Maura and soberly watching TV while the ball dropped in Times Square. On the first morning of the New Year, Clay seemed to awaken inside the body of a fallen man from whom he felt peculiarly detached. Propelled into a role he didn't understand, he picked himself up, splashed water on his slugged face, climbed into the saddle of his Exercycle and rode for a hard hour until his juices began running and he was ready to give his lawyer a decision.

"Clay, don't you have a right of first refusal?" I asked.

"It expired at midnight."

"No, it didn't, you weren't allowed to exercise it."

"Still? Are you sure?"

"I'm no lawyer, but your own lawyer at Skadden, Arps—what's his name?"

"Pirie, Bob Pirie."

"He said you have fifteen days to match any offer by a third party."

"Jesus, why didn't I remember that?"

"You never thought you'd have to. Pirie told me you could get a temporary restraining order." All at once he snapped into command. He reached for the phone.

"Bob! Clay here, let's go for a TRO." The old leonine confidence surged in his voice. Pirie called back to let us know he'd found a judge at home, playing the harpsichord, and persuaded him to interrupt his baroque pleasures to execute a temporary restraining order. It would block Burden from selling to Murdoch on the basis that he and his lawyer, by refusing to accept Felker's $7.50 offer, had denied Clay his right of first refusal.

The stakes were control of a company that in 1976 had had revenues of $26 million. Burden owned 24 percent of the stock. Clay's equity had been diluted to 10 percent when he bought the *Village Voice*. The battle was on.

Overnight, three posses of urban cowboys were headed for a showdown—the moneymen, the lawmen, and the pen men and women. The members of each posse rode into the showdown, saw into one another's minds, and were shocked at how different were their values, their conduct, and their codes.

Two of the magazine's top political writers, Richard Reeves and Ken Auletta, spent the siege week of January 1 getting in direct touch with key board members. The moneymen showered the writers with praise. "We're such fans!" They sounded positively starstruck.

"Fools, you're fools!" Byron Dobell told the writers each time they called in to report on conversations with moneymen who assured them the board would love to meet with the writers to resolve this thing. "You're talking to the enemy!" Byron shouted into the phone. He was histrionic, but he was right. "These people are in on it."

Hard news first came in late Sunday, January 2. Even as board members were mollifying Auletta by phone, Rohatyn called to notify Clay that Patricof and those same board members had just sold. They were on their way to a gala signing party at Murdoch's Fifth Avenue apartment.

That weekend the moneymen learned how easy it is to play to the narcissism of "talent." And the writers learned a phrase that helped us to understand the moneymen: "On Wall Street, loyalty is a quarter of a point."

CLAY AND I WALKED INTO the bite of winter's morning on that first Monday of January with a buoyancy that had something of our old frontier spirit in it. Clay was off to meet with the lawmen, I to meet with the journalists.

"Well, sweetheart," he said at the corner, "we may have to start from scratch and put out a little country journal."

"I'm with you," I said.

A summit of the magazine family had been called for 8 A.M. at *New York*'s new offices on Second Avenue. One hundred twenty-five people filled the room, faces of underpaid staff regulars, secretaries, people who had medical bills, mortgages, and new babies to worry about. A great deal was made over the fact that no pressure would be put on anyone to quit. If and when the moment of truth came, it would be up to each person to make the best decision. All this did was insult people's loyalty. Mailroom people, clerical newcomers, switchboard operators, all wanted to be given the chance to act as few of us ever have the opportunity to do—on principle.

I read a statement from Clay: "Despite recent developments, I intend to fight and fight as hard as I can to keep what we have all built from being damaged. And I expect to win." It cheered everyone. In the first half hour we arrived at a definition of ourselves. We were a "talent package." We were not up for "barter." And we meant to demand our right to "protect the company from deterioration." Our support was behind the editorial leadership that had brought us all together.

Steve Brill, the lawyer-writer, was asked to work with me to draw up a statement for a press conference. From the moment we turned into activists we also grasped a reality that continually eluded our brethren. Phrases like "editorial integrity" and "creative community" stuck to the roof of the mouth with their piousness. What bound this family together was too emotional to be expressed. It was loyalty, self-respect, and, yes, love. By noon we had closed ranks around a clear consensus. It startled many of us to discover how intimately our sense of self-worth was tied to *New York, New West,* or the *Voice.* Our extended family was under siege.

When we met the press, it was not as pals, not even as colleagues. From that first news conference, the story was covered like the Super Bowl of publishing. A decisive board meeting was set for 7 P.M. that evening. The writers were jumpy. What did we know about takeovers and the rights of employees? Martin Lipton, a wizard of tender-offer law, agreed to advise us gratis. The rumor reached us that a lynching party was waiting at the offices of Clay's company lawyer, Ted Kheel. The board of directors was set to meet there. Brill, Bernard, Auletta, and I rushed into the canyon of Park Avenue and began half running uptown. Dusk had swallowed the light. It was cold. I had forgotten my coat. Entering the reception area, it was impossible not to feel the suspense of walking into the OK Corral.

"Clay's in the back," someone said.

The writers' delegation was escorted to a holding room. Kheel sent in a half gallon of Chivas Regal. We waited to see if the directors would hear us. Restlessness in the holding room bubbled up like gas in a shaken bottle. A runner from the boardroom gave us a blow by blow. "They" had thrown Kheel out as corporate counsel; two of Felker's directors had been kicked out; Rupert Murdoch and his banker took over those seats. Clay and Milton had just had their balls crushed. The raiders—by some arcane maneuver—had dissolved the board meeting altogether and were now holding a stockholders' meeting. Blood was running in the halls. Events were becoming deranged.

At 8:05 P.M. Auletta picked up the phone. He dialed New York State's attorney general Louis Lefkowitz at home, hoping to initiate an investigation. Patricof walked by and darted in. "Ken, don't be upset. You have to understand."

"Hello, Mr. Attorney General," Auletta said into the phone.

A spasm shook Patricof. He walked away twitching like a marionette. Five minutes later he was back. "We'll take the writers now," Patricof announced. "Do there have to be so many?"

Five people rose, including me. The body-heated boardroom temperature was in the mideighties by the time we were admitted. Everyone was in shirtsleeves. Another door opened. Murdoch. He stood with one hand in the pocket of his black suit, his voice utterly composed. Everyone began speaking heatedly. Except Rupert Murdoch. With the calm of the conquerer, he said, "I quite understand why there would be some nervousness on the part of the staff. It's natural to be concerned about their jobs with a new owner . . ."

"Patronizing," I hissed under my breath.

"He can't conceive of people acting on principle," Auletta fumed to Reeves.

Byron Dobell was the keynote speaker. "I don't know you people," Dobell fervently addressed the antagonists, "and I don't want to know you. But I do know you people have been living off Clay Felker's genius for eight years. Going to your cocktail parties and pretending you had something to do with building this product. You don't have the right to sell people!"

The man was on fire. Murdoch's face registered no reaction.

"It's not even a question of genius," Byron went on. "It's a question of skill. This man is a tremendously skillful person and he's put together the fragile structure of a magazine—the writers, editors, artists, photographers, everybody is in tune with one another. And you're going to smash that."

When he sat down, not a person spoke. Auletta finally talked out the options. His speech built power as he came to the point about staff feelings. "You can't treat us like widgets, or pieces of meat." Nervousness and sweating increased.

"Now wait a minute," interrupted Robin Towbin, a prominent investment banker on the board. "I was trying to do the right thing. You know how hard Clay is to deal with. You know," he addressed the writers with an injured tone, "it was me who tried to work this thing out . . ."

"You're a liar." Clay glared at Towbin.

"I will ignore the attack."

Auletta pushed the board member hard. "You told me Sunday you wanted to do business with the *Washington Post*. And you would delay any action until you had the session with the writers we kept talking about. Even as you were giving us that story, you were selling your stock."

Towbin tried to wiggle out. "But events forced me—"

"You fucking liar!" Clay escalated. It was not the first time this manner of address was used, but this was the only time when the addressee confirmed its accuracy.

"Well, you're right . . ."

Stan Shuman, Murdoch's investment adviser, a sequoia of a man with an incongruously gentle voice, tried to tamp it all down by repeating the phrase he had used throughout: "Nothing has happened. Relax. This is just some paper changing hands."

"What do you mean nothing has happened!" Clay shouted. "You've humiliated my board members. Two of the finest people I know."

Patricof rose. "Whoa, whoa now, let's not go into that! Let's not go into that!"

"Shhhh! Shhhh!" Now Shuman came off his chair with his big arms fully extended, the lion tamer, calming the crowd. Dramatically, he announced, "Rupert wants to speak."

Murdoch injected a sedative tone of voice. "This is very unfortunate," he said. "Can't we get together, Clay?"

Clay was sitting right beside him. "Rupert," he said quietly, "you and I once talked about this and agreed we could never work together, right?"

"Yes, but I meant we could never work together as publishers," Murdoch replied. "We could work together if I were publisher and you were editor."

This civilized intermission was brief. Burden cut through the cordiality between Murdoch and Clay with the accusation, "Clay, you went behind my back and tried to sell the company to Murdoch yourself."

"Carter, you're a goddamned liar," Clay replied.

I was shaking with rage, but I had never heard Clay talk this way. Murdoch affirmed that Clay was correct.

"He knows what you are," Clay said matter-of-factly to Carter. "An incompetent dilettante. No one is going to give you what you want, a tin star marked 'publisher.'"

Murdoch went back to wooing Clay. He needed Carter on Saturday, the other players on Sunday, but this was Monday and now he needed an editor. "Clay, I think you're an editorial genius. I want you to stay and run the magazine."

The men he had already bought picked up the cue. Board member Bob Towbin said he thought Clay was an editorial genius. Another board member, Tom Kempner, said he thought Clay was an editorial genius. Patricof added, "We all know Clay's the best editor in the world." Murdoch said, "I agree," but cut back slightly lest this gush of hot air could get expensive, "Clay Felker is the best editor in America."

Clay looked at Murdoch as he said evenly, "I, like you, am a publisher."

Kempner said coolly, "I think maybe we've had enough of the writers. They shouldn't witness this behavior."

Stan Shuman, speaking for Murdoch, repeated the preposterous fiction, "Nothing has changed." Kempner looked at our writers' group as if at an eighth-grade civics class. "You people don't understand," he said. "In America, anyone can sell anything he wants at any time. You're going to have to get that straight. That is just American capitalism."

As Clay and I left for our apartment along with Milton, Patricof came running behind us. "Milton," he called. "I'm counting on you, Milton, to protect the corporate asset."

"There is no corporate asset, Alan," Milton said, with factual indifference. "That's the point. People—that's all there ever was."

WELL AFTER MIDNIGHT, Bob Pirie arrived at our digs with his full team of Skadden, Arps crisis troops. Looking as angelic as Casper the Ghost, the white-haired attorney came into the kitchen and kissed my cheek and whispered, "I've got a splendid settlement. You're really going to like this settlement."

I pulled back. "Who the hell asked for a settlement?" We were all ready to go to court the next day to hear the judge decide on Clay's temporary restraining order. Pirie soothed us with sweet talk and called us to sit down together in the living room while he laid out the terms. When he was finished, I demanded, "But if we're right, why are we giving up?"

Pirie was nonplussed. He explained what is rudimentary thinking in the law: one should try to cut a deal between this moment and court because that is the only time one has a negotiating position. Pirie suggested that Clay and Milton and I go off and talk it over in private.

"It's unfair for anyone else to make a judgment on what Clay should do," Milton chided me in the study. "No one else has the same to lose. Clay is the only one who can be castrated by Murdoch, financially ruined and left out in the cold with a noncompete clause for three years." Milton had hit the central nerve. If Murdoch enforced the noncompete clause, in the publishing world, Clay would be a vegetable.

Pirie broke in on our private meeting. He concentrated his full powers of persuasion on convincing Clay that settlement was the only rational course. If Pirie lost a motion on the preliminary injunction, he said, the judge would form an opinion on the case, Murdoch could go ahead and buy the stock, and Clay would be left out on a limb fighting for months with his own funds. "If we have full-blown litigation here, it could cost Clay a half-million dollars."

At 4 A.M. Bob Pirie left with the nod he wanted. Clay turned mournfully to his closest friend and partner, Milton. "They've stolen everything we've created. We have nothing left."

"We have our talent left," Milton said. "And our integrity."

FRIDAY, JANUARY 7, 1977, was a long, dull ache of a day. A delegation of editors and writers met with Clay and Milton to save the senior members of the family. Ten people were given the protection of two-year contracts. As the joyless day deepened into evening, forty members of the magazine's talent package walked out, quitting in support of Clay and rejection of Murdoch. They gathered at a restaurant ironically called Chicago, across from the magazine's home on Second Avenue. There they waited for Clay and Milton to arrive and give direction.

I sat with the two men in Bob Pirie's office above P. J. Clarke's and watched as the last breaths of their offspring were stilled by a signature. Clay's broad shoulders drooped. I had never before seen him give up.

"Let's look to the future," I said to Bob Pirie. "Neither of these men was born rich. But they have exceptional talent and they work very hard. What's to prevent this happening all over again?"

"Nothing," Pirie said. "The laws of this country are set up to protect the free flow of capital."

The staff called to warn Clay to use the restaurant's side door when he arrived. They wanted to protect him from a phalanx of press numbering about fifty and from a climate that came close to the hysteria of covering a politician's downfall.

When Clay at last appeared inside Chicago, he jumped up on a table and stood tall in a suit and tie. His first words were those of the father looking out for his flock. "I cannot tell you how much it means to me to see you all on this side of the street, but"—and suddenly his voice kicked up half an octave with conviction in it—"don't quit on my account. Stay and get some money out of these bums!" *That's a man,* I thought, *looking out for his progeny before himself.* He expressed his affection for each and every one there and promised to help find good positions for those who were determined to leave. He finished by saying, "Rupert Murdoch's ideas about friendship, about publishing, and about people are very different than mine. He should know that he is"—now the voice of leadership broke—"breaking up a family, and he does so at his peril."

Men and women wept. "Impossible," people murmured. "This can't be happening."

Clay walked out the door into the crazy neon of Second Avenue, into the leer of transient bars, TV lights, the heave of shoulders and elbows. His body lurched through the reporters, looking for a hole, a dignified way out.

"The publisher once feared for his piercing attacks was pinned, crucifix style, against a no-parking sign," the NBC reporter shouted into her microphone.

"Look, I haven't been thinking about what I'm going to do next, but it's going to be in publishing," Clay replied to the cacophony of questions. "I'm a journalist and that's what my life is." His face was waxen—a mixture of humility and humiliation.

"What kind of day was today for you?" he was asked.

"A terrible day. It's also the best day of my life."

"Why is it the best day?" a reporter interrupted.

"Because of the support and the love these people have shown me."

I hoped the cameras would not pick up the streak of his tears.

A WEEK AFTER HIS LIFE was kicked apart, Clay awoke next to me on a Caribbean island and shuddered. "I realize how fragile my life is," he said.

Saint Martin's was a refuge from all the friends and curiosity seekers who wanted a replay of the disaster with full dialogue. I had persuaded Clay to turn down offers of hideouts from Barry Diller, Kay Graham, and others. Why be obligated to anyone? He was a free man. Why not hole up in a bungalow on some beautiful deserted beach and forget the world for ten days?

A silent-footed waiter had left a glistening pineapple wrapped in orchids at the foot of our bed. A fist of sun punched over the horizon and stretched its fingers into our eyes. We kissed. Clay sat up and rested against the headboard, opening a history of Napoleon and Talleyrand across his chest, and began to fight the panic of age, fat, self-doubt.

Clay believed in the great-men version of history. He needed to believe that greatness could be his. He was dispassionate and mostly correct in judging the value of other people's work. About the lasting value of his own work he was now uncertain. Would the stamina be there to start all over again? Was there time to dream the great magazine of the 1980s?

Yes, of course, I said.

We began running the beach. We swam a mile in the morning, another mile in the afternoon. A storm built up for two days. The sea turned wild and communication to the island was severed. I opened the fat package of letters of cheer and condolence that Clay had received before we left New York. I read some aloud. Clay was moved. It was the first step toward healing.

I wanted to make love. I could not bear to see my man unmanned by events. My motive was not exclusively therapeutic. He had bought me a string bikini in Philipsburg. Its red and white checks were deceptively innocent. A large keyhole peeped at the inner swell of my breasts. The strings of the halter begged for loosening. I backed close to him as he lay reading on the bed. Cupping the tanned half-moons beneath my full white saddle would be, I knew, irresistible. He rose and drove me to the full-length mirror. His hands explored every curve and crevice of my body. My knees went weak. He turned me.

"Are you having a trembler?"

"What do you think?"

We both loved these surprise stand-ups that made our knees tremble. In the middle of a noisy summer party he often pulled me outdoors and pressed me against a dark side of the party house. It might even happen in Paris, well, okay, that's Paris, but in an alley in London, too. I loved being wanted so urgently that Clay would forget his normal propriety. We were lost in rapture when I heard a sound. Opening my eyes, I caught the waiter standing in the doorway, frozen, stiffer than a deer in headlights. Clay saw the waiter in the mirror. In his old voice he boomed out his familiar welcome:

"Look who's here!"

The absurdity of it relaxed us. The next day the storm withdrew. We were feeling loose and even a little homesick when a stranger approached our hotel terrace where Clay was answering more letters. "Congratulations," called the American with his hand forthrightly extended. He must have recognized Clay from TV coverage of the takeover. "From what I read, that's what's in order," he said. "Guess you won't be running *New York* anymore. It won't be quite the same, but it'll keep going all right."

Clay forced a slight smile and nodded.

"So what's this new publication you're going to start?" the stranger asked innocently. "If you need any money, Alan Patricof is a close friend of mine. I know he'd be interested in investing."

ON OUR LAST DAY, we sat on the terrace and studied the surf, rolling its great barrels of energy into the shore. We watched it leave behind a silken sheet of water relieved of tension. The sea surprises us with what our ears have never heard, our toes have never touched, our eyes have never seen before; it is a place of endless beginnings. Each moment is a miracle, and we have to be present for it.

Just then we heard the phone ring from inside the bungalow. I ran to pick it up.

"Mr. Felker has a call from London, from a Mr.—I beg your pardon—from a Lord Harmsworth?" said the operator with a note of awed surprise. "Yes, put him through." Vere Harmsworth, the third Viscount Rothermere, was a British newspaper magnate who had founded the *Daily Mail*. He had talked to Clay in the past about searching for a new American magazine to buy, possibly *Esquire*. Clay saw me beckoning. When I mouthed the name of his caller, he ran. I held out the phone for both of us to hear.

"Vere?"

"Let's go!"

WHEN THE BOARD SOLD *NEW YORK* MAGAZINE, the *Village Voice*, and *New West* to Murdoch in 1977, the value generated for the shareholders was only about $15 million. By 1992, Murdoch's News Corp.

had amassed huge debts and sold off many of its American magazine interests, including *New York,* which then had a value of $150 million, and the *Village Voice,* which then brought $55 million. Ken Fadner pointed out to me later the board members' limited understanding of the media business: "They claimed that Clay was no businessman. But the man who was not a businessman created properties worth well over $200 million, while the 'businessmen' sold out cheap."

CHAPTER 25

FOR THE LOVE OF EDITORS

AN EDITOR WITHOUT A PUBLICATION is like a jockey without a horse. *New York* was the equivalent of Clay's only child. It was hard to imagine that he would be able to pick himself up and find another winning horse. There were nights when he awoke with a sob snarled in his throat; one night in particular, when he dreamed of falling down a bottomless black hole and bolted upright gasping for air. He could not talk to me about the terror. Only years later did he admit that he decided that night to throttle all thoughts of murdering his betrayers. The terror and anger would fester in his throat with consequences we could not imagine.

But on he galloped, excited by the prospect of partnering with Vere Harmsworth to buy the only other publication he had loved, *Esquire*. Those negotiations, begun in 1977, would take almost two years. Meanwhile, he found a hometown shopper to buy in Northern California, the *Advertiser,* and tried to pretend that selling discounts on day-old bread had some redeeming value.

With the success of *Passage*s continuing unabated, I was being pursued by literary editors to write the next book. I must admit I fell a little bit in love with every editor who worked with me over the years. Not surprising. Pairings between writer and editor are naturally intimate, a dance between dominance and submission. The writer is the vulnerable one, always wishing to say, "Do you love it?" Translation: "Do you love me?" To risk surrendering some creative control, the writer must have faith that the editor wants to enhance the author's book, not turn it into the editor's own. It takes polite lunches and panicky late-night phone calls and missed deadlines and making up to build the necessary trust.

Need I say that in the '70s few men in senior positions respected any boundaries between professional relationships with women and the desire for conquest of any attractive female who moved through their daily orbit. The most amusing effort was made during a hiatus in my romance with Clay. He was a senior editor beloved around Random House as a brilliant mind inside a shambling recluse. Joe Fox could hardly be seen behind the two-foot-high wall of yellowing newspapers that sat on his desk, behind which he chain-smoked and pored over the manuscripts of some of the finest writers of his generation, including James Salter, Peter Matthiessen, and Truman Capote. But that barrier disappeared once he invited me to dinner to discuss my next book.

Our dinner conversation veered off topic and into the usual first-date questions and answers: his divorce, my divorce, our dreams and disappointments. The restaurant was around the corner from Central Park South, which allowed Joe to make the casual suggestion that he show me his dramatic apartment in the Gainsborough Studios.

The façade of the Gainsborough was unique, lavishly ornamented with classical sculpture and carved latticework on the lower floors, but breaking out into intensely colored tile work above. Inside, Joe's duplex gave a dazzling view through double high windows of Central Park's soft yellow lampposts glowing between spongy trees. Over snifters of brandy, Joe gave me the history of the building, designed to reflect the status of well-established artists. Then he excused himself to prepare the surprise. Ten minutes later, he reappeared sartorially transformed in a white tie and tails, perfectly pinched bow tie, a top hat rakishly tilted to one side, dancing shoes, and confidently twirling a cane. His hunched spine was upright, the lead shaken out of his feet. Shod in tap shoes, he was transformed into a suddenly graceful, light-footed artist of the dance, and he was not bad! He wanted to show me his secret self—Fred Astaire.

That performance led to a brief flutter of a romance, but not to an editorial marriage. My heart still belonged to Clay. But I never again thought of Joe Fox as "shambling." Sadly, in 1995, while smoking, the secret Fred Astaire expired at his desk behind the wall of yellowed newspapers.

HILLEL BLACK, THE EDITOR IN CHIEF of William Morrow, made his own unique impression in 1978. He invited me to lunch at Tavern on the Green. A warm man with a mischievous twinkle in his eyes and a crooked smile, he made me feel good within our first hour. He did this by listening, his body language always leaning in, his gentle prodding, "Tell me more," conveying genuine interest in me as a writer.

"I want to show you something you have written," he said. "Take a look and see if you like what I do." He had taken a copy of one of my magazine pieces and pencil-edited it, to demonstrate, he said, "that I get your writing and I can make it even better."

I was humbled; he did make it better. And I liked Hill. We talked about my concept for a book about people who make successful passages through failure and heartbreaks and the normal vicissitudes of life. In the couple of years since publication of *Passages,* its thesis was not only being absorbed by popular culture, it was being adopted by academia as a part of the growing field of study of adult development and healthy aging.

With the boomer generation approaching the dreaded "middle age"—then thought to begin in the forties—and intensely interested in itself, important longitudinal studies of midlife were launched.

I was eager to pursue my research in a similar fashion. There were now more Americans in their forties and fifties than had ever existed in any country of the world, and no one had closely mapped such a population to see who prospered in health and enjoyed well-being, who among them was negotiating the treacheries of tough passages and finding uncommon paths to growth in the physical, emotional, social, and spiritual dimensions of their lives. These were the people I would call *pathfinders*.

By the spring of that year I was still desperate for money. It's always a struggle to get paid as a writer. My new literary agent, John Hawkins, discovered a killer clause in my *Passages* contract with Dutton. It so drastically limited the amount of yearly income I could take from royalties on the book sales that I wouldn't see the full proceeds from a bestseller until I was too old to care. Clay sent me back to his friend Tom Baer, the lawyer. During the seemingly interminable weeks that Baer tore into the Dutton contract and disqualified the income holdback, Hill and I played tennis and got to know each other.

I believed I had to validate the success of *Passages*. I used at least a third of my large advance for the follow-up book to fund an academic-level study. Only later did I understand how women often think we must justify success. Men don't second-guess being rewarded monetarily, but I was still dragging along my '50s socialization behind my '70s radicalization. I took three years to travel and research *Pathfinders*. It paid off with many vivid stories of people who had made passages successfully and achieved high well-being.

What made pathfinders different? I wanted to know. All of us have stood at a point where two roads diverged and doubted our wisdom to choose. Some refuse to choose and remain in a rut; others take the safest path; but pathfinders take the risk of choosing the less-traveled path. It can lead to a new beginning, an opportunity to make themselves more. What could they teach us about the qualities we need to cultivate to build toward well-being?

The elusive concept of well-being is more than happiness, which is only fleeting. Happiness generally conveys relief from pent-up frustration or deprivation of pleasure. Well-being is an accumulated attitude that registers deep in our unconscious. It grows into a sustained background tone of equanimity behind the more intense contrasts of daily events, behind even periods of unhappiness. To find such pathfinders among us, I worked with a team of social psychologists at New York University to develop an extensive Life History Questionnaire. It probed the self-perceptions, values, goals, coping styles, and experiences at each stage of life of adults between the ages of eighteen and eighty. Within the questionnaire was a complex instrument for measuring well-being; it identified the women and men who were finding the keenest contentment in the many dimensions of a full life.

During 1978 and 1979, I gathered questionnaires from a wide diversity of Americans who were recommended by their peers: corporate chiefs, members of Congress, men and women lawyers, women brokers and bankers, homemakers, professional athletes, military officers, union representatives, automotive workers, women returning to school for professional degrees, and working people attending community colleges. By the end of 1979, I was ready to cast the widest nets of all, by publishing the Life History Questionnaire in two mass-circulation magazines, *Redbook* and *Esquire*.

Altogether, we collected sixty thousand questionnaires. A computer team at NYU tabulated the data. Dialing up people who scored at the highest and lowest levels of well-being for maximum contrast, I made hundreds of telephone interviews. Some sounded like contestants for *To Tell the Truth* while others were more sincere and willing to collaborate on probing their life stories with me. I narrowed the selection to people who passed my "no b.s. test."

The next two years were an exciting odyssey that took me across thirty-eight states, four Canadian provinces, three European countries, and many occupational, racial, ethnic, and social-class boundaries. Most phone or paper surveys skip this step. In my view, subjective understanding of a human being can come only from face-to-face experience.

To reduce my conclusions to the very essence, I learned that people who gain high well-being share at least three hallmarks. They say . . .

1. I have a willingness to take risks.
2. I have experienced one or more important transitions in my adult years, and I have handled those transitions in an unusual, personal, or creative way.
3. My life has meaning and direction.

While I was researching this book, I saw that it had resonance in my own life. I had taken risks in my career; some had not paid off, but others had catapulted me into new levels of curiosity, craft, and success. I hadn't been brave enough to take the risk of marrying again, and I ached to have another child; in those areas I was sorely incomplete. Would I ever find the confidence and creativity to make those passages?

Becoming a pathfinder, I came to understand, requires small acts of courage. It means bucking the status quo, striking out on a less-traveled path, and using one's ingenuity or creativity to meet the challenges of a difficult life passage. If it leads to a failure, a pathfinder will learn from it, resist panic and self-recrimination, and find the resilience to pick him- or herself up and try a different path. Coming out of such a passage with a sense of completion may take several years. But the boost in self-esteem and well-being is worth all the effort. The pathfinder gains a new sense of mastery.

WHILE I WAS BURIED in analyzing questionnaires for *Pathfinders,* Clay gave me the chance to meet with a world-class pathleader. At the time, Clay and Milton Glaser owned *Esquire,* together with Viscount Vere Harmsworth. Clay sent me to Egypt in November 1978 to write about President Anwar Sadat. This was a year after Sadat had found the courage to journey from Egypt to Israel to meet Prime Minister Menachem Begin and address the Knesset. It was widely regarded as one of the most innovative acts of peace in the twentieth century.

Before I went to Egypt, I learned that this was a man whose devotion to his predecessor, Gamal Abdel Nasser, earned him the nickname "Nasser's poodle." When Nasser's envy caused him to denigrate Sadat for his heroic exploits as a young revolutionary, Sadat withdrew. As he wrote, he took up the position of a detached observer. A government functionary, he did nothing self-destructive. He did not give up hope. Remaining in this state of suspended animation for eighteen years, he adapted to a reality he could not change. How, I wondered, was he able to come back in his fifties, after nearly two decades of passivity, and emerge with every fiber of stifled intuition intact, ready to risk taking a less-traveled path that no Middle Eastern leader had ever dared?

The Egyptian leader was invited by President Carter to meet with him and Begin at Camp David in September 1978. Over twelve days, with Carter using real muscle to challenge each of the adversaries in one-on-one meetings, a historic peace agreement was reached. It was a month after Sadat had returned from Camp David that Clay sent me to Cairo on the faint possibility that I might get an interview with the now-celebrated Egyptian leader.

Confined for a week in a hotel room in Cairo across the hall from a Saudi family that cooked chickens in their room, I stared at the phone praying for a summons to the presidential palace. To pass the time, I composed a history of the man's life and studied his Muslim philosophy. Warned that I would have only twenty to thirty minutes with him, I color-coded the question cards according to their urgency. It turned out to be time well spent.

"GOOD MORNING!"

Sadat did not enter ceremoniously. He appeared out of nowhere like a puff of smoke. Dark, gaunt, looking like a prisoner of war—or was it a prisoner of peace?—his energy and theatricality quickly engaged me. An introductory conversational gambit explained why he was so thin. He had been fasting since August and the holy month of Ramadan. But he had kept up the fast through the Camp David summit and come home to Egypt to start a social revolution by first consuming himself.

The three months of fasting, he told me, helped revive the mental discipline he had learned when jailed as a terrorist in his twenties. He explained that he regarded his time in prison as the happiest period in his life. His narrow self ceased to exist. In fasting and meditation, he came to believe that depending on outward success alienates a man from himself. And self-alienation was the worst fate to befall a man, leading to the loss of inner light and the end of any possibility of vision. He came to experience friendship with God—"the only friend who never lets you down or abandons you."

I began my formal interview with a different kind of question: "Mr. President, you have proved Egypt to the world, proved yourself to the world, and you no longer have to be quite so careful. It is important for people to know you in your depth. No one is without some frailties, some imperfections. Will you join with me in the objective of following your passages—by that I mean the transitions between stages of adult life when we have the chance to grow or to go backward?"

"Very interesting, your approach," he purred, puffing on his pipe. "For me it is like this: since my childhood, even when I was very poor but proud, I was asking to be a different guy from the others." That interview gave me an insight that offered another dimension to the *Pathfinders* book. Two hours later, we were still talking when his muscle-bound secretary waved his arms frantically to shut me up. Sadat brushed him off. He was about to reply to my final question: "What is your personal attitude toward death?"

"I don't fear it at all," he replied. "No one will rob me of one hour of my life. God has put it. So I am at ease. Great ease." I was amazed by his serenity. He let me know that it was part of his Muslim faith, believing in predestination. Having prayed and fasted and prepared for months before making the decision that it was his destiny to go to Israel with the offer of peace, he was not responsible for the outcome of his action. To me, as a product of Western Judeo-Christian thought, it was a novel concept: he carried no burden of guilt if things did not turn out well. This was a wholly unfamiliar way of faith. For Sadat, it settled him into a serenity that was palpable.

"Do you expect to be killed for breaking with the tragic history of Muslims and Jews by offering peace?" I asked.

Sadat sucked on his pipe, not a pinch of anxiety anywhere in his face. "If it is so, I am not surprised; I have done my work in this world." He let me know that he expected his hour was not far away.

Sadat's peace treaty with Israel enraged Islamists. On October 6, 1981, during an annual victory parade held in Cairo, Anwar Sadat was gunned down by members of a jihadi cell in his own military. The *New York Times* carried a memorable cartoon on its op-ed page. Little people wandered, baffled, through what appeared to be a featureless desert landscape. They were saying: "We want to follow in his footsteps—but where are they?" Ironically, they were stumbling in the middle of a footprint so gigantic, they could not see it.

Clay was delighted to publish the first in-depth portrait of the Egyptian leader's personality, titled "The Riddle of Sadat." After his assassination, the article was widely reprinted as prophetic.

OVER THE YEARS, MY EXPERIENCE with editors has been magical: Tina Brown at *Vanity Fair* and the *Daily Beast* and, later, Graydon Carter, a Renaissance man who greatly enhanced *Vanity Fair* beginning in 1992. As an author, I was thrilled to be published by Random

House under the leadership of Harry Evans. There I worked on five books with one of the last of the classic gentlemen editors, Robert Loomis. His authors were mostly men, from William Styron, Calvin Trillin, and Neil Sheehan to historians Edmund Morris and Shelby Foote. Maya Angelou and Shana Alexander were two of his star women authors. I was much younger than they and hungry to learn more about writing at book length.

Loomis was famous for his cryptic comments penciled on the manuscript. "We know this." Even more astringent were the barely audible critiques emitted from beneath his white pencil mustache as we worked over long lunches at Mediterraneo, an Italian café on Second Avenue around the corner from the Random House building. The food was banal, the service worse. But while Loomis sipped his Jack Daniel's on the rocks, I scribbled notes from one of the masters of structure and style.

At HarperCollins I have had the pleasure of working with two fine women editors: Mary Ellen O'Neill was a compassionate companion while both of us were acting as caregivers for loved ones. She helped me to combine my personal story with practical help in my last book, *Passages in Caregiving*.

The process of writing a memoir is different from anything else I have done. The patience and painstaking effort required to burrow into one's past and salvage the richest memories begs for an editor of the rarest tolerance. I have been blessed in having the skill and enthusiasm of Jennifer Brehl while working on this book.

I have other passions, of course—skiing, tennis, and, later, theater and opera—but what is more satisfying than almost anything else is the marriage of minds with a trusted editor as we chisel words into a well-sculpted book.

CHAPTER 26

THE MISSION THAT FOUND ME

HONG KONG'S VICTORIA HARBOR was suddenly ablaze in the plane's window, a dazzling light show of neon reflections coloring the water crimson, orchid, orange, garish green, any color but that of real water. It announced the purpose of Hong Kong: the creation of money.

"Come meet me in Hong Kong!"

Who but Clay would call out of the blue after months of separation with a command to fly halfway around the globe to meet him? "Trip of a lifetime!" was his headline. It was 1981 and his third call from Indonesia inviting me to spend two weeks seeing Asia with him. Clay knew how to tempt me to dive off the edge of the world into an adventure. I was thrilled, but wary.

He was waiting for me at the airport with an armful of exotic flowers and a hungry kiss. We were driven across the busiest bay in the world to Kowloon by his hosts from the *Far East Economic Review* to the Peninsula Hotel, veddy, veddy British. Hong Kong was still under British control, but the days were numbered before China would reclaim it. Cranes swung between the stacks of deluxe hotels and corporate flagships as if in a race against a Communist future. The incessant noise of the city was of slums being leveled and girders being pounded into landfill.

Gazing out from our luxurious room overlooking Victoria Harbor, where ocean liners began in the 1920s depositing European gentry at the doorway to Asia, Clay mused prophetically, "I'm glad we're living when we are—probably the last ten years when we can indulge ourselves in some sentimental colonialism before the Chinese take over the world."

I was excited to show him Temple Street. My seatmate had tipped me off about Hong Kong's vast outdoor kitchen hidden behind the public square. We gasped at the sea of bodies squatting on sidewalks and in the gutters and all up the side streets, countless families all cooking Mongolian hot pot over coal fires. Everyone dipped into the same pot and scuttled the morsels into their mouths quick as birds. Fortune-tellers moved between the makeshift tables offering to read bumps on one's head or released birds from cages to pick fortune cards. Sidewalk entrepreneurs fashioned false teeth and hawked snake venom for potency. To us, the only Caucasians in sight, the Chinese paid no mind. These were people fully enculturated in their own freewheeling style of street-corner capitalism.

Singapore and Malaysia were enthralling. But it was Christmas in Thailand that would change our lives.

Midnight of Christmas Eve passed in the confines of an airless plane while we awaited a delayed takeoff from Singapore. Clay was next to me slack in sleep. My daughter was half a world away. Eighteen years had passed since her conception. I remember thinking about that when I felt that month's clot drop; the blood apple of something like the three hundred and sixtieth ovum, falling, waste. A wind of emptiness seemed to blow through me. I began crying softly for what it was too late to have.

"Melly Kismis!" At three thirty in the morning we were welcomed into the Oriental Hotel in Bangkok by a Buddhist bellhop. Red satin bows were tied around the giant teak temple bells hung from the soaring lobby ceiling. We walked outside and down to a veranda over the *klong*, the wide canal, feeling embraced by the humid air and dizzied by the sweet rotted scent of jasmine. We discovered the Author's Wing, a genteel green-shuttered structure; its suites were named to call up the fateful attraction of the East to Western writers . . . Maugham, Conrad, Michener. A floor boy brought wild orchids, mangoes, and a split of champagne.

"This is the Colette room, in case you didn't know."

Hours later, we awoke slashed by sunlight through the uncurtained glass. Christmas Day, Bangkok, on our backs running musky with sweat. Now what?

Then we were on the verandah, mesmerized by watching the great hippos of rice barges nuzzle through the *klong*, up to their noses with cargo, when Clay pointed out a story in the *Bangkok Post*.

"Honey, this will interest you." He passed me the paper.

> Thousands of children, most of them under twelve, orphaned by the genocide in Cambodia, have been existing in holding centers inside Thailand for over two years. Many suffer from persistent malnourishment and other medical problems. They have scant hope of being adopted or resettled in third countries.

"Maybe there's a child for you here," Clay said.

Adoption was an idea as foreign to me as the hippo barges, but that was Clay and his leaps of imagination. I had been deeply moved by TV images of survivors of Pol Pot's genocide. After four years of forced labor and extermination by starvation for the crime of being educated, the survivors had to flee the 1979 invasion by the Vietnamese army. They kept coming that year, a surge of a half-million Cambodians, tuberous bodies with faces devoid of animation, minds frozen by years of trauma. By 1980, Cambodia was a land that had disappeared from Western consciousness.

Prior to this trip, First Lady Rosalyn Carter had invited me to join one hundred prominent Americans on her Cambodia Crisis Committee. We sat on gilt chairs in the East Room of the White House and discussed how to mobilize support to get Western rice and seed to survivors in the interior, past the Vietnamese political blockade.

On the verandah, now, I read the newspaper item again and shook my head. "We raised millions to bring starving Cambodians to the border after the Vietnamese invaded, and then what? We're leaving them to rot in holding centers?"

"Don't beat yourself up, honey," Clay said. "Cambodia is ancient history to American TV viewers now."

"Clay?"

"Hmmm?"

"We have to visit those camps."

"On our last day in Asia?"

"What better to do?"

He looped an arm around my hips. "I planned not to let you out of the room."

The lure of a last day devoted to your standard decadent Western pleasures held appeal for me, too, but as we crossed the Oriental's lobby toward the cool elevators, I broke away.

"Where are you going?" he said.

"To hire a driver."

"I'll go with you."

WE STAYED AN EXTRA DAY to get the necessary permissions to visit a holding center at the border, Khao-I-Dang camp. The Thais were jumpy about allowing journalists into these camps, for fear that news stories would swell the already indigestible mass of human refuse from ten years of war in Southeast Asia.

After five hours on bumpy, mostly dirt roads to the border, we were admitted to a camp that was nothing like what we expected. Neatness and order prevailed. Thousands of thatched dwellings showed little carpets of vegetable gardens in front. International relief agencies were providing food, birth-control injections, even electrification for rock bands. This was obviously the show camp.

The UN director of the camp, Erkki Heinonen, a reedy Finn, was not pleased to receive us. "We cannot allow foreign visitors to see the children," he said.

"Why not?"

"It could put ideas into their heads."

"Ideas?"

"These are simple children," he said, offering us tea. "They lost their families. The Khmer Rouge taught them the world is flat, nothing beyond the rice fields. Why give them ideas? Let them go back to Cambodia."

"Haven't they endured enough?" I asked. "Couldn't some be resettled in the West where they could have new families?"

"None of these people want to resettle in the West." The director was emphatic.

"All eighty-five thousand of the Cambodians in this camp are just waiting to go back to the horror of the killing fields?" I asked, incredulous.

"Some have already gone," he said, dodging a direct answer.

I stalled long enough to ask about the three giant plastic bags stuffed under his work table with what looked to be letters inside. "Oh, those." The director brushed off my question. "Resettlement fever. People write letters whenever they see some movement—a few children were accepted by France the other day."

The director excused himself. Alone in the office, I bent down to examine the plastic bags more closely. They were coated with dust. Crammed inside were hundreds of letters written by refugees in the camp and addressed to embassies, mostly to the U.S. Embassy. Pleas obviously smothered before they were heard.

"There's a story here," I said. Clay came up with the headline. "The People America Forgot."

THE PLANE RIDE HOME seemed interminable. I couldn't wait to get to a pay phone in the airport and call the editor of the *New York Times Magazine,* Ed Klein. I wanted an assignment to go back to Thailand. A few bags of unsent letters was hardly worth a story, but Klein didn't give me a total brush-off. I had some reporting to do. Every call I made referred me to a man who was said to know more about Cambodian refugees than anyone in the world: Peter Pond, a New Hampshire minister with an extraordinary family of five adolescent survivors of Cambodian genocide. A humanitarian hustler, he found me first.

"I thought we should join forces," he said on the phone.

"I don't know much yet," I said. "But the pipeline for resettlement seems to be shut down."

Pond told me it was the new Reagan administration's policy. Because the United States had closed the door on Southeast Asian refugees, other Western countries were following suit. That left the fate of the child survivors in the hands of the Thai military. "The silent policy of the Thais is that these kids oughta go back and fight with the Khmer Rouge against the Vietnamese, never mind coming to the United States."

"But they're still children, aren't they?"

"Mostly teenagers now," Pond said. "They were held hostage by the Khmer Rouge for three or four years. Separated from their parents and trained as the future of the country. No intellectual training, school was the rice fields. Some were forced to carry guns at the age of eleven or twelve."

"How many survived?"

"At least half died, but about three thousand managed to sneak across the border into Thailand. They've been in the camps ever since."

My interest was growing far beyond the personal. This was not just a story, this was becoming a mission. I called Klein with more ammunition.

"Thailand," Klein said. "That's a hell of an expensive travel budget."

"I'll pay half."

A week later, I was back in Thailand to write a story about the child survivors of Cambodian genocide—the pawns of war.

PANIC WAS SPREADING THROUGH a different refugee camp, Sakeo, on the day I returned to Thailand. The first movement of refugees to a third country in a full year had taken place the day before. Rumor had it that this would be the last. As soon as I stepped out of the car, my pale face and red hair attracted a swarm of camp inmates. Hundreds of people pressed letters for the U.S. Embassy into my arms. I was trapped.

"Guide for you, okay?" A pair of muscular teenage shoulders appeared above the mass of short people, then a broad smile; he introduced himself as Nhep Sarouen and opened the crowd like a gate. Sarouen was hungry to speak English, forbidden by the Thai guards. He held out his battered English copybook and spoke in a hushed voice. "This my best friend, I sleep with, I play with." In it, he had copied out an entire English dictionary.

"You America?" he asked.

"Yes, American."

"America means freedom, something no one can smash out of our minds."

"Do people here have serious hopes of going to America?"

"All people here very afraid they send back to Cambodia, Vietnamese kill them." Sarouen looked over his shoulder at the Thai guards and sucked in his breath. "Take people, at night, in a truck to the border, no one see them again."

Sarouen led us to the Thai commander's office. Children scampered beside us, their shy smiles followed by the traditional Khmer greeting, their fingertips and palms pressed together in the shape of a lotus blossom. Then they dipped their chins to their fingertips. They never looked me in the eye. I knew that Cambodian children were taught as a sign of respect not to look directly at grown-ups. That was what I found strange about the girl with hungry eyes. I was vaguely aware of her, a child of maybe ten or twelve, darting behind bamboo fences but following me like a deer through the forest. Her wary eyes kept reappearing, and just as quickly disappearing. I took out my Nikon.

The Thai commander received me, scowling. "No camera. Not stay long. We do not consider these people refugees. Illegal immigrants." He motioned to a mustached guard wearing orange lipstick to bring tea. I asked the official if Cambodians were still fleeing across the border and into his camp.

"Camp closed," he barked. "Border closed. Must put in your story!"

Sarouen led me to a sequestered area of the camp known as the Children's Center. It was under the supervision of volunteers from the International Rescue Committee. The young American woman in charge introduced herself as Margie de Monchy. She was prepared to use the full deck of her bureaucratic powers to keep me from interviewing any unaccompanied minors, as the teenage survivors of Pol Pot were called.

"But why? Don't you want publicity, to help them get out?" My official role now was the newspaper lady writing a story for the *New York Times*.

Margie laid her cards on the table. "Look, these children see a *farang* and go a little crazy."

"What's a *farang*?"

"A foreigner. Us—French, British, American—we all look the same to them. They write more letters. Then you get back in your plane and forget."

I asked Margie if the IRC had been able to trace any of the children's family members who were still alive inside Cambodia. She looked at me wearily. "We've had a tracing program for almost two years. No hits."

Using all the charm I could muster, I persuaded Margie that I would not forget. A story in the *Times* might put some pressure on the United States to open the doors again for resettlement. She relented. As I walked back through the camp to the car, I caught another glimpse of the phantom girl whose hungry eyes continued to follow me.

The next day four boys and girls were lined up for me outside the Children's Center. A diminutive Cambodian woman, Darvy, was assigned as my translator. By late afternoon the tragic stories of massacre, mutilation, starvation, and seeing half-dead bodies tossed into pits had left me numb. But I had not yet seen a child from an urban background. There was a delay; the child scheduled for that interview was not available.

The girl with the hungry eyes suddenly appeared. In the midst of the dust and chaos, she was perfectly groomed. Her black hair was freshly washed with the comb marks still visible; it ran down her back like a waterfall. Her miniature body was wrapped in a flowered sarong.

"She offers to substitute," Darvy said. "She has twelve years, okay?"

"Okay." This girl had something else, that indefinable gravity we call presence. I asked the translator to tell her it was all right to look at me. She did. I smiled. She did not. We contemplated each other for a long time. For the next hour, she never took her eyes off my face.

"Do you remember a happy time?" I asked.

Such a frivolous question caught her by surprise. Her face brightened to the innocence of a child—almost. "Yes, she has happy memories." The translator painted the picture of an educated urban family who lived in a prosperous quarter of Phnom Penh. She and her brothers and sisters enjoyed picnics by the river and movies with their parents. Her grandparents had a gold-working shop. Her mother was part Chinese, which would explain her light amber skin. This made her family a prime target in July of 1975 when the illiterate peasant army of Pol Pot drove two million of the educated, urban populace on brutal marches out of the cities and into the war-wrecked countryside to do hard labor, deprived of schooling, money, or authority over their children.

"What happened to your family?" I asked.

The child spoke in a soft monotone, quickly but without inflection, digging the nails of one hand under the nails of the other, then flicking them apart with a high, clicking sound.

"Her father a soldier," the translator conveyed. "He fight on side of United States. When Pol Pot come, father return with soldiers and white flag to . . ."

"Surrender?"

"Yes, surrender. Her mother first one Pol Pot soldiers take."

"Why?"

The girl clicked her nails.

"She doesn't know why."

"*Slap,*" said the girl.

"*Slap?*"

"She mean kill," the translator said.

"*Slap,*" the girl repeated.

Did she have brothers or sisters?

Click click.

"Small brother and sister, very sick, only eat roots."

"Dysentery?"

"Yes. Then soldiers take her away. Send her work in forest. Send older brother away."

"Did she see her small brother and sister again?"

"She sneak in fields at night to dig crab for them, but when she lie to go home see her sister, the sister die three days before."

"And her little brother?"

"He starve."

"Did she see that?"

Click click.

"She see."

"Did she—did she see anybody beaten or killed?"

"She see woman and man, for love."

"For love?"

"They punish woman and man in public. Beat with stick."

Horror flickered in the child's eyes.

"Beat them to death?"

"Yes. To death."

"And she saw this, too?"

"She saw."

"Oh, God, what did she think?"

"She think of her parents, maybe they die like this."

Tears began to smear the girl's expressionless eyes, but they did not spill over. She held up her arm in front of her face and dropped her head to the table. Soundless moments passed, a slight trembling in her back the only visible sign of distress. The sobs I heard were coming from the translator.

"I never see her like this before," Darvy whispered.

"She's never told her story before," Margie said. "We don't have time to ask."

I massaged the child's back and waited for her to compose herself. The Thai guard demanded to know when I would leave.

The girl lifted her head. Her face was bland as a Buddha's.

I asked for permission to take her picture. Through the lens of my camera she looked like the *apsara,* shapely young celestial nymphs in Buddhist mythology that dance seductively in stone around Cambodia's ancient temples. I mumbled endearments to the child.

"She thank you from her heart, and she—" The translator broke off in midsentence.

"What else did she say?"

Click click. The child worked her nails.

"Nothing. She confuse."

"Please, what is it?"

"She think you take her to free country."

"Oh my God—can you explain, I mean, this is for a newspaper story . . ."

The child immediately entreated the translator to put things right. "She very sorry she make mistake."

The child backed away. The spell was broken. She stood straight and dry eyed and bowed her head to her hands, forming the Khmer good-bye, waxen and closed. Outside I was besieged by a new crowd of letter bearers.

"What's her name?" I shouted over the heads to Darvy.

"Who?"

"The last one."

Darvy shook her head; she didn't understand.

"The girl who couldn't cry."

Darvy's lips formed the words *Srey Mom.* Surviving children had had their family names wiped from their memories to avoid being victimized as offspring of the intelligentsia. *Srey Mom* in Khmer meant simply "beloved girl." It was not a name. Frantic grown-ups pressed in from all sides until I couldn't see a thing. Only an airborne observer—one of those crisp officials in a UN helicopter—might have seen below the figure of a pale-skinned woman, blowing a kiss to the girl who could not cry.

CHAPTER 27

SEPARATIONS

MY STORY CAME OUT in the *New York Times Magazine* in June 1982. The refugee children haunted my dreams. In particular, I could not forget Srey Mom. I had decided I must find a way to adopt her. On a crusade to spread awareness about the survivors of the Cambodian genocide, I persuaded Don Hewitt, the producer of *60 Minutes,* to do a story on them. But personally, I was frustrated. How could the letter I sent to Srey Mom—the only name I had—ever reach her? Calling around to social agencies, I could not find anyone who could help me to sponsor a Cambodian refugee. It looked hopeless.

That summer, when Maura and I returned from Scotland after our last vacation together before she left for college, neither Ella nor I could bear to let her go. We made all her favorite dishes and ironed all her clothes, even jeans, anything to stay connected awhile longer. Before the designated day of letting go, the nineteenth of September 1982, Maura asked me to drive her to Brown University two days earlier than planned. I lied to myself: maybe she was just anxious to get a head start. That rationale didn't stick. Feeling unloved and unappreciated, I had one of my flashes of temper. I scolded Maura in the cold, censorious voice she hated. She walked out of the apartment. I called Clay to tell him my life was over. I remember him saying, "Listen to yourself and you will realize that, rationally, none of the things you've just said are true. It's all an overblown neurotic reaction to your daughter leaving home."

What came out of this was an emotional collision with my daughter. She let me know how her self-confidence could be corroded by my outbursts. She didn't get enough of me. Sure, I took her on trips across the country and halfway around the world while I did stories on famous people, but how often did I hang out with her, in her room, listening to her music, wanting to be there just for her?

Of course, I knew she needed to separate. Still, I was devastated. Instead of just listening with my heart, I offered excuses. It wasn't easy being a single mother. I hadn't chosen it. I had to work all the time to pay for our lives. On and on. It was Maura who patched up the rift, suggesting that I stay over in Providence for a day or two so our parting would not be so abrupt. We shopped for a bedspread, books, a pair of black Reebok Freestyles. By the time I left, she said she felt confident and enthusiastic about doing well at college.

"Would you like me to walk you to the car?" she asked on that parting day.

"No, darling. It's time. It's your time."

A FEW DAYS LATER, a two-sentence letter arrived from the girl who couldn't cry. Over her handwritten Khmer, a translation had been penned: *I miss you. I want to live with you in America.* Even after nine months, she remembered. Our connection was profound.

Clay and I were not living together in 1982. By then, he was in Hollywood half the time, working for Twentieth Century Fox, occupying one of those movable chairs given to producers whose movie projects seldom get a green light. I hadn't seen him for several months. When I called him with news about the letter, I hoped that he would share my delight. After all, he was the originator of the compassionate idea of adopting a Cambodian refugee. He was not happy.

I had found a rent-stabilized apartment on Fifth Avenue, near the Metropolitan Museum of Art, for the then-miraculous price of $1,300 a month. It had a terrace overlooking Central Park. A small glass cubicle sat on one end of the terrace, where I wrote as if suspended in the sky. I could watch the leaves turn from scarlet to lemony pale and sit snug in a winter storm like being enclosed in a snow globe. It was as close to a writer's heaven as one could get.

Unheated, the cubicle was also ideally suited to keeping the neurons jumping. In winter I typed in a hoodie, my feet encased in Alaskan mukluks. In spring, the terrace became my first garden. I filled the window boxes with swaying tulips. Tubs held bonsai mimosa trees and dwarf crabapple trees that bore fruit in the fall. It was a magical place to invite friends for drinks and outdoor supper.

"CLAY? OH, YOU FRIGHTENED ME." It was after midnight. "C'mon up." Buzzer, dash for the bathroom mirror, splash of cold water on sleep-puffy eyes; I wasn't expecting Clay to be in New York. He came in with his rakish smile and his clean male smell. It was months after our Asia trip, but the magnetism had lost no pull. My heart turned over. The part of him that lived within me, impervious to time or events, was a separate and authentic thing—love. We couldn't finish a glass of wine before we came together.

In the after swoon, he said he couldn't stay over. My bed, the way it stuck out in the middle of the room—he knew would make it impossible for him to get a decent night's sleep. I said I would have a hard time sleeping, too, with his coming and going whenever the mood struck him.

"I thought you were glad to see me," he said.

"I was, I mean, oh, God, Clay"—spilling it now, not having meant to—"they're going to keep me from getting her out."

"Who?"

"The State Department, the immigration people, I don't know

who exactly. Our former ambassador to Cambodia told me the Reagan administration is going to punish me for my *Washington Post* op-ed about the refugees American bombs created and now want to forget. They won't let me bring her out."

"Bring who out?"

"You know. Srey Mom."

"Agghh, God, Gail." He was up and pulling on his pants with that air men get when something is revealed as out of their control. "You can't expose a traumatized child from a primitive background to the lack of acceptance she'd find in New York."

"Compared to a childhood spent in a refugee camp?"

"You have no idea what traumas she's been through. Why would you take such a chance?"

"Because I want another chance to be the right kind of mother."

I remember Clay stuttering with concern. "Gail, this, I mean, it's noble, but it's not a good idea." He couldn't find his sock. Our dog Ms. had a thing for smelly socks. I put on Clay's shirt and walked barefoot out onto the terrace. The night had deepened into silky last-of-the-summer black with a veil of clouds, a night when love should not be uninterrupted.

"What're you doing out there?"

"Planting tulip bulbs." Oh, I was on a tear now.

"I just want to say good night."

I looked up the terrace steps at him: maybe he was not, after all, the man of my life. "Who was it who got me started thinking about adopting a Cambodian orphan?"

"The reason that I—"

"Push-pull, push-pull, there's a real fear for you in getting close, Clay."

"You're wrong about that. I can't reason with you." Suddenly he was talking about premenopausal panic.

"Of course. I'm just a woman!"

"It shows how desperate you are, to consider taking in a teenage child from another culture."

"Desperate? Because I fell in love? With a child? She's only twelve."

"Everyone knows that women get irrational when they're afraid of losing their looks."

"I don't need middle age to be irrational."

"Not that *you*, I mean you're prettier than ever—"

"It's not about looks—it's about the family you would never agree to have!"

"Don't attack me!"

He ran for the door. We had exhausted our tolerance for open warfare. I had to rip off his shirt and hand it to him.

He said at the door: "It's really very simple."

"What?"

"The reason we haven't gotten married. You know."

"I don't know."

"I need you to pay more attention to me."

It hit me. Hard. Thinking about Clay took up more of my time than sleep.

"So *you* want to be the child!"

These last accusations were too true to be forgiven. We had unmasked each other's fears. Standing there in nothing but my panties, arms folded angrily over my chest, I finally replied. "Clay, you once told me that if I make a major decision on my own, I do it fine."

He grunted assent.

"I'm going to make this decision on my own." I saw his startled look. "I think we ought to take a vacation from each other," I said.

"Fine. Good."

"I mean it."

"So do I."

———————————

EXACTLY NINE MONTHS AFTER I had met Srey Mom in the camp, I walked across the street after a dinner at the typewriter and sat beside the rowing lake in Central Park. I gazed at the lovers enjoying their postprandial idylls and felt my aloneness. Back in the apartment, a quick check of messages on my answering machine turned up an unfamiliar voice.

What? Who? When? WHEN? I listened again. Yes, I must have heard the astonishing message correctly: *Srey Mom arriving tomorrow night, September 30, Northwest Airlines, flight 8, JFK, 8:30 P.M.*

Just like that, a new life began.

CHAPTER 28

DISCOVERING MOHM

"EXPECT LICE."

"Assume she's been raped repeatedly."

"They're very manipulative, refugees are, maybe even violent."

These were warnings from resettlement workers. I knew nothing. Who was this child who had lost her name, her family, her country?

Maura was thrilled, yet concerned for the child. Were we really doing her a favor with such a drastic dislocation? I wondered myself.

My mother was wonderful. She had demonstrated that the best way to defeat the numbing ambivalence of middle age is to surprise oneself. "Don't let anyone talk you out of it," she said over the phone from Florida. "Listen to your heart." At forty, my mother seemed old. At fifty, divorced by my father for a much younger woman, my mother had bounced back, begun a new business, dropped three dress sizes, and within a few years had been courted by and married to the love of her life. More than once she had pulled me out of anomie by chirping, "If I could start a new life at fifty-three, why you, honey, with what you have to offer [etc., etc.]—and besides, you're still young!"

I had a strong intuition that this child was meant to move on, that she had the will to endure another transmigration, that the adventure would be right for both of us. Margie de Monchy, the former director of the Children's Center in Sakeo, called to reassure me. No matter how traumatic the transition, she said, resettlement was the only alternative left.

What were the essentials? Nightgown, toothbrush, a Khmer-English dictionary, a globe—and something to give her self-respect. I dashed to Asia House to buy a poster of Angkor Wat. She must know that we respected her culture. As the hours before her arrival raced by, my preparations grew more feverish. But underneath I was singing.

Peter Pond, the humanitarian hustler who had been helping me, arranged for General Chana, Thailand's former ambassador to Cambodia, to ride with me to the airport and interpret. My sister, Trish, wanted to come. Fearing Clay might bring negative vibes, I did not invite him. Best to keep it simple. We set off for JFK in my green VW Beetle.

Halfway around the earth, a small orphaned survivor who had already run from the Vietnamese through forests, eating fruit dropped by monkeys that she knew was not poison, who had walked across the border of the damned, stepping over corpses into Thailand to reach a United Nations truck before she collapsed from malnutrition, this survivor had taken another risk. She had given away her sarongs, found homes for her bird and her cat, said good-bye to Darvy, her camp housemother, and stepped off the edge of a world she had been taught was flat, all for a crazy hope called "future."

How did she get out? The pipeline to America was opened for only twenty-four hours. I learned that Margie de Monchy and other American volunteers with IRC had shrewdly seized the last day before the fiscal year ended—a day when the ceiling for refugees expired and before Congress could vote to close it again—and hustled Srey Mom and fourteen other unaccompanied minors onto a plane bound from Bangkok to the United States. Officials gave her no name, no address, no fix in the galaxy to set her internal compass for, nothing but a mimeographed map of America with a yellow highlighting over the magic words *New York*.

After waiting for nearly an hour, at 9:42 P.M. a slip of a girl with enormous eyes and a LOVE T-shirt emerged from the jetway. We held each other's gaze as we moved through the crowds of passengers and family members. I embraced her. She was tiny but well formed. Her hungry eyes, looking up at me, were filled with light and hope, a child's eyes in a face no longer a child's.

I heard my sister, Trish, say, "She's beautiful, Gail."

General Chana had taught me a few phrases. "*Chum riap sua.*" Hello. I introduced my *bong srei*—sister. Was she cold? Yes. I had brought one of Maura's sweaters for her. Then I tried the phrase that means, in Khmer, I love you. "*Knhom sralanh nea.*"

Her face whirled up at me, astonished. Such an intimacy from a near-total stranger must have seemed odd, but then she seemed to relax.

"I think you said the right thing," whispered General Chana. He asked Srey Mom how she felt.

"*Sok sabai,*" she said, an expression that sounds exactly like what it means: "calm, content, well in spirit." She slipped her arm around my waist and we began to walk briskly into the bedlam of Kennedy Airport. Her long legs fell into synchrony with mine. A good sign. We were in step from the start.

The drive into New York was nightmarish. Cars and cabs coming at us with blinding lights, sirens screaming, skyscrapers looming up taller than mountains and looking, from where she lay in my sister's lap on the backseat, as if they would fall over on her from both sides. She was carsick.

At home, I showed her the terrace. She seemed to like seeing all the trees across the street. I picked a flower for her. She picked one for me, copying my movements precisely. I showed her the room that would be hers, all to herself. She looked dismayed. A room alone, a bed alone, so different from Sakeo where the children slept together on straw mats, all in a row.

She gravitated to the photograph of Maura. *Bong srei,* sister, I told her. She smiled. We turned on the light inside the new globe and I traced her flight path from Bangkok to Tokyo to Seattle and across the United States. A frown rippled across her forehead. Then, recognition. She ventured her first English words, "New . . . New Yawk!"

She wanted to know about the two little animals who kept sniffing at her sandals, my Lhasa apsos. We looked up the word *dog* in the dictionary. *Chkai.* My sister gave her a pretty nightgown. She pulled it over her fully clothed body. I motioned for her to take off her jeans. She dipped her head modestly. We had to leave the room.

Maura telephoned from college. "Snuggle with her." One thing I knew for certain: demonstrations of physical affection were severely inhibited in her culture. The head, the part of the body closest to God, must not be touched. We took off the bedcovers together and I tucked her in. One of the dogs jumped up and worked his rump into the indent of her waist. Would she like the *chkai* to sleep with her? I indicated. Her expression read as if I'd suggested she sleep in a tree. Dogs in Cambodia were seldom domesticated. Fully aware that I was taking a chance but unable to hold back, I brushed her cheek with my lips.

"Good night, angel."

I said good-bye to my sister and sat down with a glass of wine to look through the plastic bag that represented the sum total of Srey Mom's worldly possessions. A tin spoon, the torn half of a file card stamped by the U.S. Immigration Service, three pictures—Margie, Darvy, and the Buddha—and a tiny red plastic pocketbook. Inside, worn and folded in a cloth, was the first letter I had sent to her. I wept. What if I had been away on a trip when the call came? Call it luck, I chose to think of it as destiny. Srey Mom was one of the first Cambodian refugees to be settled in New York State. Together with Catholic Guardian Society, we could establish a precedent and help to foster others.

ON HER FIRST DAY, I wanted to keep the frenzy of the city at bay. It was mild for the beginning of October and I took her rowing on

Central Park Lake. It was the best activity I could think of to connect to her old life . . . nature, water, trees, peacefulness. Rowing did not require words. She quickly mastered the stroke and we pulled the oars in unison, just as we had fallen in step walking through the airport. As our boat glided under the wishing bridge, we lay back and gazed up at the trees bending to the water. Light filtered through the stone cutouts of the bridge and played over her face. She sighed aloud.

For a picnic, I bought her what I thought would be her first American treat. A hot dog. *Chkai,* I said. She accepted it, took a bite, then held the specimen away from her body the way a child does a dead snake. I went to find her an ice cream cone. When I came back, I found her burying the hot dog. She thought I wanted her to sleep with a dog and then eat a dog.

Early mornings she would climb into my bed and we would play word games. She had come without a word of English. Strict linguists stated there was a cutoff age at about twelve—her age—after which learners lose the ability to fully acquire a second language. But this child's appetite for learning was insatiable. She began sticking labels all over the apartment, sounding out the English words—*light, wall, floor, door*—as she wrote their Khmer equivalent above. Language gives voice to one's uniqueness. If I did nothing else, I had to give this child a voice. Every night, after I half closed her bedroom door, I would hear her reciting words she had memorized—*bus, car, subway, street, apartment*—words that reflected her fate in dropping out of the sky into the fast lane of a sophisticated Western metropolis.

When she called me "Mom," and I called her the same thing, we fell to laughing. I got a towel and we had a tug of war, then a pillow fight—who was going to be the mom around here? I had an idea. I found a box of letters and moved them around, putting an "h" inside the "Mom." Her name could be Mohm, pronounced like "Ohm." She liked it.

Maura let Clay know that the child had arrived. He called, hurt that he had been left out of the welcome, and asked, "How is she?"

"She's magic."

"I'm terribly excited to meet her." His tone was honest and sweet.

"I should have invited you to come to the airport. I didn't want to take the chance of marring that precious moment. But I'd love for you to meet her now."

Week three. We made the rounds of private schools. On the Upper East Side the reception was mostly chilly. One principal looked down his long Anglo-Saxon nose at the Asian child and shook his head. "We would, of course, have to suspend traditional educational goals in her case." All the school could provide, he said, was a rich social setting in which she could learn what it is to be an American teenager.

After being rejected by many schools, we were fortunate to find Friends Seminary, a gentle Quaker school on a tree-lined street downtown. All at once Mohm flew from my side and down the hall after two girls with black hair and amber skin, shrieking, "Same me!"

They were indeed two Cambodians. Friends had learned that the new refugees were languishing in a public school and reached out to offer them a place in the seminary, part of the mission of the American Friends Service Committee. The headmistress told me that the school was committed to instilling the concept of service in young people. Mohm was warmly accepted.

SEARCHING FOR POCKETS OF CAMBODIAN CULTURE, I found the principal teacher of the royal Cambodian dancers of Prince Sihanouk's palace, most of whom had been killed by the Khmer Rouge. Madame Kamel was alive and well in Brooklyn. She assessed Mohm, found that she was double-jointed and exceptionally graceful, and agreed to give her a tryout. On my return, I found Mohm squeezed into a string of children on a sofa, happily swaying together to Cambodian music. She looked totally grounded.

"Mohm can be a fine classical dancer," said the teacher. "But we must ask, is she serious?" Mohm nodded enthusiastically. I was elated. But pulling her out of a familiar cultural setting and plunging her back into the aridity of a Manhattan apartment with just the two of us, I watched a visceral change take place. Like a delicate shrub pulled up before its frail roots can support transplanting, she shrank into herself.

Drifting out onto the terrace, Mohm began walking in circles. She leaned over the railing and stared down eight stories to the street, turning her face away, trying to hide the last futile contortions before it turned into scowls of fear, anguish, or was it fury? I could not look at the wild discord in her face. She could not succumb to tears. I wrapped my arms around her shoulders. Her body felt like broken bird bones.

She put one foot up on the railing. I shuddered. Here in her glass-enclosed high-rise, she must have felt a prisoner, separated from her culture, lost, with me as her jailer. It began to grow dark and cold. "Will you come inside, sweetheart?" I tried.

"No."

The last sun drained from the clouds. I heard the doorbell. Mohm couldn't be left alone. A voice was calling; I couldn't make it out, then, amazed, I heard the name of Mohm's camp director. "It's Margie! Are you all right?" I had no idea Margie de Monchy was back in the States. "The door's open." Mohm's trance was broken. Margie quickly sized up the situation and joined us to talk to Mohm. They stood side by side, silent, Mohm hanging over the railing. Seven o'clock came and went. Finally, Mohm began to speak. Margie later told me what she said.

On the long plane ride from Bangkok to New York, she had watched the sun set, then rise, then set again. She thought she had landed on another planet. *I don't like to live here, all big apartments, no children. I can't speak. My family all gone, torn away. I'm already broken. I make a beginning of new life in the camps. Maybe I have to go the rest of my life without seeing anybody I love. I'm not even myself anymore. I don't think I want to go on.*

The doorbell rang. Another incredible coincidence. This time Mohm rushed inside to peek through the peephole, on guard. Seeing a man, she opened the door and instinctually butted her head into Clay's belly. He laughed. I let her know that this man was my friend, come to welcome her. She bowed her head in respect.

Clay had brought a big picture book about ancient Cambodia. He read his inscription to her in his deep voice, so unlike high-pitched Asian voices. It seemed to intrigue her. "Welcome to your new home. Here are some beautiful scenes from your other country. Now you have two home countries, the U.S.A. and Cambodia. I hope you will love it here."

Margie motioned for her to sit on the sofa between Clay and me and turn the pages. Seeing monuments of ancient Cambodia transported her to the deepest layers of memory and fantasy. She devoured the book page by page, narrating the zenith and decline of her culture. She pored over the visions of hell carved into the sandstone temples of Angkor Wat—people being yanked up by the hair, bludgeoned with shovels, led away in chains—images that could have been taken from news footage of Pol Pot's reign of terror. She drew a finger across her throat, letting us know that she had seen people's heads lopped off like fruit. "No go, *slap* . . ."

She looked for a long time at the sandstone carvings of *apsaras*. I tried to convey, through Margie, that Angkor Wat had not been touched by the Khmer Rouge. I'd read that only one of the hundreds of *apsaras* had been damaged over the centuries.

Mohm breathed. In Khmer, she said, "Oh, God, so good."

She excused herself and went into her bedroom. Was she sulking? We waited. Presently, she emerged in a green silk sarong with gold ornamentation, given to her by Madame Kamel. Her hair was wound up in a formal topknot, her feet bare with bracelets around the ankles. She switched on a tape player and we heard the endless loop of classical Cambodian ballet music.

Slowly, gently, her body slipped out of its bones. She began to undulate like the long stems of lotus blossoms that sway underwater in harmony with the currents, even during fierce storms, and never break. Her fingers turned into flocks of birds. Her hips rolled. Her face was serene. She was as beautiful as an *apsara*. Clay was besotted.

AROUND THE SAME TIME, we were given an opportunity to bring political awareness to the plight of refugee women and children around the world. One of my best friends, Catherine O'Neill, a tireless political activist, worked for the United Nations. She was appalled to learn that women and children displaced by war were left invisible, without livelihoods or health care, and easily victimized.

"Did you know that four out of five of the forty million refugees in the world are women and children?" she demanded of me and other of her friends. I was embarrassed to admit I didn't. Catherine's novel idea was to rally activist professional women to make fact-finding field missions to countries ravaged by war. We traveled on our own nickel but quickly buddied up into a bulwark of determination.

Maura joined me on our first trip, to the border of Cambodia. It was too dangerous to take Mohm back; the country's new leader was a former Khmer Rouge and vowed to recover children who had fled. Our delegation learned firsthand what the women and girls most needed and wrote our notes on the plane ride home.

"Did you finish yet?" Catherine prodded. She had already secured a congressional hearing. We were barely off the plane before we were testifying on the need for new policies that would improve the safety and offer basic services to refugee women and unaccompanied children, like Mohm. No one turned Catherine down—she was that savvy and bold. She could call up Charlie Rose and say, "You better put us on your show tomorrow, because we have up-to-the-minute news on what is happening in Cambodia," or, later, Bosnia or Afghanistan. The advocacy group we created, the Women's Refugee Commission, eventually became a legal arm of the world-renowned International Rescue Committee and to this day rallies the UN to engage women worldwide in conflict prevention and mediation.

THE WORK OF HEALING MOHM proceeded organically in the many hundreds of hours we spent together reading about Cambodia's history and mythology, playing its music, considering its religious mysteries and magic, and mostly talking heart to heart. I read to her from *The Diary of Anne Frank*. It touched her, as did *Siddhartha* about the spiritual journey of the prince who became venerated as the Buddha.

By the middle of her second year, the barrier of ice around Mohm's heart began to melt. "I wasn't welcome anyplace," she said. "That's why I had to forget about family and love and caring and just be, you know, how I was in the beginning, remember?"

"Yes, I remember."

"I could never wish. I could not have a dream. I have so much angry inside of me, remember, Mom?"

"Yes, I remember. You could not cry."

"Whole first year. Could not." She moved closer. "But now I can talk about the past with you," she said. "So many things I lost, so many mistakes I make . . ." Tears began to tremble on the edges of her lower lids.

"Let your tears come, Mohm." Hot tears streamed forth. She let me draw her into my arms, her head on my chest. She cried softly, not for long. She sat up.

"First time. Because now I believe I have a new life."

By spring, Mohm was warming to the idea of using her travails to help identify the plight of refugee children. She would work even harder to learn English so she could testify, too. One day I asked her, "What would you think if I wrote a book about the people who came out of Cambodia and used your experiences to show what a survivor is?"

"I can help you with that, I think," she said.

Smiling at her understatement, I asked if she knew the meaning of the word *survivor.* When she hesitated, I explained it.

"Oh, that's an easy one. I have good *veseana.*"

I remembered that in the Buddhist belief system, a person may be born with good *veseana* as a consequence of good actions in a previous life, but it's also a projection of a person's life force. Did Mohm have it?

"Of course I have good *veseana!*" Mohm looked at me almost in-credulously. "Why was I not kill and all my family die?"

I suddenly grasped that survivors with her beliefs have a rationale with which to answer that awful spiritual question: "Why me?" I asked Mohm if she felt guilty for surviving. She told me it had pained her terribly in the first year.

"But if I'm the only one in the family alive, probably God have some purpose I am saved for."

"Then let's concentrate on survivor merit instead of survivor guilt," I said.

A month later, Mohm asked me, "Did you write that book yet?"

"It's not such an easy one for me." I laughed. "Shall we do it to-gether?"

"If what I go through can give people a different idea, maybe it's not for nothing," she said. "So I think it's good."

Over several years, we pieced together the shattered story line of Mohm's past. The work of healing and the writing of the book became indistinguishable. The result was published in 1986, as *Spirit of Survival*.

CHAPTER 29

A PASSAGE FOR KEEPS

IT WAS A SHOCK to walk into Clay's apartment at the end of a happy summer in the country we shared with Maura and Mohm. The place was an excavation pit. A wall in the upstairs hall was missing. Plastic sheeting hung everywhere. His bedroom was blocked off. The carved four-poster in the guest bedroom was hung all around with his ties. They looked like flags hung from the balconies of Siena when we traveled there to watch the Palio horse race.

"Are you expecting someone?" I asked.

"I hope so." He mumbled something about making a new bedroom, closets, a family dining area.

"Family?"

"We'll see."

The summer must have stirred Clay's glacial emotions into movement, I thought, but I resisted nudging him. There was no win in pressing Clay on any personal question; he would only withdraw. That was the irony of Clay as an editor. On the most important matters in life, he was at a loss for words. He was a man of action.

Two months later he took me to London, ostensibly for a long theater weekend and to celebrate his birthday on October 2, 1984. Mohm had been invited to stay with Peter Pond's family of a half-dozen Cambodian refugees. They were going to meet the Dalai Lama.

I loved going to London with Clay. We always stayed at the Stafford, hidden in the heart of St. James on a quiet cobblestone mews. In a rare gesture of frugality, Clay would book one of the "cozy rooms" in the Carriage House, former stables. After a few days in a one-horse stall, he inevitably broke down and booked an adjoining room. The hotel backed up on Green Park, which allowed us to jog outdoors. Clay, jog? friends asked in disbelief. Okay, I jogged. He fast-walked for a mile or two, then gladly destroyed the results by lunching at Overton's on creamed shrimp on toast and a pudding studded with candied fruit.

We couldn't miss Peter Nichols's *Passion Play*, "a scorching depiction of modern marriage as an irresistible invitation to sexual infidelity." That resurrected our mutual fears of marriage. Clay took me for after-theater omelets and champagne at the Garrick Club and recounted a joke about Moses coming down from Sinai with the tablets and announcing: "First the good news—I got 'em down to ten. Now the bad news—adultery's still in."

On our final day Clay and I drove to Oxford and cozied up for an intimate lunch in a classic pub, the Carving Board. His behavior became even more comically incoherent. With the prickle of Buck's Fizz in our noses and the unctuousness of Stilton cheese on our tongues, we grew mellow. Dusk settled. Our faces were lit by an amethyst-and-gold stained-glass window. Only then did Clay make mention of *the date*.

"We should probably set the date before we go any further," he said.

"The date?"

"Not too close to Christmas."

"Definitely not too close to Christmas," I teased.

"The living room is big enough, don't you think?"

"It depends on what you're using it for." Was it my imagination or did he look uncomfortable?

"Would you like another Buck's Fizz?" Yes, he was uncomfortable.

"Darling, is there something else you want to ask me?"

"Is that really necessary?"

"You might get lucky and I'll say no."

"Gail, why do you think I've been turning my apartment upside down?"

"You want a family?"

"I *have* a family—you and Maura and Mohm—my three angels. *You're* my family and I can't stand it anymore—we have to live together!"

I could not resist. "What the hell are you trying to say?"

He grinned at hearing himself. Reaching across the table, he clasped my hands and drew them toward him and leaned in for a kiss. From his pocket he drew a jewelry box from James Robinson and opened it to reveal an heirloom circlet of diamonds and rubies. It was the prettiest engagement ring I had ever seen. With a shy smile, he punched out the headline: "Clay Felker asks Gail Sheehy to be his wife."

I LATER LEARNED THAT MAURA had been a catalyst. She was then working as an intern at *Adweek,* where Clay was consulting, and the two of them were able to have long, soulful talks. Clay's old housekeeper, Iris Mendoza, had come back from Argentina to replace the infamous Angeles, and Iris knew Clay well enough to whisper in his ear before he got out of bed, "Mr. Felker, it's time you get married to Miss Gail." He didn't stand a chance.

Once we became serious about marriage, we became very, very serious. We applied to formally adopt Mohm. We sought out the Reverend Carol Anderson, one of the first women to be ordained into the Episcopal priesthood. Carol had broken the stained-glass ceiling at a tall-steeple church, All Angels parish, not by being a militant feminist, but because she was a passionate evangelist and a very down-to-earth woman. Carol agreed to marry us on the condition that we take instruction with her on the meaning and obligations of the sacrament of marriage. We agreed. Those sessions were humbling. We were chagrined that we had hesitated so long, separated so often. Marrying would allow us to be dependable as parents and consistent as friends. We would hardly have anything left to fight about.

We decided to be married at home in a candlelight ceremony. Clay's living room was easily converted into a chapel. Lighted wreaths hung at the huge windows turned the room into a cathedral. The stone fireplace served as the altar, banked with lilies. After the ceremony, the room would be turned into a banquet hall with long red-clothed tables.

The sixteenth of December 1984 was as warm as spring, summer even. We had to break out iced tea along with the Kir Royale. My girl-friends kept trying to hurry me to get dressed. I had found a vintage gown by Elsa Schiaparelli, left over from the late 1920s, a slither of ecru satin cut on the bias to give a moving awareness of the body beneath. But I couldn't resist sneaking out onto the upper balcony of the duplex and peeking through the railing to watch the guests enter below.

Lesley Stahl and Aaron Latham were first to arrive, bringing their strawberry-blond daughter, Taylor, to be our ring bearer. Clay took pride in helping to godfather the conception of this beautiful child. As only the second TV anchorwoman in the history of the male-dominated CBS News (the first one, Sally Quinn, having been fired), Lesley thought her career would be finished if she dared remind her bosses she was female by taking maternity leave. Once Clay's love of Mohm made him an enthusiastic convert to fatherhood, he prosely-tized the unmarried couple over dinner one night with the fervor of a Mormon missionary. Less than a week later, the couple conceived. Aaron liked to say, "That advice gave our lives a new focus and mean-ing for the years to come."

Gilt banquet chairs had been set in a semicircle facing the fire-place altar. We had invited only fifty guests. Given our age and our capricious courtship, we needed to stand before our most cherished friends and seek their endorsement of our commitment. This was the whole purpose of having the wedding at home. The ceremony would mark our passage into the mystery and vulnerability of marriage.

The *New York* family took up most of the seats. Walter and Bina Bernard brought their daughter, Sarah, a talented writer of the next generation to carry on at *New York* magazine. Byron and Elizabeth Dobell took seats near my literary agent Lynn Nesbit. Tom Wolfe came decked out in his white suit, blue-and-white cravat, and white spats, with his attractive wife, the art director Sheila Berger, at his side.

As I started down the spiral staircase, the warmth of the room and perfume of the lilies melted my nervousness. And there was Clay, standing still for once, facing me with what felt like open arms. He was the other cover on the book of our life. How could we have waited so long to bring our story together?

The Reverend Anderson spoke simply. She finished by laying a satin sash over our clasped hands and pronouncing us man and wife. Clay bent to kiss me and nearly lifted me off my feet. He whispered in my ear, "Promise you will never leave me again." I put my lips to his ear. "Never."

Later, friends would compete for giving the most comical toast about our many breakups. "Thank God we don't have to keep updating our Rolodex," someone quipped. Amid hearty laughter at David Frost's jokes, I noticed women long divorced retreat into their private thoughts and weep a little, women who, like me, for so long had feared to take a second chance; I felt for them. But the fact that we had finally seen what all our friends had seen—that we were meant for each other—satisfied everyone that they had contributed to a story with a happy ending.

It was Milton Glaser who presided as the family rabbi to give a homily on marriage. The thrust of his message has stayed with me. He asked the guests to consider their own marriages, to dismiss their grievances and renew their own vows. "Let's see new hope in this marriage," he said. "And let's give it our full approval. That, as much as a religious blessing, will seal the vows of Clay and Gail, in the presence of their two daughters."

I could hardly keep my eyes off the two girls who stood to make their own poignant toasts about what this marriage meant to them. One from the West with her pearly skin and fiery Irish red hair, one from the East with her amber skin and demure lowered eyes—they were the angels who had brought us together. They were the meaning in this day. Seeing Maura and Mohm side by side, I felt a shiver of ecstasy. This was the family for which I had longed for so many years. This was the happiest moment of my life.

CHAPTER 30

FINDING A NEW VOICE AT *VANITY FAIR*

FORTY-SEVEN. A POPULAR AGE for a midlife crisis. Not for me. I had been there and done that back in my midthirties, when the violence of Bloody Sunday plunged me into a premature mortality crisis. By the time I turned forty-seven, I was ready to dare to reach for new life in every dimension. Finding the courage to marry the love of my life and create a new family was the culmination of a long passage through the fear of intimacy. From the start, our marriage brought me happiness beyond my imagination. But that very same year, 1984, when I turned forty-seven, I was also offered an open door to a brand-new career direction.

The catalyst was Tina Brown. She was only thirty, an ambitious English editor with one magazine success behind her. Condé Nast had turned to her in desperation to revive one of its most storied publications, *Vanity Fair,* a romantic title from the 1930s. Two other editors had tried and failed; circulation and advertising were virtually nil. Newly arrived in New York in January with all the arrogance of youth, Brown thought she could give *Vanity Fair* new life by analyzing American culture through its class divisions. But this was not Britain. Americans don't like to acknowledge our class divisions.

To revive *Vanity Fair* was a much more daunting project than Brown had thought. She asked to have lunch with Walter Anderson, a protégé of Clay's. The hard-driving marine was transforming the Sunday magazine supplement *Parade* into a hot property for Condé Nast, bringing in serious writers like David Halberstam and Norman Mailer. I was lucky to be one of his writers. Anderson told Brown she needed a hard-nosed reporter with a name who could write about politics.

"I don't want the pedestrian political stuff that you see in Metro sections," she told Anderson. He recommended me as the kind of literary journalist she needed. Brown was familiar with my writing but only in connection with *Passages*. "Would she be interested in writing politics?"

"If you really want human-interest stuff in politics, Gail's your girl," she remembers being advised. Such is the power of networking.

Brown called me out of the blue on March 12, 1984. I had written a sum total of three political profiles thus far in my career: the Bobby Kennedy story for *New York,* Anwar Sadat for *Esquire,* and a profile for *Parade* of Cory Aquino, the shy wife of an assassinated candidate for the presidency of the Philippines. I had followed her as she stunned the country by leading a revolution and ascending as the first woman to the presidency. Brown would be taking as big a chance on me as I would be in writing for a magazine that hadn't found its legs.

When we met in the Condé Nast building, then on Madison Avenue, I was startled by how much Tina Brown resembled Princess Diana, with her youthful beauty and tousled blond hair. The resemblance ended there. Brown fixed me with her steely blue-eyed intensity and talked at the speed of a fast-forwarded tape. Her restless energy was infectious. She told me she liked a high-low approach to the news, with the flash of celebrities, glamour, and crime to balance highbrow culture and serious investigatory journalism. Could I write humanized political profiles? Could I! I told her I'd love to experiment with using my psychological approach to probe the character of political figures.

"Great! Find out who Gary Hart really is, can you?" We were on the same wavelength from the start. She gave me a month to do the story.

It was a presidential election year, 1984, and Hart was the most tantalizing challenge. A Colorado senator whose campaign had been virtually ignored for a year, Hart had just burst onto the national stage in February with his upset victory in the New Hampshire Democratic primary. He was the Gentleman Caller of American politics—the illusory romantic figure with "new ideas"—who shocked the political establishment and the media by beating the old guard, Vice President Walter Mondale. Hart himself had been quoted as saying, "I'm an obscure man, and I intend to remain that way. I never reveal who I really am." The mystery became all the more intriguing as I heard the same refrain in preliminary interviews with his political associates: "When you find out who Gary Hart is, let me know."

The traveling press was tracking his daily public appearances. Expert political analysts were already dissecting the issues. But research had shown that in presidential elections, most people were not voting on issues. They were voting on character. And the importance of character was something I had done a lot of thinking and reading about, starting with Plutarch's *Lives* and Arnold Toynbee's *A Study of History* (a twelve-volume magnum opus I only grazed to get the gist of his model, tracing the stages of development and decay of all the major world civilizations).

The study of character, as I see it, starts with placing the individual in his or her subculture; for that, I had the tools of social anthropology from my studies with Margaret Mead. Then I would trace his or her development through each stage of life, looking for the pivotal turning points and threads of experience that form a pattern of behavior. My fascination with character, I surmised, might be shared by Americans who had bought one president after another for neatly packaged virtues they turned out not to have. The "new" Nixon.

Lyndon "the peacemaker." The "competent" Carter who pledged to eliminate federal deficits but allowed interest rates to skyrocket, inflation to explode to 12 percent, and unemployment to climb to 7.7 percent, close to the disastrous numbers of Americans thrown out of work by the 2008 global financial crisis.

As always, I started by interviewing all around my subject, usually compiling a list of about forty sources—parents, if living; siblings, a must; the family housekeeper, childhood friends, coaches, the pivotal teacher, the religious guide, the first love, the spouse, the early political staff. It always surprises me how much I can learn from the underlings who worked for the candidate when he or she was a nobody: Could he connect with people? Whom did he listen to? Was he seriously concerned with helping people or full of himself?

My first clue to Hart's character was revealed in April in the back of the chartered plane. He had been virtually sealed in the plane for two months since his win in New Hampshire. Both he and his wife were suffering from a honking bronchitis. Lee Hart kept trying to cuddle up on the armrest next to her husband. He ignored her. She struggled to lift the armrest and back her hip close to his. He was oblivious, talking issues. No one could get close to Gary Hart. Not his wife, not even his own closest Senate staffers. They told me how, when they all huddled with Hart late at night to mark up a bill, he would suddenly command, "Back off!" What was he hiding?

When Hart walked back to the press section, there wasn't a wrinkle in his fitted western shirt. The only sign of campaign wear and tear was in the run-down heels of his cowboy boots—a man as controlled physically as he was emotionally.

I dropped a name: Marilyn Youngbird.

"Do you know Marilyn?" Suddenly his voice was buoyant. "She's been my spiritual adviser for the last few years."

My jaw must have literally dropped. The mysterious Marilyn was a full-blooded Native American introduced to me by a campaign staffer. Marilyn had assured me that she was Hart's closest friend, a soul mate. She had described in vivid detail their peak moment at an Indian ceremony that had brought them close both personally and spiritually: a Comanche powwow in a Denver park.

"It was so romantic," she said. "They brushed the front and back of our bodies with eagle feathers. It was sensual. He would look at me, smiling from ear to ear. We didn't know whether to laugh or cry."

I had been certain this was merely the wishful memory of a lonely female supporter who became infatuated with a handsome presidential candidate and wildly exaggerated her importance to him. Now, I wondered.

"Marilyn asked me to tell you that you should take time for a spiritual-healing ceremony," I reported.

"I know." Hart sighed. "Marilyn's been telling me for a long time I need a spiritual purification."

Suddenly I remembered the note Marilyn had given me to pass on to Hart. When she'd shown me the contents, I thought I would never have the nerve to hand it to a serious man running for the most serious office in the land. But Hart was eager to read it.

Get away from everybody. Go to nature. Hug a tree.

What was more, Marilyn had told me that her parents, both medicine people, had heard the prophecy. The Great Spirit, their god, had chosen Gary Hart to save nature from destruction. I repeated the prophecy for Hart.

"I know," he said gravely. "She keeps telling me that."

"Do you believe it?"

"Yes."

He wasn't kidding. This was a man with an unusually serious case of grandiosity. When his own words were reported in my first *Vanity Fair* story that July, "The Hidden Hart," the candidate's immediate reaction was to charge: "It's terribly inaccurate journalism." This was the first evidence of what we all later learned was Hart's knee-jerk reaction to being caught at anything. Lie first, then blame others.

Fortunately for both journalists and voters, lying stirs plenty of media attention. *Time* and *Newsweek* both called me to ask how could I back up what I had written. It was the first time my veracity had been challenged. Hart's people would stop at nothing to discredit me. Suddenly, all the work I had put into this story had led to me to a cliff, over which I might lose my career. I invited editors from both magazines to listen to my audiotapes. They were satisfied. Walter Mondale's campaign backed away from any interest in Hart as a running mate and began dropping references in news stories to "the flake factor."

Tina was thrilled. "You knocked it out of the park!"

IN 1987, AS CANDIDATES BEGAN lining up to run as the successor to President Ronald Reagan in the 1988 election, Tina was on the phone with an urgent assignment: this time she wanted me to write a whole series of character portraits. I had no hesitation about taking up her offer, but it was a risk. The more successful you are, the harder it becomes to walk the plank. More people notice and more sharks start circling in the water. Still fresh in my mind were the attacks I had received at the '84 Democratic Convention from some well-respected, classical male profile writers—a few of them personal friends.

"How dare you?" said one, suggesting that I was to blame for dooming Hart's chances of being on the Democratic ticket.

"Would you trust me as a journalist if I backed away from what I'd learned, to avoid controversy?" I replied. No response.

I had to have confidence that when trying out a new form, in any field, one must expect a backlash from top practitioners of the currently accepted form. I was an upstart, and a woman journalist to boot.

My defense was simple. "Issues are today. Character is what was yesterday and will be tomorrow."

I was convinced that in Hart's second presidential race, it was not a question of *if* he would destroy himself, but of *when*. This time, I traveled through the various worlds of Gary Hart and found a tortured and divided man.

Hart was shaped—one might even say malformed—by a highly punitive fundamentalist religious sect. The Church of the Nazarene forbade all sentient pleasures—no dancing, no movies, no listening to the radio, and of course no drinking or unmarried sex. Young Gary had to hang around outside the movie house and ask his friends to tell him what they saw. His mother drilled into the boy her own dark, evangelical beliefs: that man is born with a sinful nature and his appetites must "continue to be controlled" by "putting to death the deeds of the body." Compulsive about cleanliness, his mother moved the family to sixteen different houses before Gary finished high school. He went on to Bethany Nazarene College.

"You do everything right, you go with a girl, you get married," he told a friend, Tom Boyd, "then six months later you wake up in the middle of the night and ask yourself, 'My God, what have I done?' "

Hart admitted to me, "The one Protestant quality I suppose I've got my share of is guilt." His pastor, whom I met, had made certain that guilt would follow him forever. The Reverend Earl Copsey told me that Gary Hartpence (his real name; he changed it because his classmates called him "hotpants") was a dead soul as far as the church was concerned. The pastor remembered the exact date on which that death occurred, September 20, 1968—"he left the church to go back out to the world of sin." Soon, Hart would abandon his wife and family and his new law practice and volunteer to work for a near-hopeless cause called the McGovern campaign. And there he met the man in whose image he remade himself, Warren Beatty, the sybarite who introduced him to guiltless philandering.

The twenty-five-year-old Hart, still imprisoned by his evangelical upbringing, began beating on the cell floor. David Barber, a Duke history professor, told me that Hart, a married senator, had slept with many young volunteers on the McGovern campaign, but when the women wanted a relationship, he acted as if he didn't know them. Finally, he went over the wall, gravitating toward the furthest extreme and using hedonists and fixers to find him girls. That led him into the kind of suspect scene where party drugs were ubiquitous.

What demon was loose in the mind of the fifty-year-old front-runner of the Democratic Party when he frequented Turnberry Isle, home of the party boat *Monkey Business*? He lurched across the chartered yacht, drink in hand, to tell a model friend of Donna Rice's to pass a message to the lanky blonde that this was her big chance to play with the next president of the United States.

When Hart was confronted by reporters from the *Miami Herald,* who had staked out his town house on Capitol Hill and verified a weekend liaison with Ms. Rice, the senator denied any immoral conduct and stalked off the public stage in furious defiance.

Initially, Tina and I thought it best to leave Hart to indecent obscurity. But the Hart tragedy continued to obsess Americans. Here was a smart and charismatic new-generation politician; why should we lose a potentially great president because of a sexual peccadillo? Network pundits reminded us nightly that we had lived through the adulterous presidencies of FDR and JFK. So was Hart the victim of a prurient press?

"To Gail Sheehy, he was not," as Tina Brown wrote in her *Vanity Fair* editor's letter. "Hart's sexual adventures were only a symptom of a character malaise . . . she made us realize how the true character of a presidential candidate can remain a secret to the public despite what he feels is excessive scrutiny."

"The Road to Bimini," as we headlined the story, seemed to register with a critical mass of Americans. It suggested an answer to the question: Why would any man in his right mind defy a *New York Times* reporter who asked about his alleged womanizing, challenge him to "put a tail on me," and then arrange a tryst at his Washington town house with the same Miami party girl?

Because Hart's double life had finally imploded. He could not be both worthy and sinful. He needed to be caught.

Despite all evidence, Hart continued to lie and attack me. When we appeared together on *Nightline,* with Ted Koppel questioning us on split screens, Hart flatly denied that he had ever been to Turnberry Isle. Unbeknownst to him, however, hours earlier I had remembered a photograph I'd seen in the resort manager's office while I was researching the piece for *Vanity Fair,* showing a rakish-looking Hart and his sidekick Beatty on the boat. I'd made a copy of it, thinking the magazine might want to use it. Two hours before showtime, I scrambled for the image, then recalled I'd given it to the fact-checkers. I called Pamela Maffei McCarthy, *VF*'s managing editor, who went to the office, retrieved it, and got it delivered to me minutes before the monitor light went on in the remote studio. When Hart asserted he'd never been on the *Monkey Business* with Donna Rice, I held up the photo. Hart's lie was exposed.

ONE SATURDAY IN 1986, Tina called me in the country to say, "You need to get into the character of George Bush."

I couldn't wait to start. Back in the 1980s, we still wanted our leaders to be macho. Brick walls were made for Jack and Bobby Kennedy to walk through. Lyndon Johnson humiliated people to make certain they were afraid of him. Richard Nixon compiled a secret enemies list and bugged reporters. Ronald Reagan projected cowboy courage as a movie idol. But nobody seemed to be scared of George Herbert Walker Bush. The core question in my mind would become the title of my story: "Is George Bush Too *Nice* to Be President?"

To explore the character of George Bush, I talked with forty of his friends and family, aides, and close observers before I traveled with him on campaign. What made this lengthy and tenacious process worthwhile was being able to gather enough of the puzzle pieces of my subject's life to propose a pattern that might surprise even him. Bush's sister, Nancy, told me she often said, "Damn it, George, why won't you say what you really think!" According to his brother Jonathan, "You just can't get him in there fighting."

He was the kind of guy who would step out in his pin-striped suit in the middle of a downpour to help his chauffeur fix a flat. He was always a teacher's pet, never a bully. "Too little," he admitted to me. The secret to his sense of humor was that he knew how to plant the punch line in someone else's mouth. He was also loyal to a fault. Bush served under three presidents—as UN ambassador, GOP chairman, envoy to China, and director of the CIA—unable to see, much less admit, the most egregious mistakes of the men for whom he worked. During the Watergate scandal, when Bush was GOP chairman, even his mother tried to persuade him that Tricky Dick was lying. But Bush was the last man in the party to believe ill of Richard Nixon.

I asked everyone I interviewed if he or she knew of a gut issue with George Bush, something for which he consistently stood. Most answered like Malcolm Baldrige, secretary of commerce, who said, "I dunno. He probes everybody about what they think before he makes up his own mind."

"Poppy" was his feckless nickname. His habit of a lifetime was to avoid at virtually any cost tackling anyone head-on. It wasn't hard to see the antecedent in his childhood. His father, Prescott, was austere, a towering Wall Street banker and former senator with a basso profundo voice who invited no argument and brandished a belt to punish his children. The vice president later affirmed to me, "Dad was really scary." The parallel between his relationship with his father and with Reagan seemed palpable. George H. W. Bush would do anything to keep from making the father angry.

When I finally got a green light to interview the vice president, it was after he had barnstormed through three states in a twelve-hour day. His hair was mussed and his clothes were an incongruous combination of a banker's pin-striped pants and a baseball jacket. I was ushered into his private cabin on *Air Force Two* and stood before him as the plane began rolling down the runway. Bush stretched out and put his stocking feet up on the couch.

"So is this gonna be a deal on where I'm coming from, a complete psychiatric layout?"

It was so Bush; there was almost nothing he avoided more assiduously than introspection. So I began by asking to talk about his war experiences. "I get in trouble with my mother if I talk about being in combat," he said. Why? I asked. Talking about it would sound like bragging. Bush had never told the whole story to a reporter up to that point. I cajoled him.

What went through his mind, I asked, when that eighteen-year-old string bean of a pampered suburban boy, the youngest pilot in the U.S. Navy, climbed into his barrel-chested bomber and sat on top of two thousand pounds of TNT? In seconds he'd rev up his single engine, then reach over to signal the tower and push forward on the throttle and—*swooock*—he'd be catapulted into the Pacific mist. Minutes later, he would be grinding through heavy antiaircraft fire.

"I thought I was a kind of macho pilot," he finally admitted. "You were trained, you knew what to do. There wasn't any 'Wonder if it's going to work this time' feeling to it." On the morning of September 2, 1944, the young American fliers on USS *San Jacinto* were readied to hit Japanese installations on Chichi-shima. They were warned that their ship wouldn't be around to pick up anyone who went down—it was turning south. Bush was in the second pair of Avengers to go in. He looked out and saw fluffy little clouds all around, black flack filling the sky; it would only be luck to get through it. "I was aware that the antiaircraft fire would be heavy, but I was not afraid. I wasn't thinking: This next one's going to hit me."

But it did. Suddenly his plane slammed forward. Black oily smoke belched out of the engine and streamed through the cockpit. Bush admitted that, for the first time, the macho pilot was scared. "We were going down. I never saw what hit me, but I felt this thing. I had to finish my bombing run." He continued his dive and hit his target. When he bailed out, he pulled the rip cord too early. The slipstream caught his body, all 152 pounds of it, and flung it at the tail of the plane. He hit his head. His chute tore. He was falling fast. He managed to slip out of his harness before his boots smacked the water.

He climbed into a tiny life raft and vomited. "I didn't know whether I'd survive. It seemed like the end of the world."

A few hours later, he saw a periscope break the monotony of the sea. For a moment, he said, he feared it was a Japanese submarine. But American sailors fished him up. For the next month, he knew what fear really was, he said, as the sub was continually attacked by Japanese ships and aircraft, depth charged, and surface bombed. But six weeks later, although he had the option of rotating home, Bush elected to return to combat.

IN STARK CONTRAST TO HIS BRAVERY in wartime, Bush's overweening need for Ronald Reagan's approval made him appear weak. He spoke emotionally of the president and "the closeness we have." I asked him how he had cultivated such trust from Reagan. "It took awhile, but the president knows now, which he probably didn't know, that I'm not going to betray him." He admitted that his refusal to separate himself from the president had "cost me something. Politically."

Bush was ridiculed for saying he wasn't great at "the vision thing." He gave a revealing look at his concept of Reagan's "miracles" in an ad-libbed speech. "Ronald Reagan and I believe in the miracle that is America. But the funny thing is, when you look at miracles, they're nothing. It's hard work."

The deadline to close my piece was early December 1986. On November 13, the Iran-Contra arms scandal blew up and President Reagan addressed the nation with an outright lie: "We did not, repeat, did not, trade weapons or anything else for hostages, nor will we." The president's magic was suddenly tarnished, and the scandal put Bush under relentless questioning. Bush ducked for almost a month. He denied any knowledge of the policy. I had to call my editor and beg to tear up the front and back of my story to shoehorn in an update on Bush's behavior. The vice president's only comment to me was that "mistakes were made." He never did let on that he knew Reagan's hands were all over the Iran-Contra deal. Reagan's agreement to sell arms to the Islamic state of Iran, in exchange for the freeing of the hostages, had assured his win as president. Reagan then used the proceeds to finance a secret war in Nicaragua.

Bush maintained that "I'm for Mr. Reagan—blindly." He wrapped one arm in another and rubbed it. In the end, his slavish loyalty to Reagan worked. Bush was elected president.

TODAY, IN LIGHT OF THE CATASTROPHE of his son George W.'s two fruitless wars in Iraq and Afghanistan, George H. W. Bush looks like a great foreign policy president. He showed strong leadership when it came to the biggest crisis to confront a president: the necessity to take the nation to war in 1991. Using his skillfulness as a former ambassador to the United Nations, President Bush persuaded fifteen countries on the Security Council to pass a cease-fire resolution in November of 1990 against Saddam Hussein for invading Kuwait. To lead Operation Desert Storm, he assembled an overwhelming force of ten countries including Syria, Egypt, and Saudi Arabia. It was arguably the last time an American president would be able to gather a worldwide coalition including Muslim states to oppose aggression in the Middle East.

THE FIRST BUSH PORTRAIT was followed by character pieces about other 1988 candidates: Michael Dukakis, Albert Gore Jr., Senator Bob Dole, and civil rights activist Jesse Jackson. I later expanded versions of these profiles, adding a chapter on President Reagan, for my 1988 book, *Character: America's Search for Leadership.*

The *Vanity Fair* pieces often made front-page news and gave me a chance to spread the word further on the *Today* show or evening news programs. The "gotcha reporting" criticism often surfaced, but by the end of the campaign, the character portrait was pretty well established as a new and respectable genre of political writing.

Before the election, Tina was on the phone to me: "Guess what? The *Washington Journalism Review* just called me. You were voted the best magazine writer in America."

"You must be kidding."

"It's brilliant, Gail, brilliant. And I get to throw a cocktail party for us in Washington."

CHAPTER 31
START-UPS

THE GO-GO 1980S STIMULATED both Clay and me to dare to head in new directions. Clay tried a cold start-up of a weekly newspaper, the *East Side Express,* in October 1983. It had the same sassy attitude as *New York,* but focused on the social life of young Upper East Siders.

"Every morning when Clay walked into the office, it was like estrogen shock," Cyndi Stivers, then the entertainment editor, recalls. The newsroom was all women: Patricia Leigh Brown, who would become a feature writer for the *New York Times;* Lisa Gubernick, who would go on to *Forbes* magazine; and Bethany Kandel, who during her career has written on every topic from homelessness to breast cancer.

Being Clay, he couldn't help himself from plunging into the politics of a prepresidential election year. "It's time for a woman vice president," he said casually as we rode up in the elevator to our apartment. I was startled but I knew to trust his prescience.

"What kind of a woman would that take?"

"Any politician who makes that radical leap has to pick a woman who is otherwise safely conventional."

"Obviously she has to be a Democrat."

"A conservative Democrat," he said.

Out of the air he pulled the name Geraldine Ferraro. I'd never heard of her and I was sure that very few other people had. Clay told me that she was a three-term congresswoman from Queens. Italian, married with children.

"She's a woman, she's ethnic, she's Catholic, and she has the support of blue-collar and union voters." Clay rattled off her bona fides.
"She would excite a lot of women."

"And maybe men, too."

IN THE WAITING AREA for a shuttle flight to Washington, I looked
around for a middle-aged, dumpy Queens housewife. Instead, a vivacious woman with blond-streaked hair steamed up the ramp wheel-
ing her suitcase behind her. She stuck out her hand to shake mine.
She was friendly and funny and pretty and we immediately hit it off.

On board the American flight I complimented her on her blue-
rimmed designer glasses. "My husband hates them," she said. I asked
her how long she'd been married—twenty-three years it turned out.
Cleverly she turned the interview around to me. "How long have you
been married?"

"Mmmm, once briefly. I've been seeing the same man"—I stopped
to calculate how long—"for sixteen years."

"SIXTEEN YEARS?!" she practically shouted. "What are you
thinking?!"

"I thought it was okay when it was just a ten-year stand."

She laughed, and every time I saw Geraldine Ferraro after that,
her opener was "SIXTEEN YEARS!"

But on that flight I had only forty-five minutes to learn what she
was about. From my research I knew that domestic policy was her
strength with an emphasis on women's issues. She was also active on
the environment and critical of Reagan's handling of toxic cleanups. I
was impressed, but a journalist has to probe: "I can't write a puff piece
about you," I said. "Tell me a weakness."

Immediately she said "foreign policy."

This was her first mistake, as she would later acknowledge. She
probably knew as much about foreign policy as most members of

Congress. Only a woman would be so eager to admit her weakness. It turned out that Ferraro had never given the vice presidency a thought. She was angling to be named the party's platform chair.

My piece ran in the *East Side Express* in October 1983 with the headline: "Will This Queens Housewife Be the Next Vice President?"

At the Democratic Convention nine months later, the presidential nominee, Walter Mondale, blew the roof off San Francisco's Moscone Center by announcing that his vice-presidential pick would be the first woman ever. Ferraro, a forty-eight-year-old former teacher and assistant prosecutor, broke into a wide grin as Mondale said, "I'm delighted to announce that I will ask the Democratic Convention to ratify her." Mondale congratulated himself for taking the "difficult decision" to choose a woman, but added: "Gerry has excelled in everything she's tried, from law school at night to being a tough prosecutor to winning a difficult election, to winning positions of leadership and respect in the Congress."

Mondale said her political rise was "really the story of a classic American dream." TV viewers saw women delegates weeping tears of joy when Ferraro gave her acceptance speech.

Clay was spot on. Mondale had been a tepid vice president during Jimmy Carter's single term and desperately needed pizzazz for his presidential ticket. Ferraro gave him an immediate bounce of sixteen points, pulling him even with President Reagan. But Mondale's people had devoted only forty-eight hours to the vetting of Ferraro. They missed red flags going back to 1978 when her husband, John Zaccaro, a real estate developer-manager, had contributed $110,000 to her congressional campaign and violated election law. The media began raising questions regarding Ferraro's family's finances and why she and her husband filed separate tax returns. She promised to release both their returns, then reneged, then made a joke: "You people who are married to Italian men, you know what it's like."

That quip brought charges of ethnic stereotyping, which escalated the media frenzy. "I had created a monster," she reminisced.

But the real monster was another woman. As the longtime Republican presidential strategist Ed Rollins later revealed in his book, *Bare Knuckles and Back Rooms,* the person who ordered him to create a covert operation to undermine Ferraro was none other than Nancy Reagan. The operation was successful.

When Ferraro debated George H. W. Bush, women who heard it live, including me, thought she had won. But much of the country was unable to forget the snarky sound bite by another woman, Barbara Bush: "That four-million-dollar—I can't say it, but it rhymes with rich."

After that experience, I expected that any woman pushed forward to run for national political office would have to be squeaky clean. When Senator John McCain chose Sarah Palin as his running mate in 2008, it would be another instance of a desperate male candidate needing to add flash to his moribund campaign. This time the vetting process was even shorter. No one was writing about Palin's religious beliefs; the McCain camp refused even to state her religion. I found out that she had been "anointed" by a firebrand Pentecostal preacher from Kenya, and her fanatic supporters belonged to something called "the tea party." Too good a story to miss. So, without an assignment but working with an equally passionate cohort, Deirdre English, a Berkeley journalism professor, we jumped on the next plane to Wasilla, Alaska.

Following Palin from church to church, we heard her exhort parishioners to join her in an evangelical cause: "Alaska will lead the nation in a Christian revival," she proclaimed. "We are the head, not the tail." Our story, "Palin's Pastor Problem," was snapped up by Tina Brown for the first appearance of her digital magazine, the *Daily Beast.*

Of course, the "mavericky" Palin was quickly exposed as an egomaniac, intellectually vapid, and an expensive clothes horse who would sink the McCain campaign. But the blaze of publicity fired her up as the pilot light under the tea party. Ferraro's naïveté about how to counter dirty tricks made me sad. Palin made me ashamed. When a woman candidate becomes a figure of national ridicule, how many women of true character are discouraged from daring to step forward on the national stage?

CLAY'S NEW BABY, *East Side Express,* had a very short life. He and his original backer, Philip Merrill, had screaming matches in the office. Along came the Hartz Mountain birdseed king, Leonard Stern, thinking he could turn this little paper into the new *New York* magazine. Clay projected the *Express* would be profitable in the third year. Stern expected to make a killing right away. He dumped the paper less than a month after he bought it.

This was just one small step in the long march toward extinction of small news and literary publications, which later extended to major print magazines and fine newspapers. The massive conglomerates that have come to dominate the U.S. media landscape do not have a primary interest in informing the public. Their interest is in using free airwaves and digital portals to make billions by concentrating their control over what we see, hear, and read.

AMERICA WAS SOARING on a joyride of wild excess, go-go greed, and faster-than-light computerized stock-market trading. Everyone seemed to believe the Dow Jones would continue rising indefinitely.

"When doormen want to share stock tips with you," Clay remarked to me in the mid-1980s, "you know everybody is thinking about one thing: money."

The fixation on money did give Clay the impetus for another hit magazine, *Manhattan, Inc.* The glossy monthly captured the values of Wall Street in the mid-1980s, even as crime and racial and cultural tensions in the city were boiling over. Clay saw the chance to make it the must-read publication about the magicians of money manipulation. Men like junk bond king Michael Milken, Ivan Boesky, Ron Perelman, and Carl Icahn—the inspiration for the Gordon Gekko character in Oliver Stone's film *Wall Street*—were making historic changes in the ethos and ethics of Wall Street.

Clay delighted in luring a new team of twentysomething financial geeks to give up their outrageously inflated six-figure salaries on Wall Street for the promise of proud penury as stars on newsstands. Michael Lewis, a hotshot twenty-four-year-old bond trader for Salomon Brothers in London, was Clay's number-one target. From our first dinner with the witty New Orleans native, Clay knew that Lewis was a natural satirist. Lewis admitted it was his dream to be a writer. What's more, he had kept notes on the epic mismanagement of his company. Lewis enthralled readers with articles about the coming wreckage on Wall Street. The book that grew out of his work with Clay, *Liar's Poker,* assured Lewis of a lifetime as a bestselling author and media darling.

When the American stock exchange crashed in 1987, Herb Lipson, executive chairman of *Philadelphia* magazine, Clay's backer for *Manhattan, Inc.,* was at Claridge's in London. Returning from dinner, he tore off the ticker tape in the lobby and read about the largest drop in history. Certain the world had come to an end, he returned at once to New York to meet Clay for lunch, expecting to see no limos, no lights in the penthouses, and tumbleweed blowing down Park Avenue.

It didn't happen. *Manhattan, Inc.* survived for two more years. The crash only made Wall Street—and *Manhattan, Inc.*—more of an obsession for readers, who salivated over seeing how the mighty would fall. The magazine did begin to bleed financially. But Lipson, the sole stockholder, personally kept the magazine afloat by taking more than a $20 million loss. Years later, he told me he had no regrets: "It was a great ride for us all."

ONE WEEKEND IN THE VILLAGE of Sag Harbor, I bumped into a classmate from UVM. Bill Pickens was the only African American who had graduated with me. We had danced together at Greek fraternity parties while I was dating the only genetically Greek guy admitted to Alpha Epsilon Pi, the Jewish fraternity. My classmate, now a handsome middle-aged international business consultant, was the grandson of an NAACP founder. Pickens told me that he and William Denby, a black novelist and college professor, had been sharing their frustrations over social in-activism with Betty Friedan: Why weren't the thought leaders of both the black and white communities of Sag Harbor village teaming up to maximize our voices politically?

By the '80s, Sag Harbor was becoming a smart and sophisticated retreat for writers, editors, and journalists whose politics were socially progressive. Even as artists opened galleries along its main street, the old charm was preserved with the windmill at the long wharf, the original Five and Ten, and the family-owned Schiavoni's Market (all remain to this day).

The village was also home to one of the first upper-middle-class black enclaves in the country. Some of the most prominent African Americans of the twentieth century had at one time bought vacation homes here, including Lena Horne, Langston Hughes, Colin Powell's parents, and more recently the restaurateur B. Smith and the novelist Colson Whitehead.

Our mutual friend, E. L. Doctorow, already recognized as a pillar of American literature for his early novels, *The Book of Daniel* and *Ragtime,* called the state into which many of us had slipped "somnambulistic." Mentally asleep. "With all the brainpower out here," Bill said, "why don't we hold a convocation, a kind of publicly held think tank?"

At one of our first brainstorming meetings in one or another's homes, Pat Pickens, Bill's wife, came up with the name: Sag Harbor Initiative. Both communities accepted some of the responsibility for the social divide. Nobody had forced it or even much thought about it; it just happened. Clementine Pugh, an outspoken black professor from Lehman College in the Bronx, pointed out that "The ideal in the '60s was integration. We were moving toward trying to be accepted by white people. That's over."

I agreed with Clem Pugh. "Like everything else in the past ten years," I said, "the spirit and energy that was trying to bring people together just petered out." Pugh said, "Now we are joining in the formation of the agenda."

Other socially conscious writers were roused from their guarded solitude, including Robert Caro, who was deeply engaged in writing the second volume of his monumental biography of Lyndon Johnson; Kurt Vonnegut, whose most recent social realist novel, *Galapagos,* had raised concerns that the "oversized human brain" was ironically leading mankind to possible extinction; and Blanche Wiesen Cook, a gay activist who surfaced from her monumental research on Eleanor Roosevelt to join us.

We were to convene the first Sag Harbor Initiative town meeting over Columbus Day weekend, 1987. The weekend before, I was in Florida, sleeping at the foot of my mother's hospital bed. She had awakened in the middle of the night and asked me to recite for her the 23rd Psalm. I got as far as ". . . he maketh me to lie down in green pastures, he leadeth me in the paths of righteousness—" when Mother pulled the oxygen mask off her nose and corrected me: "What about 'he leadeth me beside the still waters. He restoreth my soul'?"

She was still determined to stay in the game. The next morning, a young intern had told me that my mother's blood gases didn't look good. "She won't have any quality of life going forward, so we should think about suspending further treatment."

I looked into this callow man's face. "You don't know my mother."

By the following morning, her blood gases had returned to near normal and she was well enough to go home. The attending physician told me that my mother could be expected to live possibly another year or more. She told me that I should go back to Sag Harbor.

Our first town meeting attracted 250 people to the community for three days of intense round-table discussions. We were early in addressing the growing divide between haves and have-nots. But on the way to the first evening panel, a phone call from Florida notified me that my mother had died. I was heartsick.

EARLY IN NOVEMBER I TOLD CLAY, "We'll have to cancel our Thanksgiving party."

"Why?"

"I'm just so blue about my mother."

"What would your mother say?"

He knew, just as well as I, Mother would never cancel a party. And this party had been conceived as a broadening of the friendships made through the Sag Harbor Initiative. It was to be a Saturday-night soiree on Thanksgiving weekend, a buffet dinner for forty or fifty. Maura and Mohm and I would turn the window-walled living room into a grand café. We picked the last of the mums and arranged them in cornucopias with winter pears and grapes and lady apples on tables draped in green felt. We had great vats of paella cooked up by an Irish caterer, Janet O'Brien, with fresh-caught clams and lobster, chicken and homemade Italian sausage. The last preparation would be to light what looked like a thousand candles once they multiplied their flickering gaiety on the windows.

The party was a grand reunion. The faces of friends not seen since the end of summer brought forth gusts of pleasure all around. Along with the Pickenses and the Pughs, we got to know Bruce Llewellyn, the Coca-Cola franchise holder in Philadelphia, and his wife, Shahara, a major supporter of Hillary Clinton. Tom Wolfe had just published *Bonfire of the Vanities* and was the talk of our first party. Paul Davis was painting portraits of world leaders and becoming the toast of Japan. Myrna Davis, along with managing Paul's studio, was named executive director of the Art Director's Club. Richard Reeves was becoming a celebrated presidential biographer. His wife, my dear friend, Catherine O'Neill, was on a mission to make our Women's Refugee Commission an official arm of the United Nations.

Peter Jennings, then anchor of *ABC World News Tonight,* appointed himself toastmaster and gave a gentle ribbing to each guest as he lauded their most recent accomplishments. I moved from table to table, ever eager to talk to Bob Caro and his author-wife, Ina, who brought back from Texas startling new revelations about Johnson's mastery of the Senate. Bob Loomis, the senior Random House editor famous for publishing William Styron, Maya Angelou, and Shelby Foote, as always offered encouragement on what I was working on. A few years later, I would humbly join his tribe and we would do five books together over ten years. Robert Emmett Ginna, the charmingly garrulous Irish American editor, enchanted me and his whole table with stories of writers he had published from the revolutionary playwright Sean O'Casey to the impossible Lillian Hellman.

Our Thanksgiving soiree became a tradition that enriched our friendships for the next fifteen years. The conversations among that extraordinary circle expanded my thinking.

As modest as was the Sag Harbor Initiative, it had a long reach. Walter Isaacson, a charter member and, back then, a young political correspondent for *Time,* never forgot the purpose and format of the

Initiative. He ran with the idea years later in a much grander public think tank. As president and CEO of the Aspen Ideas Festival since 2003, Isaacson has used the same template to create the quintessential Olympics of the mind, inviting thought leaders from across the United States and the world to spar over the newest and most pertinent issues of the day.

Gail and Clay at the beach, 1983. *Courtesy of the author*

Clay announcing the takeover of *New York*, 1977.

Mass walkout of *New York*. (*Left to right:*) Byron Dobell, Burt Glinn, Ellen Stern, Gail. ©*2014 United Press International*

Gail, Clay, and Maura in Mexico with a piñata, 1974.
©Elena Prohaska Glinn for the Estate of Burt Glinn

Gail reporting in a Cambodian refugee camp.
Courtesy of the author

Clay's seventeen-year-delayed proposal, 1984.

Courtesy of the author

Mohm (*right*), twelve, meets her new sister, Maura, eighteen, a freshman at Brown University, 1982. *Courtesy of the author*

"Familymoon" in Egypt. (*Left to right:*) Mohm, Gail, Maura, Clay.
Courtesy of the author

Gail with
Hillary
Clinton, 1992.
Courtesy of the author

Gail with British
prime minister
Margaret
Thatcher, 1989.
Courtesy of the author

Gail and Clay at Literary Lions gala,
New York Public Library, 1992. ©2014 *Bill Cunningham*

CHAPTER 32

TWO WHO CHANGED THE WORLD

IN THE LATE 1980S AND EARLY 1990S, Tina Brown gave me the opportunity to expand my character portraits by writing about leaders who changed the world. I was fascinated by the power symbiosis among Margaret Thatcher, Mikhail Gorbachev, and Ronald Reagan. Of these, the smartest was Britain's prime minister Thatcher, the catalyst who brokered the relationship between the men who ran the world's two superpowers. The result would be no less than the end of the Cold War.

"She has eyes like Caligula and the mouth of Marilyn Monroe." That memorable description by French president François Mitterrand suggested a fascinating dualism in Thatcher's nature. I couldn't wait to go to London and discover more. This was what I loved most about literary journalism. Who could make up a middle-aged right-wing woman leader who possessed the dual character of a domineering male and a seductive female? Who could make people believe that a peasant boy born into famine in a hut in the Russian steppe was destined to lead a country of 290 million people?

It was early in 1989 when I began studying Thatcher. She was completing her tenth year in office. No one had enjoyed such a political reign over the monarchy in the twentieth century. At home, she had vanquished the opposition, gagged the media, and silenced or sacked the critics in her own party. She was a fearsome force, hell-bent on putting the spine back into an enfeebled Great Britain.

My first exposure to this force of nature was from the gallery of Parliament where I watched her thrust and parry with her opposition at Question Time. Thatcher's entrance was unexpectedly deferential. She hunched over and tiptoed in, starkly smart in a black silk suit with a white tuxedo collar, almost a parody of a gentleman's garb. She sat on the edge of the government's front bench, fingers threaded through her briefing books, and crossed her legs, confidently displaying her slender knees sheathed in sheer black stockings.

A debate ensued. Thatcher leaped up to the dispatch box only a few feet from her opponent, mano a mano. Her warmed-milk voice turned quickly to a scald: "Fact is, fact is, fact is . . ." she repeated, refusing to be outshouted until their exchanges became ear-splitting.

"Order!" shouted the speaker of the House. Sometimes these debates became so rough, the speaker had to call a break for "injury time." But something other than Thatcher's voice captured my attention. Her legs. Each time she rocked up from her seat to debate the opposition, she would rub the back of one black-stockinged calf with the toe of her other foot. "She has sexy legs" was a comment I heard from both her devotees and detractors. One of her ambassadors told me that he found Mrs. Thatcher "sexually attractive, in a sort of packaged way."

Thatcher, sexy? Friends laughed when I mentioned what I was beginning to find out. The "Iron Lady," a sobriquet attached to her by the Soviet press, was one she relished—how sexy was that? The supernanny who "hand bagged" the men in her cabinet if they failed her tests of manhood—sexy? Unimaginable! But I remembered Clay telling me that when he was introduced to the PM socially by David Frost, he came away as impressed by her flirtatiousness as by her ferocity.

———————————

A FRIEND LENT ME his flat in Mayfair for a month and I set about contacting fifty-plus members of the prime minister's coterie, almost all of them male, her "star boys." The stories they told me were startling and amusing. Once, when all her party officials were lined up for a photo op, she stopped the proceedings. Her eyes fell on a handsome young buck of an Irishman, John Ranelagh, a television producer chosen by the PM to be a member of her economic think tank. His double-breasted jacket was not buttoned up. Over lunch, Ranelagh told me he had felt her hand on his tie, slowly sliding to the top. Then her hand inside his jacket, feeling for the inside button. She purred, "John, if you wear a double-breasted jacket, you must always keep it buttoned."

"The sensation was one of hardening of the organs." He chuckled in the retelling. "She is sexy and very interested in sex. You feel it when you work for her." He speculated that, given her strict background, "she's never had enough sex, and now that her husband, Denis, is a little old and a little louche, she's more demanding of other men. She seems to be always searching for a man who can stand up to her."

THE DAY BEFORE I WAS TO INTERVIEW Margaret Thatcher, a press officer took down my questions and warned that the prime minister was granting no interviews at all in connection with her tenth anniversary. However, Mrs. Thatcher had given her word that she would see me, and so, on the appointed day, I turned up at the famous door at No. 10 with a bunch of flowers. Precisely at eleven, Mrs. Thatcher burst in at a canter. The helmet hair, the pursed lips, the crisp white handkerchief in her breast pocket—all suggested a woman as tightly wound as a brussels sprout. Pains would have to be exerted to peel away some of her psychological reserve. Not one of the fifty-five sources I had spoken to claimed to be close to her.

"You have gone to so much trouble," she purred disarmingly, "it would be a terrible pity, you know, if I couldn't find a little time."

Translation: *I've heard how many people you've talked to and I want to find out what they've said about me.*

In person, the most remarkable features of this lady of sixty-three were the terrifying eyes that penetrated her guest. She asked if coffee was on the way. I had learned that she lived basically on coffee, vitamin C, and royal jelly—a wallop of minerals right from the hive, as befits a queen bee.

I had been warned that she had no time for discussing how she ruled as a woman. Just the facts. But she totally surprised me. Since Mrs. Thatcher had agreed to talk about how her character was formed, she seemed determined to do it, as everything else, exceptionally well. She had read my questions and done her homework.

"We'll go *straight* in at the *deep* end," she began.

Growing up in Grantham where young Margaret Roberts lived over her father's grocery store, she was never accepted by her peers. Before meeting the PM, I had visited Grantham. Her home was without hot water or an indoor toilet. Standing in her former bedroom told me much about the formation of her rigid political belief in individual enterprise. Out her back window was the worst slum in town, a breeding bed for the thieving class. But across the street, she could see her future. There stood a row of upmarket Edwardian houses with members of the smug professional class coming and going with dignity.

Her origin in the social stratum considered most contemptible by the incurably class-conscious British—the lower middle class— ensured that Thatcher's accomplishments were held against her. "That awful, jumped-up woman" was how the upper classes often referred to the grocer's daughter who had vaulted class lines. A top Conservative Party official scoffed, "She is a very ordinary person."

Once this "ordinary person" made herself the most powerful woman in the world, people began referring to "Thatcherism" as if it were a coherent, worked-out ideology. What it really was, I began to infer, was a reflection of her character. The ultimate self-made woman, she was out to remake Britain from top to bottom in her own image.

She attained that goal in her midlife passage. At the age of fifty-three, she became the first woman to lead a major Western democracy. After ten years of her rule, she was admired and abhorred on all six continents.

In our interview, I observed, "Being a leader who is a woman seems to present no hardship to you."

She quoted Kipling. "'The female of the species is more deadly than the male.' So it's nothing unusual—it's just that people have got this strange thing that to be strong you have to be a man."

I began recounting the insults she had had to endure. She nodded impatiently. "What I can't stand is when they say, 'Oh well, she's the only man in the Cabinet.' I say, 'She's *not*. She's the only *woman*.'"

One source of her power, I observed, was that she didn't care if she was liked. She only cared about being obeyed. When I asked if this was how she intimidated her opposition into submission, Thatcher bristled.

"You see me in the House, I'm *driven* to be confrontational. I had to learn to be combative. To get it across. Of course, when you're a woman and you're combative, they say you're an Iron Lady. Let me tell you"—and she snapped to like a bow after it's flung its arrow—"if you hadn't got a *spine* which was strong and firm, and a *will* which was strong and firm, we would never have got through. It is so much easier to"—contempt oozed over the next words—"be liked."

SOMETHING HAD CHANGED DRAMATICALLY since Mrs. Thatcher entered her sixties. She looked younger and prettier than the plump, gray, matronly Thatcher from the early '80s. Back then she had a mushy jaw and crepey neck and a prominent gap between her teeth. It almost looked now like she was enjoying a second girlhood, or maybe her first. I uncovered her real secret.

For rejuvenation of the aging body and skin, Thatcher had relied in recent years on a certain Indian woman whose identity was as closely guarded by her clients as their real ages. My source, a client, had to recommend me for an appointment. Madame Véronique, as the Indian woman called herself, practiced the ancient Hindu health system of Ayurveda. She had updated it with electrical underwater stimulation. The price of admission was a thousand dollars' worth of her natural flower oils.

I found the imperious madame in a village on the outskirts of London. Her establishment looked like a cross between a medical clinic and a massage parlor. But Madame Véronique carried herself with the air of an Indian queen, a rani. "I have the most high-powered women in the world," she informed me. "Some run empires," she said, a not-so-veiled boast regarding her most famous client. She also mentioned the Churchill family and Pamela Harriman.

Madame Véronique directed me to disrobe and climb the steps to her formidable electrified tub. First, she explained, she would sprinkle garlic and salts in the water as it warmed. Then she would manipulate the .3 amps of current to "recharge the nervous system and release blocked energy." Shivering at the top step, I was frankly terrified. I'd gone to great lengths to get a story, but I drew the line at electrocution.

"My dear, I have had kings and princes and little bitty emirs in my tub," she asserted in her high-pitched rani voice.

I decided it was worth it to get the straight skinny on the prime minister from a woman who knew her inside and out. Sinking into the water, I allowed myself to be poached. As the current began needling my ankles, then calves, and tingled up the sides of my body, I found the sensation mildly pleasant. I imagined Thatcher allowing herself a rare hour of relaxation, although there was nothing sybaritic about the electrical tub. It was the equivalent of plugging in one's phone charger overnight. Indeed, Madame Véronique warned me to go home and go to bed and not to drink or eat for the next twelve hours. I found the result of mild electrocution was a supercharge of energy and a slight halogen glow. It lasted for at least a month.

I felt I could learn more from the rani. I had to call Tina and ask if *Vanity Fair* would stake me for a second session; she agreed. The next time, Madame Véronique became more loquacious. "Mrs. Thatcher is a very, very feminine woman," she told me. "We are strong but not *hard*. Some men run from us." But not strong men, she indicated. I kept prodding and was staggered when she revealed that one of her strong male clients was "Mr. Gorbachev," leader of the Soviet Union. Definitely a referral by Thatcher.

THATCHER HAD BEEN the very first Western leader to pluck a little-known provincial Communist Party boss, Mikhail Gorbachev, out of the pack of those vying to replace the dying chairman of the Soviet Union. Back in 1984 she had invited Gorbachev to England and ordered a full-dress reception for him as if he were already general secretary. Their weekend at Checkers was so intimate, waiters had to remove their dinner plates, untouched, then stay late to refill their brandy glasses. "Maggie" had already given her heart to "Ronnie," as she called the American president. But her Russian caller challenged the Great Communicator at his own game—leadership through personal chemistry.

This was how Gorbachev won her over, as Thatcher herself described to me in our interview: "President Reagan and I have always been close, but right from the beginning I found it easy to discuss and debate with President Gorbachev in a very animated way. Neither of us giving an inch." The Russian leader questioned her on how Britain let go of its colonies and exchanged the empire for a commonwealth. He was looking for a formula to shed the Soviet satellites in Eastern Europe as a way of rescuing his desperate economy. When he insisted to his English hostess that Russians were really Europeans, Thatcher snapped back: they would never be accepted by Europe as long as his Eastern bloc was still barricaded behind the Iron Curtain. "It's archaic," she railed.

A month after their marathon debate, Gorbachev began to spell out his vision for unyoking the outer Soviet empire. It was a watershed. Thatcher saw the first sign of change in Soviet expansionism. It was this startling shift that prompted her to put her seal of approval on the new leader.

"I like Mr. Gorbachev," she announced to a stunned capitalist world in 1984. "We can do business together."

The prime minister's transformation into a seasoned coquette had coincided with her momentous trip to Moscow in 1987. That was when the relationship with Gorbachev became surprisingly intense. In preparing for her trip, she changed her look entirely. From tidy suits with tortured dressmaker details and floppy bows, Thatcher had the chief designer of Aquascutum lower her décolleté and hike up her skirts to show more of her fine legs.

Thatcher described for me how she felt stepping off the plane in Moscow. "I was more nervous than I've ever been." The thirteen-hour tête-à-tête between the Iron Lady of capitalism and the Iron-Toothed Man of communism was unprecedented, the longest time Thatcher had spent with any head of state. Their meeting was described by observers with voluptuous adjectives—"vigorous," "deep," "passionate." Mrs. Thatcher emerged, tossing her head back with an uncharacteristic cascade of laughter.

During their talks, Gorbachev confided his frustration over his first two meetings with President Reagan, Thatcher told me. The Russian leader exploded, "He doesn't know policy!" Thatcher could sympathize. She said she enjoyed hearing Reagan's Hollywood stories, but given his lazy work habits, she despaired of discussing "privatization" with him, a term she had invented. Instead of reading his briefing books to prepare for the 1983 summit in Williamsburg, Reagan had watched *The Sound of Music* on TV.

I learned later that the prime minister and the general secretary had once become locked in conversation at a Kremlin banquet. They ignored the ballroom full of guests, pecked at their food, arms touching, with eyes only for each other. On their night out at the Bolshoi they held up the second act of *Swan Lake* while they debated methods of grain silage. When they finally reentered their box, Thatcher, resplendent in black lace, rudely inserted herself between Mikhail and his wife, Raisa. Highly displeased, Raisa muscled her way into their discussion of Western nuclear policy.

THATCHER HAD THE SAME kind of affinity with the other superpower leader. Both she and Reagan were out-of-fashion conservatives when they first became friends. Some predicted that historians would cast them as the leaders who together gave capitalism back its confidence. White House insiders confirmed that she flirted with Reagan, to their mutual advantage. He taught her about teleprompters and gave her clearance to use a base on Ascension Island for staging strikes on the Falklands. She lent him her bases to launch the bombing of Libya. Thatcher had no compunction about giving her Ronnie a dressing-down. Nevertheless, the Reagan-Thatcher axis was, in the words of her biographer, Hugo Young, "the most enduring personal alliance in the Western world throughout the 1980s."

Ultimately, the results of her debates with Gorbachev about nuclear disarmament were world changing. Thatcher finally gave her blessing to the new peace formula that he and Reagan devised to replace MAD—mutual assured destruction—which marked the beginning of the end of the Cold War.

Thatcher wound up our interview at 10 Downing by returning to her view of dissent as a socialist-communist conspiracy. It was "them," the counterculture radicals, who used intimidation to prevent free speech and shut down universities, she insisted. When I raised the liberal argument, she lifted her arms skyward with a war cry: "That is why you've got to stand up for what you believe in, and thank goodness there are some people who *always* will."

"But look at you now—you have survived all of these attacks," I said, expecting we could end on a positive note.

"I HAVE TO FIGHT EVERY DAY, STILL," came the thundering reply.

My final question elicited a surprising reply. Who did she see as her historical counterpart? "You go back to the person who really had to fight for what he believed in and—I couldn't begin to compare myself with him—it was Abraham Lincoln."

WHEN MY STORY APPEARED in *Vanity Fair* in June 1989, "The Blooming of Margaret Thatcher," it stimulated a lot of talk and talk-show fodder. But the response in England was literally electric. "THE ION LADY" blared the *Daily Mail*'s front page. Rivals as well as the opposition taunted the PM during Question Time over her watery vibrations.

Following on the success of the Thatcher piece, Tina Brown asked me if I would like to go to Russia and write the first character portrait of a Russian leader, Mikhail Gorbachev. I was intrigued. Gorbachev was all over the news in 1989 as Westerners tried to decipher whether his startling reforms would really change the one-party Communist state. But Gorbachev refused interviews with print journalists.

The more I thought about reporting on the convulsions in the Soviet Union, the more fired up I got. The real draw was studying a formerly rock-solid Communist boss whose persona had already been "transformed" two or three times, according to my sources at the CIA. As Gorbachev tried to lead his "revolution from the top down," he would surely go through another mind-bending change.

On my first trip in the summer of 1989, I discovered that nothing could be done in the Soviet Union without a "connection," meaning a fixer. For starters, there were no phone books. Every call had to be preceded by an introduction. Using my wretched Berlitz Russian, I hired one of the new mercenary entrepreneurs as my translator. Young Sergei appeared, miraculously, with just the part I needed to make my portable printer work on Russian current. I was in good hands.

One evening I entertained some writer friends for dinner, including the novelist Anatoly Pristavkin. When his English-speaking wife, Marina, began to translate for her husband, Sergei butted in aggressively.

"I will translate," he demanded with a rap of fingers on the table.

The next time I had dinner with the Pristavkins, it was alone.

"Gail, you must know something," they said. "Sergei is KGB."

"What gave you the clue?" I asked, astonished.

Marina explained in a typically Russian way. "His fat face, his perfect English, his sudden appearance in your life with everything you need—why?" I explained that an American woman associated with our embassy recommended him. Marina's eyebrows shot up. "You must think this way—in probabilities. One out of every three Soviets is connected to the KGB. So why not Sergei?"

At least, I hoped, my driver was okay. Oleg was a great fixer. His parents were highly cultured members of the Moscow intelligentsia, but Oleg had the sunken-cheeked, wolfish look of many young Soviets. He was utterly amoral. Shortly after I returned home from that extended stay in the Soviet Union, I learned that my every move and contact had indeed been reported to the KGB. From what they learned about me, I deduced that the informer was not Sergei, my translator. It was Oleg.

The day before my next trip, I was waiting on tenterhooks for my visa. Suddenly a fax came in from Moscow! I dived for the machine, expecting it to be from the inner sanctum of the Kremlin.

"You bring me another Sharp Wizard. I know your arrival time. I meet you at airport. OLEG."

Amazing. People didn't have phones. But a twenty-six-year-old black marketer could fax me his extortion order for a computer worth $350. On my next trip, I managed to evade Oleg at the airport. He was outraged. When I didn't respond to his phone calls, he chased me down the street. He finally had the audacity to lure the wife of a top diplomat out of the U.S. Embassy compound. On the street, the young thug raged at her about my having shortchanged him and threatened that the Americans wouldn't get away with this. It was a stunning display of the power of the new Russian "mafia" born in the vacuum between state power and dollar power.

I was getting nowhere in finding a fixer. Just then, Clay called to tell me to jump on a plane. We were invited to a dinner in New York by Mort Zuckerman, the real estate tycoon and publisher of *U.S. News and World Report,* who could introduce me to a real Russian poo-bah. Nikolai Shishlin was a consultant to the Central Committee, the ruling body of the Soviet Communist Party. I made my case for the importance of a character portrait of Gorbachev. Shishlin was in favor: "Perhaps in six months or a year I can talk him into such an approach."

"Wonderful!" I pretended, whereupon Shishlin peered over his thick glasses with a sardonic smile and added: "If nothing happens."

What happened, of course, was the collapse of the Soviet Union's Iron Curtain, culminating in November 1989 in the teardown of the Berlin Wall and the hurtling exodus of East Germans out of Communist confinement. I developed the habit of rising well before six every morning to phone Moscow before the measly thirty-eight trunk lines that serviced the entire country overloaded for the day. There were no answering machines, no secretaries, just the hit-or-miss chance one might catch the fixer at his office. When I would be just about to scream, the voice of this quintessential apparatchik would suddenly answer.

"Da."

"Nikolai?"

"That's me." Sound of a whipped dog.

Shishlin would never say no. Always "Just now it is not possible." Or "Call me back at four." With a promise from Shishlin that I might go to Gorbachev's home village, I flew to Russia in September. Nobody knew anything about my "permission" from the top. Over and over again, I was able to talk my way through barriers and interview his teachers, friends, his first girlfriend, and on up to the party apparatchiks who were dying to learn something personal about the top dog. Soviets appreciated a foreign writer who wasn't afraid of flouting the rules.

To go to Privolnoye, Gorbachev's village, was a journey back in time to Chekhov's Russia. In the country people, one could see the blows of history in their twisted bodies and pained eyes. In the eight precious hours allotted to me in Gorbachev's village, what impressed me the most was how young Misha had survived. He was born into the first year of a Stalin-made famine that killed thirty thousand people. If the Gorbachev family of free farmers had not swung over early to the Communist government's side, earning the scant privileges of local officialdom, they would not have been able to keep the baby Misha alive.

Tina Brown was bold enough to put my first Gorbachev story on the cover of the February 1990 issue: "Red Star: The Man Who Changed the World." For readers of Vanity Fair to see the face of a bearish old man was a startling departure from the usual come-hither Hollywood starlet, but Tina was thrilled. "That was a real breakthrough for us; nobody ever wrote a thing about Russian leaders' private lives." The story got tremendous buzz.

I asked Shishlin if President Gorbachev had read my piece in *Vanity Fair* and if he had any reaction. He said, "I think he rather enjoyed it."

IN THE SPRING OF 1990, my Russian writer friends alerted me that Gorbachev was having a series of "emotional accidents." They sent me translations of his lengthy public diatribes where he veered off into streams of consciousness: "Sometimes I have this crazy idea . . . that I should withdraw my candidacy." He accused his so-called democratic deputies of trying to drive him crazy. "They want to make the leadership come off the track!"

My hunch was that we were beginning to see the disintegration of Gorbachev's inner control. Events were now rushing past him as if on some cosmic slide, scattering even his powers of improvisation into a shower of quickly extinguished sparks. Could Gorbachev change himself once more, this time liberating himself from the Communist ideal implanted in him from the age of sixteen? This story was worth a book. HarperCollins signed me to expand my stories about Gorbachev into a biography.

So I moved to Moscow for the month of March 1990 to watch firsthand the transformation of "the New Gorbachev." This time I was prepared to approximate living within the economy like a Moscow housewife. Friends made on previous trips generously offered an apartment in the Lenin Hills, not far from Moscow University. I had packed a huge trunk full of packaged food and soups, vacuum-packed salami, cans of tuna and sardines—stuff I hated, but, hell, it would keep me fed. Before leaving the luxurious cocoon of an international jetliner, I squirrelled away airline sugar, salt, pepper, and butter. It felt as if I was "going under."

The Lenin Hills were leafy and pretty with the pleasant energy of a university town. My apartment building was an eight-story Stalin-era redbrick block just off the most modern boulevard in Moscow: Leninsky Prospekt. When I first entered my own kitchen, it was with a shudder of dismay. Nothing helpful to a woman was made in the Soviet Union: no paper towels, aluminum foil, or plastic wrap; no napkins or toilet paper; no mops or brooms; not even sanitary napkins.

Most Soviets I met believed that their weaknesses had been engineered genetically. This belief was murderously self-fulfilling. Whenever I asked my Russian friends how long they thought it would be before they would feel truly free, the answer was deeply pessimistic. "You have to be born free to feel it." The most optimistic predication was "Maybe for our children's children."

Whenever I spoke about Gorbachev with my neighbor Irina Peterhov, her soft voice took on a harsher cast. "This is the question I would ask if I ever had an interview with Mr. Gorbachev. 'Who is responsible for the wreckage of our society for the last seventy years? The Communist Party, or Mickey Mouse?'"

I had become almost obsessed with finding out what lay inside the Central Committee complex, the citadel of power in the USSR.

Finally granted an interview with the number-two Soviet power figure, Alexander Yakovlev, Gorbachev's propaganda chief, I entered the cavernous building. Hush of a vacuum. No evidence of work. No secretaries, no aides with computers, no phone banks or fax machines or printers spewing out briefing papers. Just miles of blond veneer, bare bookshelves, closed doors.

Alexander Yakovlev's massive forehead protruded as if his brain was almost too big for his skull. Deep lines flared above his eyes like lightning flashes. His skin was colorless. I asked if Gorbachev was shaken by reports that he had lost the support of the intelligentsia. It was a raw wound. "We are very respectful of the intelligentsia," Yakovlev said defensively. "All of us can be called intelligentsia."

I reminded Yakovlev that he had once written that ultraleftists were the curse of any revolution. Was this how he saw Boris Yeltsin, Gorbachev's challenger on the far left?

"The ultraleftists must be isolated," he said darkly.

"How?" I asked the propaganda chief.

"Moral isolation."

After this chilling answer, I felt bold enough to ask the number-two power in the country if he worried that Gorbachev's enemies were poisoning his mind. "Are they trying to drive him crazy?" Yakovlev's answer spoke volumes about the Russian people

"We are not always stable people," Yakovlev said.

AFTER A YEAR AND A HALF of research and four extensive trips to the Soviet Union, I sensed that Gorbachev could be overthrown at any moment. Even though I had not met him in person, I felt I knew him, almost killing myself in the summer of 1990 to write his biography in three months. My editor impressed upon me that the manuscript's drop-dead deadline was Labor Day. Only then could they publish before December, when we anticipated that Gorbachev would win the Nobel Peace Prize.

Clay shut me in my study in East Hampton and Ella brought me lots of iced tea. I wrote six and a half days a week with breaks only to swim or eat. The morning after Labor Day, I pushed Send to my editor. Her return e-mail took my last breath away:

> I know you will understand, as the author of *Passages*,
> that the time has come for me to leave publishing and go
> climb a mountain.

It almost made me sorry I'd ever written that damn book about life transitions.

In December 1990, Gorbachev was indeed awarded the Nobel Peace Prize. Eight months later he was summarily overthrown. For all his courage in changing the psychology of his people, he was left in the dust by the horsemen of history. The last line of my biography of Mikhail Gorbachev cast him as a tragic figure. He was the man who changed the world but lost his country.

BOTH THATCHER AND GORBACHEV WERE scuttled off the world stage ignominiously, both shouting their unshakable beliefs in themselves. For Thatcher, it was neither the socialists nor the communists she hated who engineered her abrupt downfall. It was a coup by her own star boys who plotted a revolt behind her back. On November 20, 1990, the "perpetual prime minister" lost her place as Conservative Party leader. She returned home from a state visit to find her nearly twelve years in power finished off by her own MPs. Rarely seen in tears, on the traumatic day that Thatcher was ushered out of her home at No. 10 after announcing her resignation, she broke down and wept. She confided to her Ronnie that she felt "betrayed."

Reagan left office venerated around the world. He and Thatcher are the only two world leaders in modern times whose political philosophies became memorialized in "isms." Reaganism and Thatcherism live on today. Indeed, together the two leaders set the developed world on the conservative course of free-market capitalism, including the new Russia. It would take almost twenty years before the near collapse of the American economy exposed the danger to the world of government run by rich people's political bribery and the slow starving of the middle class.

Charmed as I was by the animal magnetism between Thatcher

and Gorbachev, I had been working on a play about a fantasy romance between the two leaders. *Maggie and Misha* even had a two-week workshop production off Broadway. So I had a very personal reason to be disappointed when both were sent off to political Siberia. Incurable romantic that I am, I wanted the fantasy to come true!

CHAPTER 33

THE SILENT PASSAGE

"I WANT YOU TO DO THE POPE."

Tina Brown was deliciously cocky after seven years of growing *Vanity Fair* into the most talked-about magazine around town and actually making it profitable. By 1991, she thought we could "do" anybody.

"The pope! Jesus, Tina, I'm not even Catholic!"

I had come to her apartment on East Fifty-Seventh Street early that Saturday in January armed with an equally preposterous idea. "I want to write about menopause."

"Excuse me?"

It took Tina an uncharacteristically long time to respond—maybe more than a minute. She had just had a baby. She was in that cotton-brained dither of hormonal chaos that overtakes the newly postpartum woman, not unlike the static in my brain brought on by menopause. We were living in alternate realities. The last thing on Tina's mind was the end of fertility. But being Tina Brown, she knew a taboo when she heard one and she liked nothing better than breaking taboos.

"Brilliant, Gail! It's the one thing nobody can talk about. You can talk all you want about sex, but menopause—I've never even heard the word spoken aloud."

I WAS AS IGNORANT AS anyone else when the first bombshell of the battle began. It was a Sunday evening in 1985. Snug inside our marriage, a pillow's throw away from Clay, we were both contentedly reading while jazz lapped at our ears and snow curtained the window. Every so often we looked up and congratulated ourselves on staying home in the cocoon of love and comfort we had created in what was now *our* apartment on East Fifty-Seventh Street. As I wrote then, "What was that?" I mumbled.

"What?"

"Nothing."

It felt like a little grenade had gone off in my head. I tried to go back to reading. But some powerful switch had been thrown. I couldn't concentrate. When I looked down at the page I had just finished reading, I realized that its imprint on my brain had washed out.

A little while later, my heart began leaping against my chest like a frog caught in a jar. I lay down. But I was too agitated to sleep. In the months that followed, I sometimes felt outside of my body. My memory was as solid as Swiss cheese. Clay and I began having Thermostat Wars.

"It's freezing in here," Clay would moan. "No, it's boiling." "Did you turn the thermostat below fifty again?" "I'm sorry, I just have to open a window."

It was the little crashes of fatigue that really disturbed me. Having always enjoyed abundant energy, I was furious at myself for crawling home from a day of writing and falling into bed for a "nap," from which I had to drag myself up to make dinner. I said nothing to Clay. But it's not like he didn't notice my mood swings, which were becoming more like the arcs of a trapeze.

This couldn't be the dreaded Change, could it? But I was only forty-eight.

The first friend with whom I raised the dreaded subject was a sultry-looking woman of fifty who prided herself on her body, her tennis game, and her youthful-looking husband. I asked if she had ever talked with anyone about menopause.

"No, and I don't want to," she said.

"Women don't bring up the subject around you?"

"One friend did," she said sourly. "I haven't seen her since."

The wake-up call came at a Park Avenue dinner party. It was one of those high-protocol parties where the place cards look like tracings from the Book of Kells. I was feeling especially pretty in my new black velvet suit with its white satin collar, when from nowhere, a droplet of something hit my collar. What the—was the waiter dribbling wine? Could there be a leaky ceiling behind all the beautiful wood beams? I noticed Clay's gaze from across the table turn to alarm: What horrible thing was happening to me? I put a hand to my face.

My forehead was swampy. *Oh, no, not me!* The moisture began running down my face in rivulets—plop—onto my satin collar. Should I pick up the white linen napkin and mop my forehead? I reached for the five-hundred-thread-per-inch napery, hesitated—*No, all the makeup will come off on the napkin.* Trying to pretend this wasn't happening, I turned to the titan of industry on my right and tried smiling and mopping, chatting and fanning, laughing at his jokes and dabbing, when what I wanted most in the world was to disappear into the kitchen and tear off my clothes and open the freezer door—never mind that it was February—and just *stand there.*

It was time to see my gynecologist. I had always prized him as a solid clinician. I asked if I could be in menopause.

"Not yet," he said flatly. "You're still menstruating."

"But I have these weird symptoms . . ."

With coaxing, he measured my hormone levels. I was very low on estrogen.

"Could I be a candidate for hormone-replacement therapy?" I asked.

"You have to be menstruation free for a year before I can give you estrogen replacement."

Finally, shamefaced and stumbling over my words, I tried to spit out my worst fear. "I've always enjoyed a wonderful sex life with my husband, but I'm not feeling . . . you know . . . juicy."

"Decrease in sexual response is a natural part of aging," he said curtly. "I can't help you with that." I had just been handed a one-way ticket to the Dumpster. *What's happening to me? Why can't I fix this? Am I the only one?* But I knew too much about passages by now to know that if I was feeling like this, probably a lot of other women around my age were too. And we weren't all crazy. I put on my research hat. It didn't take long to discover that most male gynecologists in the late '80s were woefully ignorant about the mysteries of menopause. It was only when I found a knowledgeable female gynecologist that I began learning about a passage that is universal among half the world's population.

It was Dr. Patricia Allen, an attending physician at New York Hospital, who identified what I was experiencing as perimenopause—a preliminary phase of this long transition—the three or four years leading up to the end of menstruation, which is often the most symptomatic and anxiety-provoking phase.

We hit it off from the start. She let me know that she didn't accept passive patients, only those willing to participate actively in their own health care. Fine with me. I guessed Dr. Pat's age to be early forties. From her appearance—coppery hair swept off her beautiful face, makeup applied sparingly to her delicate features, an intentional switch of her hips when she walked, and a raucous laugh—this was not a woman who would give up on sex after fifty, or probably ever.

"I believe in treating each patient as an individual," she said. "This perimenopausal period should be a transformation," she explained, "so that a woman gets to become—physically, emotionally, and spiritually—the best that she ever was."

"Why do I feel like I'm not me anymore?" I asked.

She leveled with me. "The forties are the decade of greatest anguish," she said. Women begin to sense a momentous change coming on, but often feel embarrassed to discuss it. Or they cling to the fantasy of endless youth and report to her, when their periods stop at forty-eight, "Surprise! I must be pregnant!" Of the several hundred patients who consulted her about managing their menopause, she said quite a few mentioned feeling depressed, although they had no rational reasons to be. I told her that was true of me.

I was in a thrilling, mind-stretching period of creative redirection in both my career and my new family life, traveling around the country and the world, and coming home to an adored husband and newly adopted child. But I knew I couldn't take Scarlett's fiddle-dee-dee approach any longer.

She asked if there was a history of osteoporosis in my family, which brought to mind memories of my mother suffering in her seventies as she sat on her powdery bones. Dr. Pat sent me for a bone density test to the only facility available in the city at that time: the Hospital for Special Surgery. I was a prime candidate for osteoporosis—fairskinned, thin, small-boned, Northern European extraction—but no one paid attention at the time to Asian women and Hispanic women, who were at just as high risk.

I was already a runner, thank goodness. But now I was educated to add weight-bearing exercises to constantly replenish bone mass. Three mornings a week I tumbled out of bed early to run down to Gilda Marx's studio on East Fifty-Seventh and pound the boards in a hot and heavy aerobics class. My midsection had thickened. No amount of crunches deflated that tube—infuriating!—until I discovered yoga. Stretching helped. But they could have put me on a medieval rack and I still wouldn't have recovered my usual trim figure, not until I came out the other end of the transition.

Dr. Pat also took seriously my distress over changes in my libido. "You're a good candidate for hormone therapy," she said. But I had read some reports that suggested synthetic estrogen might increase a woman's chance of getting cancer.

"We just don't know," said Dr. Pat. "Why don't you do some research on different regimens."

I attended an FDA (Food and Drug Administration) meeting where the question was asked, "What proportion of the female population over age fifty would be suitable candidates for long-term consumption of estrogen alone, or combined with progestin?"

"Virtually all" was the answer from the FDA committee. It was a blank check.

"How do they know?" I asked Jamie Grifo, a gynecologist at New York Hospital.

"They don't," he said. "The bottom line is, the right studies need to be done for the right length of time, and, clearly, for economic and political reasons, they're not. Why? Who supports most research? The drug companies."

I learned that no study had been completed in North America on the possible carcinogenic consequences of combined-hormone therapy, or the long-term consequences for women's health in general. I asked a public health expert, Dr. Lewis Kuller, "Is it even conceivable that millions of men over fifty—those at the highest levels of the power structure—would be herded by physicians toward chemical dependence on powerful hormones suspected of causing testicular cancer?"

"It's the largest *uncontrolled* clinical trial in the history of medicine," he charged. This was my introduction to the scandalous politics of menopause. Activism was the only answer. I had to talk to the few women in Congress about pushing for a government-controlled study of menopause and the impact of treatments on women's health. And I had to try to upend the stereotype. "The change" was not a curse that turned older women into victims; it was a freedom that allowed older women to stop trying so hard to please.

That settled it. I had to be willing to go public with my own menopause to start a national conversation about the silent passage. Tina paired me off with a young editor, Elise O'Shaughnessy, to dig through the trove of information and pare it down into a trim article. Years later, Elise admitted that working with me had given her "a fake menopause" twenty years in advance.

When my article was ready for publication in October 1991, Tina told me, "I'm sorry, Gail, we can't put it on the cover. We have Jessica Lange on her back with her legs in the air." Only the tantalizing headline was fit to print: "Breaking the Last Taboo."

Immediately following publication, I was off to Moscow to research a follow-up story on Gorbachev. I tried valiantly to phone Clay, but the wretched Soviet infrastructure made it impossible to connect with New York for two weeks. Until my last day.

"You have to come home, right now!" Clay pleaded. "I can't stand it anymore."

I was touched by his ardor, until he told me, "Every party I go to, women crowd around me and insist I tell them about menopause."

We laughed. He changed tack. "You should think about doing a book."

"Are you crazy! Who would want to read a whole book about menopause? It's bad enough going through it."

BOB LOOMIS, MY RANDOM HOUSE EDITOR, was keen on the book idea. He was dead right in advising, "This should be an experience book," rather than a medical approach or a historical tome. I committed to moving around the country and *listening* to women of as many different class and color backgrounds as I could find to talk to me. The deadline was daunting. Loomis gave me two months, from October to Christmas 1991, to finish. He wanted the book for the 1992 spring list. In those same two months, I had to finish the second *Vanity Fair* cover story on Gorbachev, "Red Star Falling."

In kid gloves and high heels, Dr. Pat took to the trenches with me to co-lead focus groups with midlife women from Kentucky to California. We found previously confident and highly competent women suddenly feeling helpless from the ignorance, shame, and fear that surrounded the subject. "Menopause!" shrieked a producer who called from Hollywood. "God, I've never seen that word written until I read your article." It was Lynda Guber, wife of then-head of Sony Pictures Entertainment, Peter Guber. She told me she had run into Joanna Poitier and asked innocently, "How are you doing?" The actress-wife of Sidney Poitier wailed, "I'm a lunatic. I'm going through menopause and empty nest at the same time."

Losing the magic of fertility—that was a deeper mutation and harder to accept. "For many of us who waited until we were well into our thirties and even early forties before having children, the physical power of giving birth is still palpable—it touches something very deep and instinctual," ventured Suzanna Rosenblatt Buhai, a Los Angeles psychotherapist.

Vicki Reynolds, then the fiftysomething mayor of Beverly Hills, told me, "I have seen women my age go through menopause totally ignorant of what you are saying. We're looking to you, boomer generation women, to talk about this openly and explore the benefits of menopause. That's exciting!"

The vestigial attitudes surrounding menopause would be changed by the way women of our time handled it. I was determined to upend the sorry stereotype and showcase the bold new faces of women in middle life.

MOTHER'S DAY IN MAY 1992 was the publication date for *The Silent Passage*. Again, I hit the road three full weeks in advance and began giving speeches and feature interviews. Those little sparks set off a word-of-mouth blaze like a spontaneous forest fire. Once the seventeen-city book tour began, I quickly learned that talking about menopause demanded a sense of humor, especially with male talk-show hosts. They were stuck with interviewing this sassy woman about a subject they had never heard mentioned, until a producer shoved an introduction under their nose a few minutes before airtime.

"Menopause," gulped a Cleveland man on the midday news. "Is that like—impotence?"

"Um, no," I murmured lamely. Only later did I come up with the right answer. "Baldness. Is that like—Alzheimer's?"

Stunned to realize the level of their ignorance about such a fundamental physiological process, women listeners responded with a desperate "need to know" urgency. The book began flying out of the stores. My most memorable public appearance on *The Silent Passage* was in the California Bay Area. Alta Bates Hospital in Berkeley was getting threatening calls from women who were refused when they tried to make a reservation to hear me speak. A protest was being planned. One woman swore she was going to look for her gynecologist in the audience. "If I see him, I'm going to say, 'If you keep refusing to give me hormones for my hot flashes, I'm going to shout out your name and tear off all my clothes!'"

The hospital's auditorium would hold only 250. The hospital administrator told me they were afraid that something like a thousand women were planning to beat down the doors. The day before the event, the venue was moved to an old burlesque theater in Oakland. When I arrived, there was a double line of women around the block.

But that wasn't what hit me. It was seeing my name up in marquee lights for the first time:

GAIL SHEEHY IN MENOPAUSE

THE CALL FROM OPRAH WINFREY'S TALENT BOOKER was a magic wand. In 1992, Oprah was the model of the new self-made celebrity. She had established the ultimate compassion pulpit. Having broken the silence on so many of our secret shames and wounds, from the eternal battle to shed pounds to the revelation of incest, certainly Oprah wouldn't flinch from talking about middle age, menopause, and how to bring back a woman's sex drive. Oprah incorporated my attitude into the philosophy of her pulpit, shepherding women beyond self-doubt into believing this is the stage when we can become our most authentic selves.

After that appearance in June of 1992, Random House began printing books at five thousand a clip; a few days later it was ten thousand, then fifteen thousand, and on one Friday, forty thousand books were slapped together. "That oughta hold 'em," said Loomis. Demand began to spread to the most remote little burgs in Alaska, Virgin Islands, Hawaii—it was a phenomenon.

The first leap onto the *New York Times* Bestseller List—at number 8—came a month after the first shipping. That same Sunday, the *Times* reviewed it, giving the assignment to Barbara Ehrenreich, an angry feminist, who wrote, "One can imagine Ms. Sheehy ... scanning feminist works and deciding they just weren't—well—scary enough."

Ouch! Was Ehrenreich trying to say we should keep the realities of menopause in the closet, since it pointed out how women are different from men?

By the time Tina and Harry threw me a book party at Barbetta's on June 30, 1992, a Random House executive told me they had shipped four hundred thousand books. Liz Smith, the reigning gossip columnist sitting next to me, printed it.

Clay and I were in London with Mohm, having our own idyll with Shakespeare, when Loomis called to report the good news. "Well, now the *Times* is going to have to print you're on the bestseller list whether they like it or not." By that time, the book was review-proof.

Only four days later, we learned the book would leap to number 1 the next Sunday—astonishing! I was sitting in a publishing escort's car in Toronto when the Random House representative called me. I sat mute for several minutes. That said it all. The taboo had been lifted, the silence broken. The experiences I had related did reflect what millions of women were going through or anxiously expecting. Once more, I was speaking for strangers.

Then came streams of flowers, masses of white roses from Tina and peonies from Harry Evans, with a card reading, simply, "Natch!"

The bidding for softcover rights began. These rights had not been sold before because Loomis wanted to see what happened to the hardcover, figuring Random House might want to keep the hardcover in print beyond the normal one year. Random House's paperback line, Ballantine, offered $25,000. My agent, Lynn Nesbit, said, "That's insulting."

At a delightful book party thrown for me by Lesley Stahl and Aaron Latham on a sunny summer evening in June, we had just spilled out onto their penthouse terrace when Harry Evans burst in and made a beeline to my side to say, "I just got an offer for $650,000, it's fabulous, but from here on it will start falling back. It's a twenty-four-hour offer," he panted urgently. "I'm off to London tomorrow, so I hope you'll take it."

I had to catch the last shuttle to Boston, but I stayed up half the night to finish writing a speech for a League of Women Voters convention. Before six, I was up to take a run in the Boston Commons and back just in time to dress. When I spoke about *The Silent Passage,* I received warm applause. A long line was waiting for me at the book-signing table, probably 150 to 200 women out of the audience of 1,200. Each one had a story to share. I listened avidly. I have always loved connecting with my readers one-on-one. But I was late getting back to the hotel. Rushing to pack in time to make the next shuttle, I almost didn't answer the door when a bellman knocked to deliver an urgent message. *Call Mort.* Heart in my mouth, I phoned Lynn Nesbit's senior partner, Morton Janklow.

"We made the deal," he said.

"You what . . . ?" I choked. My accountant had lectured me sternly not to allow my financial future to be decided in a competitive spasm. "How could you, without talking to me?"

"Hey, you gotta have faith in your representatives. It was eleven forty-five. I had a twelve o'clock deadline. I couldn't reach you."

"But, but," I sputtered, "what about the royalty rates and when are the payment periods—I was afraid this was going to happen!"

"Don't you wanna hear the deal?"

I could tell, Janklow was feeling ten feet tall.

"Sure."

"A million dollars." He let it sink in.

"A million dollars?"

He moved right to self-congratulations. "You gotta believe it." He rattled on. "So Avon was at six-fifty and I called up Dick Snyder [Simon & Schuster/Pocketbooks] this morning at ten, I tell him, 'Look, a low editor at your place says she's interested in this book but I don't know how real that is. I want you to know it's hot. The demographics alone—forty-three million American women—do the figures yourself—what can you give me for this book?'" Janklow hurried on: "Snyder gets all excited. He said he'd published *Passages* when he was at Bantam and he knew what he could do with this book. It's all about you gotta believe, and with this wonderful book you wrote, these guys only needed two hours to check the demographics, and they believe. Snyder called me back with his High Noon preemptive bid—a million bucks. He said, 'I need an answer in fifteen minutes.' He got it. Avon had dropped out at seven-fifty."

It was a sweet ironic moment of triumph. Men would only take a subject like menopause seriously when it generated numbers like forty-three million potential buyers.

I thanked Janklow profusely and went home eager to share the excitement with Clay. When we came together, we began dancing and giggling like kids who'd pulled off a great caper.

TWO WEEKS LATER, I had my first meeting with Graydon Carter. He had taken Tina Brown's place as the much-anticipated editor in chief of *Vanity Fair,* a handsome, Byronic man-about-town and Hollywood connoisseur. He took me by surprise when he said, "God, all those candidate profiles starting in '87, then Gorbachev, then your menopause article, and a bestselling book—the last five years have probably been your best."

Probably so. They coincided with being happily married—and menopausal. Dr. Pat had been right about postmenopause. I felt buoyant, surging with a new kind of energy, not so start-stop but more sustainable. It's what Margaret Mead had described as "postmenopausal zest." My waist had returned. My memory was more reliable (but don't expect me to remember your name the first time we're introduced).

I had written it. I had declared it in speeches. But living it is believing it: the most satisfying stage of our lives as women is our fifties. Not for everyone, of course. But for the majority of healthy women, as studies have documented, this is the stage of highest well-being. I could not, and did not, imagine anything of the sort when I was in my thirties and writing *Passages*. Back then, I had stopped parsing the stages of adult life at fifty-five. I thought then, What could happen of any interest after fifty? How quaint.

But it wasn't just postmenopausal zest. It was the accumulated force of the women's movement that coalesced around that time. The show "trial" of Anita Hill in 1991 had awakened millions of women and men to the spectacle of an all-white, middle-aged male phalanx of senators shaming a prim, thirty-five-year-old attorney and academic, who calmly exposed an assault against women that then had no name—sexual harassment. It took the daring of Anita Hill and millions of boomer women who stood up and demanded a respected place at the table. We empowered one another.

The media dubbed 1992 the Year of the Woman. Barbara Mikulski, the first woman ever to be elected to the U.S. Senate without following a husband, made me laugh when I interviewed her about it. "Calling 1992 the Year of the Woman makes it sound like the Year of the Caribou or the Year of the Asparagus," she scoffed. "We're not a fad, a fancy, or a year." She knew that we had to be prepared for a long, slow, never-give-up, nonviolent war until 51 percent of the American population was fairly represented in the Senate. President George H. W. Bush was not supportive. In a debate at the University of Richmond, he voiced his contempt for women in politics. "This is supposed to be the year of the women in the Senate. Let's see how they do. I hope a lot of them lose."

But they didn't. Mikulski galvanized other women to step up and run for office. Patty Murray, an education activist from Washington State, won a Senate seat despite being ridiculed as "a mom in tennis shoes." Carol Moseley Braun was the first and only African American woman to be elected to the U.S. Senate. Barbara Boxer and Dianne Feinstein became the all-female face of California's representation in the Senate. By 2013, it took a woman in the Senate, Patty Murray, to start talking with her conservative male counterpart in the House, Paul Ryan, and break through the partisan gridlock, avoid another government shutdown, and revive the art of compromise to come to a friendly agreement on a budget deal.

By now, I like to think we are living in the Century of the Woman.

CHAPTER 34

LIONS AND TOADS

WE ARE CLIMBING THE STEPS to the Parthenon of the printed word. From behind its grand pillars the New York Public Library on Fifth Avenue glows and beckons through a blur of rain. The fantastical lions, Patience and Fortitude, sit astride stone steps too high for ordinary mortals. It is the night of the Literary Lions gala, an award coveted by practitioners of fiction and nonfiction, who will be draped in red sashes and bronze medals, warriors in the battle of wits to create something that might last.

My toes, slippered in satin, float upward step by step, my arm buoyed by the man who sculpted my career as a writer. "Clay!" people call out. It's Tom Wolfe and Gay Talese and Vartan Gregorian, then president of the library; everybody knows Clay. He has done far more to deserve recognition than I, having given countless writers their voice. But tonight, he takes pride in the fact that I am one of the new literary lions. His throat inflates like a bullfrog who commands the pond. I am happy too, and sick with fear.

At the top step, jaded news photographers pretend to be thrilled to see each couple. "Over here! Oh, yes, divine!" Air kisses are blown. Embraces carefully avoid dislodging hairpieces. Those who have to be asked "Your names?" suffer a crisis of fading social status, quickly assuaged by the feigned apology "Oh yes, of course." Clay and I are recognized as a power couple.

I lift the skirt of my long beaded gown, taking care not to let droop the swath of black satin in which I am caped. I have never dressed so grandly. The usually hushed halls are suddenly deafening with jollity. Glasses clink and silken hems are lifted when the command is sounded to descend for dinner. Among the twenty writers to be lionized tonight are William Styron, Neil and Susan Sheehan, Maya Angelou. Through this portal have walked giants of the word, carriers of the narrative of our species. I feel humbled.

My mind lurches back to a few hours before when Clay and I waited in a cramped examining room. Clay sat with his naked limbs poking out from a paper gown. We were propped side by side, on stools, like dolls. When the imperious Indian surgeon entered, he rolled on his stool toward Clay. I was in the way. I skittered to one side. In the cut-crystal accent showcasing his posh British education, the surgeon delivered his dictum.

"Radical neck surgery—it is your only option."

I wanted to say, "There is never only one option," but I was invisible.

"I need your full consent," the surgeon told Clay.

"Full consent—what does that mean?"

"To do whatever is necessary." The surgeon stepped out while we considered. Clay's head lurched forward. His shoulders slumped. I pulled him to my shoulder before he fell off the stool. I had never seen him faint.

THE GONG RINGS FOR DINNER, summoning me back to the library. The swarm suspends its ritual calculus of status positioning and descends to another vast room beneath a glass-and-steel dome. We look for name cards. I am seated next to a King Kong of publishing. He has discarded the wife who helped him build his company. She is a friend of mine and the editor on my next book. Conversation will be forced, but nonetheless he loudly boasts about his new lady, a younger, sexier, more accommodating accessory.

I catch Clay's eyes, distant in thought. He smiles. He isn't scared. He had told me earlier that day, "We'll get through this, together." But he wants me to make a promise. "Don't tell anyone."

"Why not?"

"The minute people hear the word *cancer,* they move away."

"Not everyone."

"Oh, yes. It's like you're contagious. You must promise me. Not a word."

"Well, I'll tell Maura, of course."

"No! Not *anyone.*"

How could I shut out my daughter? She would never forgive me. She is my rock. But how could I go against the wishes of a person who is looking death in the eye? Loyalty demands that I seal this knowledge. It scalds my throat.

Clay's booming voice suddenly summons our whole table of literary lionizers into a single scintillating conversation. No one knows that we are not what we appear to be. We are about to be turned into something else, unknowable, a powerless couple up against mortality.

WEEKS LATER, WE SOUGHT A SECOND CONSULT, this time with Dr. John Conley, a pioneering head and neck surgeon. We sat long enough in his waiting room on Central Park West to learn that he was a violinist and a self-published poet. We liked the idea of a surgeon who was an artist. A tall, elegant gentleman appeared and summoned us into his consultation room, treating us like guests who had stopped by for tea. He poured Lapsang souchong into porcelain cups and casually offered Clay the same solution: radical neck surgery.

"Don't let the name scare you," he said quickly, soothing the shock. He told us he had pioneered a procedure that spared deformity.

I had looked up this physician in the Columbia Presbyterian Medical Center database. There was only one item of alarm: he was seventy-nine years old. How steady could his hands be in a lengthy operation? Clay did not have to verbalize his fear to another man. Instinctively, Dr. Conley moved closer to Clay, knee to knee in fact, and held out his long tapered hands.

"I do three or four of these operations a week," he said. "They take from three to five hours. I'm as steady as I ever was, or I wouldn't still be doing surgery." All the while he described the procedure, his hands remained still as gloves on a table.

Dr. Conley's approach was collaborative. He wanted Clay's complete buy-in and he included me, the caregiver, in endorsing his care plan. We agreed.

"And now, I want to ask something of you two." We were enthusiastic. "On the morning of surgery, I want you to tell me 'You are going to do a splendid operation.'" He was showing us that this truly was a collaboration based on acceptance and trust.

Across the street, Central Park was beginning to awaken from the dreary winter with a splurge of cherry blossoms. Clay grabbed me around the waist and pulled me to him, giddy with the euphoria of disaster.

"Hope. We have hope!" He led me into the park to find a tree to hide us, "while I kiss you all over."

We took the time to walk up and down the grassy hillocks from Eighty-Sixth Street to 110th and stop to look at the Shakespeare Garden. It was poetry in color, each bed a bright verse of English flowers from the bard's plays or sonnets: columbine bells, primrose, quince, eglantine, and the deadly rue. I vowed then and there, one day I would create a Shakespeare garden as a paean to the *aHa!* moment of this day.

The toad of cancer crouching on the back of Clay's tongue had been caught early and would be cut out. Dr. Conley was confident that radiation would finish the job. We were buoyant with victory.

We were not a powerless couple. We were partners in fighting for life.

PART THREE

THE BONUS YEARS

AND NOW LET US BELIEVE
IN A LONG YEAR THAT IS
GIVEN TO US, NEW,
UNTOUCHED, FULL OF THINGS
THAT HAVE NEVER BEEN.

—RAINER MARIA RILKE

CHAPTER 35

THE HAPPINESS PRESCRIPTION

"IT'S INDOLENT." The oncologist broke the news slowly. "This is a low-grade non-Hodgkin's lymphoma. The median survival rate at your age is ten years. But since you have no symptoms and early treatment with any drug won't improve your life span," and here his voice rose cheerily, "I'm going to leave you alone."

It was 1993 and the new diagnosis came out of the blue. An invisible killer had been sleeping in Clay's blood for who knew how long? It was my friend Dr. Pat who had sent us to see Dr. Morton Coleman, director of the Lymphoma Center at New York Hospital. She had told us he was known for his humanistic approach.

We were stunned at being "left alone"—did this mean giving up?

"My advice is this," Dr. Coleman said in a voice pulsing with confidence. "Go out and live your life—the two of you. Do something wonderful you wouldn't have done before." He smiled. "Do it together."

This was the secret of true power, I thought. Not external success, not the overkill of Big Pharma. Why not try to tap into the powers of the mind to mobilize the body's astonishing capacity for self-healing? By changing the way one thinks, one could mitigate the emotions that translate into harmful chemicals in the body. We made a commitment to try. Most weekends for close to a year, we took long, meditative walks in Central Park or, when the weather was good, in the Mashomack Preserve on Shelter Island. Meandering along paths through dense oak woodlands and crossing a latticework of tidal creeks, we would suddenly emerge on the shoreline. Sitting, hushed, we would wait to be startled by the soaring of a great-winged fish hawk. Osprey were protected there. The ultimate thrill was to see the acrobatic swoop of an osprey diving for its dinner.

When we spoke on these quiet walks, it was to wrestle with the next great existential question: Stripped of title and setting, what was it about his work that Clay most loved? What could revive the excitement and purpose he had felt in putting out his own publications ? It would take a full year before he found the answer.

After *Manhattan, Inc.* folded, Fairchild Publications gave Clay another command as editor of a men's magazine called M. For the first time in his life, Clay was locked into a contract and had to go through the motions of a corporate employee with no passion of his own. Where was the bodysurfer I knew who had an unquenchable zest for catching the next wave? The man who always dared his protégés to go beyond? The man who transmuted his cocksure smile into a Roman candle under his writers' fearful feet with the emphatic words "You can do it!" Now he was a man stopped in his tracks. Not running, not looking for the next wave, not getting out of his sweatpants until noon. It didn't require another doctor to tell us that he was suffering from chronic low-grade depression.

Secretly, Clay's network of grateful colleagues and protégés, people whose careers he had fostered, including me, had been meeting for months to share ideas for how to get him back in action. The group had approached several journalism schools. We heard from the journalism school at the University of California, Berkeley. The dean there, Tom Goldstein, a native New Yorker, was excited about luring Clay to the West Coast. I thought Clay would be thrilled, given the loss of *New West* and his interrupted dream of exploring California lifestyles and politics. Instead, he was phlegmatic.

Here I was, at the peak of success in my work, while Clay was beginning a descent. Not surprising, given that he was a dozen years older. We were changing places. He had been the guide and inspiration that allowed me to become what I was meant to be. How could I, in essence, be as valuable to him—slow his descent?

I HAD A JOURNEY OF MY OWN to make. It had been seven years since I began research on the sequel to *Passages*. In that earlier book I had stopped tracking the stages of adult life at the age I was now—at fifty-five. Back then, in my thirties and midway through that brilliant decade of endless promise, I could not imagine what would be of interest about life after the midfifties. How naive!

Now, two decades later, science and medicine were stretching our life spans by some thirty years. A Western man in 1900 had a life expectancy of about fifty-five. Nearing the year 2000, his average life span was eighty-five, and the average woman's life span was eighty-eight. One in four baby boomers was expected to live to one hundred. These facts threw off by miles our calculations about middle and later age—nothing short of a revolution in the adult life cycle. In a single century we had created almost a different species.

Why wait until we were old to take advantage of those extra years? Whole new stages were springing up at several points along the landscape of adult life, offering new opportunities and discontinuities that had never before appeared on the maps in our minds. To investigate how people were adapting to this startling expansion in lifetime was a thrilling prospect.

From beneath my bed I dragged out the zippered suitcase containing all the journals and hundreds of pages of transcripts from interviews I'd conducted thus far with men and women in their late forties, fifties, sixties. I was on top of the mountain. If I stopped long enough to look around, the view was breathtaking, a 360-degree panorama of the roads taken, hills climbed, foolish detours, and crash sites. But I had survived—more than that, I had thrived. Now the specter of mortality had once again invaded our dreams.

My own fears were also stuffed inside that zippered suitcase. What Furies would fly out? From all my research and interviews, I expected to brace myself to accept the inevitable decline at this time of life. Would I cry a lot and come out the other side with the crisp, dispassionate composure of Older Woman?

Concentrated work on writing *New Passages* demanded discipline and solitude. I would have to walk away from my public platform and turn inward for at least a couple of years. A plan took shape when a friend offered to share her office in a resort town in Southern California. There I could drop out for a month, let fall the masks of public life, escape offers and deadlines, even ignore the rituals of grooming to get to work.

Clay promised to join me in California as soon as he closed the next issue of *M* magazine. Having found a modest condo to rent a block from the beach, I set up a Spartan routine. Rising at dawn, I stretched, inhaled coffee, spooned organic yogurt, and tried to work up the nerve to do what I had always enjoyed doing with no sense of danger: swim in the ocean.

Why not? I reminded myself that I had been comfortable in the water since I was a tadpole being tossed back and forth between my parents in the shallows of Long Island Sound. But this was the mighty Pacific. And I was no longer young.

Walking to the beach under the rattle of palm leaves, I melted from the warmth of the West Coast in winter. Abruptly, I came upon a little strip of beach. The backdrop was an outcropping of tall reddish rocks. With very little room between water and rock, I began running cautiously along the shoreline, considering the waves. These were not surfer waves, but they tumbled in with a careless energy that I began to sense as malevolent. Instead of thinking, as I had in the past, *I can't wait to dive under and come up on the other side,* my imagination was invaded by thoughts of drowning. I returned quickly to the condo.

Over the next several days I waited a little longer each morning to walk to the beach, hoping the strip of sand would expand as the tide lowered. My fear only increased. Fear of losing my footing; fear of no longer being carelessly agile; fear of Clay's body breaking down. When the thought of death is too terrifying to confront, it comes back in various disguises. Those waves represented everything that could overpower me and take away what I loved.

One night Clay called. For the first time in almost a year, his voice was booming with brio. "It hit me!" he said. "Today, while I was walking in the park—it's like you were with me—I suddenly knew."

"What?"

"What I love to do."

"What, what?"

"I love to identify and shape young talent."

"Of course, yes! You can do that as a teacher!"

He grunted. "But I don't want to occupy a stuffy academic chair."

"No, darling, Berkeley has something else in mind—actually making magazines with your students."

Because he had pinpointed his core passion, he was suddenly open to a possible new container for it. Berkeley was about as remote from Manhattan as one could get, but its graduate school of journalism was among the most prestigious in the country. The very originality of the idea—to establish a brand-new center devoted to the hands-on creation of magazines—appealed to both of us. Clay was now eager to join me sooner in California and we would fly up to the East Bay together. He couldn't wait to meet the graduate students.

The morning after that call, I waded into the ocean beyond my waist. An aberrant wave caught me off guard and broke over me. I was startled, but not frightened. That was the surprise: it was a gentle dunking, like that of a playmate. Foam gurgled around me. I suddenly felt girlish. I looked out at the big waves, playful as white-bellied dolphins, leaping and tumbling and inviting, *C'mon in and dive through us. You'll see, you'll come out the other side.*

No, this passage was not about decline! Our midlife can be a progress story, a series of little victories over little deaths. We have time for a *Second Adulthood.* This was one of those small epiphanies that Virginia Woolf called "moments of being." It's when a shock pulls the gauzy curtain off our everyday resistance and throws a sudden floodlight on what our lives are really about. Now I knew: faith over fear is what it would take.

I dove into the cold waves and came up on the other side, laughing. There it was. The challenge—the anchor for all of us in the sea of our Second Adulthood—is a rebellious purpose. Mine would be to redefine middle life and put out the word: this is a gift.

THE GREAT UPROOTING. The move from the East Coast to the West Coast in January 1994 fulfilled a long-held fantasy of Clay's and mine to try living in Northern California. We would gain some release from the toxicity of New York's unrelenting competitive struggle. And we'd be exposed to the wild creative energies of the new digital revolution.

But the break was also agonizing. Clay's apartment had been his home for thirty-five years. As we boxed hundreds of books and rolled up carpets, Clay groaned and turned gray. I tried to cheer him up with a brilliant insight from one of our best friends, Ciji Ware, whose book in progress redefined downsizing as *rightsizing.* But pain was literally hammering at Clay's heart. Dr. Pat dispatched us to the cardiac unit at New York Hospital. He lay all day on a gurney, nearly bored to death. Once doctors snaked a balloon into one of his vessels and began stretching open an artery, he became animated. He couldn't stop interviewing the doctors. "How close did I come?"

"Ninety percent blockage."

In the recovery room, he was humbled. "It's about time we opened up!"

Moving into a cramped faculty apartment turned out to be the best medicine of all. Even though we were back to living like graduate students, with brick-and-board bookcases and fighting over one bathroom, we also awoke to the music of goldfinches and woodpeckers. On walks through the woods, we might spot a quail or a preening blackbird. We found a running track that overlooked San Francisco Bay. Steep steps took us down to the original Peet's Café. At first glance, I thought it must be a methadone clinic. A line of regulars would be standing outside, sleepy-eyed, clutching their own mugs and waiting for the 8 A.M. opening. For Clay and me to sit outdoors in T-shirts in January, reading the *New York Times,* while we lazily devoured oatmeal and lattes, was sheer bliss.

Clay swapped his tailored British shirts and big lunch ties for denim and rolled-up sleeves, driving to the campus wearing a jaunty cap and shades. He was crazy about his graduate students. They all seemed to know several languages, at least one of which was Chinese or Farsi. They were as in love with making magazines as he had been at their age.

I spoke to Clay's class about what's involved in writing for *Vanity Fair,* organizing a long-form story by themes. At the end of each semester, Clay and I entertained the class with a buffet at our home and talked about their aspirations. Carla De Luca, a star student and later documentary maker, remembers, "We got a twofer with you and Clay."

On the exciting day when their magazine came out, Clay took his budding writers and editors to dinner at the Chez Panisse Café, where Alice Waters was pioneering the slow food movement. The Berkeley campus in those days was a veritable Garden of Eden where there were enough African Americans, Asian Americans, Hispanic

Americans, Arab Americans, and Native Americans along with preppie easterners and proper midwesterners to feel comfortably represented amid the swarms of supercool Californians. Clay often said he wished he had come to teaching sooner.

For me, it had to be a bicoastal life. My children, my hoped-for grandchildren, my sister, my editors, my publisher—so many of the important people in my life were on the East Coast (did I mention my hair colorist?). A week spent in New York, running to *Vanity Fair* to close a story, and on to Random House to talk about my next book, kept my adrenaline pumping. The returns to Berkeley always felt like being on vacation.

After two years, we bought a sun-filled house clinging to the hills, with a backyard garden full of exotic tropical plants. I would come back from a morning run up and down the hills and, while descending our steps, pick a clementine or a sweet Meyer lemon to suck on while I gathered an armful of camellias or pink dogwood. It was a paradisiacal environment for a writer. Except for one thing. I couldn't find an assistant with a New York work ethic. They always had to leave early for a pottery class or chanting circle or to feed a camel (honest, two people in our neighborhood kept camels as pets).

On weekends, Clay and I might drive up to the wine country or down the coastal road for an overnight in Big Sur, indulging in the sybaritic life for which we had never had time as young strivers. We were young again. We were in love again.

That lymphoma never came back.

JOIN THE FELKER FEST!

It was a happening. A pack of literary journalists at the gate! It took a ballroom to contain all the luminaries who came to support Clay's new dream—the Felker Magazine Center at the University of California, Berkeley. Nearly a thousand people turned out to pledge contributions—writers, editors and publishers, business tycoons, art-

ists and agents, even salespeople and switchboard operators who belonged to the original *New York* magazine family—all crowded into
the ballroom of the Pierre on Fifth Avenue for the "Felker Fest" on
an unforgettable evening in April 1995.

Tom Wolfe embodied the pop idiom in his winter white suit,
lime tie, and—of course!—his white spats. There's Gloria! Long legs
in black leather and streaked hair curtaining her beautiful, ageless
face. And Clay himself, rather shy and nervous at first. I overheard
snatches of conversation with the same phrases: "He gave me my first
job"; "He changed my life"; "He loved me and left me, but I forgave
him"; "Can you believe how many of us came out of that one place?"

Everyone wanted to say hello to Clay, so we formed a reception
line in the Cotillion Room. Abe Rosenthal, the formidable former
executive editor of the *New York Times,* had mellowed enough since
leaving that post to be able to say to me, "I didn't so much know Clay
as steal from him. He gave me the idea of giving readers information
to enjoy—service reporting. That's when we added enjoyment to the
New York Times." Mort Zuckerman, for whom Clay had been a consultant, dropped a punchy compliment: "He dumped all over everything
I did. He's a genius."

It was better than a wedding. No infighting relatives among this
bunch; every face that came past me was someone I cared about—
Milton, Lesley Stahl, Helen Gurley Brown, Kurt Vonnegut, still
playing the old fart smoking his fags; Chris Buckley, who would later
write the spoof *Thank You for Smoking;* Pete Hamill, who would later
write his moving memoir, *A Drinking Life*. Ken Auletta recalled Clay
descending for the first time on the offices of the *Village Voice,* "like
an astronaut landing on a strange planet. I remember wanting to
strangle the bastard. I thought he was a showman, but I found out
he is much more. The showman is a servant of his blinding talent as
an editor."

Terry McDonell remembered Clay telling him, when he was trying to raise money to start *Smart* magazine, "'It's impossible.' Then he'd give me another idea for how to make it happen. He helped all sorts of people launch new magazines."

Cyndi Stivers called herself a Claymate, from her brief but indelible stint as a member of the female cast at *East Side Express*. She had created a fifty-page booklet of reminiscences from Clay's protégés, titled *Uncommon Clay*, and recalled the first important lesson she got as a Claymate. "He would look into the middle distance, rake his fingers through the few remaining hairs, and tell you that your latest opus, felt, uh, thin and bloodless. 'Go back and write it like you told it to me,' he'd dictate. 'You've got to add your point of view.'"

Walter Bernard had one of the best stories. When the magazine moved uptown in 1974, it was suddenly transformed from a cozily choked garret to a large but sterile space. Clay designed himself a separate office with Georgian paneling and a private bathroom. "How could we overhear his private phone calls?" Bernard griped. "How could he hear our complaints and sniping? Would we have to knock on his door? Could we use his bathroom?" The move took place over a weekend. "On Monday, Clay was barricaded by paneling. By Tuesday, the staff felt out of touch and isolated. On Wednesday, managing editor Jack Nessel marched into Clay's office and used his bathroom. On Thursday, Clay moved his desk out of the office and into the newsroom. He never went back. We all used the bathroom."

The witty literary jester Mary Ann Madden, of the famous *New York* magazine competitions, assembled a toast by combining the title of a percussion band, Adversity Breeds Malice, and a line from *Macbeth*: "Clay fostered unknown talent by instinct and smarts. From the *New York* of the *Herald Trib* to the *New York* ripp'd untimely by Rupert Murdoch, Clay remained wantonly original, gutsy, graceful. Success becomes him. And *in adversity, malice is not his gift*."

Seeing Clay as the object of such deep affection and respect from the whole upstairs to downstairs of our profession, I was in awe. I couldn't believe how many people felt a personal attachment to this midwestern nobody who showed up in New York with no money, no connections, yet was able to transform journalism. He had changed so many lives.

By the end of the night, a little more than a million dollars was pledged, enough to create a foundation and endow the center, assuring its longevity. Clay had the last word. "This is kind of a tribal gathering of the magazine world," he said. "Magazine people like each other. Even if I wasn't the honoree, I'd still really want to be here!"

CHAPTER 36

THE HILLARY DECADE

THE 1990S WERE FULL OF NEW PASSAGES for my entire family. When Mohm graduated from Wellesley College and devoted herself to becoming an artist and an activist working with refugees of war, Clay and I were deeply moved. Eventually, she would have to go back to Cambodia to discover who she was.

Maura started out as a journalist—a successful staff and freelance writer for several major national publications. She earned an M.A. in cultural studies and a second degree as a master of social work. She found a new career as a psychotherapist in private practice. Early on, she and Tim Moss committed to an egalitarian marriage and were part of the great social shift of their generation, seeking an urban village where they could support a family-centered life. Settling in Brooklyn, they tag team as parents and self-employed professionals.

My own new passage began with the excitement of setting up a new bicoastal life for Clay and me in 1994. Six golden years would follow. Despite anxieties over Clay's health, the 1990s were also the most fertile years in my career. Looking back over my Day-Timer diaries from that decade makes me wonder what I was smoking. But now I think I know how I was able to do so much: in 1990 I was riding high on the booster rocket of energy that Mead defined as "post-menopausal zest." It was exhilarating to feel healthier and stronger than ever. Who would have thought? This was nothing like the dreaded middle age that women had been conditioned to expect.

I felt fortunate to be able in those ten years to write five books about which I was passionate: *Gorbachev: The Making of the Man Who Changed the World* (1990); *The Silent Passage* (1992); *New Passages* (1995); *Understanding Men's Passages* (1998); and *Hillary's Choice* (1999).

Through all the creative ferment of my writing life, there was one figure, and one story, that captured my attention more than any other. Hillary Rodham Clinton. I followed her from her entrance to the national stage in 1991 and wrote about her turbulent evolution over the next ten years, culminating in her own dramatic midlife passage—at the age of fifty-three—when she ran for and won a seat in the U.S. Senate. I found it fascinating that Hillary was the same age as Margaret Thatcher when she reached her goal of becoming elected to high office in her own right.

From my first exposure to Hillary in January 1992, I had a strong hunch that she would become the most important woman in American politics. I had never met a woman like her.

We met at Little Rock airport on the morning after she appeared on *60 Minutes,* a maternal arm around Bill Clinton as she leaned in to coach and cover for her husband while he weakly ducked one question after another about an alleged affair. He blew their strategy of total denial. Hillary jumped in and shook her fist and declared, "Ah'm not sittin' here, some little woman, standin' by my man like Tammy Wynette. Ah'm sittin' here because I love him . . ."

When all hell broke loose the next day, I was standing by Hillary's side. We had just entered the lounge of a nondescript motel in Pierre, South Dakota. Hillary flipped on the TV. The screen filled with the come-hither countenance of a black-rooted blond lounge singer, Gennifer Flowers, who was playing tapes for the media of the love-talk she used to "deflower" Governor Clinton. Not a whit of surprise showed on Hillary's face. Her eyes took it all in with the glittering blink of a lizard. She ordered her tearful campaign manager, "Get Bill on the phone."

Returning from that call, she scowled and said Bill had brushed it off. "He said, 'Everybody knows you can be paid to do anything.'" Hillary was furious, not at her husband's unfaithfulness, but at his carelessness. "Everybody doesn't know that," she had told him. "Bill, why were you even talking to this person?"

An hour later, fortified with a mask of equanimity, she swept into a Pork Producers' Rib Feed and charmed the whiskers off the farmers—until her press secretary whispered in her ear, "All three nets led with the Flowers press conference." Hillary made a beeline to another pay phone. Another woman had been offered a million dollars to say she had a one-night stand with Bill Clinton.

Squeezed into her six-seater plane, I sat knee to knee with this publicly scorned woman and listened, openmouthed, as she vented her frustration above the grinding hum. "If we'd been in front of a jury, I'd say, 'Miss Flowers, isn't it true that you were asked this by AP in June of 1990 and you said no? Weren't you asked by the Arkansas *Democrat Gazette* and you said no?' I mean, I would *crucify* her."

Jotted in my notebook: *She is angry. Not all of the time. But most of the time.*

I listened as Hillary rehearsed a retaliation strategy. "In 1980, the Republicans started negative advertising. In 1992, we have paid political character assassination. What Bill doesn't understand is, you've gotta do the same thing: pound the Republican attack machine and run against the press."

We had scarcely bumped down through the black hole of the Dakota night before Hillary, coatless, clicked across the field to a shack with a sign reading RAPID CITY. "Get me Washington and Little Rock on the line," she ordered. George Stephanopoulos and James Carville and the other baby-faced staffers were about to be "inspired" by the candidate's wife. "Who's getting information on the *Star*? Who's tracking down all the research on Gennifer?"

Hillary's ire was totally focused on the other woman. Not on him. Never him.

When I asked Hillary if she thought her husband had told her everything she needed to know, she dissembled. "Yes. I have absolutely no doubt about that," she replied, her blue eyes unblinking beneath the dark hedgerow of brows. "I don't think I could be sitting here otherwise. That's been, over the years, part of the development of trust." The real answer, I surmised, was that Hillary didn't know what she didn't *want* to know.

After years of protecting the philanderer's secrets, Hillary had built so thick a guard wall that it seemed to paralyze her judgment when it came to revealing almost anything at all, even to herself. The stories of her husband's infidelities appeared to register, consciously at least, as having nothing to do with her or their marriage, but rather as evidence of the depths of degradation to which the hit men behind George H. W. Bush would stoop. The face Hillary showed to the world was that of an innocent victim.

I later learned that Hillary mounted a counteroffensive to stanch further "bimbo eruptions." After checking with her attorney on how far she could go legally, she joined with her sidekick Betsey Wright in a sub-rosa black arts campaign against the mounting list of women claiming sexual involvement with Bill Clinton. They hired a private detective, Jack Palladino, to handle the matter. When the detective ran into resistance, he would visit relatives and former boyfriends and develop compromising material to convince the women to remain silent. Palladino eventually gathered affidavits from six of the Jane Does who were later subpoenaed by the special prosecutor Ken Starr. For Palladino's services, Hillary and Wright arranged to pay him $100,000 out of federally subsidized campaign funds, initially disguising the payments as "legal fees," monies they later repaid.

I often watched Hillary brush past her husband to the microphone while Bill Clinton danced in the background like a prizefighter trying to stay warm. Who was really running for president, she or he?

Hillary invited me to sit beside her at a Hollywood Women's Political Committee luncheon during the '92 campaign. She was warm and we eagerly engaged in conversation. After she gave a brilliant speech, a questioner asked when and if we would see a woman president. With the certainty of the *Farmer's Almanac,* she prophesied, "By 2008."

The question on my mind, and voiced by just about everyone I interviewed, was obvious: Why did she stay with Bill Clinton? Did she love the boy in the hound dog, or was she simply unwilling to forfeit her seventeen years of investment in their political partnership?

WHAT MATTERED MOST TO HILLARY was winning. Bill Clinton liked that.

She had the structure. He had the natural political sensibility. Hers was the precise, disciplined world of the tort, the logical argument. Bill had the common touch. He could slice through complex policy ideas and serve them up as simply as doughnuts and coffee at the local diner. From Bill's first campaign for Congress, Hillary took on the role of maker and shaper of the future president. She was the lawyer who bagged big clients like Tyson foods and Walmart and supported the couple financially. She was the avenging angel who flew in to rescue her wounded warrior every time it looked as if he was finished.

But after hitching her wagon to his star, like so many women of her generation, she resented having to do so. I have no doubt that they loved each other, and always have. They started out with a shared vision for the way they wanted to change the country. And both of them seemed to believe in 1992 that one couldn't do it without the other.

At each juncture of the couple's perilous political journey, people I interviewed would say with blind certainty, "She'll divorce him when . . ." "Now, for sure, she'll divorce him . . ." I became convinced that she never would.

They became symbiotic.

I understood that kind of interdependent relationship. It was what made my off-again, on-again love story with Clay endure in the face of countless tests. We, too, believed that in working together and helping each other, we made a contribution to the national conversation about ideas and issues. That bond enlivened our work and sustained our mutual respect. It added another dimension to our love, building in surprises as constant as the daily news. These parallels were a good part of what continued to fascinate me in following the Clintons.

Tina Brown's reaction to my first story about Hillary was visceral: "I hate her!" she erupted. "She's too fucking perfect."

I was stunned. On reflection, I imagined many accomplished women of her generation seeing Hillary as a rival. She was supersmart and intensely ambitious, but she also came across as having no human vulnerabilities. She could speak in paragraphs, without notes. Her confidence appeared impregnable. Never a hint of fear or tears. She held up a new standard for women of high aspiration, an impossible standard for most mere human beings to match.

That first *Vanity Fair* story, "What Hillary Wants," evoked extreme reactions. Some women embraced her for her courage. Others, mostly high-status white women who did not owe their identity to a man, felt almost voyeuristically degraded by Hillary's acceptance of blatant unfaithfulness. The constant comment I heard was: "Why doesn't she leave him?"

I found the answer the first time I interviewed Bill Clinton. It was early in his '92 campaign. He and Hillary were sitting at opposite ends of the plane. Hillary always had her nose buried in briefing books. Casual Bill played cards with aides. When I interrupted his game of Hearts, he gave me a window on the couple's vision. What did their unique relationship—"Buy one, get one free"—bode for a future Clinton dynasty? I asked. He replied without missing a beat.

"Eight years of Bill, eight years of Hill."

FOR ME, THE SAGA OF BILL AND HILLARY continued to dominate the decade. It was clear to me by the mid-1990s that the Clintons were different from every other presidential couple in history. The saga of Bill and Hillary had echoes of Franklin and Eleanor, as well as Tracy and Hepburn, with a dash of Bonnie and Clyde. They gave our country eight years of peace and financial well-being. What made their partnership unique was that no matter how many times they were at each other's throats, or gunned down by their enemies, they arose, together, to fight another day. His recklessness and her eagerness to step in and save the day created a dynamic of perpetual crisis (his) and crisis management (hers). They seemed to thrive on it. Every time he went down, she reared up and turned into a lioness, ready to rip the flesh off their enemies. Bill Clinton could sit through an assault with the passivity of the Buddha while Hillary worked out the counterattack with their attorneys or campaign operatives and flak catchers. And each time she saved him, he rewarded her with ardor and gave her more power.

But it had taken a toll.

CLAY AND I ENJOYED GOING to Renaissance Weekend every year, an intellectual and spiritual refreshment that brought together political junkies from the north and south who had a peculiar taste for sitting through four days of nonstop panels on every issue, including

"What's Been Bugging Me Lately." We had signed up for the 1992 weekend between Christmas and New Year's. It turned out to be a lovefest for the surprise election of Bill Clinton.

A year before Bill Clinton's reelection race, I ran into Hillary at the 1995 Renaissance Weekend in South Carolina where women really talk—in the ladies' room. Dragging a comb through her untended hair, she looked depleted—even depressed. The crushing defeat of Democrats in the '94 congressional election had been laid by many critics at her feet, for her handling of the health-care initiative. She had confided in her strategist, Dick Morris: "Everything I do seems not to work. I just don't know what to do anymore."

I had been feeling sorry for her. As I saw it, she was the lightning rod for people's fear of change: the change of generation from Bush to boomers, the change in equation between men and women, the huge social dislocation as we moved into a new information-based economy. Bill Clinton himself had talked about "anxious white males," but he hadn't figured out how to connect with them.

On seeing me, Hillary's eyebrows shot up and she stretched out her hand. She immediately made me feel important by making reference to my 1992 book about menopause, *The Silent Passage*. I must admit, I was momentarily surprised by her warmth.

"I thought of you when I heard a comedienne refer to menopause," she said. The comic had quipped, "I've decided I'm not going to do that." Hillary laughed somewhat ruefully. "Yeah, right, let's do away with that."

I told her I'd heard the president express empathy for anxious white males, and I had some thoughts. "The whole theme of your campaign was one of change as good, as a chance to make things better," I said. "But most people don't like change. They fear change. They'll do almost anything to avoid change. Maybe what you can do is connect with the wives of those anxious white males and offer them some ideas for helping their families manage change."

Hillary began spinning out a strategy right there in the ladies' room. She told me about a recent study that showed most teenage boys still saw their future as primary breadwinners who expected their wives to stay home and take care of them, the house, and the kids. Teenage girls saw an opposite future: completing their education, getting a good job, enjoying the independence of a career, and, *if* they married, having a husband who would share the housework and child care. "So we're on a collision course," Hillary concluded.

Then, in an unusually candid self-analysis, she ascribed some of the white male backlash to herself. "I know I'm the projection for many of those wounded men," she said. "I'm the boss they never wanted to have. I'm the wife they never"—she caught herself—"the wife who went back to school and got an extra degree and a job as good as theirs. It's not me, personally, they hate—it's the changes I represent."

During that reelection campaign, many women began to revise their opinions about Hillary. Even Tina Brown became an admirer. "Hillary's changed, she's grown," Tina told me.

During their last year in the White House, after Hillary was blindsided by the Monica Lewinsky scandal, the Clintons went through the Couple Crossover I had written about in *New Passages*. The couple agreed to marital counseling. Hillary described herself as "shell-shocked." She received consolation from old friends such as Stevie Wonder and Nelson Mandela, who, after making a speech to the UN, told Hillary gently, "Our morality does not allow us to desert our friends." When Mandela made a plea to Americans to end the impeachment spectacle, Hillary took to heart his philosophical guidance: "The greatest glory in living lies not in never falling, but in rising every time we fall." Hillary later confessed that during that year, she tried every day to rise and start over, one day at a time. Trying to forgive Bill.

———————————

BUT HILLARY HAS A REPUTATION for holding grudges against almost anyone who isn't a total adherent. That is not the role of a journalist. Hillary had told me in our first interview that one of her key strategies was to "run against the press." I learned, firsthand, that included me. Her anger over my first 1992 *Vanity Fair* story became palpable seven years later. In 1999, my biography *Hillary's Choice* was published. It looked at the Clinton presidency through the lens of the Clintons' unprecedented partnership. My first TV appearance was on *Larry King Live,* where King gave the book an enthusiastic buildup.

Returning to the green room after my interview, I ran into Hillary's bellicose press secretary, Howard Wolfson. For months, he had refused to take my calls to check facts, a stonewalling that was highly unprofessional. We grunted at each other. He followed me on King's show and savaged the book.

I sat before the monitor, stupefied, and waited to confront him when he returned to the green room. "Why didn't you answer my phone calls?"

He shrugged.

"Howard, it was a sympathetic biography and you know it!"

"We don't need you" was all he said before walking out.

I was furious. The Clintons and their attack dogs played rough. What was most painful about that imbroglio was that I really admired Hillary and I wanted to see her succeed. But as a journalist, I had to adopt a mind-set similar to that of a doctor or psychologist, detaching my personal feelings from the responsibility to report the truth, even—or especially—when it is uncomfortable to do so.

It seemed clear to me that, without Hillary, Bill Clinton would not have become president. And most likely, without Bill, Hillary Rodham would not have had the platform to cast herself as one of the most remarkable women of the twentieth and twenty-first centuries. How long would it take Hillary to dare to strike out on an independent political path of her own?

The answer came during a pivotal afternoon in the Clintons' last year in the White House, which was the hook for my third article for *Vanity Fair* on the saga of Hillary Clinton. February 12, 1999, was the day the Senate met to vote on impeachment. Hillary waited in a separate corner of the residence from her husband. She was meeting with a man who had floated between the his and her sides of the White House for two years: Harold Ickes. The abrasive political strategist had a great deal in common with Hillary. They shared a passion for liberal causes, and he, too, felt betrayed by Bill Clinton, having learned the president fired him as an adviser by reading it in the *Wall Street Journal*.

Finally, Hillary was ready to talk to Ickes about her suspended dream of building a political platform of her own. When Clinton wandered by and looked in to greet his wife's guest, Ickes noticed that Hillary barely glanced up. Bill was not invited into their huddle.

Hillary was clearly interested in running for the Senate, Ickes found. But from a state not her own. New York. She showed an urgency to speak with her own voice. The strategist knew the frustration she had endured. He laid it out for me when we met in his Washington law office: "After the pillorying of Hillary and the constant effort to drive the president out of office, for her to run and win a very prestigious seat would permit her supporters to say, 'There was a lot more here than anybody thought—you guys were wrong!'"

After four hours of discussion that day, Ickes found out the bottom line for Hillary. She declared, "This is a race for redemption. It's really that simple—redemption."

Hillary interrupted her meeting to watch TV as the Senate voted to acquit her husband of the impeachment charges. There was no elation. Ten minutes later, Hillary resumed planning her own political future. Her poll numbers had hit an all-time high, close to a seventy favorability rating. Bill Clinton's favorability ratings had trailed into the low fifties. In the hearts of the public, the couple had traded places. She was at the peak of her power.

Still, she had to wait.

WHILE BILL CLINTON WAS UNDER virtual house arrest throughout the fall of 1998, Hillary went out of her way to establish a very public parallel social life in New York. After a makeover, gone were the dark dominatrix eyebrows and the barrel-bottomed suit jackets and treacly pastels. A newly glamorous Hillary emerged, with a golden helmet of shorter, straighter hair, softer matte makeup, a slimmer silhouette, even showing a little décolleté. Suddenly she began appearing at name-dropping cultural events, elegantly dressed by Oscar de la Renta and wearing designer jewelry commissioned by her husband.

"I want independence," she declared emphatically to me that spring, as she psyched herself up to plunge into electoral politics. "I want to be judged on my own merits." Although it sounded strange coming from a woman the world saw as iron-willed, Hillary confessed, "Now for the first time I am making my own decisions. I can feel the difference. It's a great relief."

She appeared for her first fund-raiser as a senatorial candidate on March 3, 1999, in the grand ballroom of the Plaza Hotel. In the back of the ballroom where an army of video camera operators was stacked up on risers, the comments were typical of New Yorkers' cynicism:

"She's probably coming to New York for therapy."

"Nah, she'd rather run for Senate than look inside herself. Besides, running for Senate is cheaper than therapy."

That night, she was entertained at a private dinner party. The atmosphere inside the town house was surreal and artificially serene. At the same time, seventy million people were watching Barbara Walters showcase Monica as the femme fatale. The hostess from the dinner

party told me, "This has to be one of the worst days of Hillary's life."
I saw it as the start of the most significant passage of her life.

FOLLOWING HILLARY IN THE EARLY MONTHS of her 2000 Senate
campaign, I found her as stiff as Queen Elizabeth in a cartwheel
hat on a windy day. But First Lady Hillary had learned an important lesson. The American public did not relate to a woman of regal
bearing. Hillary's sense of entitlement had always gotten in her way.
Mocked for her "listening tour," she paid no attention to the ravening
media. Upstate, she began to project humility, meeting voters on their
own turf, at state fairs and on small farms and in economically depressed towns that had never before been visited by a national Democratic figure, much less a rock star of Hillary's fame. She took careful
note of their concerns. When she got to the Senate, she worked hard
to send business to those same upstate constituents who had helped
win her an impressive 55 percent of the vote.

Just about every political pundit predicted that Hillary would fail;
she would never get along in the tightly knit boys' club of the Senate
chamber, especially since nearly half of the opposing side had tried
to throw her husband out of the White House. Again, surprise! Un-
bound at last from the ill-fitting bodice of First Lady, she seemed
newly at ease. I found it fascinating to watch her stride around the
Senate chamber in mannish pantsuits with hands clasped behind her
back. Her most disarming strategy was to seek out rabid conservative
Republicans and tell them funny stories and flutter her hands at their
jokes. Really!

I watched her allow Orrin Hatch to lay his hand on the small of
her back. Hatch was the moralizing Mormon who played the judge at
the Puritan witch "trial" of Anita Hill. He had also pronounced Bill
Clinton guilty on both counts that helped to impeach him. Ignoring
all that history, Hillary showed an interest in his pet charity. Hatch

asked her to be his cohost at the first gala fund-raiser. Picture Our Lady of Forgiveness as she swept into a downtown hotel on the arm of Senator Hatch, who praised his "date" to reporters: "Let me tell you, it's been a wonderful thing to work with her."

Instead of inviting the jealousy of other senators, Hillary turned her celebrity spotlight on them and their bills, especially conservative Republicans, who came to respect and even like her. She won her race for redemption. The groundwork was laid for her to make Bill Clinton's prophecy come true: eight years of Bill, eight years of Hill.

I could hardly wait until 2008.

CHAPTER 37

RECURRENCE

WE BURNED DOWN THE DAYS when we were young. Who counted the years? The arithmetic of life was different now. When did we begin counting backward? At fifty? No, at fifty I reset my counter. Time to start over. Coming out of the three-year emergency of menopause, I felt revived. I was homing in on the important things. I had sloughed off the superfluous.

Once we married, everything had come together. Clay was home for dinner. Maura came home for holidays. We had another daughter to adore. A kitchen I could call my own. Life. Love. Work. Together. It was the most sublime time of my life. Before the cancer.

The year 1997 was the darkest. After a six-year reprieve from the original cancer of the throat, a test introduced us to the ugliest word in the English language. *Recurrence.* Another toad had appeared at the back of Clay's throat and was dangerously close to crawling across the midline of his tongue. Reluctantly, Clay's oncologist, Dr. H, saw us on his last day at Memorial Sloane-Kettering. Dr. H was leaving the institution and in a hurry. He skittered across the consulting room on a rolling stool toward Clay, ignoring Maura, Mohm, and me, giving a sales pitch for "the standard curative option for you in this setting—surgery." About the side effects, he was brutally casual. "The voice box frequently has to be removed as part of the process—even if it isn't involved with the cancer. You can discuss the details with the surgeon."

I was aghast. Removing Clay's voice was a detail? Clay Felker without a voice? Without the instrument of his purpose, a voice that gives others their voice? Unthinkable. The girls and I tried to ask questions. We were ignored. The oncologist rolled to his light board, displayed the picture of Clay's throat, and wound up his argument like a prosecutor to a hostile jury. "You have to make a bottom-line decision—am I going for broke with my life?"

Clay could not answer.

We dragged out of the hospital doors late on a summery Friday afternoon, dodging weekenders who rushed past us pulling their designer bags toward cars and jitneys. We were going nowhere.

LATER, CLAY REMEMBERED only one thing about that day. "We were all together." That meant everything to him. "I'm not alone in this. I have people who care for me. People I love. If I'd just been lying in bed that weekend all by myself, I would have been . . . hopeless."

Serendipitously, only a month before, Dr. Pat and I had made a bold move. We decided to share the rental of a pied-à-terre in Manhattan. With Clay living and teaching in California, and Pat's husband working weekdays in Chicago, Pat and I both needed a base in the city for our work. We teased our husbands, "If you're good, you can come for conjugal visits." It was one of the best decisions the four of us ever made. That apartment became the comfort zone where Clay could recover.

When I had to be out at night, Dr. Pat would sit on the edge of Clay's bed in her pajamas and keep his spirits up with her wicked sense of humor. After a month in free fall, we found hope in Boston at Massachusetts General Hospital. A renowned Chinese radiologist. Dr. C. C. Wang, known as the Gauguin of radiation therapy, was candid.

"So I hear you're big shot in New York. But they want to cut out your voice box—so you come to me."

"You know how they are in New York—cutthroat," I teased back.

Dr. Wang chuckled. He kept up a lively banter while he examined Clay's throat. Then came the magic words: "Your condition still has chance to be cured—our odds very good!" He was a pioneer in the development of a technique called *hyperfractionated radiation*. He would give Clay two brief treatments a day, five days a week, for about a month. The goal was to shrink the tumor to the point where his surgical colleague, Dr. William Montgomery, could safely remove it.

Dr. Wang left us with a Chinese proverb. "When chase a tiger, must run very fast."

We moved to Cambridge for six weeks, renting an apartment on the hospital grounds. With the help of a concierge service, I was able to set up a home office with Internet access, overnight, while Clay prepared to go through prolonged radiation. Maura guided us to Herbert Benson's Center for Mind-Body Medicine. We joined a cancer support group and took sessions on meditation, visualization, cognitive restructuring, yoga, nutrition—the works. Clay embraced the mind-body philosophy. We walked for an hour every day to stimulate his immune system. Those walks along Beacon Street and over flying footbridges and along the historic Boston harbor were a joyful break. Mohm, now living in Cambridge with her new husband, came over to help. Ella, bless her heart, insisted on taking the train up from New York and staying over three days a week to make the special bland meals Clay needed. At night, I sat vigil for the sound of choking. To keep my sanity, I wrote in the gaps of the night.

"WILL I BE ABLE TO TALK AFTER SURGERY?" Clay asked the speech pathologist.

She chose her words with precision. "Some healthy tissue has to be taken from around the tumor, to catch any floating cells. So Dr. Montgomery is going to take out a fair chunk of the base of your tongue."

My head swam. Clay began negotiating. "The thing is, I don't do anything but talk in my work. I teach seminars and give lectures and even when I do consulting, all I do is talk."

The pathologist told Clay he could not use his voice at all for a week to ten days after surgery. And then? he asked. "You will need to work with somebody like me to restore intelligibility. The base of your tongue is important for speech." She paused. "Also for pushing down food in swallowing. You will need a feeding tube. At least temporarily."

Another unexpected blow.

Clay asked about timing. "My second semester starts the third week of January." His surgery was scheduled for December 27, 1997. The speech pathologist frowned. Definitely not enough time to heal.

The night before the operation, Clay's friend the writer Aaron Latham called from New York. He offered to come out to Berkeley and team teach with Clay for the spring semester. Clay was moved, but he protested that he could not allow Aaron to take on such a burden.

"Clay," said the gentle surrogate son, "I'll be your voice."

Before we walked to the hospital, Clay pulled me close. "I don't know how to say this, to be politically correct, but, sweetheart, you are the center of my life. You create beautiful homes wherever we are and find vacations we can enjoy with the children even when I have, you know, limitations. It all comes from you—and I want you to know I think about it all the time."

I must have fallen asleep while waiting for word from the surgeon. A tap on the shoulder. As I looked up, Dr. Montgomery pulled off his face mask and gave me a smile. "The cancer is gone. He has great margins."

"Can I kiss you?"

"Please."

MY JOB FROM THEN ON would be to widen the margins of our life. For assistance, I found a psychotherapist who specialized in working with cancer patients and their family members. Dr. Ruth Bolletino, a cancer survivor herself, turned our thinking around. She was a colleague of Lawrence LeShan, a famous holistic psychotherapist who spent thirty-five years working with several thousand cancer patients before publishing his classic 1989 book, *Cancer As Turning Point*. Instead of focusing on what was wrong with Clay and how to fix it (the traditional psychotherapeutic approach), Dr. Bolletino focused on what was *right* with him—and with us. To rebuild a compromised immune system, she guided us in using psychological change and creativity in a search for new purpose. We learned from her and Dr. LeShan how to view cancer as a potentially victorious passage.

Clay was able to get back to teaching right on time. With a lapel mic and strong coffee before his three-hour classes, he was able to make himself mostly understood. He confessed up front that he couldn't pronounce his own name—"l"s were hard for him. His doctor's quick solution: "Just change your name to Izzy Cohen." In class, Aaron was on hand to take over when Clay tired. The magazine that class produced was among Clay's favorites.

The hard part was finding a way to make sure he could enjoy meals. Just managing the secretions in his mouth gave him trouble. Swallowing was dangerous. The paddles at the back of the throat that collect chewed food and pass it down the esophagus to the stomach had been frozen by all the radiation. The slightest particles of food that slipped down the windpipe and into the lungs could cause pneumonia.

At our dinner parties, Clay now often dropped out of the quick and jaunty badinage, not wanting to break the tempo. The brilliant intelligence in his eyes would dart from one speaker to another, the only reminder of how his voice and ideas used to dominate any dinner table through the sheer force of his intensity about getting to the heart of the story.

On my next trip to New York, I had a sleepless night and sank into despair. I found Pat at six in the morning in the antiseptic setting of a hospital examining cubicle, where she was waiting for a patient to deliver a baby. I knew Pat kept in touch with Clay's doctors. I asked her why Clay was having more trouble than ever speaking and swallowing.

"His trachea—his windpipe—is beginning to narrow," she said in her even, professional voice. "It's the radiation effect. Tissue necrosis." She sat opposite me in a metal chair, drained of sleep, draped in her pallid green scrubs. She encouraged me to spill my scattered fears. Then she pulled them together and shaped them into one sharply pointed question.

"You chose this man," she began. "You engineered his return to life and a new dream on the West Coast. What you're really asking yourself at the deepest level is 'Do I want to stay with Clay during his long, not-yet-dying years?'" She didn't wait for me to reply. "You're at the peak of your flaming fifties, sexy, toned, terrific, wise, energetic, and still climbing in your career. Do you want to put in the next ten years with a man you love who is older, aging faster, and not healthy— knowing, when he goes, you could be near seventy, in descent yourself, and alone? Clay's no fool. He knows at some intuitive level that's the question you're wrestling with. Most women couldn't even ask it of themselves."

A long pause. I stared at her solemn face, her clear blue eyes and pale freckly skin—a mirror of myself, ten years younger. We were both survivors, self-made successes but vulnerable to the losses of aging like everyone else. Then Dr. Pat said something that made her eyes spill over with tears.

"Generosity becomes you. I'm a beneficiary." I had stood by her during her wrenching decision to remarry a man she adored, despite hostility from other family members. Given her professional position, I was one of the only friends in whom she could confide.

In that brief conversation with Dr. Pat, the dare that would shape the rest of my life was boiled down into a few simple words. *Stay with Clay.* My proper destiny was to see the war through. For so long, Clay had been the strong one who encouraged and mentored and supported my efforts to become a good writer. It was my turn to be the strong one. I would just have to work out how to meet my own separate needs.

AFTER SIX MONTHS OF HIDING OUT at home for meals, I blurted, "Let's go to Paris for a week. And eat escargot."

"Are you crazy? How could I eat?"

The feeding tube had become a permanent fixture in our lives. That meant liquefying Clay's every meal through a laborious process. Ella had come out to live with us. She and I took turns parboiling a stew of organic vegetables and pasta, chicken or fish, protein powder and olive oil, then whipping it up in a blender and straining it through a sieve, so he could pour it into a quarter-inch tube that entered his stomach through a perforation just below his beltline. It was a nutritionally impeccable diet. He could live for years on it. But who would want to live a tasteless existence?

"I'll forage for gourmet food," I told him. "I don't know, we'll figure it out."

He took the risk. But after a twelve-hour trip from California to Paris with only a can of Ensure, Clay could barely stand up while we waited for a taxi at Charles de Gaulle. He had to ask—and I know he felt humiliated—"Don't leave my side." I hated myself for thinking I could drag this sick man across the Atlantic and make something joyful of it.

I was playing God.

But the next morning, while he slept, I ran out to find a blender and bought Greek yogurt and organic eggs, oatmeal and ripe fruit, and came back to the hotel to whip up a hefty breakfast for Clay. I half roused him from sleep and poured a café au lait into his feeding tube. Then, what the hell? I poured in another café au lait.

Clay bolted upright. "Let's go to the Louvre!"

And so we did. But what about dinner? Not in the hotel room. I had noticed a baby bistro on our street. The Rotisserie d'en Face looked informal with high red banquettes, all the better to hide our unusual table manners. I asked to speak to the chef. A young man appeared, eager to please. I explained that my husband couldn't take any food or wine by mouth, and I showed him the blender and what needed to be done.

"*Quel dommage!*" the chef exclaimed with a look of horror. In France, to be unable to indulge the sense of taste was unimaginable. I told the chef that Clay could enjoy the meal through the sense of smell, and the ambience of his lovely bistro. The chef was delighted to help us.

That evening, Clay dressed impeccably. He carried his own strainer in a shoulder bag, not at all convinced that a busy chef would be able to accommodate such an extraordinary request. I ordered escargots and held them under Clay's nose so he could inhale the scent of snails and garlicky butter. He groaned with pleasure.

The chef sent out two waiters with trays held high, bearing two silver pitchers, one for his soup, one for his blenderized main course of chicken, mashed potatoes, and haricot verts. The waiters stood around us to partially block the view while my husband poured his lovely meal into the tiny tube below his waist. I ordered whipped cream for dessert and dabbed a bit on his tongue. Two couples from neighboring tables came over to welcome us to Paris. It was one of the most romantic evenings of our lives.

After that experience, we became fearless about eating out. If we could do it in a Paris restaurant, we could do it almost anywhere, as long as I asked the chef's cooperation in advance. We learned that normal is as normal does.

CHAPTER 38

NEW MILLENNIUM, NEW BABY

PARIS WAS THE TONIC WE BOTH NEEDED. We rejoined social life. Over the years, Clay and I had become great friends with Richard Reeves and his wife, Catherine O'Neill. We'd explored the world together, often invited by Reeves-O'Neill to their rented summer places in France and England. But the ultimate experience came at the end of the 1990s, when America was feeling especially flush. The Clinton presidency had left us with a fat budget surplus and Wall Street was soaring on the Internet bubble and e-commerce boom. The value of equity markets swelled and the technology-dominated Nasdaq index rose from less than 1,000 to 5,000. Richard was riding high on the successes of his presidential biographies. It was Richard and Catherine's twentieth wedding anniversary, so Richard gave Catherine an order:

"Get us a castle!"

We arrived in grand style in a chauffeured Mercedes at the gates of the eleventh-century Castello di Brolio in lush Chianti country. As we gasped at the 140-room brick manse, Catherine assured us they had rented only one wing. It had lots of bedrooms but Catherine warned us that she had invited twenty of their journalist friends and some of us would have to double up. Sleeping rough in a castle was a delicious irony. But looking out on the countryside, preserved in its natural beauty as a living Renaissance painting, we quickly joined in Catherine's fantasy. Playing the part to the hilt, we all dressed for dinner and swanned around the balconies with drinks in hand, while Richard's son Jeffrey affected the role of the young Ricasoli family duke and called a welcome to "our ancestral home" to tourists gaping from the gardens below. Mary Murphy, a fellow journalist, staged with me a little musicale called *The Chianti Tales*.

One night at dinner in the baronial great room, after copious refills of the castle's premium Chianti, one of the guests had the temerity to make this toast:

"Here's to us—we're rich!"

That fantasy would quickly fade with the dot-com bust of Y2K. But that inevitability did not inhibit Clay or me from living every moment we had together and sharing our gratitude for another reprieve by throwing the best Thanksgiving soirée ever. We decided to welcome the first day of the next thousand years in the style of a turn-of-the-century dinner party in the Hamptons. Fifty friends came, all dressed up in bustiers and boots, into the high-ceilinged room lit by dozens of candles mirrored in the window walls. It was magic.

Gail and Clay's little "castle"—the old farmhouse in East Hampton. (Counterclockwise:) *Clay, Catherine O'Neill, Mohm, Maura, David Aaron, Richard Reeves, Chloe Aaron.*

The birth of a new century could not hold a candle to the birth of a first grandchild, which took place seven months into the new millennium. Maura chose to deliver naturally in a homey room at Roosevelt Hospital's birthing center. Her serenity through the whole process was remarkable. Moments later, it seemed, Maura was holding her son, blue-eyed like his mother, to her breast and talking about being hungry. It was the most natural of passages. I found myself out on Amsterdam Avenue at one in the morning with Clay, scavenging for cold cuts. Delirious with my assignment, I brought back bagels and lox and chocolate chip cookies for everyone. More than anything in the world, I wanted to be a good grandmother. This was my year to give back, to Maura as a new mother, to my grandbaby as he reached out like a tendril seeking attachment.

The year's rental on the apartment Clay and I shared with Dr. Pat and her husband was up. I had found a charming loft near Lincoln Center. It was a miniature version of Clay's old bachelor pad, with a high ceiling and tall windows and a near replica of his great fireplace. The loft was badly in need of renovation. And as everybody knows, the contractor always takes twice as long as he contracts to take. You wait, and pay, and wait. Clay went back to Berkeley in the fall. I stayed in New York to do battle with the contractor. But the truth was, I welcomed the excuse so I could stay close to Brooklyn and see my new boyfriend.

Declan would greet me at the door in his mother's arms with a full pumpkin-head grin. "Hi, darling," I'd coo. He'd duck his head shyly behind his mother. Then we'd be off on our giggly scales—I trilled, he trilled, I gurgled, he gurgled, delighted by the mirroring. I bathed him, singing "Rain in Spain" while dribbling water from his washcloth and watching him try to catch it. I couldn't get enough until Maura had to discipline her mother to mellow out and move on to a lullaby, time for bed.

Grandma Gail (called "Nonnie") with Declan at eighteen months, 2001.

When Declan was six months old, I was entrusted with babysitting privilege while his parents went to a movie. I gave him a soft terry rabbit. He laid it over his eyes and dropped right off. Maura gave me clear instructions before leaving her apartment: "If he wakes and cries, lean down and croon to him, just for a moment, then kiss him and let him pacify himself again. Sure enough, when the baby stirred, I sang to him. He rubbed his hand over the silky square that was always nearby and dropped back into a deep sleep.

I curled up on the sofa to daydream. The phone rang.

"Mo?"

"No, she's out at the movies."

"Who's this?" Rather alarmed.

"Gail."

"Gail Sheehy—I know Gail Sheehy. Gail Sheehy is someone I know."

"Albert?"

"You'll laugh, but I just called to see what Declan did today."

"That's exactly why I'm here—to see for myself."

We giggled together. The encounter of two foolish first-time grandparents, both of us were hungry to catch the day's droppings from this delicious creature whose every new sound and movement seemed utterly miraculous.

I described for him watching Maura take Declan to a body movement class.

"What's that?"

"Something like baby aerobics. He reaches for balloons and learns to roll over."

"And gets to play with his mother for an hour. Isn't Maura a spectacular mother?"

"Isn't she?" I said. "Nurturing comes so naturally to her. She seems to know exactly what to do and how to do it."

He mocked himself for being a stupid gooey grandparent.

"It's one of the few things that's great about getting old," I said.

"How about only?" Albert was sixty-nine. "The only other good thing is getting a senior discount on dog biscuits." We laughed again.

"Maura has turned out to be an extraordinary young woman," Albert said with great depth of feeling.

"A most extraordinary young woman," I quelled.

"Being a mother becomes her absolutely."

"So does being a psychotherapist," I said. "And she'll be able to balance it all because she's married to a supportive husband."

"Right!" He said we should shake hands, phonetically, on how well Maura had turned out.

"Yes, let's shake."

Suddenly, Albert said, "I'm so pleased we had this talk."

"I cherish it."

CHAPTER 39

LOSING CLAY

"YOUR HUSBAND HAS ENTERED the cycle of slow dying."

An intensivist they called him. He was a pulmonologist with critical care training who saw patients when they were wheeled straight up to the intensive care unit. The intensivist had taken Clay into the bronchoscopy unit at Lenox Hill Hospital in New York three or four times and tried to dredge the sludge out of his lungs. It was 2006 and a fourth and final cancer was arrested. Recurring lung infections were the only problem. Seemed simple enough. But surgery had removed the part of the tongue that pushes secretions into the right pipe. And after chemotherapy, Clay did not have the strength to cough up the secretions that kept reinfecting him.

"How long does slow dying take?"

"He could live another year like this," the intensivist said. "Maybe two."

This sounded to me worse than a death sentence. Would this be like the polar bears who are slowly dying from global warming? As their icy habitat melts away earlier every spring and their swim from shore through rougher seas becomes longer and more treacherous, they lose so much weight and strength, they drown. Where does one go to do the work of slow dying? I asked the intensivist.

"The next time he gets a lung infection, don't send him back to the hospital."

Give up? Quit? Surrender? I was the bird who flies into the glass window. I hadn't seen this coming. Clay was not actively dying, but he was beyond curing. This is what they call *serious chronic illness*. Our health-care system has no affordable solution for serious chronic illness. We were medical refugees.

Clay made the decision: "No more hospitals!"

I covered Clay with my coat and exchanged a decisive look with our Senegalese aide, aptly named Safoura Tall—six foot one and fearless. Safoura and I wheeled Clay into the elevator and past the protesting security guard and out the hospital's front door with the IV needles still stuck in his wrists. Just taking back that little bit of power felt like a triumph. We danced him into a taxi. Clay was smiling.

BY THE SUMMER OF 2007, Clay was recuperating from another pneumonia and had to be moved to a nursing home for rehabilitation. I was relieved when he was accepted at the Jewish Home Life Care facility on the edge of Harlem. It was a safe place for him to gain strength while I sorted out our future. I was having trouble making the mortgage payments on my house in the Hamptons. The IRS was breathing down my neck for back taxes. For too long I had been paying for private aides for Clay and copays for his many hospital admissions, while trying to maintain a semblance of our old lifestyle. With each of his medical emergencies, I had to cancel a speech or forgo a story assignment. My income was stagnant. Meanwhile, the housing market kept overheating, and my upkeep expenses kept climbing. I was not alone in using the perceived golden value of a resort property along with low interest rates to turn my home into a virtual ATM.

At Lally Weymouth's Fourth of July party that summer, I was seated again next to one of the gnomes of Wall Street. We had always joked about the sky being about to fall, and I would ask him, "Is it time, or can I have one more year in my house?" He had told me what he was telling his private investment clients: not to worry yet, housing prices were still climbing and the market wasn't about to blow up. But this summer he did not smile when I asked, "When do I have to sell my house before the sky falls?"

"Yesterday."

As if to resist this ignominious fate, the East Hampton house developed all kinds of problems: scabs on its shingles, holes in its roof, plumbing backups of a severity that seemed to call for a colonoscopy. At first it felt like a reprieve. How could I sell the house that *Passages* had bought? It had been my family home for thirty years. All the best things happened here—watching my children splash in the pool and bounce on the trampoline, letting grandchildren try out their rubber legs on first tricycles, planting rosemary and rue and foxglove and cowslips to create a Shakespeare garden, picking lunch from our herb garden, doing yoga on the sun-dappled grass, entertaining friends under a bower of wisteria for long lazy Sunday lunches, and the solitary pleasure of early Monday mornings, when I could plunge into the pool and swim laps and settle in my favorite writing room, gazing out the bay window at the linden tree and watching for the resident pheasant to parade by until the words came and I lost myself in writing. At 10 A.M. Ella would arrive from New York, bringing me a container of coffee and a jelly doughnut and ordering, "Get up off your meat, Miss Sheehy. Time to take a walk!"

I bit down hard and put the house on the market. Nobody wanted it. It cried out for renovation. Where to begin?

I began by trying to let go of control. Starting the morning with meditation in my Shakespeare garden, I would sit in the sunlight below a row of life-size Madonna lilies. Their huge white bulbs would be clasped as if in prayer. I prayed, too, for the serenity to accept the things I could not change. And then I asked for help. By the time I opened my eyes, the Madonnas would have opened their ivory trumpets and be pointing to the sky. I could have sworn they were playing Bach.

One morning as I was leaving a village coffee shop, I stumbled over help in the form of an exceedingly long leg.

"Sorry," said a tall, gray-haired man. His eyes were deep-set and sad, mischievous but a smile played around his lips; I suspected he had tripped me up deliberately. I ignored his faux apology and went back to my sidewalk table. He followed me, mouthing more sincere apologies and bad jokes. I stared at my newspaper. He told me he designed and built houses. Did I live here? I turned my back. Then he let me know he was a recent widower. That got my attention. He had cared for his partner for two years after her stroke, he said. His eyes clouded. He recalled lovingly how he walked her up and down this very street, slowly, daily, until her life had ended six months earlier. I couldn't help but sympathize.

How did he know I was on the same journey? He didn't.

I mentioned that I had to sell my house, but I worried that it wouldn't pass inspection. He lit up.

"Why don't I come over and take a look at your place and see what we could do to increase its value?"

I declined his offer, said good-bye to the widower, and forgot about the impudent encounter.

It wasn't long before the widower bumped into me on the street, this time definitely on purpose. He introduced himself as Richard.

"Any offers yet?"

I had to admit there were none.

This time I allowed him to follow me to the house. He marched around the property like an African hunter, taking a machete to the thicket of vines and dead shrubs that obscured a good quarter of an acre of the land. I was suitably impressed by his strength. He was a man of about seventy, I guessed, but his legs in shorts looked to be made of rock and rope. He mentioned that he was a skier, world class; he was not shy.

"I could clear all this out and then buyers would see a vista straight into the woods," he tantalized me. "It'll raise your price by half a million." For emphasis, he performed an excavation of a rotted tree stump with his bare hands.

"I couldn't pay you very much."

"Don't worry about it. Whatever you can, when you sell." He would be my property manager, he said. To have anyone managing anything for me sounded tempting.

The next morning I awoke to the sound of a chain rattling and the groan of an overtaxed engine. It was Richard, hauling out the stump of a thirty-foot arborvitae with his truck. If he was an angel sent by the Madonnas, they knew how to find one tough angel. From that day on, the widower worked miracles on the house. He hired day workers to acid wash the stucco and repair the roof and spackle and paint. He rewired the electrical system and replaced faulty water pipes, and when I told him I couldn't afford to replace the pool, he dove to the bottom and plugged the leaks without a snorkel.

Within weeks, the house and grounds were handsome and virtually inspector-proof. A movie actress made a solid offer and put down a hefty deposit. I was, literally, home free.

Until the fickle buyer backed out. Her check had never been "cleared" for deposit. A crushing blow.

BY MIDSUMMER, MY DAYS AND NIGHTS ran together in the pallor of a midtown hospital where double pneumonia kept Clay confined for weeks in and out of an ICU. When I finally got away to Long Island to arrange another house showing, the molten sun of late summer made me ache with longing. I knelt in the Shakespeare garden and wept as I cut back the wilted roses. I felt enveloped in darkness. Richard appeared. Suddenly the balance between light and dark shifted. I felt a jolt of masculine energy.

He insisted on taking me to his favorite spot, the walking dunes on the Atlantic Ocean. The sun there was still strong. The beach deserted. I tossed my sandals aside and slipped off my sweater and began running. My leaden legs loosened up. My white skirt billowed. The warm sand on my bare feet, the spanking breeze, the sparkling water, jolted my senses awake. How could I have forgotten the joys of nature? The delight in feeling again like a woman?

Richard asked if he could carry me to the top of the dunes. To be touched again was electric. Long-deadened desire erupted like a madness. Melting into his arms, I felt an explosion of joy and surrender. It was all wrong but I couldn't stop the wanting, it took me beyond thinking. And then we were rolling over and over down the dunes, laughing like kids and kissing.

I had to stop. I couldn't do this. "You are a delivering angel, Richard. But Clay is the love of my life."

"I know." He told me he was a rescuer by nature. He needed to fill the hole left by his partner's death. He saw me as another "damsel in distress." Helping me helped him.

"I wish I could bring Clay out here," I moaned. "For the last weeks or months before we give up our home."

"Why not?" Richard offered to set up a hospital room in the country house. It sounded like deliverance.

BEFORE LONG, CLAY WAS SITTING in his favorite chair in the dining room, a dominant presence again, supervising the interior repair work on the country house. We ate lunches together, the three of us. I no longer felt isolated.

A unique bond formed between these two men, both grown old enough that their macho urges were tempered by the rise of tenderness and need for connection. One day, when Richard helped to pull

Clay up from his chair, they stood for a long moment, chest to chest. I watched Clay size up Richard. Clay had always been possessive and proud of being my protector. Although his mind was still fully functional, his body betrayed his efforts to help me. His shame was palpable. Clay raised his right arm. I froze. He clapped his hand on Richard's shoulder. Then, leaning on Richard, the two men walked the house with Clay pointing out cracks in the ceiling that needed patching. An understanding passed between them, man to man, without words. Clay let it be known that he appreciated what Richard was doing to help me. He needed to know that I could survive without him.

Richard insisted that I claim at least an hour a day to restore myself. "Just an hour when you take your mind completely off what's happening with Clay and not happening with the house." It was my own mantra to other caregivers, coming out of his mouth.

Before the world woke up, Richard would come by with a thermos of coffee and sweet buns and drive us to a cove where he would slip his canoe into the still water and we would paddle out to a bank and spread a blanket. Silently, we would open our senses to the birdsong and the fiddling of rushes in the breeze, watch for fish jumping and maybe a tiger salamander slithering, for just an hour as the sun came up, a hidden hour, to feel fully alive. Those sunrise sojourns, I believe, restored my capacity for joy.

WEEKS BEFORE THE IRS THREATENED to put a lien on the house, I had a solid offer. This time I was smarter; I asked that the deposit be nonrefundable. This buyer agreed. My *Passages* house was about to become history. So, sadly, were our Thanksgiving soirées.

Yet Thanksgiving that year was never truer. Maura gave birth to a third grandchild, a golden redhead she gave the very Irish name Mairead. Bringing Clay out to the country for three whole days required elaborate arrangements. It rained like hell. When we arrived, I struggled to get Clay out of the car. We came close to the two of us sprawling in the mud. I called Richard. Racing over, he picked Clay up and carried him inside to his makeshift hospital room. Neither of them said a word. They didn't have to. Faced with the cruel limits of aging, people form attachments beyond the ordinary, and that summer and fall, we three helped one another survive.

The family all came and we cooked a traditional turkey dinner. Sitting in his chair by the window, Clay spoke with his eyes. His mind had always been engaged day to day, but he was seldom emotionally involved. He had seen himself as an outsider, extraneous. His transformation on that Thanksgiving was remarkable. He was an organic part of all that happened. Presiding over the family, he experienced himself as belonging again.

In the middle of carving the turkey, I stopped. This was Clay's role. I handed him the great knife. As I leaned over to kiss him, I saw his eyes glow. The muscles in his face relaxed, he looked around at everyone and smiled. Warmth and love radiated from him, and his presence once again filled the room.

I saw Richard wipe away his tears. He whispered, "I love him, too."

THE DEADLINE FOR TURNING OVER the house was January 1. I spent the month of December ransacking the archives of both our lives. Miraculously, an antique dealer surveyed the furnishings of the house and bought them, lock, stock, and barrel. That left the art and books and the precious pieces that Clay and I had collected over the years. Call it procrastination. On New Year's Eve I was still packing up books. It felt like I was closing the book on our lives. Alone in the house, I watched dense milky fog seal the windows.

I couldn't help myself, I called on Richard again. I hadn't seen him since Thanksgiving, when I told him we could not continue our relationship. He had wept. I felt horrible. But I did not return his love, and I did not have the emotional strength to support a double life. Clay needed all of me now.

Richard came over on New Year's Eve and became even more of a hero in my eyes, helping me as a friend through this most excruciating passage. At 4 A.M. after we taped up the last box, he dropped me at a local inn. When I awoke and meditated, I felt cleansed. Ready to dare a new day. A new year. Undivided.

CHAPTER 40
LOSING MYSELF

THE LONGEST WALK. From the edge of Harlem. It had started with Clay's first admission to the Jewish Home Life Care rehab unit. After languishing there for several months, he had asked me to turn off the light before I left for the night. He whispered the words: "I can't read."

I realized it had to be dark for him to dredge up this shameful confession.

"Oh, darling, why not?"

"Concentration."

He tried to explain. But he could hardly speak intelligibly. Only much later did I learn that problems with reading comprehension are not uncommon in serious illness. His mind was so splintered from the rallying of emergency forces to save his major organs from malfunctioning, there wasn't much help left in the twenty-some stations of the brain needed to work together to accomplish one of the most complex tasks—reading—an indispensable skill for an editor.

I lay down by his side. We shared the silence of despair.

I thought the longest walk of my life had been down the back stairs from the Women's Department at the *Trib* to cross the DMZ of the city room and present myself at the door to Clay Felker's world. No, it was this walk. The nightly trudge along Columbus Avenue around midnight: a woman alone, indifferent to her safety, no future she cared to contemplate, shambling down the long dark blocks from the edge of Harlem, deserted on weeknights, then ducking into the meanest bar. A noisy sports bar.

I had no interest in contact sports, but I had a need for noise and a place where I wouldn't be known or noticed. Only the late-shift waitress recognized me from other nights, but she knew not to chat. I was just the lonely lady who dropped in late and sat opposite a vacant chair, waiting for my companion: a glass of cheap chardonnay. A generous pour. I would scribble in my journal. My new companion did not talk. Did not judge me. So I'd ask for another. And another, but just this one time. That's how I would put it to myself: I'll have a third glass, just this once.

When I went to Dr. Pat for my annual gynecological checkup, I mentioned that I was drinking more than usual, it wasn't really a problem, but . . .

"How much?" she demanded.

"Two, sometimes three glasses of wine."

"Every night?"

"Oh, no, not every night," I lied.

In her utterly precise, clinical voice, Dr. Pat spelled out her prescription: "It's simple. Just pour four ounces of wine into a glass, not one drop more, and have one glass a night, six nights a week, at most."

"I'll try that!" I said with genuine enthusiasm. Within a few weeks, I was back at the sports bar. I was a late-blooming problem drinker. A shame, really. I missed all the fun years. I'd never gotten to drink margaritas all night and dance on tables and enjoy the delirium of imagining myself to be as devil-may-care as Drew Barrymore and brilliant as Marie Curie—after all, she died lit (albeit by radiation exposure).

In recent years, Clay had warned me more than once that I needed to cut back on drinking. "It will dry out your skin and give you wrinkles and take the sparkle out of your eyes." If that weren't dire enough, he added, "You'll end up looking like Bill Buckley." Clay knew how to get to a woman. He pointed to a recent magazine photo of the eighty-year-old bon vivant whose TV debates amused even us liberals with his polysyllabic exuberance. It was a horrid mask of radishy skin and red-rimmed, rheumy eyes.

A year passed before I had another checkup with Dr. Pat. "I filled your four-ounce prescription. It didn't work."

She picked up the phone and introduced me to her friend Peggy, a veteran of a twelve-step program. Peggy invited me to go to a meeting with her that very night. She met me on the street, a blonde in a cowboy hat who was proud of being on the north side of sixty. Before I had a chance to make excuses, I was being welcomed into the nave of a huge Presbyterian church packed with what I called Uppies—well-dressed urban professionals over thirty—hundreds of them. Who knew that everyone under forty in Manhattan was in recovery?

One after the other people introduced themselves the same way: "Hi, I'm Bev, I'm an alcoholic," or "Good evening, I'm Rob, I'm an alcoholic." I couldn't bear the thought of raising my hand and making such an announcement. Peggy sensed my trepidation. She whispered to me: "Just say your first name and 'I have a desire to stop drinking.'"

"That's enough?"

"That's the only requirement."

I was fine with that. The speakers came up two by two, a man and a woman, each couple more nauseatingly upbeat than the last. I'd expected downbeat tales of self-loathing. But as I listened, it dawned on me that people were seeing themselves in these stories. Gradually, I began to recognize myself as well. The laughter around me was startling, even uproarious. I found myself laughing. That's what shocked me about this fellowship. These people were high on something. I wanted some of what they had.

At the end of the meeting we all held hands and recited the serenity prayer. It had never been so meaningful. Women huddled around me, the newcomer, and pressed their contact numbers into my hands.

Then Peggy took me out for pizza and introduced me to her drink of choice: cranberry juice and seltzer. "Keep coming back," she said.

I found a meeting closer to my apartment and began showing up every day, as advised. It felt good to start the day at seven by entering a church basement for a spiritual booster shot with a cast of characters I couldn't have made up: opera lovers and moving men, a young dancer and a feisty octogenarian. Gay, straight, black, white, socialite, sybarite, they were all endearing—well, almost all. As we reviewed the steps of the program, I learned that any life run on self-will cannot be a success. Even though my motives might be good, unchecked self-will almost always put me in collision with someone else, even people who were trying to be helpful.

When I had to go to a *Vanity Fair* party, anxious that I wouldn't be able to resist a glass of wine "to take the edge off," I called my sponsor. She gave me a few simple tools. Stay away from the bar. Ask for Pellegrino with a lime. Eat, talk, go home early if you feel temptation. It worked. When I passed couples sitting in the spring sunshine at an outdoor café and sipping wine, did I feel a surge of envy? Of course. So I'd have a wicked dessert like profiteroles doused in chocolate sauce. When I repeatedly declined to be served a drink, my Irish friends would look at me as if I was suffering from cognitive decline.

"You don't drink?" they would shriek.

"No."

"At *all*?" they would scold.

Later, I came up with a self-deprecating answer that also happened to be true. "I'm at a stage where I can either drink right or think right. I'd rather do the latter." I let other people do most of the talking, and they enjoyed hearing themselves talk a lot more than listening to me. The next morning, I actually remembered what we'd talked about! I called my sponsor with this revelation. She had a droll response.

"If the solution works, consider that *you* might have the problem."

The meetings offered a fellowship that began to feel like a rope bridge across the chasm of living like a widow in rehearsal. I depended on those familiar faces, the smiles of recognition, the outrageous laughter, the agonized sharing. I began to learn humility. These were not losers. These were finders. We were helping one another interpret the steps and find our own way back to equanimity.

I quickly learned that the fellowship was a spiritual program, but not religious. Although the twelve steps often refer to "God," it is clear that the interpretation is left to the seeker. One's Higher Power is "God as I understand Him." As I found my way to belief in my Higher Power, I finally acknowledged that I was willful, selfish, and dishonest with myself. My mother had been an alcoholic and I knew that alcoholism was a progressive disease. For most of my adult life, I had been a moderate drinker but always on guard. The long vigil with Clay had shredded my defenses. I was exhausted—physically, mentally, and emotionally.

Giving up my riotous self-will freed so much energy. But only if I kept up my spiritual fitness program. As my sister, Trish, said, "To pray without meditation is like calling up God to tell him your problem and hanging up before you get the answer." I found the best way for me was to start the day with a prayer and meditation. And when I didn't have the time or inclination to do the good-girl morning routine, I remembered Mike Love's liberation theology: once in a while, you blow a meditation.

"CLAY SHOULD HAVE BEEN DEAD YEARS AGO," his primary doctor told me. Dr. Orsher spoke like an old friend, and he was. "You've given him ten extra years of life. Nobody has gotten the care and attention you have given this man. That's why all the doctors who've worked on Clay have made every effort to keep him alive—because we've seen the devotion between the two of you."

I was deeply touched. But I still wasn't ready to let Clay go. And he was nowhere near ready to give up. I had written a piece for *Parade* magazine, "Who Cares for the Caregiver?," and I remembered learning about something called *palliative care*.

Weeks later, Clay was running a high fever and choking on blood in his tracheostomy. His nighttime aide and I managed to clear his throat. But even though I was now paying for twenty-four-hour coverage, I was overwhelmed. That bleak morning—was it winter?—I made a cold call to Mt. Sinai's Palliative Care Center. The director, Dr. Diane Meier, gave me the name of the geriatrician who worked with her, Dr. Sean Morrison. The doctor himself answered. I gave him a capsule history of Clay's condition and told him Clay refused to go to the ER.

"Good," he said. "Our whole goal is to keep people with chronic illnesses out of the hospital."

"Is palliative care like, um"—the dreaded word—"hospice?"

"No, hospice is support for dying," he replied quickly. "Palliative care is support for living with chronic illness and the best quality of life. There is no deadline. And the patient can continue with medical care if it makes him more comfortable."

"Where do we go, then?"

"I think it's best if I make a house call," he said.

I almost dropped the phone.

It was another godsend. A surprisingly young man turned up at our apartment, gave me a warm handshake, and went straight into the bedroom. He asked for a footstool and sat at Clay's bedside, intentionally beneath him, to invert the usual doctor-as-God posture. He kept asking Clay what *he* wanted. At first, Clay's speech sounded mushy, schlurpy, like a really bad telephone connection. For an editor who had cultivated the precise speech of the mid-Atlantic man, what could be more humiliating?

With only a few questions, Dr. Morrison was able to construct a clear narrative of how Clay's many victories over cancer had depleted his body's strength and weaponry. He would start him on antibiotics to reduce the inflammation. But more important, he said, he wanted to hear Clay's life story. "What are your goals?"

"*My* goals?" Long pause. Clay spoke up more fully and clearly than he had for the past year. "I want to get back to walking."

"What are the important things in your quality of life that we need to preserve?"

"Gail."

"Your wife. What else?"

"Just being able to get out—see the world. I'm a journalist!"

The doctor and I assured Clay we would make that a priority. We talked for a long time about things we could do together that would make his life worth living. Then came the hard questions.

"What about the ability to recognize people and talk with them?"

"I don't know," Clay said.

"Neither do I," I interjected. I had to speak up. "Let's say you had a massive stroke. I need to know if you would want to be prolonged in that kind of state."

Dr. Morrison backed me up. "It helps to know, because then I can guide your wife through decisions like this, rather than putting everything on her shoulders. That's why I'm asking these hard questions."

Clay and I looked at each other. Honesty was cruel. "I don't know all the answers," he said. Dr. Morrison suggested we talk about it and then write out our values and our goals for care—"Your wishes in your own words." As I walked him to the door, the doctor emphasized that we were entering a partnership, the three of us. He would also provide a team, including a nurse practitioner to monitor Clay twice a week, a social worker to walk me through the phases, and possibly a volunteer chaplain. I had to tell him the truth. "I'm willing to do this. But, honestly? I don't know how to walk Clay through the valley of death."

"Nobody does," he said. "We'll walk it together."

MORE AND MORE, EACH DAY, I thirsted. Not for wine. It was a spiritual thirst, to calm the burning within. I needed to reach for the invisible thread that could connect me with the sacred, the source of wisdom. In some deep recess of my imagination, I could almost see that thread. Sometimes I glimpsed it in nature; only occasionally in church; often, gaily, in the moment of playing make-believe with my grandchildren. Most memorably, I saw it while walking a labyrinth.

On a daylong retreat for caregivers in Oregon, I was encouraged to try using this ancient practice to find the spiritual thread. A labyrinth is the opposite of a maze. A maze is a riddle, with many different misleading paths meant to trick you. A labyrinth is one continuous spiral meant to lead you to the center, where you meditate and seek guidance, and then, perhaps with a recognition or an inspiration, the path will lead you back out into the world.

At first, I felt a sense of shedding. Then a flowing with the other walkers, in a silent shared intimacy. Coming upon abrupt twists and turnings, I thought, *Oh, I recognize this, it's the pattern of caregiving.* Nonlinear. Unpredictable. Sometimes it felt as if I were going backward, moving farther than ever away from the center of understanding. Then, by surprise, I found myself in the center. The mind chatter mostly stopped. I felt a quieting. It was a place of inner knowing. Aware of my shadow self, that scrap pile of unacceptable emotions—infantile fears, self-pity, resentment, rage—I began to pray.

> *Dear Mother-Father God, I am lost, help me to move beyond these feelings*
> *and take the next right step. Show me how to use my gifts. Grant me the*
> *serenity to accept what I cannot change, the courage to change what I can,*
> *and the wisdom to know the difference.*

Resurfacing, feeling refreshed, it came to me: the inspiration I had prayed for. *Write about the journey of the family caregiver.* Advocate for them. Caregivers don't take care of themselves. Eventually, I walked around labyrinths enough times to use the experience as a metaphor for the psychological turnings faced by the caregiver. If I could map out those turnings in words and examples, a book might help other pilgrims to make some sense of the journey. I thought of the title: *Passages in Caregiving: Turning Chaos into Confidence.*

Another fear surfaced from a place too terrifying to go. I had not told anyone, had not even articulated it to myself, so fractured was my attention, so numbing my mind chatter.

I was terrified I could no longer write.

DR. MORRISON TOLD ME what needed to change was myself. "Didn't *Vanity Fair* ask you to cover Hillary Clinton's campaign?"

"Yes, but how could I leave Clay?"

"Gail, who are *you* now?"

The question stunned me.

"You're a different person than when I first met you. You're losing yourself. You won't be Clay's caregiver forever. You're a writer. You must get back to being who you are!"

Just the thought of plugging back into a society that was electrified by a presidential primary contest between the first woman and the first man of color sent a frisson of excitement surging through me. Dr. Morrison called a family meeting at Clay's bedside to ask his blessing. By now, the doctor had outfitted Clay with a simple speaking valve. And our round-the-clock home-care team was solidly established. The doctor had barely articulated his prescription for me before Clay exclaimed emphatically, "Go! You must go! Just call me with the gossip."

The minute I tossed a bag into the trunk of a cab and said, "LaGuardia, please," the fog of depression lifted. Plunging into the breakneck schedule of debates, spot interviews with fiercely divided mothers and daughters, hoofing it from school gyms to buses to planes to scant sleep in Best Westerns across Texas and Ohio, my feet stopped burning.

Hillary in the bubble of her campaign plane was surprisingly radiant, considering that just a month earlier, in February 2008, she had lost her commanding lead over Barack Obama. My friends in the traveling press corps were boarding the 737 with the sullen obedience of inmates after an outing in the yard. "Are you here for the death watch?" one of them said. But Hillary welcomed me and several other journalists to cross the line from the quarantined press section into her private cabin.

"Hi, Gail, I'm so glad to see you back out here!"

Recalling Howard Wolfson's parting words to me almost a decade earlier, I was pleasantly surprised by her friendliness. She needed me now.

What continued to impress me deeply was Hillary's persistence. She had never given up, not once in her life. She tried valiantly to revive her poorly managed campaign. I watched her virtually bleed when stalwart supporters like the Kennedy family and the African American congressman John Lewis pulled away. But she hung on until her old friend Congressman Charlie Rangel had to call her up in June and tell her bluntly, "It's over." After seventeen months of running for president, it took Hillary four days of internalizing the loss of her dream before she could let go.

When Hillary conceded on June 7, 2008, in the finest speech of her career, she sounded to me like a woman of full humanity. Yes, ruthless, nakedly aggressive, hawkish, and often tone-deaf—qualities common among politicians who dare to compete at this level. But she was also extraordinary: killer smart, empathetic, unsparing of her energy and commitment, and so resilient, she could eat scandal for breakfast. Hillary would not allow her heartbroken supporters to dwell on the what-ifs. "Life is too short, time is too precious . . . We have to work together for what still can be."

Like millions of women, I took that message to heart. I would work for what still could be—for our country with its first black president, for Clay's best last days, for a life of meaning after Clay. If I dared to begin walking the back half of the labyrinth, maybe I could come back.

DR. MORRISON HAD TOLD ME that the chief worry he heard from people with serious illness was not about themselves: it was about the well-being of the loved ones they will leave behind. I assured Clay that he was leaving me a world of people who had been a part of our life together. "You've left a part of you in each of them. I'll feel it when I'm with them. That's what I'll hold on to."

"But what about your writing?" he insisted.

I fell silent. When I tried to sit down and compose a coherent narrative out of the four months of reporting on the dazzling presidential campaign, I froze. My mind was splintered between the twenty-four-hour cable-news squawk cycle and our own twenty-four-hour life-or-death vigil. I had one week to capture the whys and wherefores in a ten-thousand-word story for *Vanity Fair*. I also had to plan a funeral. My powers of concentration deserted me. The fear persisted: *Could I still write?*

My sister told me that she and Maura hardly recognized me anymore. I had lost myself. And they couldn't bear to lose both Clay and me.

Dr. Morrison called another family meeting at Clay's bedside. He told Clay that he was ordering me to go somewhere in the country for a week, to do nothing but write and rest. He wanted Clay's endorsement.

Clay gave an enthusiastic thumbs-up. He would wait for me to finish the story.

In my week's getaway to a farm in Upstate New York, blanketed by the simplicity of the buzzing and greening and mooing of early June, I began to find myself again. An early bike ride, freshly laid eggs deposited on my porch, a day of writing, a late-afternoon walk to the song of frogs, and a night for a second burst of writing, was the best medicine anyone could have prescribed.

Clay couldn't wait to hear me read my first draft when I returned. We reverted to mentor and disciple. He commented. I listened. I felt a surge of his old intellectual force. More important, he felt it, too. One night, after I came home from closing the story at the magazine, I found Clay sitting up with a broad smile.

"I'm feeling happy," he said.

I looked at this man propped up in a hospital bed with a special valve that permitted him to speak, and I could barely ask the question: "Why are you feeling happy?"

"Because they liked your story."

WE HAD NOW BEEN THROUGH nine months of palliative care with no emergency we could not handle at home. It was time to decide whether to treat the next episode of pneumonia or to suspend feeding and let nature take its course. Shortly thereafter, Clay sent us all a message without speaking. He pulled out his feeding tube. When Safoura tried to reconnect it, he pushed it aside. She sensed it was deliberate. But when I later asked Clay if he meant to disconnect it, he insisted it was just an accident.

"Don't keep asking him!" Dr. Morrison chided me. "Look, a husband can't admit to his wife, 'I don't want to fight anymore,' because that would be abandoning you. Leave that role to me. Your role is to keep him living as long as he's alive."

I had to ask Clay, "Sweetheart, you've been in and out of pneumonia for two years now, what keeps you going?"

"I don't know," he said.

"Are you doing it for me?" A long pause.

"Yes."

The secret was out at last. I had to let him know that I was ready.

CHAPTER 41

ALL THAT JAZZ

IT IS EASY TO SLICE MUSHROOMS with a sharp knife but this knife is like so much of my life now. Blunt. Worn down, eroded, made weary by constant overuse.

This is probably the smallest kitchen of the many kitchens of my life. It is unusually hot for June. The fan on top of the refrigerator has to be small so it will clear the ceiling. It groans as it swivels and barely parts the air. I am slicing astragalus mushrooms because the Chinese speak highly of their potency in boosting the immune system. I still can't give up.

Could he have left already?

Once the hospital bed invaded our apartment, everything changed. We no longer sleep beside each other. We occupy different realms. He sleeps now in our former sitting room, not facing the window, facing inward. So unlike him. He was always looking out, looking ahead.

I hear the TV droning in there. Somebody is haranguing. Who? I know the voice. It must be Bill O'Reilly. The substitute aide must be a Fox fan. Is Clay too weak to change the channel? Or does he not care?

I am slicing earth-moist organic ingredients for his breakfast, or is it lunch, whatever. Shiny purple aubergine, baby-skinned zucchini, garden-grown garlic. I like to imagine the clove rubbing all the insides of his anatomy down to the smallest intestine, to give him flavor.

I remember the first time he took me to his apartment not far from the East River. When we came off the elevator, his door was held wide open by a pair of brass lions, his avatar, with a view out a pair of cathedral-size windows to the ramp of one of Manhattan's grand bridges. I felt as if the world itself was opening to me.

Now I am alone. With the blunt knife. In the dim kitchen. A blunt knife is more dangerous than a sharp knife. When a blunt knife cuts you, it leaves a ragged wound.

He has been slow-dying for two years now.

Don't leave yet. Stay another day.

It will take another twenty minutes to simmer the whole mixture down with pasta and protein. Then whirl it in a blender, mash it through a strainer, thin it to a stingy soup, and pour it into a feeding tube with the diameter of a drinking straw. Praying that it will not clog.

I feel a wave of nausea. The sudden memory, so sharp it's painful, of our long lazy Sunday mornings sifting through the papers together, correcting the mistakes of the world. After breakfast we would walk through Central Park all the way up to the Shakespeare Garden at 110th, stealing kisses behind rocks, swooning under the first bursts of magnolia, returning home in time to make supper for friends. That was in the larger apartment, when we had a larger life.

Slowly, I step across the threshold into his world. He is a pale giant under a white sheet, his still face dissolved in the white vastness of a hospital bed. This is the mentor who sculpted my career, the lover who haunted me for decades, the husband who shared my life for twenty-four years, a man who never had time to sleep. I bend over him and find the place where the surgeon's knife cut out the invader.

The surgeon's knife must have been sharp. The crater it left in Clay's neck was so big, at first it looked like his head was on crooked. I kiss that place in his neck. I whisper, "Sweet as honey."

Don't leave yet. Stay another summer. Another lifetime.

———————————

IN LATE JUNE, Clay's body began to shut down. As he approached his final deadline, his life force returned once more with gusto. He asked Dr. Morrison, "How long?"

"Not long," he said. "Days to a week."

Clay accepted the news with equanimity.

"Do you want to do one great thing, darling?" I said. "Something wonderful?"

He nodded vigorously.

"Jazz?"

The light flared again in his eyes.

"Tonight?"

He shook his head up and down.

I ran to the computer. Dizzy's Club Coca-Cola had a show that night. I ran back to Clay. "The show starts in two hours—think we can make it?"

I couldn't believe my eyes. He pressed up from the hospital bed and slid himself into the wheelchair and rolled it to his wardrobe. He picked out a linen jacket and a blue shirt and a suede cap. He even let me touch up his face with tinted sunscreen, "to give you color." I wheeled him in front of the full-length mirror.

"How's that for handsome?"

He looked pleasantly surprised to see a picture of near normalcy.

A taxi driver took one look at Clay's wheelchair and tried to avoid us until Safoura snapped out a few choice words and he backed up, reduced to quivering obedience.

Dizzy's was the quintessence of New York. A window wall offered a larger-than-life vista across Central Park. A full moon. We watched it slide across the star-studded sky. Clay's attention locked on the jazz pianist, a man of his vintage.

"There's a lot of pessimism and feelings of futility out there," the pianist said. "It's the job of music to dispel those feelings." Then he played an original composition called "Life Is What You Make It." Clay's philosophy. I asked the waiter for swizzle sticks.

When the drums kick-started an up-tempo piece, Clay picked up the swizzle sticks and began drumming on the table. He was a drummer as a boy. For the next hour and a half Clay sat tall and straight in his wheelchair, drumming, and drinking in the music as his sustenance. He was young again. A drummer boy again.

We were back in our apartment shortly before midnight. Clay was not the least bit tired. He wanted to talk. He gripped my hands and said, with absolute clarity, "That was a *magical* evening."

TWO DAYS LATER, on the morning of July 1, 2008, I laid my hand over Clay's. I felt a slight movement. His eyes did not open. His lips inscribed two words on the air.

"Thank you."

"Are you saying good-bye to me?"

His lips closed in a yes.

A few stop-start breaths and he slipped the last fetters of this fragile life and floated to that imagined realm beyond time. I rolled into the bed beside him and pressed my body to his. I felt a last imprint of our mated souls, and it felt good. Safoura wrapped the blood pressure cuff and pumped it up. The numbers slid to 0.

Not more than twenty minutes later, the phone roused me from a sobbing reverie. Safoura handed me the receiver. It was a reporter from the *New York Times* obituary desk wanting to confirm the time and cause of death. I snapped into journalist mode.

"He died at eight twenty-two, of natural causes."

"We never use that. It's not *Times* style."

"But it is the style in which some people go out."

"Didn't Mr. Felker have cancer?"

"Yes, four times. We beat it four times. He hasn't had cancer for the last two and a half years. And he wouldn't want anyone to think he died suffering."

The reporter persisted. "Well, then, what *did* he die from?"

A cascade of emotions silenced me for a moment. Then I came to rest on an inner smile. "He stopped breathing."

AT NOON, MAURA AND TRISH drew me outside to escape the phone. We sat quietly over tea. It hit me when we returned and saw three men in black rocking on the curbside like great crows. Waiting to take my love away. We went in ahead of them to say good-bye for the last time. I bent to kiss his forehead. Cool. He looked like an alabaster carving of a Sophoclean wise man from ancient times, his nose aquiline and skin whitened and brow serene. An unfamiliar scent wafted through the apartment, strong, but light as wisteria. His spirit, ascending.

Out on the street again, as the black crows passed us, we nodded in mutual consent for their turn to take possession of the vacated body. Sobs began grinding through my body, rattling my ribs; heaves of emotion doubled me over. Maura held me up. The three of us threaded arms over shoulders and wept together on the street until we were spent and could sit on a bench in Central Park and reimagine the joyful times with this man.

That evening my girlfriends were summoned by Maura to smother me in food and hugs and to share stories. My dear friend Sherrye Henry took one look at my face as the last guests left and crooned in her Memphis drawl, "Pack a nightie, sweetie, you're coming home to spend the night at my place."

The funeral fell on the Fourth of July. Scores of people interrupted their holiday to come to Sag Harbor. Led by the sound of a harp's haunting sweetness deep inside a country cemetery, friends gathered under a canopy of tall trees to watch Clay lying in his final sleeping place. A navy honor guard played "Taps." The image of a skinny sailor boy Clay came to me, climbing a flagpole in the South Pacific to shout about the Japanese surrender. He didn't have to die in battle after all. He lived eighty-two years.

Tom and Sheila Wolfe invited guests for a lunch of reminiscing in their buzzing, blooming backyard. Tom gave me a long brotherly hug. It brought to mind his tenderness in visiting Clay and engaging him in talk of the world. For his last visit, he charmed someone on the New York Times obituary desk to give him a copy of the obit, always prepared in advance for any notable. He had read the first paragraph to Clay in his mellow Virginia accent.

> Clay Felker, a visionary editor who was widely credited with
> inventing the formula for the modern magazine, giving it
> energetic expression in a glossy weekly named for and devoted to
> the boisterous city that fascinated him—New York—died on . . .

Clay's face had relaxed. He was assured of his legacy.

AFTER THE FUNERAL, my immediate concern was Mohm. Having lost a second father, she was inconsolable. Her husband had recently left her. I flew back with Mohm to Cambridge and stayed close for a week. She found some peace when we visited the Asian Art collection in the Museum of Fine Arts. Then we returned to her roots, eating in a new Cambodian restaurant. It turned out to be owned by her former refugee camp counselor, Darvy Heder, who was thrilled to see Mohm and offered her a job and a room in her large home. Before leaving, I found Mohm a counselor she liked and accepted.

For the rest of that summer, planning the September memorial was a welcome absorption. I wished Clay had been there to lead Louis Armstrong's Memorial Jazz Band as it marched up Central Park West and down the aisle of the Ethical Culture Center, banging out the beat of irrepressible life. He would have loved it. His finest successor as editor of *New York* magazine, Adam Moss, gave a stirring tribute, embellished by images of Clay on a screen behind him. It was a rousing celebration of Clay's progeny: scores of writers, editors, art directors, photographers, journalism students, and the golden moment in American magazines.

AND THEN, THE VACANCY.

I returned to the Mashomac nature preserve on Shelter Island where Clay and I were inspired to change our lives. Finding the spot on the shoreline where the osprey nest was in sight, I sat quietly, eyes half closed, praying for the willingness to surrender my obstinate self-will. I couldn't play God to Mohm, to Maura, or to anyone else.

After a while, I felt a stirring. Raising my eyes, I saw a huge white-winged bird lift off its nesting pole and rise into the sky with a furious flapping of wings. Then, suddenly, it gave itself up to powerful air currents blowing in from the sound. Swept along, swooping and soaring, this great osprey seemed to trust in something unseen to allow it free flight. This must be what it means to "let go" to a power greater than oneself.

CHAPTER 42

COMING BACK

I TRIED TO THINK OF ONE GOOD THING about being a widow: more closet space. I knew the worst thing about being a widow: five to seven P.M. Here are some things I did in the first year: Made pillow covers out of his cashmere sweaters so I could still lay my head next to him. Tickled my grandchildren. Reached out to my neighbors. At Christmas, I gave his unworn silk pocket squares to editors he admired—Graydon Carter, Byron Dobell, Robert Emmett Ginna.

"Shouldn't I be moving on to the next stage?"

The wise cancer therapist who had talked Clay and me through his journey fixed me with her gently mocking smile. "Move on?" said Ruth Bolletino. "You're not there yet."

"Where am I?"

"You're in the agony of grief."

It was a year and a half after Clay had died and I still didn't have the courage to feel the sorrow. Dr. Bolletino urged me to express my feelings by writing them in a stream of consciousness. "Feel it to heal it," she said, apologizing for the trite motto. "If you don't go right through the middle of the pain, if you amputate it, cut off the feelings, or drink to numb them, the anger and resentment never go away. They fester. Unexpressed grief comes out as explosions of anger, or in a physical manifestation."

"Hmmmm, I have shingles."

She nodded sympathetically. "It takes a hell of a lot of energy to keep down the violent grief of loss."

I had kept it down by throwing myself into work. After months spent developing a proposal for a book on family caregiving, I was invited to a dinner with AARP executives. I told them my idea for a series of caregiver diaries, blogs with video, portraying families in different stages of the journey. Emilio Pardo, the chief branding officer, was a veteran caregiver himself. He enthused, "We want your caregiver diaries and your stages—what do you need from us?"

AARP gave me just what I needed. A purpose. I was teamed up with a fast-acting film producer who had a wicked sense of humor and brought along a laid-back videographer who could edit with his eyes closed. We traveled the country for months to scout caregiving families with inspiring stories to tell about how they created their own circles of care. I offered them a framework for where they were in the journey. When it fit, it was reassuring to them. It felt like I might be coming back by giving back.

But once we returned to the hotel after a day's shooting, I would fight restlessness and boredom and eat too many Snickers bars. I tried to write in my journal. Too raw to bleed on paper. Not ready yet. Losing someone to whom you could pour out your soul leaves you alone with the silent screaming self-consciousness that is too much to bear. No tinsely party or sumptuous meal or self-indulgent shopping spree would blot up the seeping fear of being solitary forever. So much of grief, I decided, is raw fear.

Would there ever be happy times again? A tearless night? A rising from bed that was not a heroic act? Careless laughter? I would not join a grief group. I'd rather join a cheerful group. Dr. Bolletino, the cancer family specialist, was correct. I had to feel it to heal it, and the best way was to write out the feelings. I joined a playwriting workshop given by my friend Milan Stitt, a veteran playwright and teacher who ran the graduate playwriting program at Carnegie Mellon University. Theater has always been the church where I go to heal. Playwriting was a long-postponed passion. I wrote a play, *Chasing the Tiger,* about love and death, based on Clay and me. Many late nights I sat in the pillowed window seat of a coffee shop and let flow my feelings on paper, from icy to scalding. Writing absorbed them.

The first staged reading, in Lakeville, Connecticut, starred Jill Clayburgh and Ed Herrmann. Jill, a friend and superb actress who had starred in *Hustling,* portraying me. I didn't know at the time, nor did anyone outside of her family, that Jill herself was suffering from cancer. She gave a noble performance, her last stage appearance. Five months later, in November 2010, under the care of Dr. Sean Morrison, she died peacefully at home.

WHEN *PASSAGES IN CAREGIVING* was published, in May 2010, I gave my maiden speech on the subject at a party thrown by my publisher.

"You must be a saint!" exploded a woman whose husband had been faltering for some years after a stroke. "Didn't you ever feel angry or resentful or even secretly wish he'd die sooner rather than later?"

Of course I had. The widow was alerting me to be less preachy. I was no saint. I hate making this confession. After two years in the program, I had "slipped." I'd like to blame my drinking problem on the book tour. After performing all day, I would wind up with a major speech at a town-hall meeting or a hospital fund-raiser. Audience response was a high. So was the intimacy of listening to people's stories while signing books. Then, suddenly, I was deposited at another strange hotel, hungry, tired, and lonely, greeted by a big gift basket of wine and cheese. So I would pour a glass to keep me company while I emptied my melancholy into a journal. Wine only made me more maudlin, so, of course, I needed another glass, and then another to put me to sleep. Four hours later, when the alcohol wore off, I would suddenly awake with a racing heart and fears stripped bare. Some model caregiver!

Gratefully, I rejoined my spiritual fellowship. My top priority every day would be to resist taking a drink. My sponsor met me for my confession and recommitment to the program. She admitted that, like me, she didn't believe that one drink, one step over the line, and you were lost. But the pattern was there. The behavior was recognizable. I was one of the lucky ones who found recovery before hitting bottom.

After the first month, the physical craving subsided. Gradually, my attitude toward alcohol changed. After six months, I didn't have to fight it. I felt almost giddy in ordering my new drink of choice, ginger ale. Once my drinking problem was removed, I found something even more wonderful about the program. It gave me a new outlook on life. I found so much more enjoyment in simple things, precious moments, lesser expectations. Going to meetings became essential to maintaining my well-being and learning humility. I thanked my Higher Power each morning for doing for me what I couldn't do for myself. And I got an answer! I printed it out and hung it over my morning mirror:

> dear gail,
> i won't need your help today.
>   love,
>   god

THE GREAT HEROISM OF A SOBER LIFE is getting up in the morning and facing the day, greeting others, going out into the world with something to give. When we are in the grave of our own thoughts, feeling like we will never be able to crawl back out, our fingernails packed with dirt, how is it that sometime later we can be laughing, and laughing hard?

One morning in the fall of 2010, an early phone call shook me out of ruminating. The voice was blithe as a clash of cymbals. "Gail, dear Gail, lovely to hear your voice! Will you be having your Thanksgiving party this year?" It was our dear friend David Frost. The memory of our traditional party gave me a flush of pleasure, though I had planned no such thing. "David, leave it to you to push my button."

Frostie must have sensed even across an ocean that I needed a kick in the pants. I promised to think about getting up a party in the country. But once I did, I was stung to remember that I no longer had a country house. I no longer had a country life. A fellow *Vanity Fair* writer, Michael Shnayerson, was a well-known host in Sag Harbor. It took only one phone call to set a plan in motion. Michael and I decided we would each call twenty people. I would try to summon the spirit to invite our old friends to another Saturday-night Thanksgiving soirée.

Boeuf Bourguignon sounded easy. Michael and I split the tasks. Shopping was my job, a delightfully tactile experience. Beef, butchered into exactly two-inch chunks, needed to be squeezed to judge its plumpness. Were the mushrooms firm enough to slice clean? Was the bacon smoked in applewood? The baby carrots fresh from the earth? Sniffing fresh rosemary, parsley, and thyme made me swoon. I bought the cognac and pinot noir to tart up the stew, planning to make my sober beef in a separate pot.

Michael was late returning from New England where he had to pick up his daughter from boarding school. The beef quivered in my hands as if eager for the pot. Only three hours until party time! I started heating the oil. When Michael arrived, we took turns tossing the meat into the deep fryer, squealing at the sizzle of fat. A fountain of fat sprayed to the floor. We kept at our task, twelve pounds of beef to be seared in hot oil, in single layers, slowly turned to brown on all sides. After an hour or so, the floor was becoming a puddle, cooling to the thickness of collagen.

I slid. Landing gently, I flailed around but couldn't get up. I coasted into Michael's shins. It brought him down, too. Not one of our feet could find a grip. Slipsliding on our bums like kids who shouldn't be left alone, we laughed, ridiculously, infectiously, unstoppably, but so good.

Friends arrived, faces I was famished to see after too long. Their precious idiosyncrasies endeared them to me more than ever. Tom Wolfe in his deliberately mismatched socks; Bina Bernard, who had shepherded me through the maze of Clay's rehabs and returns, on a health kick again; Steve Byers, a Montana writer proud of his Tom McGuane sensibility and wearing a cowboy hat.

To my surprise, Robert Emmett Ginna, my onetime editor at *Life,* appeared. I had invited him, but we hadn't seen each other since Clay's memorial. His red hair was whitened, but his crooked Irish smile was still ravishing. Showing up was a sign that he might be moving back into life himself after his wife's death seven years earlier.

Hours later after most guests had said their good-byes, I found Robert alone in the sitting room. We sat close. "How was the dinner?"

"Jolly," he said.

"And the food?"

"You were the most delicious dish of the evening."

This could easily be dismissed as a pickup line by a practiced party drunk. But coming from Robert, an entertaining storyteller but otherwise an impeccably correct and buttoned-up character, it was astonishing. He and Clay were old friends, having shared a cramped office at *Life* when they were both what Robert called "young cubs" breaking into print. Robert was a polymath, an art historian who became editor in chief of Little, Brown, who wrote and produced Hollywood films, and was a founding editor of three magazines, *Scientific American,*

Horizon, and *People.* For the past twenty years he had been teaching creative writing, mostly at Harvard.

Robert invited me to lunch at the American Hotel, the grand old duchess of Sag Harbor. Once he was sated by oysters and an ice-cold Beefeater martini, he told me that since his wife died he had lived alone in his old house in New Hampshire, and he had just sold it. His pipe dream was that in his later years, he'd creep off to Ireland and read himself to sleep on the porch of an old-age pensioner's home.

"I can live without love and sex," he said.

I smiled and said, "But why would you want to?"

I FOUND THE NERVE to call him and ask what he was doing for New Year's Eve. He mumbled that he was just getting settled in Sag Harbor and preparing to teach creative writing in a graduate M.F.A. program at Stony Brook Southampton. Moments later, he called back, "Why sure, I can come into Manhattan. What would you think of dinner and music at Michael Feinstein's?" He arrived formally attired in a pin-striped navy-blue suit, black hat, and cane and swept us off with a flourish to enjoy an evening of Christine Ebersole singing love songs. After we rang in 2011, I asked if he'd like to come up to my apartment for a nightcap. He sat in the chair normally occupied by my new dog, Chollie. I sat on the sofa. Robert didn't know he was trespassing on the dog's chair, but he must have noticed his rival sulking and prowling around our feet.

He didn't kiss me.

Later that night, he sent an e-mail:

> Sorry! Flustered. I fear that I get intimidated—
> shy?—in your company. Maybe I feared Chollie
> would disapprove if I were too forward.
> Anyway, you were beautiful this evening. To

quote a favorite lyric: "You're the top / You're the Mona Lisa."

We began to enjoy sharing our passions for books, theater, art exhibits. Later in spring, when I rented a little house in Sag Harbor, Robert would drop in at dinnertime with a freshly caught flounder and insist upon making dinner for me. It was delightful to take on the role of sous chef to an inspired cook. Over his martini and my ginger ale, he captivated me with stories of the movies he'd made, the fascinating characters he had known, from seminal physicists to his literary heroes, Sean O'Casey and James Salter. He had caroused with actor Peter O'Toole and squired a twenty-two-year-old ingenue fresh off the boat from England, Audrey Hepburn, when he was *Life*'s theater reporter. He knew just about everybody and everything. I was enthralled.

In May 2011, a workshop of my play, *Chasing the Tiger,* began rehearsals at the Bay Street Theater in Sag Harbor. Robert asked if I'd like to share a reprise of our New Year's Eve date.

Christine Ebersole was singing at Bay Street. The place was full, so we climbed to the top row and perched on the steps. I was one step beneath him. We hummed and sighed to a repertoire of Noël Coward's love songs. It was the closing song that melted me: "Falling in Love Again." Without looking, I felt my hand move behind to find his. At the same moment I felt his fingertips. His hand closed over mine like a warm glove in winter. We didn't look at each other. We didn't have to.

Afterward, on the uncomfortable sofa in my rental, we pretended to be interested in TV news. He moved closer. Nibbled my ear. He brushed a shy kiss across my lips. I had forgotten how proper he was. "I'd like to try that again," he said. Embracing, we began sliding into the gulley between seat cushions on the damn sofa.

I stood up and took his hand and led him into the guest bedroom. In the dim light I turned to face him. I lifted my halter top over my head and watched the flush of astonishment come up in his face. We fell into each other's arms.

"I've been asleep for seven years," he whispered to me, "Rip van Winkle on a mountaintop in New Hampshire, living alone ever since Margaret died." Again and again, he marveled, "I can't believe it, you've turned the lights back on in my life."

I was stunned to feel myself falling in love again. We both began giggling. The more I laughed, the harder he laughed. Embarrassment dissolved into real intimacy.

A SURGE OF VITALITY SEEMED to alert the universe that I was still alive and kicking. Suddenly the curtain began going up on a new act in my life. *USA Today* asked me to write a biweekly column about new passages. Great! I enjoyed firing off pieces for Tina Brown's digital magazine, the *Daily Beast*. The people I met and conversations I had at the Aspen Ideas Festival set my mind spinning like a top. Requests came in for me to speak about *Sex and the Seasoned Woman,* a book I had had fun researching several years earlier about women fifty plus who are marinated in life experience and still passionate about life, including sex. I found out that seasoned women rock. Seven hundred of them had responded to my online questionnaire. It had been a lark to drive across the country and meet with groups of such women to hear their stories of Internet romances, pilot-light lovers, start-up businesses, audacious travels—no one had ever asked about their passions before—I couldn't shut them up!

It was always a pleasure to return to the quiet of Sag Harbor and see Robert. What I didn't know for over a year was that he endured constant pain. This was a man who had walked the length of Ireland at seventy-five bearing a thirty-eight-pound rucksack. Despite two surgeries, the severe bend in his back could not be set right. But I would not have guessed at his pain when he accompanied me on my nightly dog walkings. These were the shortest walks of my life, but some of the sweetest. We both knew he wouldn't be in my life forever, but we would make the most of the moments.

Over numerous dinners in colorful Irish joints and his choice of French cafés, Robert goaded me to write about my life. When I demurred, he said, "C'mon, you've been fearless in exposing yourself to new experiences and challenges. You've taken LSD, you've jumped out of airplanes, you dressed up in hot pants to walk the streets with hookers; for heaven's sake, you embedded yourself in the Irish civil war before anybody ever heard of embedded reporters and got caught in cross fire! You even scared presidential candidates—I mean, my God, didn't the first President Bush shudder and say, 'Is this going to be a full psychiatric layout?' You're so alive to the people and happenings around you, you can't help yourself. You live life in the interrogative!" He sipped his martini. "It's about time you wrote a memoir."

How could I craft a story with so many disparate experiences into one coherent narrative—the fearing and daring, the writing and mothering, the succeeding and failing, the loving and caregiving and dying and starting over? They were all pieces of my puzzle, and they could not be separated, because that is how women live, always struggling to find the right balance to create harmony.

"Gail!" Robert's deep voice shook me out of my reverie. "You've had an extraordinary life." He was speaking now like a true editor. "Just start with when you sneaked down the stairs from the estrogen zone to pitch a story to Clay."

AS I NOW REFLECT ON what daring means in my life, I realize it is how I survive. When I feel fear, what I do is dare. Fear immobilizes. Daring is action. It changes the conditions. It startles people into different reactions. It's a crap shoot, but it can be the catalyst to empowering oneself.

Happily, I began daring early. I thought back to when I was twelve and began sneaking into New York on the train to watch a million private lives crisscrossing Grand Central Terminal. That gave me the confidence to write about anybody. When I worried that J. C. Penney would not hire a girl in the pre-feminist '60s, I dared to ask if I could see Mr. Penney himself. At the risk of being fired by my boss on the women's page, I crashed the all-male city room of the *Herald Tribune* to pitch my best story to the hottest editor there.

When Clay insisted that I follow Senator Robert Kennedy's presidential campaign, I almost froze. But I took the dare. It thrust me into one of the major historic events of the century.

On reflection, I can see the pattern. Try as I did, I could not figure out how to balance being a mother and ambitious author while acting as hostess and consort of a powerful man. I dared to leave him. If I had stayed with Clay and failed, we would have lost each other forever. He was the love of my life and I risked losing him in order to prove that I could stand on my own two feet. When I later found the courage to marry him, I was secure enough to feel complete. And together we dared to adopt a child of trauma. By then in my late forties, I was better able to strike a healthy balance.

To find the perfect balance between the forces in our lives is impossible. When we are going through a passage, we lose equilibrium. But once we are able to let go and adapt to the change, we can grow and find a new balance. The tai chi I practice in Central Park with a friend and teacher is leading me to a deeper understanding of the Chinese philosophy of yin and yang. It is all about balance. I love the symbol—two swirls wrapped around each other within a closed circle. The white crescent, yang, represents daylight, associated with fire, sun, and masculine traits: fast, hard, aggressive, but it encompasses a dollop of black. The black swirl, yin, designates the darkness of night, and feminine qualities of nurturance, structure, and rest. Yet it also incorporates a small circle of light. The two opposites cannot exist without each other. They are symbiotic. So it is in life.

Whenever my dark side threatens to overtake my light, I remember the mantra that has guided my life: Lean forward, shoot off the edge of the pool, and keep on swimming.

ACKNOWLEDGMENTS

WRITING A MEMOIR WAS LIKE nothing I have ever done before. To be sure, I have written hundreds of thousands of words, maybe millions in articles and books, but always the focus was on others. Seldom had I closely observed myself. After some false starts, I came to understand that memoir is a wholly independent genre. It is an act of imagination suggested by things that really happened.

To learn from a master, I took a course in memoir given by Roger Rosenblatt in the Stony Brook Southampton M.F.A. program. He tried to mute the journalist in me and release the novelist's sensibility. Yes, my memoir would be about the world I have observed and the literary circle that shaped me, but that was only the container. "All that lies outside you is inside you," Roger told us. "In that fortune-cookie truth, I think, you will find your memoir."

I riffled hungrily through the daily planners that I kept from the 1960s to the early 2000s. They segmented time into neatly uniform units. But memory is a timeless pump of feelings, a surge here, a drizzle there. A year dissolves into a placid lake; a moment inflates into a soap bubble and tempts capture; a day can be an eternity. Feelings, I discovered, believe longer than knowing remembers.

Fortunately, I had often jotted notes about vivid experiences and fragments of dialogue in those Day-Timers, and from those scraps it was possible to reconstruct the architecture of a passage. Dozens of journals evoked my feelings during times of transition and acts of daring. My younger sister, Pat Henion Klein, was a brave excavator into the family drama we lived through in different acts.

Colleagues who were generous in offering recollections include Gloria Steinem, Tom Wolfe, Milton Glaser, Walter Bernard, Ken Auletta, Amanda Urban, Richard Reeves, Barbara Goldsmith, Aaron Latham, Tina Brown, Michael Kramer, Steven Brill, Ken Fadner, Jane Maxwell, Cyndi Stivers, and Dr. Pat Allen. I also thank my trusted readers: Deirdre English, Clay's successor as director of the Felker Magazine program at Berkeley; Kim Barnes, an accomplished memoirist and finalist for the Pulitzer Prize; Muriel Bedrick, Melanie Horn, Sherrye Henry, Mary Howard, and Priscilla Tucker.

In scraping the sugar coating off my guts, I found the raw desires, the fears and frustrations, the shame and self-loathing that we all feel. Side by side were splurges of creativity, longing rewarded by love, and the laughter that saves us from taking ourselves too seriously. Dredging all this up forces the memoirist to question her choices, only to find the one right answer still elusive, but acceptance easier. I hope my story eases the minds of those who demand of themselves perfection. Everything God makes has cracks in it.

I was fortunate to have as my literary agent Richard Pine, partner at Inkwell Management, a Hall of Famer in publishing Books for a Better Life. My brilliant editor at William Morrow, Jennifer Brehl, sustained me over two years with unwavering enthusiasm and thoughtful critiques. It was my good fortune to be assisted by two remarkable graduates of the M.F.A. program at Stony Brook Southampton, Elaine Rooney, an incisive reader and researcher, and Genevieve Crane, a skillful organizer and doorkeeper against interruptions. We were kept in coffee and comfort by Yolanda Ormaza.

A month before my deadline, as I stared at a mountain of pages knowing that I still had another twenty years to write about, I fell asleep at the wheel of my life. Literally. One day on a hot summer Sunday afternoon, stone sober, I dozed off and swerved across a crowded turnpike. It was what I call a God doing, because I hurt nobody including myself, but it woke me up to reach out and ask for help. I turned to Lou Ann Walker, an accomplished editor and memoirist who teaches a highly prized course on memoir writing in the Stony Brook Southampton M.F.A. program. She identified the underlying theme of my memoir, "daring," and worked tirelessly with me to flesh out the heart of the book and snip out the rest.

I am eternally grateful to Robert Emmett Ginna Jr., my navigator and my rock from start to finish.

CREDITS

INDEX

NOTE: GS refers to Gail Sheehy. Bold numbers refer to picture captions.

DISCARD